T0189351

COMPUTER-AIDED REASONING

REASONING

ACL2 Case Studies

Advances in Formal Methods

Michael Hinchey
Series Editor

Other Series Titles:

The Object-Z Specification Language by Graeme Smith
ISBN: 0-7923-8684-1

Software Engineering with OBJ: Algebraic Specification in Action by
Joseph A. Goguen and Grant Malcolm
ISBN: 0-7923-7757-5

Computer-Aided Reasoning: An Approach by Matt Kaufmann,
Panagiotis Manolios and J Strother Moore
ISBN: 0-7923-7744-3

COMPUTER-AIDED REASONING
ACL2 Case Studies

edited by

Matt Kaufmann
Advanced Micro Devices, Inc.

Panagiotis Manolios
The University of Texas at Austin

J Strother Moore
The University of Texas at Austin

KLUWER ACADEMIC PUBLISHERS
Boston / Dordrecht / London

Distributors for North, Central and South America:
Kluwer Academic Publishers
101 Philip Drive
Assinippi Park
Norwell, Massachusetts 02061 USA
Telephone (781) 871-6600
Fax (781) 871-6528
E-Mail <kluwer@wkap.com>

Distributors for all other countries:
Kluwer Academic Publishers Group
Distribution Centre
Post Office Box 322
3300 AH Dordrecht, THE NETHERLANDS
Telephone 31 78 6392 392
Fax 31 78 6546 474
E-Mail <orderdept@wkap.nl>

 Electronic Services <http://www.wkap.nl>

Library of Congress Cataloging-in-Publication Data

Computer-aided reasoning: ACL2 case studies / edited by Matt Kaufmann, Panagiotis
Manolios, J Strother Moore.
    p. cm. -- (Advances in formal methods; 4)
  Includes bibliographical references and index.
  ISBN 0-7923-7849-0 (alk. paper)
    1. Expert systems (Computer science) 2. Computer-aided design. I. Kaufmann, Matt.
II. Manolios, Panagiotis. III. Moore, J Strother, 1947- IV. Series.

QA76.76.E95 C655 2000
006.3'3--dc21

                                00-037106

Printed on acid-free paper.

Printed in the United States of America

*The Publisher offers discounts on this book for course use and bulk purchases.
For further information, send email to <lance.wobus@wkap.com>*

Series Foreword
Advances in Formal Methods

Michael Hinchey
Series Editor

University of Nebraska-Omaha
College of Information Science and Technology
Department of Computer Science
Omaha, NE 68182-0500 USA

Email: mhinchey@unomaha.edu

As early as 1949, computer pioneers realized that writing a program that executed as planned was no simple task. Turing even saw the need to address the issues of program correctness and termination, foretelling groundbreaking work of Edsger Dijkstra, John McCarthy, Bob Floyd, Tony Hoare, Sue Owicki and David Gries, among others, two and three decades later.

The term *formal methods* refers to the application of mathematical techniques for the specification, analysis, design, implementation and subsequent maintenance of complex computer software and hardware. These techniques have proven themselves, when correctly and appropriately applied, to result in systems of the highest quality, which are well documented, easier to maintain, and promote software reuse.

With emerging legislation, and increasing emphasis in standards and university curricula, formal methods are set to become even more important in system development. This Kluwer book series, Advances in Formal Methods, aims to present results from the cutting edge of formal methods research and practice.

Books in the series will address the use of formal methods in both hardware and software development, and the role of formal methods in the development of safety-critical and real-time systems, hardware-software co-design, testing, simulation and prototyping, software quality assurance, software reuse, security, and many other areas. The series aims to include both basic and advanced textbooks, monographs, reference books and collections of high quality papers which will address managerial issues, the development process, requirements engineering, tool support, methods integration, metrics, reverse engineering, and issues relating to formal methods education.

It is our aim that, in due course, Advances in Formal Methods will provide a rich source of information for students, teachers, academic researchers and industrial practitioners alike. And I hope that, for many, it will be a first port-of-call for relevant texts and literature.

Computer-Aided Reasoning: An Approach and *Computer-Aided Reasoning: ACL2 Case Studies* are two complementary volumes in the Advances in Formal Methods series. The former provides an in-depth introduction to computer-supported reasoning with A Computational Logic for A Common Lisp (ACL2), the successor to Nqthm. It provides both technical details on computer-aided reasoning and an expository introduction to ACL2 and of how to apply it in system development and in reasoning about applications. The latter is a comprehensive collection of case studies, written by experts, illustrating the use of ACL2 in a range of problem areas. Individually, these volumes provide interesting reading and a firm foundation for those interested in computer-aided reasoning; together, they form the most authoritative source for information on ACL2 and its practical application.

Professor Mike Hinchey

Contents

Preface

This story grew in the telling. We set out to edit the proceedings of a workshop on the ACL2 theorem prover—adding a little introductory material to tie the research papers together—and ended up not with one but with two books. The subject of both books is computer-aided reasoning, from the ACL2 perspective. The first book is about *how* do it; the second book, this one, is about *what* can be done.

The creation of ACL2, by Kaufmann and Moore, was the first step in the process of writing this book. It was a step that took many years and involved many people and organizations. We only list the names of the people here, but in the Preface to the first book we give more complete acknowledgments. For help in creating ACL2 and developing many of the modeling and proof techniques used here, Kaufmann and Moore thank Ken Albin, Larry Akers, Bill Bevier, Bob Boyer, Bishop Brock, Alessandro Cimatti, Rich Cohen, George Cotter, John Cowles, Art Flatau, Noah Friedman, Ruben Gamboa, Fausto Giunchiglia, Norm Glick, David Greve, Don Good, David Hardin, Calvin Harrison, Joe Hill, Warren Hunt, Terry Ireland, Robert Krug, Laura Lawless, Bill Legato, Tom Lynch, Panagiotis (Pete) Manolios, William McCune, Robert Morris, Dave Opitz, Laurence Pierre, Dave Reed, David Russinoff, Jun Sawada, Bill Schelter, Bill Scherlis, Larry Smith, Mike Smith, Rob Sumners, Ralph Wachter, Matthew Wilding, and Bill Young. We also are indebted to those who defined Common Lisp, and the entire user communities of both ACL2 and its predecessor, the Boyer-Moore theorem prover (Nqthm). Bob Boyer deserves special recognition for his contributions to ACL2's design and implementation during the first few years of its development.

Financial and moral support during the first eight years of ACL2's creation was provided by the U.S. Department of Defense, including DARPA and the Office of Naval Research, and Computational Logic, Inc. Subsequently, ACL2's development has been supported in part by the University of Texas at Austin, the Austin Renovation Center of EDS, Inc., Advanced Micro Devices, Inc., and Rockwell Collins, Inc.

Turning from the ACL2 system to this book, we owe our greatest debt to the participants in the 1999 workshop where the idea of these books was born. Ken Albin, Warren Hunt, and Matthew Wilding were among the first to push for a workshop. We thank those participants who wrote material for the book, including Vernon Austel and all those listed in the table of contents.

In addition to all the contributors and many of the people named above, we thank Rajeev Joshi, Yi Mao, Jennifer Maas, George Porter, and David Streckmann for proof reading drafts of various portions of the book.

We thank the series editor, Mike Hinchey, and Lance Wobus at Kluwer, who patiently tolerated and adjusted to the increasing scope of this enterprise.

For many months now, much of our "free time" has been spent writing and editing these books. Without the cooperation and understanding support of our wives we simply would not have done it. So we thank them most of all.

Matt Kaufmann
Austin, Texas   Panagiotis Manolios
February 2000   J Strother Moore

List of Contributors

Piergiorgio Bertoli   IRST - Istituto per la Ricerca
                             Scientifica e Tecnologica
                             Povo, Italy
                             Email: bertoli@itc.it

Dominique Borrione   TIMA-UJF
                             Grenoble, France
                             Email: Dominique.Borrione@imag.fr

John Cowles   Department of Computer Science
                             University of Wyoming
                             Laramie, Wyoming
                             Email: cowles@uwyo.edu

Arthur Flatau   Advanced Micro Devices, Inc.
                             Austin, Texas
                             Email: arthur.flatau@amd.com

Ruben Gamboa   Logical Information Machines, Inc.
                             Austin, Texas
                             Email: ruben@lim.com

Philippe Georgelin   TIMA-UJF
                             Grenoble, France
                             Email: Philippe.Georgelin@imag.fr

Wolfgang Goerigk   Institut für Informatik und
                             Praktische Mathematik
                             Christian-Albrechts-Universität zu Kiel
                             Kiel, Germany
                             Email: wg@informatik.uni-kiel.de

David Greve   Rockwell Collins
                             Advanced Technology Center
                             Cedar Rapids, Iowa
                             Email: dagreve@collins.rockwell.com

David Hardin   Ajile Systems, Inc.
                      Oakdale, Iowa
                      Email: david.hardin@ajile.com

Warren A. Hunt, Jr.   IBM Austin Research Laboratory
                      Austin, Texas
                      Email: WHunt@Austin.IBM.COM

Damir A. Jamsek   IBM Austin Research Laboratory
                      Austin, Texas
                      Email: jamsek@us.ibm.com

Matt Kaufmann   Advanced Micro Devices, Inc.
                      Austin, Texas
                      Email: matt.kaufmann@amd.com

Panagiotis Manolios   Department of Computer Sciences
                      University of Texas at Austin
                      Austin, Texas
                      Email: pete@cs.utexas.edu

William McCune   Mathematics and Computer Science
                          Division
                      Argonne National Laboratory
                      Argonne, Illinois
                      Email: mccune@mcs.anl.gov

J Strother Moore   Department of Computer Sciences
                      University of Texas at Austin
                      Austin, Texas
                      Email: moore@cs.utexas.edu

Vanderlei Rodrigues   TIMA-UJF
                      Grenoble, France
                      (on leave from UFRGS,
                      Porto Alegre, Brazil)
                      Email: vandi@inf.ufrgs.br

David M. Russinoff   Advanced Micro Devices, Inc.
                      Austin, Texas
                      Email: david.russinoff@amd.com

Jun Sawada   Department of Computer Sciences,
                      University of Texas at Austin

Austin, Texas
Email: sawada@cs.utexas.edu

Olga Shumsky   Department of Electrical and
                          Computer Engineering
                          Northwestern University
                          Evanston, Illinois
                          Email: shumsky@ece.nwu.edu

Paolo Traverso   IRST - Istituto per la Ricerca
                          Scientifica e Tecnologica
                          Povo, Italy
                          Email: leaf@itc.it

Matthew Wilding   Rockwell Collins
                          Advanced Technology Center
                          Cedar Rapids, Iowa
                          Email: mmwildin@collins.rockwell.com

Introduction

This book shows what can be done with computer aided reasoning. Included here are descriptions of mathematical, hardware, and software systems. These systems and their desired properties are modeled with formulas in a mathematical language. That language has an associated mechanized reasoning tool, called ACL2, which is used to prove that these properties hold. With these techniques it is possible to describe components clearly and reliably, permitting them to be combined in new ways with predictable results.

The heart of the book reports on a sequence of case studies carried out by twenty-one researchers, including the three editors. The case studies are summarized starting on page 21. These studies are self-contained technical papers. They contain exercises for the reader who wants to master the material. In addition, complete ACL2 solutions for both the exercises and the results reported in each case study are available on the Web, as described below.

The book is meant for two audiences: those looking for innovative ways to design, build, and maintain systems (especially hardware and software) faster and more reliably, and those wishing to learn how to do this. The former audience includes project managers in the hardware or software industry and students in survey-oriented software engineering courses. The latter audience includes students and professionals pursuing rigorous approaches to hardware and software engineering or formal methods, who may consider applying such methods in their work. We include in this audience fellow researchers in formal methods who are building "competing" systems and who wish to keep abreast of what is happening in the ACL2 camp.

We assume you are familiar with computer programming. We also assume you are familiar with traditional mathematical notation: for example, "$f(x,y)$" denotes the application of the function f to (the values denoted by) x and y, and "$|x|$" denotes either the absolute value of x or its cardinality, depending on the context.

We also assume that you are comfortable with the idea that mathematics can be used to describe and predict the behavior of physical artifacts. This notion is fundamental to modern engineering. It is non-controversial that mathematically assisted engineering allows the construction of reliable complex systems faster than can be built by "intuitive engineering."

A major difficulty with applying mathematical modeling and analysis to the engineering of hardware and software systems is that the mathematics traditionally taught in college—calculus—is inappropriate for application to discrete systems. An appropriate mathematical framework is symbolic logic, where it is possible to describe and analyze the properties of recursive functions on inductively constructed domains. Mechanical tools exist to assist people in reasoning about such systems, relieving them of the heavy burden of logical correctness while targeting their talents towards creative insights and the high level decomposition of the problem.

If you are a member of the audience looking for innovative ways to build systems, you need not care about the mathematical details as long as you accept that mathematical modeling and analysis are the keys to better engineering and that practitioners must be trained in appropriate mathematics and tools. The operative questions are probably "What can be done by these people with their tools?" and "How long does it take?" This book addresses these questions.

If you are a member of the other audience and wish to learn how to do such modeling and analysis, we recommend that you eventually also read the companion book, *Computer-Aided Reasoning: An Approach* [58]. But the present book is of interest because it shows you what is possible. It also provides many exercises on which you can hone the skills taught in [58].

Flipping through this book will reveal a certain uniformity: Lisp expressions appear everywhere! That is because the mathematical logic used here, ACL2, is based on Common Lisp. To be more precise, it is a functional (side-effect free) extension of a subset of Common Lisp. Such a language is ideally suited to many modeling problems, because it supports formal models—of algorithms, compilers, microprocessors, machine languages— that are both executable and analyzable. That is, the formal models do double duty: they specify the results to be delivered and they can be used as efficient simulators. For example, before proving a floating-point multiplier correct, one might test it with millions of test vectors. Or, engineers unfamiliar with formal methods might compile and run Java programs on a formal model of a microprocessor. Such applications are real and are described here. Indeed, the ACL2 system itself is written almost entirely in the ACL2 language; its size (6 megabytes of source code), reliability, efficiency, and general utility demonstrate the practicality of the language.

What is surprising to many people is the range of ideas that can be discussed with such a simple language. The heart of this book consists of fourteen chapters written by various contributors. The ACL2 language is used to model and analyze problems in the following areas: graph theory, model checking, integral calculus, microprocessor simulation, pipelined architectures, an occurrence-oriented hardware description language, VHDL, symbolic trajectory analysis, floating-point multiplication, a safety-critical compiler, Trojan horses, a proof checker for the Otter theorem prover, a mathematical challenge by Knuth, and non-standard real analysis. The breadth of this collection is more impressive once you realize that all the claims are expressed in a formal mathematical system and all the theorems cited are proved mechanically. The list of authors also shows that you do not have to be the creators of ACL2 to use the system well.

One might group these case studies into four categories: tutorial, hardware, software, and mathematics. But there is much overlap. The tutorial on model checking explains, with the precision of ACL2, an algorithm used primarily in hardware verification; but the chapter then proves the algorithm correct, an exercise in software verification. The hardware models are written in executable Lisp; hence, the theorems proved are really theorems about software systems that simulate hardware. The safety-critical compiler uses modular arithmetic and hence depends on the Chinese remainder theorem, which is normally considered a mathematical exercise.

The book is divided into two parts. In Part I we deal very briefly with certain preliminaries: the effort involved in pursing this approach, followed by an extremely brief discussion of the ACL2 logic and its mechanization that is intended to provide the necessary background for the second part. The heart of the book is Part II, where the case studies are presented.

The authors of these case studies were asked to do three things that are quite unusual. First, they were asked to provide exercises in their particular applications. Second, they were asked to provide solutions to all their exercises so that we, the editors, could post them on the Web. Third, they were asked to provide us with the entire ACL2 scripts necessary to formalize the models and prove all the properties discussed in their studies. These too are on the Web, as described below. When we say, for example, that one of the case studies formalizes a floating-point multiplier and proves it correct, we mean that not only can you read an English description of the model and how it was proved correct, but you can obtain the entire transcript of the project and replay the proofs, if you wish, on your copy of ACL2. Several industrial projects were "sanitized" for inclusion here (or were not included at all). But the resulting scripts are extremely valuable to the serious student of formal methods. Every case study can be treated as an exercise in formalizing the model and proof described, and a complete solution is available to help you through the hard parts.

Recall that we edited the book with two audiences in mind. If you are a member of the first audience, looking to survey the state of the art, we recommend that you read both parts, but not pay too much attention to the formulas in the second part. Most of the case studies paraphrase the formulas. Just remember that not only can the informal remarks be made mathematically precise but they are being made precise; not only can the arguments be checked by machine, they were checked by machine. Indeed, you can obtain the scripts if you wish. We also recommend that you read the exercises, even though we do not expect you to do them. By reading them you will learn what experienced users think are reasonable challenges for people expecting to move on to industrial applications.

If you are a member of the second audience, trying to learn how to do this, then your approach to this book depends on whether you are already familiar with ACL2. If so, we recommend that you skim Part I. Then, read the first three case studies of Part II, doing many of the exercises as you go. Once you get through that, we recommend reading the rest of Part II and doing the exercises for those studies that seem relevant to your own work.

On the other hand, if you want to learn ACL2 but have not yet begun, we recommend reading this book in the "survey style" suggested above, so you get an idea of the kind of thinking required. We then recommend that you read and work your way through the companion book [58], and then return to the exercises in this book, starting with the first three case studies.

The ACL2 system is available for free on the Web (under the terms of the Gnu General Public License). The ACL2 home page is http://-www.cs.utexas.edu/users/moore/acl2. There you will find the source code of the system, downloadable images for several platforms, installation instructions, two guided tours, a quick reference card, tutorials, an online User's Manual, useful email addresses (including how to join the mailing list or ask the community for help), scientific papers about applications, and much more.

The ACL2 online documentation is almost 3 megabytes of hypertext and is available in several formats. The HTML version can be inspected from the ACL2 home page with your browser. Other formats are explained in the "Documentation" section of the installation instructions accessible from the ACl2 home page.

Important: In this book, you will often see underlined strings in typewriter font in such phrases as "see **defthm**." These are references to the online documentation. To pursue them, go to the ACL2 home page, click on "The User's Manual" link, and then click on the "Index of all documented topics." You will see a list from A to Z. Click on the appropriate letter and scan the topics for the one referenced (in this case, **defthm**) and click on it.

While the online documentation is quite extensive, it is not organized linearly. There are several tutorials and fully worked problems, but the documentation is primarily a reference manual. If you are a newcomer to ACL2 and want to learn how to use it effectively, we strongly recommend that you read the companion book [58].

Solutions to all the exercises are available online. Go to the ACL2 home page, click on the link to this book and follow the directions there. The directions also explain how to obtain the ACL2 scripts for each case study.

You will note that on the Web page for this book there is a link named "Errata." As the name suggests, there you will find corrections to the printed version of the book. But more importantly, you may find differences between the version of ACL2 described in the printed book (Version 2.5) and whatever version is current when you go to the home page. The ideas discussed here are fundamental. But we do display such syntactic entities as command names, session logs, etc. These may change. Therefore, look at the online Errata when you first begin to use ACL2 in conjunction with this book.

We believe it is appropriate to use this book in graduate and upper-division undergraduate courses on Software Engineering or Formal Methods. It could be used in conjunction with other books in courses on Hardware Design, Discrete Mathematics, or Theory (especially courses stressing formalism, rigor, or mechanized support). It is also appropriate for courses on Artificial Intelligence or Automated Reasoning.

Part I

Preliminaries

2

Overview

When people talk about "theorems" and "proofs" most of us either think of the elementary results of high school geometry, *e.g.*, "If two distinct lines intersect, then they intersect in exactly one point," or famous unsolved problems, such as Goldbach's question, "Is there an even number greater than 2 that is not the sum of two primes?".

But consider the following theorems of a different sort.

- The hardware implementing floating point multiplication produces answers in accordance with the IEEE floating-point standard.

- The desired instruction set architecture is implemented by the pipelined architecture.

- The program identifies the five highest peaks in the data stream and stores the addresses of those peaks.

- The compilation algorithm produces object code that preserves the semantics of the source program.

- The processor is "secure."

These statements are informal, but they can be made formal. And once made formal, such statements can sometimes be shown to be true: they can be proved as theorems of the mathematical logic in which they are formalized. We know, because each of the statements above has been formalized and proved, using the formal logic used in this book. Indeed, the proofs were checked mechanically by the system used in this book. Furthermore, the computing systems studied were not "toys." Each system and theorem was of interest to an industrial sponsor or designer.

2.1 Some Questions

You probably have many questions, ranging from the philosophical to the practical.

- How can anyone make mathematically precise statements about physical artifacts like computers?

- What does it mean to say that such a statement is true?

- How does the computer program described in this book work? What does it do?

- Can a computer program really help a person reason?

- Who can learn to use it?

- How long does it take to learn?

- How automatic is it? How long does it take to prove a statement like those above?

- How realistic are the problems to which it has been applied?

Most of this book is devoted to the last question. It is answered by showing you the case studies and their solutions. But we will briefly address the other questions now.

2.2   Some Answers

You cannot prove theorems about physical artifacts. Theorems are proved about mathematical models of physical artifacts. More precisely, mathematical formulas can be written to describe the behavior of artifacts. We call those formulas "models" of the artifacts. Part of an engineer's job training is to learn how to create mathematical models of structures. These models address some concerns and ignore others: the shape and composition of the supporting beams are carefully modeled, but the texture and color of the paint might be ignored. These models are then used to answer questions about the behavior of the artifact before it is actually constructed.

The same basic ideas can be applied to the design of computing artifacts. But how would you describe, say, a microcode engine or a compiler? You certainly would not write differential equations. You might write the description as a computer program. That is, you might construct a program that produces the desired behavior in response to given input. Such programs are called "simulators" in hardware design and are sometimes called "prototypes" in software design. They are models of the artifact (and they often ignore important aspects, like power consumption or user interface). But generally such models are used to *test* the artifact, by executing the code for the model on concrete examples to see if it behaves as intended.

Of course, bugs could also be found by inspection of the model itself. A clever programmer might stare at the code for the model and realize that a certain input causes "unintended" behavior. What is this programmer doing? She is not executing the model. She is reasoning abstractly— symbolically—about the model. Now imagine that we could offer her some mechanical assistance in the symbolic manipulation of the model.

To offer mechanical assistance, we need to "program" the model in a language that is unambiguous, a language that is simple enough to reason about but rich enough to model a lot of computing systems. It helps if the language is executable, so we can continue to use testing as a way to evaluate and analyze our models. What language shall we use?

The answer in this book is a functional programming language based on Common Lisp. The language is called ACL2. To the newcomer, it is a variant of Lisp, without side-effects. Models of interesting systems can be coded up in this language, compiled with off-the-shelf Common Lisp compilers, and made to execute fairly efficiently on a variety of platforms. This book is full of examples, but Chapter 8 discusses microprocessor models and simulation efficiency at length.

Now suppose we want to reason about a model. For example, suppose we want to determine whether its output has a certain relationship to its input. We do this by defining the relation as another Lisp program and composing it with the model. The question we then want to answer is whether this composite expression always return the answer t. This is akin to annotating a conventional model with a test to determine whether the computed answer is correct.

To convince ourselves that the answer is always t (or, often, to discover why it is not), we might symbolically expand the model, "running" it on indeterminate data and imagining the possible execution paths. This might be called "symbolic simulation" but in a mathematical setting it is just *simplification* of symbolic expressions.

We handle loops (or recursions) in the model by thinking about "what the loop is doing" in general. That is, we posit some property that is true whenever we arrive at the top of the loop (not just the first time) and we try to show that it is true the next time we arrive at the top of the loop. If we can do that, and if the property is true the first time, then it is always true. This kind of reasoning is familiar to all programmers and is, of course, just *mathematical induction.*

To aid the "clever programmer" in the inspection and analysis of a model, we have a mechanical theorem prover. The theorem prover provides, among many other features, a powerful symbolic simplifier and a sophisticated mechanism for inventing inductive arguments.

The system is *rule driven* in the sense that its behavior is affected by rules in a database. These rules mainly tell it how to simplify expressions but also control many other aspects of the system. The rules are "programmed" into the database by the user, after considering the model in question and the kinds of problems it presents. But the ACL2 user cannot add just any rule. If that were so, the logical correctness of the system's arguments would depend on the infallibility of its human user. Instead, every rule in the database is derived from a mathematical theorem which must first be proved by ACL2. So the user writes conjectures, which, if proved by the system, are turned into rules by the system, which, in turn, determine how the system behaves in the future. The user's job is entirely strategic. Blunders by the human might prevent the system from finding a proof, but they will not make the system assent to something that does not follow logically.[1]

This design empowers the user to think creativity about how to manipulate the concepts. Along the way, the user codifies strategies that the system will apply to prove theorems in the particular application domain.

2.3 Anecdotal Evidence from Two Projects

The ACL2 system was designed by Boyer, Moore, and Kaufmann in response to the problems faced by users of the Boyer-Moore theorem prover, Nqthm [7], in applying that system to large-scale proof projects [59]. Those projects included the proof of Gödel's incompleteness theorem [102], the verification of the gate-level description of the FM9001 microprocessor [53], the KIT operating system [2], the CLI stack [3] (which consists of some verified applications written in a high-level language, a verified compiler for that language, a verified assembler/loader targeting the FM9001), and the Berkeley C string library (as compiled by gcc for the Motorola MC68020) [9]. For a more complete summary of Nqthm's applications, see [7]. Such projects set the standards against which we measure ACL2.

How hard is it to use ACL2 to prove theorems of commercial interest? What is involved? Here are very brief descriptions of two major ACL2 projects, with emphasis on what had to be done, who did it, and how long it took.

2.3.1 The Motorola CAP DSP

The Motorola Complex Arithmetic Processor (CAP) is a single-chip DSP (digital signal processing) co-processor optimized for communications signal processing. The CAP project started in 1992 at the Motorola Government and Systems Technology Group, Scottsdale, Arizona [38]. The project lasted several years.

The CAP is an interestingly complex microprocessor. Aspects of its design include separate program and data memories, 252 programmer-visible registers, 6 independently addressable data and parameter memories with the data memories logically partitioned (under program control) into source and destination memories, and an ALU with 4 multiplier-accumulators and a 6-adder array. The instruction word is 64 bits, which is decoded into a 317-bit low-level control word within the ALU. The instruction set includes

---

[1] In order to provide greater flexibility for the proof process, ACL2 allows the user to explicitly add axioms and temporarily skip proofs.

Task	Man-Months
Microarchitecture model	15
Sequential model and equivalence proof	5
Reusable books	6
Microcode proofs	2
Meetings and reports	3

Figure 2.1: CAP Tasks Breakdown

no-overhead looping constructs. As many as 10 different registers can be involved in the determination of the next program counter and a single instruction can simultaneously modify over 100 registers. The 3-stage instruction pipeline contains hazards visible to the programmer.

The motivation behind this complexity and unusual design was to allow Motorola engineers to code DSP application programs in CAP microcode and have those programs execute extremely efficiently.

One ACL2 user (Bishop Brock) was assigned the job of providing formal methods support for the design effort. Brock spent 31 months on the project, the first seven of which were in Scottsdale interacting with the design team. The rest of Brock's time was in Austin, Texas. During the project Brock described the machine at two levels: the microarchitecture level, which includes the pipeline, and the microcode programmer's level, which is a simpler sequential machine. Anecdotal evidence suggests that Brock contributed to the design in minor ways merely by recording design decisions formally and commenting on their implications.

Using ACL2, Brock proved that the two views of the machine are equivalent provided the microcode being executed does not expose any hazards. The formalization of when a hazard is present in microcode was an important contribution. Brock defined a function that recognizes whether a piece of CAP microcode is hazard-free. The equivalence theorem he proved shows that his function is adequate. Because the function is executable, Brock certified DSP application programs to be hazard-free merely by executing the function on the microcode. About 50 programs were so certified. Hazards were found and eliminated. Brock also proved several application programs correct with respect to the sequential model. See [12, 13]. In the course of the work, Brock developed several ACL2 books—collections of theorems encoding useful theorem proving strategies in certain domains— which are independent of the CAP project and have found use in other ACL2 projects. Among the books he produced is the extremely useful integer hardware specification (ihs) library.

A breakdown of Brock's tasks and the time taken on each is provided in Figure 2.1. Because the design was under constant evolution during the period, the formal models were also under constant evolution and "the" equivalence theorem was proved many times. This highlights the advantage of developing general proof strategies embodied in books. It also highlights the utility of having a good inference engine: minor changes in the theorem being proved do not necessarily disrupt the proof replay.

It generally takes much longer for the ACL2 user to develop the models, theorems, and libraries than it does for the theorem prover to check successful proof scripts. The CAP proofs can be reproduced in about one hour on a 200 MHz Sun Microsystems Ultra 2 with 256 MB of memory.

2.3.2   Division on the AMD-K5

A considerably simpler ACL2 project was the modeling and correctness proof for the floating point division microcode on the AMD-K5[2] microprocessor. This was carried out by ACL2 authors Moore and Kaufmann together with AMD designer Tom Lynch.

The divide microcode is less than one page long. Its informal analysis by the AMD designers [66] was about 10 pages long and relied on common knowledge among floating-point designers, as well as on some subtle original arguments. Peer review was limited and time was short. Informal proofs of similar length for other algorithms had previously been found incorrect during testing of the "proved" part. Hence, confidence in the analysis was not commensurate with the risks involved and AMD decided to have the proof mechanically checked with ACL2.

Ten weeks elapsed from the time the project started to the time the final theorem was mechanically proved (June–August, 1995). At the beginning of that period Lynch explained the microcode to Moore. With help from Warren Hunt, Moore came to a partial understanding of the microcode and began to formalize its semantics and the specification. This involved formalizing many floating-point concepts. Until that time, ACL2 had never been used to prove anything about floating-point arithmetic. Approximately 80% of the project's time was devoted to the formal development of concepts and relationships that are common knowledge in the floating-point design community.

About one month into the project, Moore enlisted the aid of Kaufmann. Moore and Kaufmann divided the work of formalization and proof between them, "contracting" with each other to prove certain lemmas. Lynch was involved in the formal phase of the proof whenever the informal arguments "broke down" or were unclear. The key lemma (Theorem 1 of [79]) was mechanically checked approximately one month after Kaufmann joined the project. Moore then worked alone two more weeks to complete the proof.

The theorem has since been changed several times, most recently in response to the reviewers of [79]. The "social process of mathematics" was at work here on an accurate formal modeling of the algorithm and its desired properties. Each time the theorem was changed, Moore used ACL2 to prove

---

[2]AMD, the AMD logo and combinations thereof, AMD Athlon, and AMD-K5 are trademarks of Advanced Micro Devices, Inc.

the modified conjecture (when correct), working from the revised proof script. The new proofs were most often constructed automatically because the changes were slight (*e.g.*, narrowing by 1 the bounds of a representable exponent).

Approximately 130 functions were defined. Forty-seven of them are specific to the algorithm and its proof. The others are general-purpose floating-point concepts. Approximately 1,200 lemmas were mechanically proved. Sixty percent of them are of general interest. The other 40% are specific to the analysis of the particular algorithm. It takes approximately one hour (on a 200 MHz Sun Microsystems Ultra 2 with 256 MB of memory) to replay the entire sequence of definitions and theorems starting from scratch.

2.4 Sociology

Industrial ACL2 proof projects usually involve several people, although often only one person interacts with the theorem prover. Several people are involved because it is rare to find a single person who has the requisite skills. Some members of the group must completely understand the application in question: what informal property is supposed to be true and why. We will call these people the *implementors*. In addition, the group must include one or more people who know how to

♦ use the ACL2 logic to formalize informally described concepts,

♦ do pencil-and-paper proofs of ACL2 formulas, and

♦ drive the ACL2 theorem prover.

We will call these people the *formalizers*.

Often, the formalizers do not have an intuitive grasp of the problem at the beginning of the project. This is because they are often a late addition to a pre-existing team of implementors who have been studying the practicality of the proposed "product."

Usually the first step in a project is for the implementors to explain to the formalizers what the product does and how it does it. The implementors might not give clues to why they expect the product's design to be correct; and if they do, their notion of "correctness" may not seem anything like a property that can be nicely formalized. Indeed, the notion of an explicit, abstract statement of correctness is foreign to many implementors. From their perspective, correctness is best described as the absence of "bugs" that are obvious to the end-user. "Bugs" may be detected "by inspection" but are more likely to be exposed through testing.

It is not uncommon for the crucial first meeting to go badly. The different attitudes of the two sides are obvious. The implementors are anxious to construct something that "works" and are determined to "sell" the project. They feel that their reputations, if not their jobs, are on the line. Furthermore, they may have never presented the details of the project to anyone outside the management structure. They almost certainly have never tried to explain the internal workings to outsiders, much less to outsiders unable to speak the in-house language and not possessing the common knowledge of the field. To make matters worse, the implementors may be defensive: they feel that the formalizers are out to find fault in their design and may exaggerate the importance of their discoveries.

Meanwhile, the formalizers are asking for the impossible and the implementors are not able to deliver it. The formalizers want an utterly precise specification of the component in isolation, understandable to the non-expert. They too feel that their reputations are on the line. They know they must get results soon, because of the project deadlines and because of skepticism within the company of the worth of formal methods. But the whole project seems vague, poorly understood, and rushed. And they too are defensive; they have never tried anything quite like this project and do not know how vast a body of mathematics they have to formalize just to get to where the implementors start in their informal argument.

Consider the following a worst-case scenario. Both sides may leave this crucial first meeting feeling frustrated and alarmed. The "team" is full of ignorant people! When either side tries to speak the language of the other, they either reinforce the impression of ignorance or inadvertently mislead! Neither side seems to value the skills or objectives of the other. The mutual defensiveness exacerbates the problem. The implementors hide their main worries about the design and try to bluff their way around them. The formalizers hide their main worries about the inadequacy of their tools and try to blame the problem on poorly understood goals.

As you might well imagine, this would be a difficult beginning! Crucial to the success of the project is good communication and mutual respect between these two "sides." Indeed, the polarization into two sides is destructive. The implementors should regard the formalizers as friends: the bugs they find will be fixed before they get out. The formalizers should see the implementors as friends: their designs are state-of-the-art solutions to novel problems; bugs are inevitable but the implementors often have exceedingly well-honed intuitions about how to solve their problems. The skill-sets of the two sides are complementary and should be appreciated by all. The implementors have good intuitions—it is not random chance that enables them to produce complex designs that almost always work—but they do not have the formalization skills to prove their designs correct. The formalizers are masters at casting intuitive ideas into logic, but do not have the engineering experience to navigate through the tradeoffs of behavior, performance, cost, and time-to-market. Each side has to trust that the other will fill the gaps. Each side has to be honest with the other. The implementors must explain why they mistrust their design. The formalizers must confess that they do not understand the goal or the methods, that the extant formal work in the field is miniscule, and that the expressive power of whatever formalism they are using limits their ability to capture what is desired. All team members should agree that the goal is to produce a better understood product.

Often the main contributions of the formalizers are to foster communication and reduce ambiguity. As the team coalesces, the formalizers become lexicographers: they record the precise meanings of terms used by the team and look out for misunderstandings between team members. Bugs are often found by trying to make precise the statement of what the product is supposed to do and why the implementation works.

Once the basic ideas have been formalized and agreed upon, the implementors and formalizers can design clear interfaces between the modules and get on with their main tasks, of producing implementations and proofs. Often feedback between the tasks is very helpful. You know the team has come together when the implementors ask the formalizers whether it is permitted to assume that a certain module has a given property, or when the formalizers ask the implementors for help in proving some key property.

2.5   Toy Models

The formalizers will often be struggling with several issues at once: understanding the informal descriptions of the product, discovering and formalizing the relevant knowledge that the implementors take for granted, and formalizing the design and its specification. To a large extent this phenomenon is caused by the fact that formal methods is only now being injected into industry. Once a significant portion of a group's past projects has been formalized, along with the then-common knowledge, it will be much easier to keep up. But at this moment in history, keeping up during the earliest phases of a project can be quite stressful.

When working on a new project, we recommend that the formalizers start by formalizing the simplest imaginable model, *e.g.*, the instruction set with one data operation and a branch instruction, or the protocol with a simple handshake. Choosing this initial model requires some experience. The trick is to choose a model that exhibits the "new" problems—problems the formalizers have never dealt with—that will be encountered when the model is elaborated to the interesting case. Such toy models are extremely useful for developing the form of the model, the statement of its key properties, tool support (*e.g.*, simulation support), and the structure of the proofs. Since iteration is often required to get things to fit together properly, it is crucial that this initial foray into the unknown be done with a small enough model to permit complete understanding and rapid, radical revision.

The most common insight gained from this process is that intermediate abstractions are being used implicitly. Informal language is so flexible we often develop new models without realizing it. "Imagine that we did runtime error checking" calls into being an intermediate model in which certain conditions are checked at runtime and explicitly signaled. Often, subsequent arguments are couched in terms of the original model but in fact are being conducted about this new model. Without careful scrutiny, one may not be aware that two models are being used by the team and that the two models have important relationships, *e.g.*, that they produce identical outcomes when one of them satisfies some additional constraint *that cannot even be expressed about the other*.

Once such insights are made, they not only dramatically influence the formalization of the actual models but they influence the language used by the design team to discuss the evolving implementation.

A toy model is also a good sandbox in which the implementors and formalizers can learn to communicate and can come to a clear agreement as to what is to be modeled, formalized, and proved.

Finally, it is crucial that the project management understand the importance of these initial toy models. The premature introduction of realistic complexity into the model can delay the completion of the project. A well-chosen toy can provide a road map to a correct design, implementation, and proof.

2.6   Requirements on the User

The "typical" ACL2 user has a bachelor's degree in computer science or mathematics. We expect that reading [58] and working the exercises there will be sufficient training to prepare a newcomer for the exercises here.

How long does it take for a novice to become an effective ACL2 user?

Let us first answer a different question.[3] How long does it take for a novice to become an effective C programmer? (Substitute for "C" your favorite programming language.) It takes weeks or months to learn the language but months or years to become a good programmer. The long learning curve is not due to the complexity of the programming language but to the complexity of the whole enterprise of programming. Shallow issues, like syntax and basic data structures, are easy to learn and allow you to write useful programs. Deep skills—like system decomposition, proper design of the interfaces between modules, and recognizing when to let efficiency impact clarity or vice-versa—take much longer to master. Once deep skills are learned, they carry over almost intact to other languages and other projects. Learning to be a good programmer need not require using a computer to run your programs. The deep skills can be learned from disciplined reflection and analysis. But writing your programs in an

---

[3]The following three paragraphs are taken verbatim from our discussion of this issue in [58] because they answer the question so appropriately in the current context.

implemented language and running them is rewarding, it often highlights details or even methodological errors that might not have been noticed otherwise, and, mainly, it gives you the opportunity to practice.

We hope that you find the above comments about programming noncontroversial because analogous comments can be made about learning to use ACL2 (or any other mechanized proof system).

How long does it take for a novice to become an effective ACL2 user? It takes weeks or months to learn to use the language and theorem prover, but months or years to become really good at it. The long learning curve is not due to the complexity of ACL2—the logic or the system—but to the complexity of the whole enterprise of formal mathematical proof. Shallow issues, like syntax and how to give hints to the theorem prover, are easy to learn and allow you carry out interesting proof projects. But deep skills— like the decomposition of a problem into lemmas, how to define concepts to make proofs easier, and when to strive for generality and when not to— take much longer to master. These skills, once learned, carry over to other proof systems and other projects. You can learn these deep skills without doing mechanical proofs at all—indeed, you may feel that you have learned these skills from your mathematical training. Your appraisal of your skills may be correct. But writing your theorems in a truly formal language and checking your proofs mechanically is rewarding, it often points out details and even methodological errors that you might not have noticed otherwise, and, mainly, it gives you the opportunity to practice.

3

Summaries of the Case Studies

There are fourteen case studies, organized as follows. The first three, written individually by the editors, are especially appropriate for beginners, but contain useful information for all readers. The next six chapters are related to the formalization, specification, and verification of computer hardware. The next two deal explicitly with computer software applications. The last three focus on problems in logic and mathematics. We say "explicitly" above because all the applications can be seen as illustrative of software verification: since the logic is in essence Lisp, the models being verified are in essence just software systems.

As noted in the Introduction, each case study is supported by material on the Web, including full solutions to the exercises and all definitions and theorems discussed. See page 4.

♦ Chapter 5, An Exercise in Graph Theory, by J Moore. This chapter formalizes the notion of a directed graph and shows how to prove the correctness of a depth-first path finding algorithm. The chapter requires no specialized knowledge of graph theory and is meant entirely as an exercise in formalization and use of ACL2.

♦ Chapter 6, Modular Proof: The Fundamental Theorem of Calculus, by Matt Kaufmann. This chapter presents a modular, top-down ACL2 proof methodology and then uses the methodology to outline a formalization and proof of the Fundamental Theorem of Calculus. While the example is based on the non-standard extension of ACL2 described by Gamboa in Chapter 18, non-standard analysis is not a prerequisite either for this chapter or for the proof methodology presented.

♦ Chapter 7, Mu-Calculus Model-Checking, by Panagiotis Manolios. The Mu-Calculus is a formal logic into which many temporal logics, including CTL, CTL^*, and LTL, can be translated. This chapter presents a formal development of the syntax and semantics for the Mu-Calculus, a model-checker for the Mu-Calculus in ACL2, and a discussion of the translation of other temporal logics into the Mu-Calculus. There are several self-contained sections in which the reader is presented with exercises whose solutions lead to books on set theory, fixpoint theory, and relation theory. These books will be of interest even to readers not interested in the Mu-Calculus.

- ♦ Chapter 8, High-Speed, Analyzable Simulators, by David Greve, Matthew Wilding, and David Hardin. High-speed simulation models are routinely developed during the design of complex hardware systems in order to predict performance, detect design flaws, and allow hardware/software co-design. Writing such an executable model in ACL2 brings the additional benefit of formal analysis; however, much care is required to construct an ACL2 model that is both fast and analyzable. In this chapter, techniques are described for the construction of high-speed formally analyzable simulators in ACL2. Their utility is demonstrated on a simple processor model.

- ♦ Chapter 9, Verification of a Simple Pipelined Machine Model, by Jun Sawada. An ACL2 model of a three-stage pipelined machine is defined, along with a model of the corresponding sequential machine. Then a proof of the equivalence between the two machines is presented. More importantly, the method of decomposing the proof applies to much more complicated pipelined architectures.

- ♦ Chapter 10, The DE Language, by Warren Hunt. The DE language is an occurrence-oriented description language that permits the hierarchical definition of finite-state machines in the style of a hardware description language. The syntax and semantics of the language are formalized and the formalization is used to prove the correctness of a simple hardware circuit. Such formal HDLs have been used to prove properties of much more complicated designs.

- ♦ Chapter 11, Using Macros to Mimic VHDL, by Dominique Borrione, Philippe Georgelin, and Vanderlei Rodrigues. The purpose of this project was to formalize a small synthesizable behavioral subset of VHDL, preserving as much as possible the syntactic flavor of VHDL and facilitating verification by symbolic simulation and theorem proving.

- ♦ Chapter 12, Symbolic Trajectory Evaluation, by Damir Jamsek. Symbolic Trajectory Evaluation (STE) is a form of model checking fundamentally based on symbolic simulation. This chapter presents a formal treatment of STE, including ACL2 proofs of results presented in the Seger and Joyce paper [101].

- ♦ Chapter 13, RTL: A Verified Floating-Point Multiplier, by David M. Russinoff and Arthur Flatau. This chapter describes a mechanical proof system for designs represented in the RTL language of Advanced Micro Devices. The system consists of a translator to the ACL2 logical programming language and a methodology for verifying properties of the resulting programs using the ACL2 prover. The correctness of a simple floating-point multiplier is proved.

♦ Chapter 14, Design Verification of a Safety-Critical Embedded Verifier, by Piergiorgio Bertoli and Paolo Traverso. This case study shows the use of ACL2 for the design verification of a piece of safety-critical software, the Embedded Verifier. The Embedded Verifier checks online that each execution of a safety-critical translator is correct. The translator is a component of a software system used by Union Switch & Signal to build trainborne control systems.

♦ Chapter 15, Compiler Verification Revisited, by Wolfgang Goerigk. This study illustrates a fact observed by Ken Thompson [106] in his Turing Award Lecture: the machine code of a correct compiler can be altered to contain a Trojan Horse so that the compiler passes almost every test, including the so-called bootstrap test in which it compiles its own source code with identical results, and still be capable of generating "bad" code. The compiler, the object code machine, and the experiments are formalized in ACL2.

♦ Chapter 16, Ivy: A Proof Checker for First-order Logic, by William McCune and Olga Shumsky. In this case study, a proof checker for first-order logic is proved sound for finite interpretations. More generally, the study shows how non-ACL2 programs can be combined with ACL2 functions in such a way that useful properties can be proved about the composite programs. Nothing is proved about the non-ACL2 programs. Instead, the results of the non-ACL2 programs are checked at run time by ACL2 functions, and properties of these checker functions are proved.

♦ Chapter 17, Knuth's Generalization of McCarthy's 91 Function, by John Cowles. This project deals with a challenge by Donald Knuth [63] for a "proof by computer" of a theorem about his generalization of John McCarthy's famous "91 function." The generalization involves *real* numbers, and the case study uses ACL2 to meet Knuth's challenge by mechanically verifying results not only about the field of all real numbers, but also about every subfield of that field.

♦ Chapter 18, Continuity and Differentiability, by Ruben Gamboa. This chapter shows how an extended version of ACL2 can be used to reason about the real and complex numbers, using non-standard analysis. It describes some modifications to ACL2 that introduce the irrational real and complex numbers into ACL2's number system. It then shows how the modified ACL2 can prove classic theorems of analysis, such as the intermediate-value and mean-value theorems.

We close this chapter with a brief sketch of an interesting case study not included in this book.

ACL2 was used by Vernon Austel and Sean Smith at IBM Research in the formal analysis of the bootstrapping code for the IBM 4758 secure coprocessor.[1] Roughly speaking, a secure coprocessor is a small computer inside a container that should prevent an attacker from reading or modifying its data using unauthorized means (for example, by opening it up and directly reading the contents of memory using a probe); the device should detect such attempts and take defensive action, such as erasing cryptographic keys. In the case of the 4758, the container is about the size of a thick book and the device has successfully withstood all physical attacks mounted against it as of this writing. The U.S. government established Federal Information Processing Standard 140-1 (or FIPS 140-1) to impose requirements on cryptographic devices for use in government work.[2] FIPS 140-1 defines four levels of effectiveness concerning software and hardware, level four being the highest. In order for cryptographic hardware to achieve level four, it must withstand any physical attack; in order for software to achieve level four, it must be formally modeled.

The 4758 has been evaluated by an independent commercial evaluator according to the FIPS 140-1 criteria and has achieved level four in both hardware and software. A detailed description of the security-critical software in a state machine notation was required for the software evaluation, together with a careful description of the properties the state machine has that collectively justify calling the device "secure" for the purpose to which it is put. Translating this state machine into ACL2 was straightforward; translating the four properties that define the notion of "secure" was sometimes not straightforward.

The state machine (and hence the ACL2 model) is fairly low-level, in that all data structures in the software being modeled are represented in the state machine (albeit abstractly), and one state transition in the model corresponds to roughly ten lines of C code; however, no formal connection between the code and the state machine was established. The ACL2 code for the model is about 15,000 lines long, including comments, and required approximately three person months to develop.

This case study is not further discussed in this book because the ACL2 code implementing it is proprietary. Indeed, several of the case studies presented here are distillations of larger proprietary projects.

We believe it is good for prospective users of any tool or methodology to know about the existence of proprietary applications. Often the main obstacle to trying out a new technology is deciding whether it might be applicable. One aim of this book is to be a guide for those who wish to learn ACL2. As such, we felt it necessary to focus on reproducible results and case studies that can be disclosed in full detail.

---

[1] Information concerning the IBM 4758 may be obtained at http://www.ibm.com/-security/cryptocards.

[2] The NIST Web page concerning FIPS 140-1 is http://csrc.nist.gov/cryptval/-#140-1.

We believe that when you read the case studies you too will be convinced that formality is truly practical. The practical requirement is to learn how to be truly formal.

4

ACL2 Essentials

We present here a brief, and very informal, introduction to ACL2. Our purpose is to provide just enough ACL2 background to support reading the ACL2 formulas displayed in this book's case studies. The reader interested in learning more about ACL2 is invited to take a look at the companion volume, [58], and to visit the ACL2 home page (see page 4).

ACL2 is both a logic and a programming language. As a programming language it is closely related to the Common Lisp programming language [104, 21]. In fact, ACL2 is intended to be consistent with Common Lisp where the two languages overlap. We do not assume that the reader is familiar with Common Lisp, but point out that most of these ACL2 essentials apply to Common Lisp as well.

Data types are presented in Section 4.1 and expressions are presented in Section 4.2. Readers already familiar with Lisp can probably skip most of these two sections. In Section 4.3 we discuss definitions, how to state properties (theorems) about defined notions, and how to submit definitions, theorems, and other *events* during an ACL2 session.

4.1 Data Types

The universe of ACL2 objects consists of several data types.

Numbers include the integers, rationals, and complex rational numbers.

Strings such as "abcd" are sequences of *characters*.

Symbols such as ABC and A-TYPICAL-SYMBOL may be viewed as structures containing two fields, each of which is a string: a *package name* and a *symbol name*. The package name is beyond the scope of this introduction, except to say that it is usually implicit with one major exception: symbols printed with a leading colon (:) have a package name of "KEYWORD". For example, :HINTS is a symbol with package name "KEYWORD" and symbol name "HINTS". In fact ACL2 is case-insensitive, at least for our purposes here, except for strings. So for example, :hints and :HINTS are the same symbol, both with symbol name "HINTS". We generally use lower-case in this book except when displaying ACL2 output.

Objects of the above types are called *atoms*. ACL2 also contains ordered pairs called *conses*. Binary trees are represented in ACL2 as conses whose two components may be either conses (*i.e.*, binary trees) or atoms. These binary trees thus have atoms at their leaves.

In the remainder of this section, we discuss a few important data structures that can be constructed from the small set of data types described above.

A *true list* (often referred to simply as a *list*) is either the special atom nil, which represents the empty list and is sometimes written (), or else a cons whose second component is a (true) list. Lists are represented by enclosing their elements in parentheses. For example, (3 2 4) is a list with the following *elements*, or *members*: the numbers 3, 2, and 4. More literally, it is a cons whose first component, called its *car*, is 3 and whose second component, called its *cdr*, is the list (2 4).[1] The list (2 4) in turn has a car of 2 and a cdr of (4), which in turn is the list whose car is 4 and whose cdr is (), the symbol nil. Lists can of course be nested. The list (A 5/6 (3 2 4) "B") has elements A (a symbol), 5/6 (a rational), (3 2 4) (a list), and "B" (a string).

ACL2 uses two symbols to represent the Boolean values *true* and *false*: t and nil, respectively. Notice that this is the same nil that is used to represent the empty list. Such overloading is not generally confusing. It comes from four decades of Lisp tradition and is analogous to the treatment of 0 as a Boolean in the C programming language.

A very common data structure is the *association list*, or *alist* for short, which is a true list of cons pairs. An alist represents a mapping, so that (roughly speaking) when a pair is an element of an alist, then the car of that pair is associated with the cdr of that pair. We say more about alists on page 32.

4.2 Expressions

ACL2 expressions (or *terms*) evaluate to the data objects described in the preceding section. Expressions are, in turn, represented by certain of the data objects. There are essentially four kinds of expressions (see term for details[2]):

- ◆ the symbols t, nil, and those whose package name is "KEYWORD", which evaluate to themselves;

- ◆ all other symbols, which take their values from the environment;

- ◆ (quote *x*), also written '*x*, whose value is the ACL2 object *x*;

---

[1]The names "car" and "cdr" come from Lisp.

[2]Recall our convention of underlining topics discussed in ACL2's online documentation. See page 4.

♦ $(f\ x_1\ x_2\ \ldots\ x_n)$ where $n \geq 0$, f is a symbol[3] denoting an n-ary function, and each x_i is a term, whose value is the result of applying that function to the values of the x_i.

Figure 4.1 should clarify the above notion of *value*. It also serves to introduce some important primitive (built-in) functions, many of which are used frequently in the case studies. (Many others are not listed here, but we expect their meanings to be reasonably clear from context, and the ACL2 documentation can resolve ambiguity when necessary.) In addition, they introduce the notation for same-line comments: text from a semicolon (;) to the end of the line is treated by ACL2 (and Common Lisp) as a comment. The function symbols of Figure 4.1, including <, are all underlined to remind you of the online documentation.

We will see a few more built-in functions in Section 4.3. Note also that (car (cdr x)) may be written as (<u>cadr</u> x), that (cdr (cdr x)) may be written as (<u>cddr</u> x), and so on. Some prefer to use <u>nth</u> for zero-based access to elements of a list; so (nth 0 x) has the same value as (car x), (nth 1 x) as (cadr x), (nth 2 x) as (caddr x), and (nth 3 x) as (cadddr x).

The expression language is slightly complicated by *macros*. The following built-in macros are most easily understood as though they were operators of indeterminate arity. Let v_i be value of xi below.

```
(+ x1 x2 ... xn)       ; the sum of v1,v2,... ,vn
(* x1 x2 ... xn)       ; the product of v1,v2,... ,vn
(list x1 x2 ... xn)    ; the list (v1,v2,... ,vn)
(and x1 x2 ... xn)     ; vn if each vi is not nil, else nil
(or x1 x2 ... xn)      ; vi for the least i such that vi
                       ; is not nil, if any; else, nil
```

Two more built-in macros extend the function if defined in Figure 4.1. The macro <u>cond</u> is applied to 2-element lists each of the form (*test form*) and returns the value of the first *form* for which the *test* has a value other than nil.

```
(cond (test1 form1)
      (test2 form2)
       ...
      (testn-1 formn-1)
      (t formn))
=
(if test1 form1
    (if test2 form2
       ...
        (if testn-1 formn-1
            formn)  ...  ))
```

---

[3]f can also be something called a *lambda expression*, but it is safe to ignore this point for purposes of the case studies.

Term	Value
3	; *The number 3*
-3/4	; *The number -3/4*
x	; *Depends on the environment*
(car x)	; *If the value of x is a cons,*
	; *its first component, else* nil
(cdr x)	; *If the value of x is a cons,*
	; *its second component, else* nil
(consp x)	; T *if the value of x is a cons, else* nil
(acl2-numberp x)	; T *if the value of x is a number, else* nil
(integerp x)	; T *if the value of x is an integer, else* nil
(rationalp x)	; T *if the value of x is a rational number,*
	; *else* nil
(zp x)	; T *if the value of x is 0 or is not a*
	; *natural number, else* nil
(nfix x)	; *The value of x if it is a natural*
	; *number, else 0*
(≤ x y)	; T *if the value of x is less than the*
	; *value of y, else* nil
(1- x)	; *One less than the value of x*
(1+ x)	; *One more than the value of x*
(equal x y)	; T *if the values of x and y are the*
	; *same, else* nil
(iff x y)	; T *if the values of x and y are either both*
	; nil *or both non-*nil*, else* nil
(if x y z)	; *The value of z if the value of x is* nil*,*
	; *else the value of y*
(implies x y)	; T *if the value of x is* nil *or the*
	; *value of y is not* nil*, else* nil
(not x)	; T *if the value of x is* nil*, else* nil

Figure 4.1: Some Terms and Built-in Function Symbols

Related macros <u>case</u> and <u>case-match</u> are used occasionally. Their meanings may be clear from context; if not, we recommend consulting the ACL2 documentation. We say a bit more about macros in the next section.

Finally, we introduce the constructs <u>let</u> and <u>let*</u>. Each of these forms takes two "arguments": a list of *bindings* (2-element lists) followed by a form to be evaluated relative to those bindings. Consider first this example.

```
(let ((x (+ 5 3))
      (y (- 5 3)))
  (* x y))
```

How is this form evaluated? First, x and y are *bound* in parallel to the values of their respective forms, *i.e.*, to 8 and 2, respectively. Then (* x y) is evaluated in the resulting environment by multiplying 8 by 2 to get the final value of 16. The construct let* is similar, but evaluates the bindings sequentially. So, the following expression has the same value as the one above.

```
(let* ((a 3)
       (x (+ 5 a))
       (y (- 5 a)))
  (* x y))
```

Let us do a bit of expression evaluation involving lists. Two important built-in list manipulation functions are **append**, which concatenates two lists, and **assoc**, which finds the first cons pair having a given car in a given alist. This time we illustrate evaluation using the ACL2 *read-eval-print loop*. First we illustrate **append**. User input is on lines following the **prompt**, "ACL2 !>"; the rest is printed by ACL2.

```
ACL2 !>(append '(1 2) '(a b))
(1 2 A B)
ACL2 !>
```

Before turning to **assoc**, we introduce so-called *dot notation*. The cons pair with car a and cdr b is sometimes written (a . b). The following examples illustrate this notation. Notice that $(x_1 \ldots x_n \ . \ nil)$ represents the same value as $(x_1 \ldots x_n)$.

```
ACL2 !>(cons 3 4)
(3 . 4)
ACL2 !>(cons 'a 'b)
(A . B)
ACL2 !>(cons 3 nil)
(3)
ACL2 !>'(3 . nil) ; same as (quote (3 . nil))
(3)
ACL2 !>'(3)
(3)
```

```
ACL2 !>(cons 3 (cons 4 5))
(3 4 . 5)
ACL2 !>(cons 3 (cons 4 nil))
(3 4)
ACL2 !>(list (cons 'a 2) (cons 'b 4) (cons 'b 6))
((A . 2) (B . 4) (B . 6))
ACL2 !>
```

Now we are ready to give examples illustrating <u>assoc</u>. We use the alist shown just above. Notice that `assoc` returns either a cons or `nil`.

```
ACL2 !>(assoc 'b '((a . 2) (b . 4) (b . 6)))
(B . 4)
ACL2 !>(assoc 'e '((a . 2) (b . 4) (b . 6)))
NIL
ACL2 !>
```

For a more complete discussion of expressions see the ACL2 documentation for <u>term</u>. The description above should generally be sufficient for reading the case studies. Most of the built-in functions used in this book are either mentioned above or in the next section.

4.3   Events

The ACL2 user strives to define functions and to lead ACL2 to proofs of theorems about the built-in and defined functions. Function definitions and theorems are the most important types of **events**. In this section we give the syntax of these events and a couple of others.

4.3.1   Function Definitions

The basic form for defining a function is <u>defun</u>. Most of the built-in functions are defined (in the ACL2 source code) using <u>defun</u>. For example, the built-in function <u>not</u> is defined as follows.

```
(defun not (p)
  (if p nil t))
```

This definition says: "Define function `not`, with formal parameter list `(p)`, so that the application of `not` to such a list is equal to `(if p nil t)`."

Definitions may be used to build up hierarchies of concepts. For example, the built-in function `consp` that recognizes cons data objects may be used, together with the function `not` defined above, to define the following function <u>atom</u>, which recognizes non-conses, *i.e.*, atoms.

```
(defun atom (x)
  (not (consp x)))
```

We can take this a step further. In many cases we want a function that distinguishes non-empty lists from nil. Although atom does this, Common Lisp provides another function <u>endp</u> that may be slightly more efficient than atom. ACL2 builds in the following definition for endp.[4]

```
(defun endp (x)
  (declare (xargs :guard (or (consp x) (equal x nil))))
  (atom x))
```

The list above that starts with <u>declare</u>, inserted between the formal parameter list (x) and the body (atom x), is called a *declare form*, which unlike the body, is not a function application. It is generally harmless for the casual reader to ignore declare forms, and it is beyond the scope of this introduction to discuss them in much detail. The subform (xargs ...) is used to provide ACL2-specific information. In this case, ACL2 is being informed that the formal parameter x is intended to have a "type" specified by the indicated term, *i.e.*, x should either be a cons or nil. Through this mechanism we can allow ACL2 to use the underlying Common Lisp execution engine in a direct manner to achieve greater execution speed; see <u>guard</u> for details.

In the same spirit as with endp, ACL2 has definitions for fast equality tests: <u>eq</u> can be used when at least one argument is a symbol and <u>eql</u> can be used when at least one argument is a number, symbol, or character. *Logically*, however, endp is the same function as atom, and all of equal, eq, and eql are the same function. For example, it is a theorem that (endp lst) is equal to (atom lst). Some built-in functions use eql and have built-in analogues that use equal and eq, for example: <u>assoc</u>, <u>assoc-equal</u>, and <u>assoc-eq</u>. As with the {eql,equal,eq} family, these functions are all semantically the same.

ACL2 supports recursive definition, *i.e.*, definition where the body of the function mentions the function being defined. Here is a definition of the built-in function <u>member</u>, which checks for membership in a list. Notice that when (member e x) is not equal to nil, it is the first tail of list x that starts with e. We omit the guard below, which allows the use of eql below.

```
(defun member (e x)
  (cond ((endp x) nil)
        ((eql e (car x)) x)
        (t (member e (cdr x))))))
```

Recall that <u>cond</u> picks out the form corresponding to the first test that is true (non-nil). So for example, we can see that (member 3 '(4 5)) is equal to (member 3 '(5)) using this definition: Suppose the value of e is 3 and the value of x is the value of '(4 5), *i.e.*, the list (4 5). Then the value of (endp x) is nil, so we move past the first pair in the cond. Next,

---

[4]Certain details not germane to the discussion are omitted from some of these definitions.

the value of (car x) is 4 since car takes the first element of a list; so, the value of (eql e (car x)) is nil since 3 does not equal 4. Hence the second test in the cond does not apply. Since t is not nil, the final pair in the cond does apply, showing that (member 3 '(4 5)) has the same value as (member 3 '(5)). Similar reasoning shows that (member 3 '(5)) has the same value as (member 3 '()), which in turn has the value nil. This chain of reasoning suggests how to compute with recursive definitions, in this case computing the value of (member 3 '(4 5)) to be nil.

It is possible to introduce inconsistency with recursive definitions, for example by defining $f(x)$ to equal $1 + f(x)$ (from which we obtain $0 = 1$ by arithmetic). ACL2's definitional principle (see **defun**) avoids this problem by requiring, in essence, a proof of termination. Consider for example the definition of member, above. The recursive call of member is made only under the conditions that the first two tests of the cond are false (nil), *i.e.*, x is not an atom and e is not the first element of x. The first of these two conditions guarantees that (cdr x) is a "smaller" list than x.

In the above example ACL2 uses a built-in *measure* (see **defun**) on the size of x. However, there are cases where one needs to help ACL2 by specifying a particular measure. For example, one can add the following declare form just before the body of member, above, to specify the length (**len** x) of the list x as the measure.

```
(declare (xargs :measure (len x)))
```

4.3.2   Theorems

We have seen how to define functions using **defun**. The analogous construct for submitting theorems to ACL2 is **defthm**. Here is an example, a theorem with name member-append, which says that a is an element of the concatenation of (lists) x and y if and only if a is an element of at least one of them.

```
(defthm member-append
  (iff (member a (append x y))
       (or (member a x) (member a y))))
```

ACL2 can prove the above theorem without any help. More complex theorems generally require user assistance. Probably the most common form of help is to prove lemmas to be used automatically in subsequent proofs. In fact it is easy to imagine that one would prove the lemma above in order to cause the theorem prover, in proofs of subsequent theorems, to simplify terms of the form (member a (append x y)) to corresponding terms (or (member a x) (member a y)). Such simplification is an example of *rewriting*, a further description of which is beyond the scope of these Essentials. But sometimes one needs to give explicit hints for a proof, or to give explicit directions for how to store a theorem, which is otherwise stored by default as a rewrite rule (see <u>rewrite</u>). Here is an example called `equal-char-code`, from ACL2 source file `axioms.lisp`, which states that two characters are equal if they have the same <u>char-code</u>. The :<u>rule-classes</u> value nil says that this theorem is not to be stored as a rule, and the :<u>hints</u> direct ACL2 to use two explicit instances of a previously-proved theorem called `code-char-char-code-is-identity`.

```
(defthm equal-char-code
  (implies (and (characterp x)
                (characterp y))
           (implies (equal (char-code x) (char-code y))
                    (equal x y)))
  :rule-classes nil
  :hints (("Goal" :use
           ((:instance
             code-char-char-code-is-identity
             (c x))
            (:instance
             code-char-char-code-is-identity
             (c y))))))
```

In the case studies, the reader is often spared the trouble of looking at these details by way of "...". An example follows.

```
(defthm equal-char-code
  (implies (and (characterp x)
                (characterp y))
           (implies (equal (char-code x) (char-code y))
                    (equal x y)))
  :rule-classes nil
  :hints ...)
```

4.3.3   Macros and Backquote

Users can define macros to extend the language. The symbol <u>cadr</u> is defined as a macro in the ACL2 source code. Here is its definition.

```
(defmacro cadr (x)
  (list 'car (list 'cdr x)))
```

The body of the macro constructs an expression that is used in place of calls to `cadr`.

This macro could be written using "backquote" notation.

```
(defmacro cadr (x)
  '(car (cdr ,x)))
```

Backquote allows the exhibition of what might be called "near-constants." It is like the normal single quote (') except that any expression after a comma is evaluated and the value used as the next element. If the comma is immediately followed by @, the value of the expression is spliced in.

Macros can be defined to take a varying number of arguments and can use arbitrary processing to construct the new expression. Here is the definition of list.

```
(defmacro list (&rest args)
  (list-macro args))
```

The symbol list-macro is just a defined function.

```
(defun list-macro (lst)
  (if (consp lst)
      (cons 'cons
            (cons (car lst)
                  (cons (list-macro (cdr lst)) nil)))
      nil))
```

Thus, (list a b c) expands to (cons a (cons b (cons c nil))).

4.3.4 Single-Threaded Objects

ACL2 provides *single-threaded objects*; they are sometimes called "stobjs" (pronounced "stob-jays"). Logically, such objects are just lists containing several components. Logically, they are "changed" in the usual way, by constructing new lists of the appropriate shape from the parts of the old one. Stobjs are introduced with defstobj, together with functions for accessing and "changing" their components.

But syntactic restrictions insure that once a stobj is modified, it is impossible for any function to obtain the "old" list structure. The ACL2 system takes advantage of this fact, by modifying stobjs destructively while preserving the applicative semantics. See stobj or [8].

4.3.5 Structuring Mechanisms

Files composed of events are called books. Ultimately, the goal of the ACL2 user is to get ACL2 to accept all the events in a book, discharging all proof obligations. Once a book is thus *certified* (see certify-book), its events may be included into an ACL2 session using include-book.

Some events in a book may be wrapped with local, as in the following.

```
(local
  (defthm my-lemma
    ...))
```

Local events are proved when the book is certified by ACL2, but they are omitted by `include-book`.

ACL2 provides another structuring mechanism, **encapsulate**. This mechanism provides both a scoping mechanism and a way to introduce functions that are constrained by axioms, rather than defined. (When there are no constraints on a function then the shorthand **defstub** may be used.) Here is an example that constrains a function `fn` of one argument to return a cons.

```
(encapsulate
  ;; signatures:
  ((fn (x) t))
  ;; local definition:
  (local (defun fn (x) (cons x x)))
  ;; exported theorem:
  (defthm consp-fn
    (consp (fn x)))))
```

4.4 Concluding Remarks

The discussion in this chapter has been very informal and highly incomplete. It was designed to provide sufficient information to enable the reader to make sense of the case studies that follow. The companion volume, [58], gives a more thorough and precise introduction geared towards potential ACL2 users. We also strongly encourage anyone interested in using ACL2 to visit the ACL2 documentation and tours on the ACL2 home page, `http://-www.cs.utexas.edu/users/moore/acl2`.

Part II

Case Studies

An Exercise in Graph Theory

J Strother Moore

Department of Computer Sciences, University of Texas at Austin, Texas
Email: moore@cs.utexas.edu

Abstract

We define a function that finds a path between two given nodes of a given directed graph, if such a path exists. We prove the function terminates and we prove that it is correct. Aside from illustrating one way to formalize directed graphs in ACL2, this chapter illustrates the importance of the user's decomposition of a problem into mathematically tractable parts and the importance of defining new concepts to formalize those parts. Our proof involves such auxiliary notions as that of a simple (loop-free) path, the process for obtaining a simple path from an arbitrary path, and an algorithm for collecting all simple paths. The algorithm we analyze is a naive one that executes in time exponential in the number of edges. This chapter requires no specialized knowledge of graph theory; indeed, the main thrusts of the chapter have nothing to do with graph theory. They are: to develop your formalization skills and to refine your expectations of what a formalization will involve. Appropriate expectations of a project are often the key to success.

Introduction

Consider the obvious depth-first algorithm for looking for a path from **a** to **b** in a given directed graph, **g**: if **a** is **b**, we are done; otherwise, consider each neighbor of **a** in turn and try to find a path from it to **b**. If such a path is found, then extend it via the edge from **a** to the neighbor. Care must be taken to avoid loops in the graph; a simple solution is never to consider any path that visits the same node twice. In addition, some convention must be made to indicate whether the search succeeded or failed (and, in

the former case, to indicate the path found). We will define (find-path a
b g) in accordance with the sketch above.

The correctness of find-path may be informally stated as "if there is a
path, p, from node a to node b in graph g, then (find-path a b g) finds
such a path." This may be formalized as shown below.

```
(implies (and (graphp g)
              (nodep a g)
              (nodep b g)
              (path-from-to p a b g))
         (path-from-to (find-path a b g) a b g))
```

Now think about the theorem above. How does the existence of path
p insure that find-path will succeed? In particular, find-path will not
necessarily find p! Indeed, p may be a "non-simple" path (*i.e.*, one with
loops). Here is the informal correctness argument.

> **Informal Proof Sketch:** It is fairly obvious from the definition
> of find-path that it returns a path from a to b *unless* it signals
> failure. So the problem is to show that find-path does not
> signal failure. Now given a path p from a to b, we can obtain
> a simple path, p', from a to b. Furthermore, p' is a member
> of the set, S, of all simple paths from a to b, showing that S is
> non-empty. But find-path signals failure only if S is empty. □

ACL2 certainly cannot discover this proof! However, it can be led to it.
To formalize this argument we must formalize more than just the concepts
used to state the goal. Some concepts, *e.g.*, that of "simple path," are
introduced during the proof. Many relationships between these concepts
are left implicit. The key observations made in the sketch are not themselves
proved. All of this may leave the false impression that the theorem has been
proved and that the proof is quite short.

Learning how to formalize ideas that are informally understood is crucial
to using ACL2. An under-appreciated but essential skill, long known to
mathematicians, is recognizing when new concepts are needed, especially
if those concepts are not identified in the informal arguments. Being alert
to situations that may call for new lemmas of certain forms makes it easier
to apply The Method (see the companion book [58] or see the-method),
because you know what to look for as you inspect failed proofs.

And now for some psychological remarks: developing your expectations
of the amount of work involved can make the difference between success
and failure. Your experience of using The Method will be much more
positive if you correctly anticipate that a step will require certain kinds of
lemmas, even if you do not know what form they will take. The failure
of the system to complete the step validates your intuitions and provides
you with the information you need. In this situation, the theorem prover is

often regarded as a partner or a useful tool in the creation of the proof. On the other hand, if you are unrealistically expecting the system to complete the step for you, its failure disappoints you. Repeated disappointment leads to disillusionment; the theorem prover becomes an adversary. It is easy in this situation to abandon the project as unworkable.

In this chapter we formalize and prove the theorem above. But much of the chapter is aimed at helping you develop your expectations.

For the record, it took me about 8 hours to develop the script described here, from my first contemplation of the problem. About 20 definitions and 70 theorems are involved. It takes ACL2 less than 30 seconds to process the script. I have worked about two weeks writing up the proof, not to make it more elegant but to explain the original intuitions and the process.

The supporting material contains four books of interest. The book find-path1 contains my original script, developed more or less by following The Method. That script contains many "general purpose" lemmas about list processing. So next I segregated these into a book named helpers, and I created the book find-path2, which is concerned only with the graph-theory part of this problem. But find-path2 is still linearly structured, reflecting basically the post-order traversal of my originally imagined proof tree. So in find-path3 I defined the macro named top-down.

```
(defmacro top-down (main &rest others)
  '(progn ,@others ,main))
```

Thus, (top-down *main* $e_1 \ldots e_n$) expands into a command that first processes the e_i and then processes *main*. I use top-down to structure the proof as it is described here. Kaufmann's article, Chapter 6, presents much more flexible proof-structuring devices. After reading this chapter you are encouraged to look at the three find-path*i* books to see how proof scripts can be made more perspicuous. If you wish to use The Method to do this entire chapter as an exercise, look to find-path1 for my solutions.

5.1   Getting Started

We use two books to make this proof simpler to describe.

```
(include-book "/projects/acl2/v2-5/books/arithmetic/top")
(include-book "helpers")
```

The supporting book helpers contains a definition of rev, the list reverse function defined in terms of append rather than the tail recursive reverse native to ACL2. In addition, it contains nineteen theorems about rev and/or several native ACL2 functions including append, member (which checks membership in a list), subsetp (which checks the subset relation between two lists), no-duplicatesp (which checks that a list has no duplicate elements), and last (which returns the last consp cdr of a list). We use these results largely without noting them below.

Exercise 5.1 *Is this a theorem? Why not? Prove the theorem it suggests.*

```
(defthm member-append
  (equal (member x (append a b))
         (or (member x a)
             (member x b))))
```

Exercise 5.2 *Given the definition of* rev, *prove* car-last-rev *below.*

```
(defun rev (x)
  (if (endp x)
      nil
    (append (rev (cdr x)) (list (car x)))))
(defthm car-last-rev
  (equal (car (last (rev x)))
         (car x)))
```

Exercise 5.3 *How would you rewrite*

(no-duplicatesp (append a (cons e b)))

to simplify it? Prove the theorem.

5.2   The Primitives of Directed Graphs

The most basic notion we must define is that of a "directed graph." In this work, we use the word "graph" always to mean directed graph. We represent a graph as an alist.

Formally then a graph is a list of pairs; each pair consists of a key and a value. Each key is the name of a node of the graph. The value associated with a key is the list of neighbor nodes immediately accessible from the given node. For sanity, we insist that each node name appear only once as a key in the alist, and that the list of neighbors of a node contain no duplications. These restrictions play no part in the proof and could be dropped. Note the use of top-down to structure the presentation.

```
(top-down
  (defun graphp (g)
    (and (alistp g)
         (no-duplicatesp (all-nodes g))
         (graph1p g (all-nodes g))))
  ; where
  (defun all-nodes (g)
    (cond ((endp g) nil)
          (t (cons (car (car g))
                   (all-nodes (cdr g))))))
  ; and
```

```
(defun graph1p (g nodes)
  (cond ((endp g) t)
        (t (and (consp (car g))
                (true-listp (cdr (car g)))
                (subsetp (cdr (car g)) nodes)
                (no-duplicatesp (cdr (car g)))
                (graph1p (cdr g) nodes))))))
```

The functions for recognizing nodes in a graph and for computing the neighbors of a node are defined below.

```
(defun nodep (x g)
  (member x (all-nodes g)))
(defun neighbors (node g)
  (cond ((endp g) nil)
        ((equal node (car (car g))) (cdr (car g)))
        (t (neighbors node (cdr g)))))
```

The formal definition of a path in a graph g is given by pathp. A path is a non-empty list with the property that each element except the first is a neighbor of the preceding element.

```
(defun pathp (p g)
  (cond ((endp p) nil)
        ((endp (cdr p))
         (equal (cdr p) nil))
        (t (and (member (cadr p)
                        (neighbors (car p) g))
                (pathp (cdr p) g)))))
```

Having defined a path, it is convenient to define the notion of path-from-to, which checks that p is a path in g, with initial element a and final element b.

```
(defun path-from-to (p a b g)
  (and (pathp p g)
       (equal (car p) a)
       (equal (car (last p)) b)))
```

We test and illustrate these concepts by observing the theorem named Example1 below. The theorem is proved by evaluation! But by making it a theorem and including it in a certified book we can help document how our functions behave and provide tests should we wish to change them in the future. Figure 5.1 shows a picture of the graph g used in Example1.

```
(defthm Example1
  (let ((g '((A B)
             (B B C)
             (C A C D)
             (D A B C))))
```

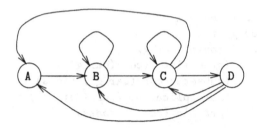

Figure 5.1: The graph in Example1

```
(and (graphp g)
     (not (graphp (cdr g)))
     (nodep 'A g)
     (not (nodep 'E g))
     (pathp '(A B C D C A B B) g)
     (path-from-to '(A B B C) 'A 'C g)
     (not (pathp '(A B D) g))))
 :rule-classes nil)
```

5.3   The Specification of Find-Path

We desire a function find-path with the following property.

```
(defthm Spec-of-Find-Path
  (implies (and (graphp g)
                (nodep a g)
                (nodep b g)
                (path-from-to p a b g))
           (path-from-to (find-path a b g) a b g)))
```

After we define find-path we will actually prove a stronger theorem about it.

```
(defthm Main
  (implies (path-from-to p a b g)
           (path-from-to (find-path a b g) a b g)))
```

Spec-of-Find-Path follows easily from Main: the first three hypotheses of Spec-of-Find-Path are irrelevant!

This is an aspect of ACL2's typeless language. (Find-path a b g) is defined to return something, whether g is a graph or not and whether a and b are nodes in it or not. Main establishes that if (path-from-to p a b g) is true then so is (path-from-to (find-path a b g) a b g), regardless of the "types" of the variables.

Many new users struggle with an apparent dilemma: which of these two theorems is to be preferred? The answer is: both! The two theorems have different purposes. The weaker theorem, `Spec-of-Find-Path`, is desirable as a specification of a not-yet-defined function: it makes it easier for the implementor because it does not overconstrain the function on irrelevant inputs. The stronger theorem, `Main`, is desirable as a theorem about an already-defined function: if a defined function actually has such an elegant property, use it! In particular, the stronger theorem is easier to use (*e.g.*, as a rewrite rule), because it has fewer hypotheses. In addition, such strong theorems are often easier to prove by induction, though that consideration is irrelevant here because we will not prove `Main` by induction. Thus, we prove both theorems. The stronger one is for "internal use" (*i.e.*, it will be stored as a rewrite rule) while the weaker one is for "external use" (*i.e.*, it will be stored with `:rule-classes nil`).

Because such theorems as `Main` are easier to use and often easier to prove, it is advantageous to define our functions so as to insure such strong properties. A side-effect is that, quite often, the definitions are simpler than they would be if we included a lot of checks for type correctness.[1] How is it possible to define `find-path` so that it "works" even for non-graphs? Before we answer that, let us reconsider our representation of graphs.

Our representation is non-unique: many different objects can represent the same graph. For example, the lists `'((A A B) (B A B))` and `'((B A B) (A B A))` are different objects that represent the same graph. Our functions are not sensitive to the order in which the keys presented. `Path-from-to` is not sensitive to the order in which the neighbors are presented. `Find-path` will be sensitive to the order of the neighbors only in the sense that the order affects which path it finds, not whether it succeeds or fails.

Therefore, we could choose to strengthen the notion of `graphp` to require that graphs be presented in some canonical order. But even if we strengthened `graphp`, the `path-from-to` and `find-path` defined here would still enjoy the relationship above, even for non-canonical "graphs."

In a similar vein, our functions are not sensitive to other aspects of the concrete representation of graphs. For example, `graphp` requires that every neighbor listed for a node also appear as a key, with some associated list of neighbors. Suppose some "graph" fails to list some neighbor as a key. All our functions behave just as though the neighbor were listed and had the empty list of neighbors. Similarly, `graphp` requires that a graph list every node only once as a key. But if some "graph" has two entries for the same key, all our functions use the first entry and they all ignore the second. Thus, our notion of `graphp` could be weakened without affecting the relationship between `path-from-to` and `find-path`. In fact, it could be weakened to accept any object!

---

[1]This discussion ignores guards. Our functions would have to be coded somewhat differently if we wished to verify their guards. See `guard`.

In the sense illustrated above, our functions "coerce" any object into some graph. By insuring that all the functions—in particular both path--from-to and find-path—coerce non-graphs to graphs in exactly the same way, we can prove theorems like Main without making restrictions on the form of graphs. This would not be the case, for example, if path-from-to used the first occurrence of a key to determine the neighbors and find-path used the last! If we defined the functions that way, we would need to include a graphp hypothesis to insure that there is only one such occurrence.

Defining all the functions in a family to coerce "unexpected" inputs in the same way is a useful skill. It is generally done—as here—by defining the primitive functions for a representation—*e.g.*, neighbors— and then using them consistently without checking for irrelevant conditions first. This is a good discipline in part because it allows one to state and prove theorems without a lot of cluttering hypotheses.

5.4   The Definitions of Find-Path and Find-Next-Step

In this section we define find-path, as follows.

```
(defun find-path (a b g)
  (cond ((equal a b) (list a))
        (t (find-next-step (neighbors a g)
                           (list a)
                           b g))))
```

Find-path finds a path from a to b, if possible. If a and b are equal, the path is the singleton list containing a. Otherwise, find-path calls find-next-step to search for a path. That function takes four arguments and, in this call, those arguments are the neighbors of a, a stack of nodes, the target node b, and the graph g. The stack is represented as a list and initially the stack has one node on it, namely a. In general, the topmost node on the stack can be thought of as the current node and the stack itself (in reverse order) can be thought of as a path from the original source node to the current node. Roughly speaking, find-next-step does a depth-first search through the neighbors, looking for the first one from which it can build a path to b without visiting any node already on the stack. If and when find-next-step finds the target b among the neighbors, it builds the appropriate path from the stack. If it fails to find a path, it returns the symbol 'failure.

Here is the definition of find-next-step, ignoring the necessary measure hint.

```
(defun find-next-step (c stack b g)
  (cond
    ((endp c) 'failure)                           ; (1)
    ((member (car c) stack)                       ; (2)
```

```
        (find-next-step (cdr c) stack b g))
       ((equal (car c) b)                        ; (3)
        (rev (cons b stack)))
       (t (let ((temp (find-next-step             ; (4)
                        (neighbors (car c) g)
                        (cons (car c) stack)
                        b g)))
            (if (equal temp 'failure)             ; (4a)
                (find-next-step (cdr c) stack b g) ; (4b)
              temp)))))))                          ; (4c)
```

Reading it clause-by-clause: (1) If there are no neighbors left to consider, return 'failure. (2) If the next neighbor is a member of the stack, continue to the neighbor after that. (3) If the next neighbor is the target, construct a suitable path using the stack. Finally, (4) call find-next-step recursively, letting the result be called temp. In the recursive call, try to find a path to the target through the neighbors of the next neighbor, after pushing that neighbor onto the stack. Then (4a) if temp is 'failure, there is no path to b through the neighbor just tried and so (4b) try the rest of the neighbors, using the input stack. Otherwise, (4c) return the path found.

Some readers may have preferred mutually-recursive definitions of functions find-path and find-next-step. However, mutually-recursive functions are somewhat more awkward to reason about formally than simple recursive functions.

Few programmers would code this algorithm. Its run time is exponential in the number of edges in the graph: we repeat the work done for a node upon each simple arrival at the node, even though a previous arrival at the node via a different path would have fully explored the simple paths from it and found that none reaches the target. By coloring the nodes we can produce a linear time algorithm. It is tempting to improve find-path in this way. We resist the temptation and explain why later.

Instead, let us consider the admission of find-path and find-next--step as defined above. The former is easily admitted after the latter. But how do we admit find-next-step? We must exhibit a measure of the arguments of find-next-step that gets smaller in each recursive call.

Exercise 5.4 *Before reading on, think about* find-next-step. *Why does it terminate?*

The measure we have in mind is a lexicographic combination of two measures. The first is the number of nodes of g not yet on the stack. Naively speaking, that number decreases every time we add a new neighbor to the stack. But not every recursive call adds an item to the stack. In particular, as we scan the neighbors of a node, the stack is fixed. Thus, the second component of our lexicographic measure is the number of neighbors left to be explored.

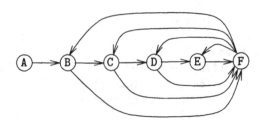

Figure 5.2: The graph in Example2

Exercise 5.5 *Before reading on, formalize what was just said. Define* (measure c stack g) *to decrease in each recursion in* find-next-step.

Here is our definition.

```
(defun measure (c stack g)
  (cons (+ 1 (count-non-members (all-nodes g) stack))
        (len c)))
```

Exercise 5.6 *Define* count-non-members.

Exercise 5.7 *The termination proof is more subtle than you might expect. The recursive call on line (4) generates the measure conjecture shown below.*

```
(implies (and (not (endp c))
              (not (member (car c) stack))
              (not (equal (car c) b)))
         (e0-ord-< (measure (neighbors (car c) g)
                            (cons (car c) stack)
                            g)
                   (measure c stack g)))
```

ACL2 proves this automatically. But is it really a theorem? The naive explanation sketched above can be elaborated as follows. "In the recursion, the stack grows by one item, (car c), *which previously was not a member of the stack. Thus, the number of unvisited nodes in* g *decreases." But this naive argument assumes that the new item is a node in* g. *What if it is not? The subtlety of this argument is the price we pay for not checking that* g *is a graph and that* c *is a list of nodes in it. The reward is a much simpler definition and main theorem. But why does* measure *decrease?*

Here is an example of find-path on the graph of Figure 5.2.

```
(defthm Example2
  (let ((g '((A B)
             (B C F)
```

```
                    (C D F)
                    (D E F)
                    (E F)
                    (F B C D E))))
      (and (graphp g)
           (equal (find-path 'A 'E g) '(A B C D E))
           (path-from-to '(A B C D E) 'A 'E g)
           (path-from-to '(A B F E)   'A 'E g)
           (equal (find-path 'F 'A g) 'failure)))
   :rule-classes nil)
```

The conjuncts inform us that g is a graph, find-path succeeds from A to
E, the alleged path found is indeed a suitable path, there is a shorter path
from A to E, and that find-path fails to find a path from F to A.

5.5   Sketch of the Proof of Our Main Theorem

Recall the strong conjecture about find-path.

```
(defthm Main
   (implies (path-from-to p a b g)
            (path-from-to (find-path a b g) a b g))
   :hints ...)
```

Here we begin to formalize the proof sketched on page 42, by stating the four
observations as formulas. In subsequent sections, we define the necessary
concepts and prove each of the observations. We will eventually prove Main
by filling in the hints above to use our observations.

Proof Sketch
     If find-path does not signal failure, then it actually does return a path
from the indicated source, a, to the indicated target, b.

```
(defthm Observation-0
   (implies (not (equal (find-path a b g) 'failure))
            (path-from-to (find-path a b g) a b g))
   :rule-classes nil)
```

(One might call this "weak correctness" because it does not preclude the
possibility that find-path fails unnecessarily often.) The proof of Main is
thus reduced to showing that find-path does not fail unnecessarily.
     If there is a path p from a to b, then there is a simple path. Rather
than use <u>defun-sk</u> to introduce an existential quantifier, we will define
a function, simplify-path, to construct a simple path from an arbitrary
path, and use it in the statement of our observation.

```
(defthm Observation-1
   (implies (path-from-to p a b g)
```

```
           (and (simple-pathp (simplify-path p) g)
                (path-from-to (simplify-path p) a b g)))
    :rule-classes nil)
```

Furthermore, if there is a simple path from a to b, then it is a member
of the set of all simple paths from a to b, as constructed by the (soon to be
defined) function `find-all-simple-paths`.

```
(defthm Observation-2
    (implies (and (simple-pathp p g)
                  (path-from-to p a b g))
             (member p (find-all-simple-paths a b g)))
    :rule-classes nil
    :hints ...)
```

From Observations 1 and 2, together with the hypothesis of our `Main` theorem, we know that the set of all simple paths from a to b is non-empty.

   We therefore conclude the proof by observing that `find-path` succeeds
precisely when the set of all simple paths is non-empty.

```
(defthm Observation-3
    (iff (find-all-simple-paths a b g)
         (not (equal (find-path a b g) 'failure)))
    :rule-classes nil)
```

☐

5.6   Observation 0

```
(defthm Observation-0
    (implies (not (equal (find-path a b g) 'failure))
             (path-from-to (find-path a b g) a b g))
    :rule-classes nil)
```

We have to prove that if `find-path` does not report failure, then it returns
a path, the path starts at a, and the path ends at b. Roughly speaking,
these theorems follow immediately from three analogous theorems about
the function `find-next-step`, in terms of which `find-path` is defined.
However, to prove things about `find-next-step` one must use induction,
because it is a recursive function. And to prove inductive theorems one
must find suitably strong statements of those theorems. So below you will
see three inductively provable theorems about `find-next-step`. The first
says it returns a path and the next two say that the source and target of
that path are appropriate. ACL2 proves these without assistance. But the
real contribution of the user here was to find suitably strong statements
of these properties. Basically, when looking for theorems like these, one
wants to ask the question: what is the most general situation in which the

function can be called? More formally, contemplate a call of the function with distinct variables in every argument position.

We anticipate the lemmas noted above from our experience, not from a detailed a look at the proof of Observation-0. In particular, our expectations are that we should seek lemmas about find-next-step, that they will be proved inductively, and that they must be general. We find them by applying The Method to Observation-0.

The first lemma is that find-next-step returns a path in the graph, when it does not report failure. For this to be true, the initial stack must be a non-empty list which, when reversed, is a path in the graph. Furthermore, the list c of neighbors to consider for extending that path must be a subset of the neighbors of the top of the stack.

```
(defthm pathp-find-next-step
   (implies (and (true-listp stack)
                 (consp stack)
                 (pathp (rev stack) g)
                 (subsetp c (neighbors (car stack) g))
                 (not (equal (find-next-step c stack b g)
                             'failure)))
            (pathp (find-next-step c stack b g) g)))
```

ACL2 proves this inductively, but finding its proof via The Method requires that we find several other lemmas. In our decomposition of the proof, we identified eleven such lemmas. All but one were list processing lemmas now in the support book helpers. They were suggested by the occurrence in failed proofs of such terms as (append (append x y) z), (last (append a b)) and (subsetp x x).

Exercise 5.8 *The theorem above requires one lemma that is not just list processing. It was suggested by a failed proof of* pathp-find-next-step *in which the following term arose.*

```
(pathp (append (rev stack)
               (list (car c)))
       g)
```

What is it about find-next-step *that led us to expect the need for such a lemma? What is the suggested lemma?*

Exercise 5.9 *As an exercise in using The Method, get ACL2 to prove the theorem above, without all of the necessary list processing helpers in the database. Start by doing*

```
(rebuild "find-path1.lisp"
         'pathp-append)
```

to initialize the database. The second argument to rebuild *tells ACL2 to to stop loading the file after processing the event named* pathp-append. *Then, prove* pathp-find-next-step.

The second lemma states that find-next-step returns a list whose first element is the last (bottom-most) element of its initial stack.

```
(defthm car-find-next-step
  (implies (and (true-listp stack)
                (consp stack)
                (not (equal (find-next-step c stack b g)
                            'failure)))
           (equal (car (find-next-step c stack b g))
                  (car (last stack)))))
```

The third is that find-next-step returns a list whose last element is the target.

```
(defthm car-last-find-next-step
  (implies (and (true-listp stack)
                (consp stack)
                (not (equal (find-next-step c stack b g)
                            'failure)))
           (equal (car (last (find-next-step c stack b g)))
                  b)))
```

Note that all three of these lemmas are made rewrite rules. These three results give us Observation-0 directly.

Exercise 5.10 *Starting with the database constructed by the successful completion of Exercise 5.9, prove* car-find-next-step *and* car-last- -find-next-step *above.*

5.7 Observation 1

The next observation constructively establishes that if p is a path then there exists a simple path with the same end points.

```
(defun simple-pathp (p g)
  (and (no-duplicatesp p)
       (pathp p g)))
```

Here is the definition of simplify-path.

```
(top-down
  (defun simplify-path (p)
    (cond ((endp p) nil)
          ((member (car p) (cdr p))
           (simplify-path (chop (car p) (cdr p))))
          (t (cons (car p) (simplify-path (cdr p))))))
  ; where
  (defun chop (e p)
    (cond ((endp p) nil)
```

```
((equal e (car p)) p)
(t (chop e (cdr p)))))))
```

When `simplify-path` finds that some element of the path occurs later in the path, it uses the function `chop` to delete from the path the first occurrence of that element and all subsequent elements up to the second occurrence, thus removing one loop from the path. The admission of `simplify-path` is mildly interesting. ACL2 has to prove that `chop` returns a list that is shorter than p. This is an inductive proof, but ACL2 manages it without help.[2]

Since the result of `simplify-path` is obtained by repeatedly applying chop to its input under certain conditions, we can expect that every inductive lemma we need about `simplify-path` will require proving an inductive analogue about `chop`. Developing this sense of expectation is important. With it, you can easily sketch a proof. Without it, you may be worn down by the continued need to state unexpected lemmas!

Here is a typical pair of lemmas. The first shown is a fact about `simplify-path` that is used repeatedly in the proof of `Observation-1`. The second is the corresponding fact about `chop`.

```
(top-down
 (defthm simplify-path-iff-consp
   (iff (consp (simplify-path p)) (consp p)))
 ; Proof:  An easy induction, using:
 (defthm chop-iff-consp
   (implies (member e p)
            (consp (chop e p)))))
```

We now turn our attention to `Observation-1`. Its conclusion is a conjunction of two requirements on (`simplify-path p`). The first is a `simple-path` condition and the second is a `path-from-to` condition. But each of these concepts is defined as a conjunction of others. The `simple--path` condition breaks down to a `pathp` condition and a `no-duplicatesp` condition. The `path-from-to` condition breaks down to the same `pathp` condition, and conditions on both the `car` of the path and the `car` of the `last` of the path. We prove these four conjuncts about `simplify-path` separately. Each requires a corresponding property about `chop`.

With the foregoing as prelude, the details, which were finalized by applying The Method, should be more or less obvious to you. After following The Method to develop the proof, we structured it using `top-down`.

```
(top-down
 (defthm Observation-1
   (implies (path-from-to p a b g)
            (and (simple-pathp (simplify-path p) g)
```

---

[2]The astute reader might notice that chop is equivalent to member. We keep the name chop for pedagogical reasons.

```
                        (path-from-to (simplify-path p) a b g)))
  :rule-classes nil)
;; Proof of Observation-1
(top-down
 (defthm car-simplify-path
   (equal (car (simplify-path p)) (car p)))
 ;; by an easy induction using the analogous
 (defthm car-chop
   (implies (member e p)
            (equal (car (chop e p)) e))))
(top-down
 (defthm car-last-simplify-path
   (equal (car (last (simplify-path p))) (car (last p))))
 ;; by an easy induction using the analogous
 (defthm car-last-chop
   (implies (member e p)
            (equal (car (last (chop e p)))
                   (car (last p))))))
(top-down
 (defthm pathp-simplify-path
   (implies (pathp p g)
            (pathp (simplify-path p) g)))
 ;; by an easy induction using the analogous
 (defthm pathp-chop
   (implies (and (member e p)
                 (pathp p g))
            (pathp (chop e p) g))))
(top-down
 (defthm no-duplicatesp-simplify-path
   (no-duplicatesp (simplify-path p)))
 ;; Proof
 (top-down
  (defthm not-member-simplify-path
    (implies (not (member x p))
             (not (member x (simplify-path p)))))
  ;; by an easy induction using the analogous
  (defthm not-member-chop
    (implies (not (member x p))
             (not (member x (chop e p)))))))
;; Q.E.D. Observation-1
)
```

5.8   Observation 2

The next observation is the key to the whole exercise. We wish to prove
that if p is a simple path from a to b, then it is among the paths collected by find-all-simple-paths. We must define find-all-simple-
-paths first. The definition is below. The reader will note that this function is analogous to find-path, and find-all-next-steps is analogous to
find-next-step. But these new functions do not signal failure when no
path is found. Nor do they quit when the first path is found. Instead, they
find and collect all simple paths. The measure justifying the admission of
find-all-next-steps is exactly the same as before.

```
(top-down
 (defun find-all-simple-paths (a b g)
   (if (equal a b)
       (list (list a))
     (find-all-next-steps (neighbors a g)
                          (list a)
                          b g)))
 ; where
 (defun find-all-next-steps (c stack b g)
   (declare (xargs :measure (measure c stack g)))
   (cond
    ((endp c) nil)
    ((member (car c) stack)
     (find-all-next-steps (cdr c) stack b g))
    ((equal (car c) b)
     (cons (rev (cons b stack))
           (find-all-next-steps (cdr c) stack b g)))
    (t (append (find-all-next-steps (neighbors (car c) g)
                                    (cons (car c) stack)
                                    b g)
               (find-all-next-steps (cdr c) stack b g))))))
```

The similarity between these two functions and find-path and find-next-
-step will be important when we come to prove Observation 3, the relation
between them. It is a good idea when defining auxiliary functions such as
these to define them so as to make the proof obligations as easy as possible.

   Observation 2 requires that we show that every simple path p between
a and b is in the list of paths collected by (find-all-simple-paths a b
g).

   Before proceeding, let us do a shallow analysis, to refine our expectations
and structure our search for a proof. How will the proof go? Clearly, since
find-all-simple-paths is defined in terms of find-all-next-steps, we
must prove a property about that function that is analogous to Observation 2. But because find-all-next-steps is recursive, the proof will be

inductive and the property we seek must be very general. So think about
(find-all-next-steps c stack b g). When is something a member of
the result?

   We may assume that stack is non-empty and contains no duplications.
Obviously, every path in the final list will be some extension of the reverse of
stack, so the typical element will be of the form (append (rev stack) p).
What is a sufficient condition on the extension, p, to insure membership?
P must start at some element of c and will end at b and will be a path.
Furthermore, p must share no elements with stack.

   Below is a formal rendering of this analysis. You will note that there is
no mention of b in the formula; instead, the last element of p is used in its
place.

```
(defthm Crux
  (implies (and (true-listp stack)
                (consp stack)
                (pathp p g)
                (member (car p) c)
                (no-duplicatesp (append stack p)))
          (member (append (rev stack) p)
                  (find-all-next-steps c stack
                                          (car (last p)) g)))
  :rule-classes nil
  :hints ...)
```

This theorem is named "Crux" because it is the hardest part of the entire
proof. Perhaps the single most difficult aspect of Crux was stating it!
However the inductive proof is somewhat subtle.

   We are trying to prove that a certain object, namely, the one constructed by (append (rev stack) p), is a member of the list returned
by find-all-next-steps. Call this "certain object" α. How is α put into
the answer returned by find-all-next-steps? Find-all-next-steps explores all the nodes in c and extends the stack appropriately for each one.
At the bottom, it reverses the stack and adds that path to its answer; at
all other levels it just concatenates the answers together.

   Most subtle formal proofs start with an informal idea. Here is what
came to me: imagine that find-all-next-steps were miraculously able to
extend the stack only by successive elements of p. Then it would obviously
build up α in the stack and put it in the answer.

   A little more formally, think of tracing the computation of find-all-
-next-steps and watching it choose just the successive elements of path
p from among the neighbors at each successive level. That is, when find-
-all-next-steps is pursuing the paths from a neighbor that is not the next
node in p, we are not too interested in the result— α will be generated by a
call further along in the cdr of c and will survive in the answer produced by
subsequent concatenations—so we just want an inductive hypothesis about

(cdr c). On the other hand, we are quite interested when the neighbor is
(car p). The addition of that neighbor, *i.e.*, (car p), to the stack builds
up part of α and the inductive hypothesis for that stack and (cdr p) tells
us that α is in the list returned.

So much for intuitions. The devil is in the details. Below, we present a
proof.

Proof Sketch
Denote the Crux formula above by (ϕ c stack p g). We induct according
to the following scheme.

```
(and (implies (endp c)                              ; Base
              ($\phi$ c stack p g))
     (implies (and (not (endp c))                   ; Ind Step 1
                   (member (car c) stack)
                   ($\phi$ (cdr c) stack p g))
              ($\phi$ c stack p g))
     (implies (and (not (endp c))                   ; Ind Step 2
                   (not (member (car c) stack))
                   (equal (car c) (car p))
                   ($\phi$ (neighbors (car c) g)
                      (cons (car c) stack)
                      (cdr p)
                      g))
              ($\phi$ c stack p g))
     (implies (and (not (endp c))                   ; Ind Step 3
                   (not (member (car c) stack))
                   (not (equal (car c) (car p)))
                   ($\phi$ (cdr c) stack p g))
              ($\phi$ c stack p g)))
```

The first conjunct is the Base Case. The other three are Induction Steps.
The Induction Step 2 is the interesting one.

Base Case

```
(implies
 (endp c)                                           ; (0)
 (implies (and (true-listp stack)                   ; (1)
               (consp stack)                        ; (2)
               (pathp p g)                          ; (3)
               (member (car p) c)                   ; (4)
               (no-duplicatesp (append stack p)))   ; (5)
          (member (append (rev stack) p)            ; (6)
                  (find-all-next-steps c stack
                                       (car (last p))
                                       g)))))
```

From (0) we see that c is empty. But then hypothesis (4) is contradicted.

Induction Step 1

```
(implies
 (and
  (not (endp c))                                     ; (0)
  (member (car c) stack)                             ; (1)
  (implies
    (and (true-listp stack)                          ; (2')
         (consp stack)                               ; (3')
         (pathp p g)                                 ; (4')
         (member (car p) (cdr c))                    ; (5')
         (no-duplicatesp (append stack p)))          ; (6')
     (member (append (rev stack) p)                  ; (7')
             (find-all-next-steps (cdr c)            ; (8')
                                  stack              ; (9')
                                  (car (last p))     ; (10')
                                  g))))              ; (11')
 (implies (and (true-listp stack)                    ; (2)
               (consp stack)                         ; (3)
               (pathp p g)                           ; (4)
               (member (car p) c)                    ; (5)
               (no-duplicatesp (append stack p)))    ; (6)
     (member (append (rev stack) p)                  ; (7)
             (find-all-next-steps c                  ; (8)
                                  stack              ; (9)
                                  (car (last p));    ; (10)
                                  g))))              ; (11)
```

Note that lines (2')–(11') constitute the induction hypothesis. Lines (2)–(11) constitute the induction conclusion. We get to assume (0) and (1), the induction hypothesis (2')–(11'), and the hypotheses (2)–(6) of the induction conclusion. We have to prove the conclusion of the conclusion, namely the member expression that starts on line (7). We know that the member expression that starts on line (7') is true provided we can show that the hypotheses (2')–(6') of the induction hypothesis are true.

By (0) and (1) and the definition of find-all-next-steps, the find--all-next-steps expression at (8) is equal to the find-all-next-steps expression at (8'). The proof would be finished if we could relieve the hypotheses (2')–(6') of the induction hypothesis. Note that (2'), (3'), (4'), and (6') are all identical to their counterparts (2), (3), (4), and (6), which are given. We are left to show that (5) implies (5'), that is, that when (car p) is in c it is in (cdr c). By the definition of member, if (car p) is in c, then it is either equal to (car c) or it is a member of (cdr c). If the latter, we are done. So assume (car p) is (car c). Then by (1) and equality, (car p) is in stack. But if (car p) is in stack, then there

are duplications in (append stack p), contradicting (6). Recall Exercise
5.3.

ACL2 does this proof without help, given the theorems in the supporting
book helpers.

Induction Step 2

```
(implies
 (and
  (not (endp c))                                           ; (0)
  (not (member (car c) stack))                             ; (1)
  (equal (car c) (car p))                                  ; (2)
  (implies
   (and (true-listp (cons (car c) stack))                 ; (3')
        (consp (cons (car c) stack))                       ; (4')
        (pathp (cdr p) g)                                  ; (5')
        (member (cadr p) (neighbors (car c) g))            ; (6')
        (no-duplicatesp (append (cons (car c) stack); (7')
                                (cdr p))))
   (member (append (rev (cons (car c) stack))             ; (8')
                   (cdr p))
           (find-all-next-steps                            ; (9')
            (neighbors (car c) g)
            (cons (car c) stack)
            (car (last (cdr p)))
            g))))
  (implies (and (true-listp stack)                         ; (3)
                (consp stack)                               ; (4)
                (pathp p g)                                 ; (5)
                (member (car p) c)                          ; (6)
                (no-duplicatesp (append stack p)))         ; (7)
           (member (append (rev stack) p)                  ; (8)
                   (find-all-next-steps c                  ; (9)
                                        stack
                                        (car (last p))
                                        g))))
```

Elementary list processing lemmas in the book helpers, together with (2),
tell us that the append expression at (8') is equal to the append expression
at (8). By the definition of find-all-next-steps, the find-all-next-
-steps at (9) is equal to the following.

```
(if (equal (car c) (car (last p)))                         ; (9a)
    (cons (rev (cons (car (last p)) stack))                ; (9b)
          (find-all-next-steps (cdr c)
                               stack
                               (car (last p))
                               g))
```

```
(append (find-all-next-steps (neighbors (car c) g)  ; (9c)
                             (cons (car c) stack)
                             (car (last p))
                             g)
        (find-all-next-steps (cdr c)
                             stack
                             (car (last p))
                             g)))
```

If (9a) is false, that is (car c) is different from (car (last p)), (9) is
(9c), and the induction hypothesis is sufficient to finish, if we can relieve the
hypotheses of the induction hypothesis. The only problematic hypothesis
is (6'), and given (5), which tells us that p is a path in g, and (2), which
says that (car c) is (car p), it is pretty easy to see that (cadr p) is
a member of the neighbors of (car p). But this follows from the pathp
hypothesis only if (cadr p) is an element of p. What if p is a singleton?
If p were a singleton, then (car p) would be (car (last p)), contrary to
our assumption that (9a) is false.

So suppose (9a) is true, *i.e.*, (car c) is (car (last p)). Then (9) is
(9b). We must show that the append call in (8) is a member of (9b). From
the fact that (car c) is both (car p) and (car (last p)), and (7), we
conclude that p has length 1. That being the case, the first element of
(9b), namely (rev (cons (car (last p)) stack)), is equal to (append
(rev stack) p), which is the append term in (8).

Given the helpers book, ACL2 needs no additional help with this argument either.

Induction Step 3

```
(implies
 (and
  (not (endp c))                                      ; (0)
  (not (member (car c) stack))                        ; (1)
  (not (equal (car c) (car p)))                       ; (2)
  (implies
    (and (true-listp stack)                           ; (3')
         (consp stack)                                ; (4')
         (pathp p g)                                  ; (5')
         (member (car p) (cdr c))                     ; (6')
         (no-duplicatesp (append stack p)))           ; (7')
    (member (append (rev stack) p)                    ; (8')
            (find-all-next-steps (cdr c)              ; (9')
                                 stack
                                 (car (last p))
                                 g))))
 (implies (and (true-listp stack)                     ; (3)
               (consp stack)                          ; (4)
```

```
         (pathp p g)                              ; (5)
         (member (car p) c)                       ; (6)
         (no-duplicatesp (append stack p)))       ; (7)
     (member (append (rev stack) p)               ; (8)
             (find-all-next-steps c               ; (9)
                        stack
                        (car (last p))
                        g))))
```

Observe that (3)–(5) and (7) imply (3')–(5') and (7'), because corresponding hypotheses are identical. Furthermore, (6) implies (6') because of (2). Thus, we have relieved the hypotheses of the induction hypothesis. That leaves us with proving that the member expression at (8') implies the member expression at (8). That is handled by the lemma Crux-cdr, below. ACL2 cannot discover this lemma by itself.

That completes the inductive proof of Crux.

□

As noted earlier, it is good practice, when searching for a proof, to *write down* the theorem you are proving and the inductive argument used. Writing down the induction hypotheses is especially important. As shown above, this can be quite verbose. But with practice you will learn to recognize certain patterns of formula formation and proof obligations, such as the effect of the inductive substitutions and the need to relieve the hypotheses of the induction hypothesis. Once these patterns are well established, you will find that the disciplined use of well-chosen notational conventions will allow you to explore a proof without writing so much. After some practice you will probably find yourself just writing down the theorem, the inductive case analysis and the substitutions, and then "reading off" and jotting down the lemmas you need. But be aware that the mental process is more like the detailed proof above.

The proof patterns manifest themselves in ACL2's output. Our tedious consideration of how to relieve the hypotheses of the induction hypothesis (*e.g.*, , showing that "(5) implies (5')" in Induction Step 1) appears as case analysis in ACL2 output. When ACL2 simplifies

```
(implies (and c
              (implies (and ...p'₅...)
                       q'))
         (implies (and ...p₅...)
                  q))
```

it will generate such subgoals as (implies (and c (NOT p'_5) ... p_5 ...) q), except that the subterms will have been simplified. By recognizing the origin of such subgoals and understanding patterns of proof, you will be able to use ACL2 as an assistant. Rather than write the proof on paper you will let ACL2 do the induction and simplifications and then read its output. That is why The Method works. Expert users of ACL2 rarely turn

to paper to work out low-level technical details. For more on this topic,
see [60]. But we encourage beginners to develop the necessary skills by
sketching proofs on paper first, until the patterns become clear.

Exercise 5.11 *To get ACL2 to do the induction above, it is necessary to
supply an induction hint. Such hints are given by exhibiting a function call
that suggests the desired induction. Our hint is*

```
(defthm Crux
    ...
    :rule-classes nil
    :hints (("Goal" :induct
                    (induction-hint-function p c stack g))))
```

Thus, `induction-hint-function` *must be defined to suggest the induction
done above. See the companion book [58] and* **hints**. *Define and admit*
`induction-hint-function`. *Note: Until we prove* **Crux-cdr**, *ACL2 will
be unable to complete the proof of* **Crux**, *even if you code the induction hint
correctly.*

We now turn to the proof of the just-mentioned lemma for going from
(8') to (8).

```
(defthm Crux-cdr
  (implies
   (and (consp c)
        (member p (find-all-next-steps (cdr c) stack b g)))
   (member p (find-all-next-steps c stack b g)))
  :hints ...)
```

This is a pretty obvious property of `find-all-next-steps` because the
set of paths found for (`cdr c`) is a subset of that found for c, when c is
non-empty. However, as stated, it cannot be proved by induction because
it is too weak. Instead, we prove the following stronger property.

```
(defthm subsetp-find-all-next-steps
  (implies (subsetp c d)
           (subsetp (find-all-next-steps c stack b g)
                    (find-all-next-steps d stack b g))))
```

Exercise 5.12 *The stronger property, above, is a fundamental and "obvious" property of* `find-all-next-steps`. *Prove it, both by hand and with
ACL2. To do the ACL2 proof, first execute the following.*

```
(rebuild "find-path2.lisp"
         'induction-hint-function)
```

Then use The Method.

Exercise 5.13 *The exercise above is made easier by the fact that the necessary list processing lemmas are in the supporting book* helpers, *which is included above. But these lemmas were originally discovered by using The Method. So, back up to the initial state, with* :ubt! 1, *and then execute the following.*

```
(rebuild "find-path1.lisp"
         'induction-hint-function)
```

Then prove subsetp-find-all-next-steps *again, using The Method. Obviously, you should place the lemmas formulated in the previous exercise above* subsetp-find-all-next-steps *in your script—unless you wish to "rediscover" them. But to prove them you will need to discover the helper lemmas yourself.*

Given subsetp-find-all-next-steps, our proof of Crux-cdr is as shown by the hint below.

```
(defthm Crux-cdr
  (implies
   (and (consp c)
        (member p (find-all-next-steps (cdr c) stack b g)))
   (member p (find-all-next-steps c stack b g)))
  :hints
  (("Goal"
    :use (:instance subset-member-member
          (a (find-all-next-steps (cdr c) stack b g))
          (b (find-all-next-steps c stack b g))
          (e p))
    :in-theory (disable subsetp-member-member))))
```

Here is the lemma mentioned in the :use hint.

```
(defthm subsetp-member-member
  (implies (and (subsetp a b)
                (member e a))
           (member e b)))
```

Recall how :use hints are implemented: the indicated theorem is instantiated and added as a hypothesis. So with the hint above we instruct ACL2 to instantiate subsetp-member-member with the substitution [a ◁ (find-all-next-steps (cdr c) stack b g); b ◁ (find-all-next-steps c stack b g); e ◁ p]. The instance thus created is added as a hypothesis, producing the goal shown below.

```
(implies
 (implies
  (and (subsetp (find-all-next-steps (cdr c) stack b g)
                (find-all-next-steps c stack b g))
       (member p (find-all-next-steps (cdr c) stack b g)))
```

```
(member p (find-all-next-steps c stack b g)))
(implies
 (and (consp c)
      (member p (find-all-next-steps (cdr c) stack b g)))
 (member p (find-all-next-steps c stack b g)))))
```

This goal is proved by rewriting the subsetp hypothesis to true, by back-chaining through subsetp-find-all-next-steps. To relieve the hypothesis of that lemma, namely, (subsetp (cdr c) c) in this case, ACL2 uses (consp c) and the definition of subsetp. Note that our hint above also included an :in-theory disabling the lemma used. We discuss the reason for this on page 67.

So where are we? We have just finished explaining the proof of Crux.

```
(defthm Crux
  (implies (and (true-listp stack)
                (consp stack)
                (pathp p g)
                (member (car p) c)
                (no-duplicatesp (append stack p)))
           (member (append (rev stack) p)
                   (find-all-next-steps c stack
                                        (car (last p)) g)))
  :rule-classes nil
  :hints ...)
```

Observation 2 follows from Crux.

```
(defthm Observation-2
  (implies (and (simple-pathp p g)
                (path-from-to p a b g))
           (member p (find-all-simple-paths a b g)))
  :rule-classes nil
  :hints (("Goal"
           :use ((:instance Crux ...)))))
```

Exercise 5.14 *Fill in the dots above with a substitution so that Observation-2 is proved from the resulting instance of Crux by simplification.*

5.9   Observation 3

```
(defthm Observation-3
   (iff (find-all-simple-paths a b g)
        (not (equal (find-path a b g) 'failure)))
   :rule-classes nil)
```

Exercise 5.15 *Prove* Observation-3.

5.10   The Main Theorem

Recall our sketch of the proof of Main on page 51. We have now completed
the proofs of the four observations, each of which was made :rule-classes
nil. Hence, in our proof of Main we must give explicit hints to use these
observations.

```
(defthm Main
  (implies (path-from-to p a b g)
           (path-from-to (find-path a b g) a b g))
  :hints (("Goal"
           :use (Observation-0
                 Observation-1
                 (:instance Observation-2
                            (p (simplify-path p)))
                 Observation-3)
           :in-theory (disable find-path
                               find-all-simple-paths))))
```

Note that we disable two functions. This illustrates a common and
bothersome aspect of the implementation of :use hints. Once the observations are instantiated and added as hypotheses, the new goal, which might
be written as

```
(implies (and observation_0
              observation_1
              observation_2
              observation_3)
         main)
```

is simplified. But if the simplifier can prove $observation_0$, say, then it is
removed from the hypotheses and we are in the same state we would have
been had we not provided $observation_0$ as a hint. That is why we chose
:rule-classes nil for our four observations: to keep the stored version
of Observation-i from rewriting the $observation_i$ away. But things are
more subtle than that. If find-path is expanded, then the simplifier can
prove $observation_0$ by appealing to the same lemmas we used to prove
Observation-0 in the first place. To prevent that, we disable the two
non-recursive function symbols that occur in the observations.

5.11   The Specification of Find-Path

Finally, we wish to prove that find-path satisfies its specification.

```
(defthm Spec-of-Find-Path
  (implies (and (graphp g)
                (nodep a g)
                (nodep b g)
                (path-from-to p a b g))
           (path-from-to (find-path a b g) a b g))
  :hints (("Goal" ...))))
```

Exercise 5.16 *Fill in the dots above to make the proof go through. Note that* Main *is proved as a rewrite rule.*

Exercise 5.17 *The introduction of* find-all-simple-paths *is not strictly necessary. It is possible to prove directly that the existence of a simple path implies that* find-path *will not fail. Formalize and prove this lemma.*

5.12   Reflexive Definitions

As noted, our find-path runs in exponential time. We can reduce it to linear time by "coloring" or "marking" the nodes as we visit them. We can formalize this by adding a new argument to find-next-step, called mt (for "mark table"). The table is just a list of all the nodes visited so far, by any recursive call. The new function should fail immediately if it arrives at a marked node. Otherwise, in addition to returning the winning path (or failure signal), it should return an extended mark table. The returned table should contain all the nodes in the old table plus any new nodes visited. The measure used for admission is lexicographic, as before, but the first component is the number of unmarked nodes of the graph (rather than the number of "unstacked" nodes). Linearity is assured by the fact that the edges from a given node are explored at most once.

But the termination argument for this new function is much more subtle. Consider exploring the neighbors, $n_1, n_2, \ldots, n_k$ of some node. Suppose n_1 is not in the mark table, *mt*. Then the new function will explore the neighbors of n_1, using (cons n_1 mt) as the mark table. It will obtain a path or failure message and a new mark table, *mt'*. Suppose no path through n_1 is found. Then the function will recursively consider $n_2, \ldots, n_k$, using the mark table *mt'* obtained from the first recursive call. Note carefully: the mark table given to the second recursive call is one of the results returned by the first recursive call. The measure depends on properties of the returned table, in particular, that it contain all the entries of the input table. (Contemplate termination if some recursive call "unmarks" a node.) But the measure conjectures must be proved *before* the function is admitted.

Such function definitions are said to be *reflexive*. Here is a sequence of exercises to teach you how to admit reflexive definitions.

Exercise 5.18 *Does the following function terminate?*

```
(defun f (x)
  (if (zp x)
      0
      (+ 1 (f (f (- x 1)))))))
```

What are the measure conjectures to be proved? Is there any measure for which the measure conjectures can be proved before f is defined? Can you admit this definition under the ACL2 definitional principle?

Exercise 5.19 *Consider the following function.*

```
(defun f (x)
  (declare (xargs :measure (m x)))
  (if (zp x)
      0
      (if (e0-ord-< (m (f (- x 1))) (m x))
          (+ 1 (f (f (- x 1))))
          'impossible)))
```

What are the measure conjectures? Can you define m so that this is admissible? Admit the function.

Exercise 5.20 *Prove that the admitted f satisfies the originally desired equation.*

```
(defthm f-satisfies-original-equation
  (equal (f x)
         (if (zp x)
             0
             (+ 1 (f (f (- x 1)))))))
```

Hint: Prove that the test on e0-ord-< always succeeds. Note that this exercise does not establish that the original equation defines a function, only that the original equation is satisfiable.

Exercise 5.21 *Prove that any function g satisfying the original equation is equal to f. That is, use* <u>encapsulate</u> *to constrain g to satisfy* (equal (g x) (if (zp x) 0 (+ 1 (g (g (- x 1)))))). *What witness can you use to show at least one such g exists? Once you have introduced this constrained g, prove* (equal (g x) (f x)).

Exercise 5.22 *Repeat what you have learned from our toy reflexive function f to admit the linear time* find-next-step. *Call the function* linear- -find-next-step. *Define* linear-find-path *appropriately.*

Exercise 5.23 *Prove that* linear-find-path *is correct. Hint: Can you prove that it is equal to* find-path? *If so, the formal proof of the linear time algorithm exploits 100% of the work done for the "toy" problem.*

The following exercise, due to Matt Wilding, is for advanced users. Our solution to Exercise 5.23 marked nodes already seen by adding them to the mark table list. A node is considered marked if it is a member of this list. While our algorithm can be thought of as modeling a linear-time algorithm, our definition of linear-find-path does not execute in linear time because the mark table is searched to determine if a node is marked.

Exercise 5.24 *Use single-threaded objects (see* stobj*) to implement an algorithm for* find-path *in ACL2 that executes in linear time. Prove that your implementation is "equivalent" to* linear-find-path*. (Hint: The single-threaded object used in Wilding's solution is given below.*

```
(defstobj st
  (g       :type (array list (100000)) :initially nil)
  (marks   :type (array (integer 0 1) (100000)) :initially 0)
  (stack   :type (satisfies true-listp))
  (status  :type (integer 0 1) :initially 0))
```

The new algorithm takes and returns this single-threaded object, which encodes the graph, the mark table, the stack, and the success/failure answer.)

It is tempting to think that reflexive functions arise only in academic settings. This is not true. Consider the termination of a garbage collector, or any program that explores and marks a global state and depends on that marking for its termination. How can you reason about such a program except to tie together its effect and its termination? That is what reflexive functions do and this section shows a method for dealing with them in ACL2.

5.13   Less Elementary Further Work

This chapter is not about graph theory. It is about how to formalize and prove things in ACL2. Indeed, one reason we chose such a naive algorithm is so that the chapter is accessible to anyone interested in this book.

But graph theory is an extremely important and well developed subject. An excellent ACL2 project would be to formalize and prove correct some of the classic algorithms of graph theory.

Here are a few pointers. We do not make these *Exercises* simply because we have not provided solutions.

Formalize and prove the correctness of Dijkstra's shortest path algorithm [25].

The Bellman-Ford algorithm [1, 35] is more general than Dijkstra's because edge weights can be negative. Formalize and prove the correctness of the Bellman-Ford algorithm.

Savitch's Theorem [97] establishes that reachability can be done in $log^2 n$ space, where n is the number of nodes. The algorithm used is similar to our **find-path**, but instead of looking at the neighbors of a node it looks at the "midpoint" between nodes. Formalize the algorithm and prove it correct.

Aside from the correctness of the algorithms, users are often interested in their performance. Dijkstra's algorithm has complexity $O(n^2)$, and the Bellman-Ford algorithm has complexity $O(e \times n)$, where e is the number of edges. Formalize and prove such results. You might start by formalizing the performance of our **find-path**. Just as we have used recursive functions to characterize the answers produced by an algorithm, it is possible to use recursive functions to characterize other aspects of the algorithm, such as the number of comparisons it makes, the number of conses created (as opposed to the length of the answer), or some other measure of the performance. McCarthy [private communication] called these *derived functions* in the 1960's.

Any modern book on computational complexity or algorithms contains a wealth of examples of interesting graph algorithms. Two good references are [84, 22].

5.14 General Lessons

We now return to the particular problem solved here and two general lessons we can draw from it.

The first lesson is the importance of the proper choice of problem. We could have attacked a published algorithm or, at least, the linear **find-path**. We chose a far simpler algorithm. But look at all the work involved! However, in this simple setting we got to explore fundamental representational issues and discover the importance of certain concepts and techniques in this formal setting. Furthermore, with these issues behind us it is relatively easy to contemplate incremental elaborations, such as the introduction of the linear **find-path**.

Many newcomers to formality make the mistake of assuming that results or algorithms they take for granted will be easy to prove. They fail to appreciate how much informal knowledge they are using. They often do not understand the trade-offs between alternatives ways to formalize that knowledge. They have not yet internalized the formal patterns corresponding to intuitive leaps in the subject area. In short, newcomers to formality often forget that they must explore formality itself before trying to apply it.

The discussion of the linear **find-path** provides a succinct example. A major issue with that definition is its reflexive character, an issue that arises explicitly only by virtue of our using a formal principle of definition. Arguing the termination of that function is technically subtle since its recursive equation is not known to define a function until termination has been proved and the termination depends on the value computed by the

function. This issue was easily explored with our toy reflexive function f
in the exercises. The lessons of that toy carry over directly to the linear
find-path, but would have been far harder to explore in that relatively
complicated function.

   So the first lesson is: Choose your problems carefully. Resist the temptation to elaborate early! Do not be afraid to start with a ridiculously
simple "toy problem" that you think you understand perfectly. Develop a
sense of what constitutes a useful "toy" and then trust your intuition that
understanding the "toy" will make your actual problem easier to solve. This
point is illustrated dramatically in [77].

   The other general lesson is the importance of learning how to turn con-
vincing informal arguments into formal ones. One aspect of this is correctly
anticipating where a given formalization will lead.

   To state the theorem we had to define graphp, nodep, path-from-to,
and find-path. Only the last two are necessary to state the Main property.
Now recall the original sketch of the proof.

> **Informal Proof Sketch:** It is fairly obvious from the definition
> of find-path that it returns a path from a to b *unless* it signals
> failure. So the problem is to show that find-path does not
> signal failure. Now given a path p from a to b, we can obtain
> a simple path, p', from a to b. Furthermore, p' is a member
> of the set, S, of all simple paths from a to b, showing that S is
> non-empty. But find-path signals failure only if S is empty. □

   To formalize this we had to define simple-pathp, simplify-path, and
find-all-simple-paths. The first is pretty obviously necessary because
the sketch mentions "simple path." The second is only implicit in the
sketch, at the mention of "p'". The third is perhaps the hardest to see
in the sketch: it corresponds to S, the set of "all simple paths." That
our find-all-simple-paths returns the list of *all* simple paths is our
Observation-2. In the "naive set theory" in which we are often taught
to express informal proofs, this concept is not defined algorithmically. The
termination of our function implies the finiteness of the "set" constructed.

   As this discussion suggests, formalizing an informally given proof requires careful attention to what is being said. Short sentences can appar-
ently lead to large "detours." But they are not detours. They are often the
essence of the proof. The function find-all-simple-paths is far more
useful and general than find-path and if our proof had one key idea in
it, it is to shift our attention from finding one path to finding them all.
Of course, this implies collections of paths and the concomitant ability to
reason about them.

   Such subtle shifts in attention happen all the time in informal proofs.
By noting them, you can save yourself a lot of grief. Many times we have
seen users rail at the theorem prover's inability to discover an "obvious"

proof when, in fact, the user has utterly failed to formalize the key notions in the proof he or she had in mind.

For example, one might overlook the observation that the existence of an arbitrary path implies the existence of a simple path. That is, one might introduce `simple-pathp` but never introduce `simplify-path`.

Our informal proof says nothing about *how* one obtains a simple path from an arbitrary one (which is to say, it does not give a proof of existence). But on page 55, we finally explain that `simplify-path` iteratively uses `chop` to remove an initial segment from a path. But `chop` is itself an iterative (recursive) process. Hence, we should expect that each inductively proved theorem about `simplify-path` will require an analogous inductively proved theorem about `chop`. This compositionality cuts both ways: it "doubles" the number of lemmas we have to prove, but it "halves" the difficulty of each lemma. Reducing the difficulty is clearly beneficial, so you must learn to anticipate it so you can manage the increase in the number of lemmas.

On page 58 we said "α will be generated by a call further along in the `cdr` of c and will survive in the answer produced by subsequent concatenations." This is a clear indication that we will need to prove that (`append a b`) contains all the elements of a and all the elements of b, *i.e.*, our `member-append`. Some anticipation of the likely lemma development makes it much easier to follow The Method.

In discussing `Crux-cdr` on page 64, we said "This is a pretty obvious property of `find-all-next-steps` because the set of paths found for (`cdr c`) is a subset of that found for c, when c is non-empty." This sentence foreshadowed two formal developments.

♦ The explicit identification of `subsetp-member-member`

```
(implies (and (subsetp a b)

              (member e a))

         (member e b))
```

for our hint in `Crux-cdr`. This shifts our attention from a `member` question to a `subsetp` question.

♦ The articulation of the relevant fundamental and obvious property of `find-all-next-steps`.

```
(defthm subsetp-find-all-next-steps
  (implies (subsetp c d)
           (subsetp
            (find-all-next-steps c stack b g)
            (find-all-next-steps d stack b g))))
```

By reading or listening carefully, you can often see the seeds of a formal proof in an informal one. You should strive to develop this skill. It makes it easier for you to fill in the gaps in an informal proof. In addition, it gives you a more realistic appraisal of the length of the journey, which allows you to manage it more comfortably and successfully.

6

Modular Proof: The Fundamental Theorem of Calculus

Matt Kaufmann
Advanced Micro Devices, Inc., Austin, Texas[1]
Email: matt.kaufmann@amd.com

Abstract

This chapter presents a modular, top-down proof methodology for the effective use of ACL2. This methodology is intended both to ease the proof development process and to assist in proof presentation. An application is presented: a formalization and proof of the Fundamental Theorem of Calculus. An unusual characteristic of this application is the use of non-standard analysis, which however is not a prerequisite either for this chapter or for the utility of the proof methodology presented herein.

Introduction

ACL2 users sometimes lose their way in the middle of substantial proof development efforts. Moreover, once the proof is complete, it can be quite difficult to comprehend the overall structure. Such comprehension is important for presenting the proof to others, and is also useful for modifying the proof, either in order to clean it up or in order to prove a related theorem.

This chapter suggests a solution to development and comprehension problems by introducing a simple modular proof development methodology, which we have used to develop a proof of the Fundamental Theorem of Calculus (FTOC). This case study also illustrates how an *outline tool* exploits the resulting proof structure by presenting a top-down view of the ACL2 proof input.

The proof of the FTOC uses a modification of ACL2, developed by Ruben Gamboa [36] to support reasoning about the real numbers using non-standard analysis. However, non-standard analysis is neither necessary for the modular proof methodology nor a prerequisite for reading this chapter. Furthermore, the exercises are designed for standard ACL2.

---

[1]The work described here was performed while the author was at EDS, Inc.

We are aware of an earlier formalization and mechanically-checked proof of the FTOC, performed by John Harrison in his doctoral dissertation [47]. The present mechanized proof may be the first employing non-standard analysis.

The first section below presents this modular proof methodology. The second section shows how this methodology has been applied to prove the Fundamental Theorem of Calculus. We conclude with some observations. Exercises appear below in several places.

6.1   A Modular Proof Methodology

The modular, top-down methodology presented below reflects common proof development practice in the mathematical community. This methodology assists both in proof *development* and in proof *presentation*, as explained in the two subsections below. See also Chapter 5 for a more primitive approach to structuring proofs, using a macro top-down.

A makefile provided in the supporting material automates proof replay as well as outline creation.[2]

6.1.1   Proof Development

Many Nqthm and ACL2 users have experienced the following phenomenon. One desires to prove a certain lemma, but requires a lemma in support of that proof, which then leads to another lemma to be proved in support of *that* one, and so on. At some point the effort seems misguided, but by then the evolving proof structure is far from clear and it is difficult to decide how to back up. Even if a decision is made to back up to a particular lemma, is it clear which lemmas already proved may be discarded?

Even if the above process is successful for awhile, it can ultimately be problematic in a frustrating way. Suppose one attempts to prove some goal theorem, and from the failed proof attempt one identifies rewrite rules that appear to be helpful, say, L1 and L2. Suppose further that additional rewrite rules are proved on the way to proving L1 and L2. When one again attempts the original goal theorem, those additional rules can send its proof attempt in a new direction and prevent L1 and L2 from being used.

Below we develop a top-down methodology that has the following properties.

♦ The methodology facilitates organization.

♦ The methodology can eliminate proof replay problems.

---

[2] We thank Bishop Brock for providing an earlier makefile that we extended for our purposes.

Introduction: A Typical High-Level Proof Outline
Here is an outline describing many proofs, both mechanically checked ones and others.

1. *Goal*
   To prove theorem THM.

2. *Main Reduction*
   It should suffice to prove lemmas L1, L2, ...

3. *Support*
   Include results from at least one "library" book, lib.

4. *Proof Hacking*
   Prove additional lemmas as needed in order to derive THM.

The outline above may be reflected in the following structure of a top-level book, which (at least initially) can use skip-proofs as shown in order to defer the proofs of the main lemmas.

```
; 3. Support
(include-book "lib")
; 2. Main Reduction
(skip-proofs (defthm L1 ...))
(skip-proofs (defthm L2 ...))
; 4. Proof Hacking
<Miscellaneous lemmas>
; 1. Goal
(defthm THM ...)
```

A common approach to completing this ACL2 book includes the removal of "skip-proofs" by supplying necessary sub-lemmas (and occasionally, definitions) in front of these lemmas. In our modular methodology we instead place the proofs of those lemmas in subsidiary books, using encapsulate in the parent book as follows. Notice that each such sub-book has the same name as the lemma it is intended to prove.

```
(include-book "lib")
(encapsulate ()
   (local (include-book "L1"))
   (defthm L1 ...))
(encapsulate ()
   (local (include-book "L2"))
   (defthm L2 ...))
; Miscellaneous lemmas (for the "proof hacking") go here.
(defthm THM ...)
```

Each sub-book initially contains the corresponding `skip-proofs` form shown earlier above, preceded by all `include-book` forms needed for definitions of function symbols used in that form. If the proof of THM requires a change in the statement of, say, L1, ACL2 will refuse to accept the `include-book` of "L1" unless the statement of L1 in that book agrees with the one in the `encapsulate` form above, so that ACL2 can recognize the latter L1 as redundant. In such a circumstance one of course changes the sub-book L1, but can probably leave sub-book L2 unchanged.

Lemma and Library Books

The proposed proof methodology relies on notions of *lemma book* and *library book*. A *lemma book* is an ACL2 book whose last event is a theorem that has the same name as the name of the book. We call this last event the *goal theorem* of the book. (The outline tool described in Section 6.1.2 exploits this naming convention.) For example, in the book skeleton presented just above, books L1 and L2 are lemma books provided their last events are `defthm` events named, respectively, L1 and L2. A *library book* is simply any ACL2 book other than a lemma book. Such books typically contain either lemmas of general utility or definitions (or occasionally, both).

Using the Methodology

Our top-down approach suggests a focus on developing reasonably short lemma books. The trick to keeping their lengths under control is first to identify the main lemmas in support of the book's goal theorem, then pushing their proofs into subsidiary lemma sub-books, especially when supporting sub-lemmas may be required. Each main lemma is handled as illustrated above with sub-books L1 and L2: an **encapsulate** event contains first, a `local` `include-book` of the corresponding lemma sub-book, and second, the main lemma.

An important aspect of this approach is that the way in which a lemma is proved in such a sub-book will not affect the certification of the parent book. That is, the use of `local` around the `include-book` of a lemma sub-book allows the sub-book to be changed, other than changing its goal theorem, without affecting the certification of the parent book. This modularity can prevent replay problems often encountered when using less structured approaches to mechanically-assisted proof.

Although our focus is on lemma books, there is still a role for library books. During the course of developing a book, it will often seem most convenient to prove some of the simpler lemmas without going through the effort to create lemma books for them. It can be useful from time to time to browse through one's current collection of books and, after backing up the whole set of them in case the process becomes awkward, to pull out the most general of these lemmas and put them into one or more library books. For each lemma book that has had at least one such lemma removed, at least one `include-book` event will be necessary in order to account for the removed lemmas. Of course, the resulting collection of books might not be accepted by ACL2 because of the rearrangement, but often one can find a way to make appropriate modifications. (At any rate, this process of moving lemmas to library books is optional.) The resulting library books can then be used to advantage during the rest of the development effort.

There are of course reasonable variations of this methodology. One variation is to include a subsidiary book at the top level, rather than locally to an `encapsulate`. For example, a comment in book `riemann-sum-`
`-approximates-integral-1.lisp` explains that its lemmas `car-common-`
`-refinement` and `car-last-common-refinement` are needed in a parent book. Hence, that parent book includes the former book at the top level, not locally to an `encapsulate`. Perhaps a better approach would have been to move these two lemmas into a lemma book, but the modular methodology accommodates such variation. Specifically, the tool we now describe is based simply on the notions of lemma books and library books.

6.1.2 Proof Presentation

We describe here an *outline tool* that assists in proof presentation by creating a top-down outline of the proof. This tool is available on the Web pages for this book, [67].

The outline tool takes a parameter that specifies the maximum depth displayed in the outline. Each entry in the outline gives the following summary of one lemma book:

♦ the lemma proved in the book, *i.e.*, the last `defthm` in the book;

♦ the lemma books included (via `include-book`) in the book; and

♦ the library books included (via `include-book`) in the book.

Each lemma book generates a sub-entry, but only to the specified depth limit. Library books do not generate entries.

For example, the Appendix at the end of this chapter shows the depth-3 outline that was generated mechanically from the books for the Fundamental Theorem of Calculus. The first entry is, as always, labeled Main; it corresponds to the top-level lemma book, `fundamental-theorem-of-calculus`. The outline tool generates an entry for each lemma book included within that top-level book: entry Main.1 for lemma book `split-integral-by-`
`-subintervals`, and entry Main.2 for lemma book `ftoc-lemma`. These each generate entries as well, but those entries generate no further entries because of the depth limit of 3.

One exception to this format is the case of a book B included in more than one parent book. After the entry for B is printed, subsequent entries for B will be abbreviated as shown in the following example from an outline of depth at least 5.

```
Main.1.1.2.1.  riemann-sum-approximates-integral-1.
<See Main.1.1.1 for details.>
```

6.2   Case Study:
The Fundamental Theorem of Calculus

We assume that the reader has seen the Fundamental Theorem of Calculus (FTOC) but has perhaps forgotten it. Hence, below we give an informal review of that theorem, from which we build its formalization. We then give a high-level description of our mechanized proof.

Before all that, we discuss briefly an unusual aspect of this effort: the use of *non-standard analysis*, which introduces a notion of *infinitesimal* numbers as described below. In spite of this twist, this chapter assumes no prior familiarity with non-standard analysis and brings it only minimally into the discussion. Our primary goal is to illustrate the modular proof methodology described above. Our secondary goal is to give an overview of our formalization and mechanized proof of the FTOC.

6.2.1   A Very Short Introduction to Non-Standard Analysis and Its Acl2-Based Mechanization

This case study uses *non-standard analysis* together with a corresponding modification ACL2(r) of ACL2 implemented by Ruben Gamboa [36]. Non-standard analysis was introduced by Abraham Robinson in about 1960 (see [92]) in order to make rigorous Leibniz's approach to calculus from the 17th century. Its main idea is to extend the real number line by adding non-zero *infinitesimals*, numbers that are less in absolute value than every positive real number. Thus, the real numbers are embedded in a larger number system that contains these infinitesimals. See also the freshman calculus book [62] for a development along such lines. A different way of looking at non-standard analysis is given by Nelson [81, 82], where there is still one number line embedded into another, but this time the larger one is considered to be the real line and the smaller one is considered to be the set of *standard* real numbers, which includes all definable real numbers (*e.g.*, 3 and π).

Nelson's view guided Gamboa's development of ACL2(r). There, the predicate realp is a recognizer for points on the larger number line, while standard-numberp is true of only the standard real numbers. In ACL2(r) there is a constant (i-large-integer) to be interpreted as an integer greater than every standard integer.[3] Thus its reciprocal is a non-zero

---

[3]By the comment on definability at the end of the preceding paragraph, i-large-integer is not definable in the real number field.

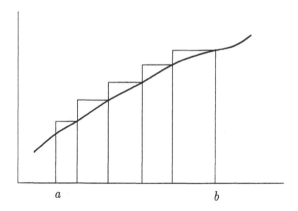

Figure 6.1: Area under the curve $y = f(x)$

infinitesimal, *i.e.*, a non-zero `realp` that is smaller in absolute value than every positive real `standard-numberp`.

Chapter 18 in this book gives the basics of non-standard analysis in an ACL2 setting. More extensive background may be found in Gamboa's doctoral dissertation [36] and also in [37]. Here we attempt to keep the discussion reasonably self-contained, introducing concepts from non-standard analysis only as needed. The full proof script can of course be found in the Web pages for this book [67].

6.2.2 Brief Informal Review of the FTOC

This section provides a quick review of the FTOC, which is often characterized by saying "the derivative of the integral of a function is the function itself." We refer implicitly to ideas presented here when discussing the formalization and proof that follow.

Consider real numbers a and b with $a < b$, together with a corresponding *partition* P, *i.e.*, a finite increasing sequence of numbers starting with a and ending with b. The *mesh* of P is defined to be the maximum difference between two successive numbers in P. Figure 6.1 shows rectangles formed by connecting successive numbers in P to form the bases and using a curve $y = f(x)$ to form the heights.

These rectangles can be used to approximate the area under this curve between a and b. The *definite integral of* f *from* a *to* b is approximated by the *Riemann sum* of f over this partition, obtained by adding up the areas of all these rectangles. These Riemann sums provide arbitrarily good approximations to the definite integral, by using partitions of arbitrarily small mesh.

If we imagine moving b a little bit to one side, then the area changes by an amount roughly equal to the height of the curve at b times the change in b. This observation is made precise in calculus, using the following idea. Given a function $f(x)$ on the real numbers, define $I(x)$ to be the definite integral from a fixed value a to x. Let $I'(x)$ be the *derivative* of $I(x)$, that is, the rate of change of $I(x)$ with respect to x. In this chapter we consider the following form of the FTOC: $I'(b) = f(b)$. Informally, the rate of change at b of the area accumulated from a under the curve $y = f(x)$ is $f(b)$.

Exercise 6.1 *Define a function* (partitionp p) *in ACL2, which is true exactly when p is a non-empty, strictly increasing sequence of rational numbers. Test your function.*

6.2.3   Formalizing the Fundamental Theorem of Calculus

The approach outlined above is formalized in the following theorem, which we have proved using ACL2(r). It reflects the discussion above: the derivative of the definite integral is the value of the function.

```
(implies (and (realp a) (realp x))
         (equal (integral-rcfn-prime a x)
                (rcfn x)))
```

In order to understand this theorem, we need to understand the functions in it. The function rcfn is constrained to be a real-valued continuous function on the reals, using the encapsulate event on page 304. The function integral-rcfn-prime is intended to formalize the notion, described informally above, of the derivative of the integral integral-rcfn (defined below) of rcfn. The following expression represents the rate of change of the integral over the interval from x to (+ x eps); thus, eps is the change in x.

```
(/ (- (integral-rcfn a (+ x eps))
      (integral-rcfn a x))
   eps)
```

The derivative of the integral is then obtained by choosing an infinitesimal value of eps. But that so-called *difference quotient* is then merely *infinitely close* to the actual derivative; that is, it differs from the derivative by an infinitesimal. In order to obtain equality, we can use the standard-part function, which produces the unique real number that is infinitely close to its argument. Here then is the definition of the derivative of the integral.

```
(defun-std integral-rcfn-prime (a x)
  (if (and (realp a) (realp x))
      (let ((eps (/ (i-large-integer))))
```

```
        (standard-part
         (/ (- (integral-rcfn a (+ x eps))
               (integral-rcfn a x))
            eps)))
 0))  ; default
```

The reader may notice the use of **defun-std** rather than <u>defun</u> in this definition. The corresponding axiom equates (integral-rcfn-prime a x) with the definition body, under the hypotheses that the arguments a and x are standard. Further discussion of **defun-std** is beyond the scope of this paper; see Chapter 18 and see [36, 37].

To be fair, the usual definition of the derivative in non-standard analysis requires the result to be independent of the change in x; see for example [62]. This property is guaranteed by the following theorem.

```
(defthm integral-rcfn-prime-exists
  (implies (and (realp eps)
                (not (equal eps 0))
                (i-small eps)  ; eps is infinitesimal
                (realp a) (standard-numberp a)
                (realp x) (standard-numberp x))
           (equal (standard-part
                   (/ (- (integral-rcfn a (+ x eps))
                         (integral-rcfn a x))
                      eps))
                  (integral-rcfn-prime a x)))
  :hints ...)
```

The function integral-rcfn represents the definite integral of rcfn between its two arguments. For standard reals a and b, its definition uses a specific partition P into a non-standard number of equal-sized subintervals, given by (make-partition a b (i-large-integer)), to form a Riemann sum (riemann-rcfn P). Standard-part is applied to this sum in order to obtain a standard real number.

```
(defun-std integral-rcfn (a b)
  (cond ((or (not (realp a)) (not (realp b)))
         0)  ; default
        ((< a b)
         (standard-part
          (riemann-rcfn
           (make-partition a b (i-large-integer)))))
        ((< b a)  ; then reverse the sign as well as a and b
         (- (standard-part
             (riemann-rcfn
              (make-partition b a (i-large-integer))))))
        (t 0)))
```

The following exercises elaborate on our FTOC formalization. They are to be done using ACL2 (although ACL2(r) should also work).

Exercise 6.2 *Define a function* (make-partition a b n) *which, for rational numbers* a *and* b *and positive integer* n, *splits the interval from* a *to* b *into* n *equal-sized subintervals by returning an appropriate sequence of numbers from* a *to* b. *Test your function, for example as follows.*

```
ACL2 !>(make-partition 3 7 8)
(3 7/2 4 9/2 5 11/2 6 13/2 7)
```

Exercise 6.3 *Define a function* (deltas p), *which returns the ordered list of successive intervals represented by* p *as in the following example.*

```
ACL2 !>(deltas '(12 13 15 24))
(1 2 9)
```

Exercise 6.4 *Define the function* (mesh p), *the* mesh *of partition* p *as introduced informally in Section 6.2.2.*

Create a book **partition-defuns** containing solutions to the preceding exercises, to use (via **include-book**) in the remaining exercises. Use the modular methodology where appropriate. The first two exercises below have a similar flavor, so if the first seems difficult, then it will be instructive to try the second after studying the solution to the first.

Exercise 6.5 *Prove the following theorem.*

```
(defthm partitionp-make-partition
  (implies (and (rationalp a)
                (rationalp b)
                (< a b)
                (not (zp n)))
           (partitionp (make-partition a b n))))
```

Exercise 6.6 *Prove the following theorem.*

```
(defthm mesh-make-partition
  (implies (and (rationalp a) (rationalp b) (< a b)
                (integerp n) (< 0 n))
           (equal (mesh (make-partition a b n))
                  (/ (- b a) n))))
```

Exercise 6.7 *Prove the following theorem with the hints shown.*

```
(defthm mesh-append
  (implies (and (partitionp p1)
                (partitionp p2)
                (equal (car (last p1)) (car p2)))
```

```
            (equal (mesh (append p1 (cdr p2)))
                   (max (mesh p1) (mesh p2))))
  :hints (("Goal" :do-not-induct t
           :do-not '(eliminate-destructors))))
```

Note. We have seen ACL2 prove this theorem automatically without the :hints *in about 7 minutes on a 1999-fast Sparc (an E10000). But with the appropriate lemmas, the proof can take less than a second.*

Exercise 6.8 *Define the dot product of two lists so that the following holds.*

```
(dotprod (list a1 a2 ... an) (list b1 b2 ... bn))
  =
(+ (* a1 b1) (* a2 b2) ... (* an bn))
```

Next, declare function (rcfn x) *using* **defstub***. Then define the pointwise application of* rcfn *to a list, so that the following holds.*

```
(map-rcfn (list a1 a2 ... an))
  =
(list (rcfn a1) (rcfn a2) ... (rcfn an)).
```

The immediately preceding exercise allows us to define the Riemann sum as described informally in Section 6.2.2. Each rectangle's height is determined by the endpoint at the right of the corresponding subinterval.[4]

```
(defun riemann-rcfn (p)
  (dotprod (deltas p) (map-rcfn (cdr p))))
```

6.2.4 Proving the Fundamental Theorem of Calculus

Our hope is that the outline in the Appendix, at the end of this chapter, provides a contribution to the exposition below, thus justifying our claim that the outline tool is useful for proof presentation.

Recall that our formalization of the FTOC says that (integral-rcfn--prime a x) is equal to (rcfn x) for real a and x. The main structure of the proof consists of two parts. First, recall the definition of integral-rcfn-prime given in Section 6.2.3 in terms of a particular infinitesimal, eps.

```
(standard-part (/ (- (integral-rcfn a (+ x eps))
                     (integral-rcfn a x))
                  eps))
```

---

[4]One typically defines the Riemann sum independently of the choices of points in the subintervals. Moreover, one considers all partitions, not just the partition returned by make-partition. Lemma riemann-sum-approximates-integral, shown as Main.1.1 in the Appendix, captures the essence of the latter issue. We have not proved results that deal with the former issue; this problem would make a nice exercise.

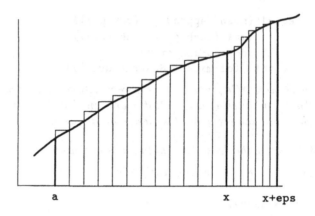

Figure 6.2: Area from a to b under $y = \mathtt{rcfn}(x)$, split in two

Figure 6.2 suggests that the difference above is equal to the definite integral from x to x+eps. The first main part of the proof is a corresponding lemma, which reduces the form displayed above to the following.

```
(standard-part (/ (integral-rcfn x (+ x eps))
                eps))
```

The second part of the proof is to show that this new form is equal to (rcfn x).

These two main steps correspond to the two lemmas just under the FTOC in the outline produced by our outline tool. In the Appendix those lemmas are shown respectively as split-integral-by-subintervals (labeled Main.1) and ftoc-lemma (labeled Main.2). Actually, the first of these lemmas expresses the decomposition in terms of a sum rather than a difference; the difference version is proved directly in the top-level book, since it is a simple consequence of the sum version. We discuss the proofs of these two lemmas below.

Lemma ftoc-lemma actually assumes that x is standard, and in fact we initially derive a version of the FTOC subject to that restriction. However, the so-called *transfer principle* of non-standard analysis, in particular as implemented by event defthm-std in ACL2(r), allows this restriction to be removed. Further discussion of the transfer principle is beyond the scope of this chapter but may be found in Chapter 18; see also [36, 37].

Overview of Proof of Split-integral-by-subintervals
Lemma split-integral-by-subintervals is labeled Main.1 in the outline appearing in the Appendix. It has the following statement, which can be viewed as a formalization of Figure 6.2.

```
(implies (and (realp a) (realp b) (realp c))
         (equal (integral-rcfn a c)
                (+ (integral-rcfn a b)
                   (integral-rcfn b c)))))
```

Each of the two integrals added together above is the standard part of the total area of a corresponding set of rectangles, much as suggested in Figure 6.2. The right-hand side of the equality above is hence infinitely close to the total area of all these rectangles, which is a Riemann sum for the interval from a to c. Thus, a main subtask is to prove the following lemma, which is labeled Main.1.1 in the outline. It says that every Riemann sum over a partition of infinitesimal mesh is infinitely close (i-close) to the exact integral, *i.e.*, their difference is infinitesimal.

```
(implies (and (partitionp p)
              (equal a (car p)) (equal b (car (last p)))
              (< a b)
              (standard-numberp a) (standard-numberp b)
              (i-small (mesh p)))   ; the mesh is infinitesimal
         (i-close (riemann-rcfn p) (integral-rcfn a b)))
```

We are now ready to sketch the proof of split-integral-by-subintervals. Its conclusion is equal to the following, by definition of integral--rcfn and for two particular terms representing partitions, which we abbreviate here as p_1 and p_2.

```
(equal (integral-rcfn a c)
       (+ (standard-part (riemann-rcfn p₁))
          (standard-part (riemann-rcfn p₂)))))
```

Lemma Main.1.2 from the Appendix reduces the term above to the following.

```
(i-close (integral-rcfn a c)
         (+ (riemann-rcfn p₁) (riemann-rcfn p₂)))
```

If we can write the sum above as an appropriate single application of riemann-rcfn, then (by symmetry of i-close) the application of Lemma Main.1.1 should be able to complete the proof.

The following theorem serves that purpose. It appears in the lemma book split-integral-by-subintervals. It may have been desirable to push its proof into a lemma sub-book instead; at least, that way it would have shown up in the outline. However, its proof is fully automatic, so it was natural not to open up a sub-book for it.

```
(defthm split-riemann-rcfn-by-subintervals
  (implies
   (and (partitionp p1)
        (partitionp p2)
        (equal (car (last p1)) (car p2)))
```

```
(equal (+ (riemann-rcfn p1)
          (riemann-rcfn p2))
       (riemann-rcfn (append p1 (cdr p2))))))))
```

Overview of Proof of `Ftoc-lemma`

Lemma `ftoc-lemma` is shown in the Appendix as `Main.2`. Its conclusion is as follows.

```
(equal (standard-part
        (/ (integral-rcfn x (+ x eps)) eps))
       (rcfn x))
```

This equality can be rewritten to the following expression, using basic nonstandard reasoning.

```
(i-close (/ (integral-rcfn x (+ x eps)) eps)
         (rcfn x))
```

Lemma `Main.2.2` in the Appendix reduces this problem to finding two values that are both `i-close` to `(/ (integral-rcfn x (+ x eps)) eps)` such that `(rcfn x)` is between them. Natural candidates for these values are the minimum and maximum values of `rcfn` on the interval from `x` to `(+ x eps)`, provided respectively by the application of functions `min-x` and `max-x` to these interval endpoints. This observation is captured in the conclusion of Lemma `Main.2.1` in the outline.

```
(between (/ (integral-rcfn a b) (- b a))
         (rcfn (min-x a b))
         (rcfn (max-x a b))).
```

Of course, many details are omitted here, *e.g.*, how non-standard analysis is used to define functions such as `max-x` and `min-x`. (See Chapter 18.) Nevertheless, the reader can see the structure of the proof of `ftoc-lemma` by looking at the outline in the Appendix, or by looking at an outline for depth greater than 3 in the supporting materials (see [67]).

6.3   Conclusion

I found it surprisingly pleasant to carry out the proof of the Fundamental Theorem of Calculus using the top-down, modular methodology presented here. It was very satisfying, when putting aside the unfinished proof for the day, to know that I had a self-contained collection of ACL2 books from which I could easily identify the remaining proof obligations. Especially comforting was the knowledge that the completion of those proof obligations would not interfere with the replayability of the completed parts of the proof.

Proof construction using ACL2 is a combination of high-level strategy and low-level tactics, a point stressed (for Nqthm and Pc-Nqthm) using an extensive example in the tutorial [60]. The top-down nature of the methodology presented here supports the user's development of a high-level strategy. The modularity inherent in the methodology supports the carrying out of lower-level tactics without interfering with the higher-level structure (strategy) of the proof.

Acknowledgments

This work was performed while the author was employed at the Austin Renovation Center of EDS, Inc., with wonderful encouragement from its manager, Joe Hill. I am also grateful to Dave Reed of Advanced Micro Devices, Inc. for his support of final preparations of this article and of ACL2 development.

Appendix: The Depth-3 Outline for FTOC

Some whitespace created by the outline tool has been manually modified for display purposes.

```
Main.  fundamental-theorem-of-calculus.
  (IMPLIES (AND (REALP A) (REALP X))
           (EQUAL (INTEGRAL-RCFN-PRIME A X) (RCFN X)))
using lemmas:
  ("split-integral-by-subintervals" "ftoc-lemma")
and library books:
  ("integral-rcfn" "nsa-lemmas" "integral-rcfn-lemmas"
   "riemann-lemmas" "make-partition" "riemann-defuns")
===============================
Main.1.  split-integral-by-subintervals.
  (IMPLIES (AND (REALP A) (REALP B) (REALP C))
           (EQUAL (INTEGRAL-RCFN A C)
                  (+ (INTEGRAL-RCFN A B)
                     (INTEGRAL-RCFN B C))))
using lemmas:
  ("riemann-sum-approximates-integral"
   "integral-rcfn-equal-if-i-close")
and library books:
  ("integral-rcfn-lemmas" "nsa-lemmas" "integral-rcfn"
   "riemann-lemmas" "riemann-defuns")
===============================
```

```
Main.1.1.  riemann-sum-approximates-integral.
 (IMPLIES (AND (PARTITIONP P)
               (EQUAL A (CAR P)) (EQUAL B (CAR (LAST P)))
               (< A B)
               (STANDARD-NUMBERP A) (STANDARD-NUMBERP B)
               (I-SMALL (MESH P)))
          (I-CLOSE (RIEMANN-RCFN P) (INTEGRAL-RCFN A B)))
using lemmas (NOT shown just below:  depth limit reached):
  ("riemann-sum-approximates-integral-1"
   "riemann-sum-approximates-integral-2")
and library books:
  ("integral-rcfn" "riemann-defuns")
===============================
Main.1.2.  integral-rcfn-equal-if-i-close.
 (IMPLIES (AND (REALP A) (STANDARD-NUMBERP A)
               (REALP B) (STANDARD-NUMBERP B)
               (< A B)
               (REALP Y) (REALP Z))
          (EQUAL (EQUAL (INTEGRAL-RCFN A B)
                        (+ (STANDARD-PART Y)
                           (STANDARD-PART Z)))
                 (I-CLOSE (INTEGRAL-RCFN A B) (+ Y Z))))
using lemmas (NOT shown just below:  depth limit reached):
  ("standard-part-equal-if-i-close")
and library books:
  ("integral-rcfn-lemmas" "riemann-lemmas" "integral-rcfn"
   "riemann-defuns")
===============================
Main.2.  ftoc-lemma.
 (IMPLIES (AND (REALP EPS) (NOT (EQUAL EPS 0))
               (I-SMALL EPS)
               (REALP X) (STANDARD-NUMBERP X))
          (EQUAL (STANDARD-PART
                   (/ (INTEGRAL-RCFN X (+ X EPS)) EPS))
                 (RCFN X)))
using lemmas:
  ("integral-rcfn-quotient-between-non-classical"
   "between-i-close-implies-i-close")
and library books:
  ("min-x-and-max-x-lemmas" "../nsa/realp" "defaxioms"
   "integral-rcfn" "max-and-min-attained" "nsa-lemmas"
   "integral-rcfn-lemmas" "riemann-lemmas"
   "make-partition" "riemann-defuns")
===============================
```

Main.2.1.   integral-rcfn-quotient-between-non-classical.
 (IMPLIES (AND (STANDARD-NUMBERP A) (REALP A)
               (STANDARD-NUMBERP B) (REALP B)
               (< A B))
          (BETWEEN (/ (INTEGRAL-RCFN A B) (- B A))
                   (RCFN (MIN-X A B))
                   (RCFN (MAX-X A B))))
using lemmas (NOT shown just below: depth limit reached):
  ("riemann-rcfn-between" "between-limited-implies-limited"
   "standard-part-preserves-between" "rcfn-standard-part"
   "i-limited-rcfn")
and library books:
  ("../nsa/realp" "defaxioms" "integral-rcfn"
   "max-and-min-attained" "nsa-lemmas"
   "integral-rcfn-lemmas" "riemann-lemmas"
   "make-partition" "riemann-defuns")
================================
Main.2.2.   between-i-close-implies-i-close.
 (IMPLIES (AND (REALP Z) (REALP X) (REALP Y) (REALP R)
               (BETWEEN Z X Y)
               (I-CLOSE X R) (I-CLOSE Y R))
          (I-CLOSE Z R))
using library books:
  ("../nsa/realp" "defaxioms" "../arithmetic/top-with-meta"
   "nsa-lemmas")
================================

7

Mu-Calculus Model-Checking

Panagiotis Manolios

Department of Computer Sciences, University of Texas at Austin, Texas
Email: pete@cs.utexas.edu

Abstract

Temporal logic model-checking has received substantial academic interest and has enjoyed wide industrial acceptance. Temporal logics are used to describe the behavior (over time) of systems which continuously interact with their environment. Model-checking algorithms are used to decide if a finite-state system satisfies a temporal logic formula. Many temporal logics, *e.g.*, *CTL*, *LTL*, and *CTL** can be translated into the Mu-Calculus. In addition, the algorithm that decides the Mu-Calculus is used for symbolic (BDD-based) model-checking, a technique that has greatly extended the applicability of model-checking. In this case study we define a model-checker for the Mu-Calculus in ACL2 and show how to translate *CTL* into the Mu-Calculus.

In the process of defining the Mu-Calculus, we develop (ACL2) books on set theory, fixpoint theory, and relation theory. The development of these books is given as a sequence of exercises. These exercises make use of varied ACL2 features; therefore, the first few sections may be of interest to readers who want more practice in proving theorems in ACL2.

Introduction

Machine-checked proofs are increasingly being used to cope with the complexity of current hardware and software designs: such designs are too complicated to be checked by hand and machine-checked proofs are a reliable way to ensure correctness. *Reactive systems* are systems with nonterminating or concurrent behavior. Such systems are especially difficult to design and verify. Temporal logic was proposed as a formalism for specifying the correctness of reactive systems in [87]. Algorithms that decide if a finite-state system satisfies its specification are known as *model-checking* algorithms [20, 27, 89]. Model-checking has been successfully applied to automatically verify many reactive systems and is now being used by hardware companies as part of their verification process. In this chapter, we develop a model-checker for the propositional Mu-Calculus [64, 30, 32, 31, 29, 85]— a calculus that subsumes the temporal logics *CTL*, *LTL*, and *CTL**—in ACL2.

This chapter is intended as a bridge between the companion book, *Computer-Aided Reasoning: An Approach* [58], and the other case studies. There are several self-contained sections in which the reader is presented with exercises whose solutions lead to books on set theory, fixpoint theory, and relation theory. We expect that the exercises in these sections are at the right level of difficulty for readers who have read the companion book. These exercises make use of diverse, less elementary features of ACL2 such as congruence-based reasoning, refinements, packages, the use of macros, guard verification, encapsulation, mutual recursion, and functional instantiation. We also discuss *compositional reasoning*; specifically we show how to reason about efficient implementations of functions by using rewrite rules that transform the efficient functions into other functions that are easier to reason about. Therefore, we expect—at least the first part of—this chapter to be of general interest.

If you are not interested in developing the required set theoretic results, but are interested in formalizing the Mu-Calculus in ACL2, then, instead of solving the exercises on your own, download the appropriate books from the supporting material for this chapter.

This chapter is organized as follows: the next three sections develop the set theory, fixpoint theory, and relation theory discussed above. In the three sections after that, we present the notion of a model, the syntax and semantics of the Mu-Calculus, and proofs that the fixpoint operators of the Mu-Calculus actually compute fixpoints. A section on the temporal logic *CTL* and its relation to the Mu-Calculus follows. We conclude with some directions for further exploration.

Conventions on Exercises

Whenever we introduce a function or ask you to define one, admit it and add and verify guards; this is an implicit exercise. Many exercises consist solely of a term or an event; interpret this as a command to prove that the term is a theorem or to admit the event. The supporting material includes a macro that you may find useful for dealing with guards. The file `solutions/defung-intro.txt` describes the macro and contains exercises.

7.1   Set Theory

In this section, we develop some set theory. We represent sets as lists and define an equivalence relation on lists that corresponds to set equality. It turns out that we do not have to develop a "general" theory of sets; a theory of *flat* sets, *i.e.*, sets whose elements are compared by equal, will do. For example, in our theory of sets, '(1 2) is set equal to '(2 1), but '((1 2)) is not set equal to '((2 1)).

We develop some of the set theory in the package SETS (see defpkg) and the rest in the package FAST-SETS, in subsections labeled by the package names. When using packages, we define constants that contain all of the symbols to be imported into the package. We start by guessing which symbols will be useful. For example, we import len because we need it to define the cardinality of a set and we import the symbols x and x-equiv; otherwise, when using defcong, x-equiv prints as ACL2::x-equiv, which strains the eye. As we develop the book, we notice that we forgot a few symbols and add them.[1]

7.1.1   SETS

Here is how we define the package SETS.

```
(defconst *export-symbols*
  (union-eq *acl2-exports*
       (union-eq
        '(len  ...  *export-symbols*)
        *common-lisp-symbols-from-main-lisp-package*)))

(defconst *sets-symbols* (union-eq *export-symbols*  ...  ))

(defpkg "SETS" *sets-symbols*)
```

We use the simplest definitions that we can think of so that it is easy to prove theorems. Later, we define functions that are more efficient and prove the rewrite rules that allow us to rewrite the efficient functions into the simpler ones. In this way, once rewritten, all the theorem proving is about the simple functions, but the execution uses the efficient versions.

The definitions of in (set membership), =< (subset), and == (set equality) follow.

```
(defun in (a X)
  (cond ((endp X) nil)
        ((equal a (car X)) t)
        (t (in a (cdr X))))))
```

---

[1]Due to some technical issues (see package-reincarnation-import-restrictions), this unfortunately means that we have to start a new ACL2 session.

```
(defun =< (X Y)
  (cond ((endp X) t)
        (t (and (in (car X) Y)
                (=< (cdr X) Y)))))
```

```
(defun == (X Y)
  (and (=< X Y)
       (=< Y X)))
```

Notice that == is an *equivalence relation*: it is reflexive, symmetric, and transitive. The macro **defequiv** can be used to show that a relation is an equivalence relation. Use :**trans1** to print out the translation of the **defequiv** form in the exercise below before you do it.

Exercise 7.1 (defequiv ==)

We make heavy use of congruence-based reasoning and will therefore discuss the topic briefly. For a full explanation consult the companion book [58] and the documentation on **equivalence**, **defequiv**, and **congruence**. Congruence-based reasoning can be seen as an extension of the substitution of equals for equals, where arbitrary equivalence relations can be used instead of equality. We motivate the need for congruence-based reasoning with an example using the equivalence relation ==.

Consider the function **set-union** which computes the union of two sets. This function is defined below and is equivalent to **append**. We might want to prove

```
(implies (== X Z)
         (equal (set-union X Y) (set-union Z Y)))
```

so that ACL2 can replace x by z in (set-union x y), if it can establish (== x z). Letting x be (1 1) and z be (1), it is easy to see that this is not a theorem. However, the following is a theorem.

```
(implies (== X Z)
         (== (set-union X Y) (set-union Z Y)))
```

If stored as a congruence rule (see **congruence** and **rule-classes**), ACL2 can use this theorem to substitute z for (a set equal) x in (set-union x y), in a context where it is enough to preserve ==. More generally, a theorem of the form:

```
(implies (eq1 X Z)
         (eq2 (foo ... X ...)
              (foo ... Z ...)))
```

where **eq1** and **eq2** are known equivalence relations can be made a congruence rule. Such a rule allows us to replace x by z in (foo ... x ...) if x and z are eq1-equal and we are in a context where it is enough to preserve eq2. This should make it clear why congruence-based reasoning is a generalization of the substitution of equals for equals.

The macro def cong can be used to prove congruence rules. Use :trans1 to print out the translation of the defcong forms in the exercise below before you do it.

Exercise 7.2

1. (defcong == equal (in a X) 2)

2. (defcong == equal (=< X Y) 1)

3. (defcong == equal (=< X Y) 2)

4. (defcong == == (cons a X) 2)

We now give the definition of set-union.

```
(defun set-union (X Y)
  (if (endp X)
      Y
    (cons (car X) (set-union (cdr X) Y))))
```

Exercise 7.3

1. (equal (in a (set-union X Y)) (or (in a X) (in a Y)))

2. (=< X (set-union Y X))

3. (== (set-union X Y) (set-union Y X))

4. (equal (== (set-union X Y) Y) (=< X Y))

5. (defcong == == (set-union X Y) 1)

6. (equal (=< (set-union Y Z) X) (and (=< Y X) (=< Z X)))

The definition of intersect, a function which computes the intersection of two sets, follows.

```
(defun intersect (X Y)
  (cond ((endp X) nil)
        ((in (car X) Y)
         (cons (car X) (intersect (cdr X) Y)))
        (t (intersect (cdr X) Y))))
```

Exercise 7.4

1. (equal (in a (intersect X Y)) (and (in a X) (in a Y)))

2. (== (intersect X Y) (intersect Y X))

3. (implies (=< X Y) (== (intersect X Y) X))

4. (implies (or (=< Y X) (=< Z X))
             (=< (intersect Y Z) X))

The definition of minus, a function which computes the set difference of two sets, follows.

```
(defun minus (X Y)
  (cond ((endp X) nil)
        ((in (car X) Y)
         (minus (cdr X) Y))
        (t (cons (car X) (minus (cdr X) Y)))))
```

Exercise 7.5

1. (implies (=< X Y) (equal (minus X Y) nil))

2. (implies (=< X Y) (=< (minus X Z) Y))

The functions set-complement, remove-dups, cardinality, and s< (strict subset) are defined below.

```
(defun set-complement (X U) (minus U X))
```

```
(defun remove-dups (X)
  (cond ((endp X) nil)
        ((in (car X) (cdr X))
         (remove-dups (cdr X)))
        (t (cons (car X)
                 (remove-dups (cdr X))))))
```

```
(defun cardinality (X) (len (remove-dups X)))
```

```
(defun s< (X Y) (and (=< X Y) (not (=< Y X))))
```

Exercise 7.6 *Define* perm, *a function of two arguments that returns* t *if its arguments are permutations and* nil *otherwise. Prove* (defequiv perm) *and* (defrefinement perm ==). *(Perm is defined in the companion book [58].)*

Exercise 7.7
```
(implies (s< X Y)
         (< (len (remove-dups X)) (len (remove-dups Y))))
```

7.1.2 FAST-SETS

Although the definitions of the basic set operations defined above are good for reasoning about sets, some are not appropriate for execution. For example, set-union is not tail-recursive[2], hence, even if compiled, we can easily get stack overflows. In this section, we define functions that are more appropriate for execution and prove rewrite rules that transform the new, efficient versions to the old, simpler versions in the appropriate context (specifically, when it is enough to preserve ==). This approach is *compositional*, *i.e.*, it allows us to decompose proof obligations of a system into proof obligations of the components of the system. Compositional reasoning is routinely used by ACL2 experts and is essential to the success of large verification efforts.

The functions we define below have the same names as their analogues, but are in the package FAST-SETS. FAST-SETS imports symbols from SETS, *e.g.*, == (we expect this to be clear from the context, but one can consult the supporting material for the package definition, if required). The definition of set-union, in the package FAST-SETS, follows.

```
(defun set-union (X Y)
  (cond ((endp X) Y)
        ((in (car X) Y)
         (set-union (cdr X) Y))
        (t (set-union (cdr X) (cons (car X) Y)))))
```

Exercise 7.8 (== (set-union X Y) (sets::set-union X Y))

Recall that the above rule allows ACL2 to replace occurrences of set--union by sets::set-union in a context where it is enough to preserve ==.

The definition of intersect follows. Note that its auxiliary function is tail recursive.

```
(defun intersect-aux (X Y Z)
  (cond ((endp X) Z)
        ((in (car X) Y)
         (intersect-aux (cdr X) Y (cons (car X) Z)))
        (t (intersect-aux (cdr X) Y Z))))

(defun intersect (X Y) (intersect-aux X Y nil))
```

Exercise 7.9 (== (intersect X Y) (sets::intersect X Y))

Exercise 7.10 *Define* minus, *a tail-recursive version of* sets::minus, *and prove* (== (minus X Y) (sets::minus X Y)).

---

[2] See the companion book [58] for a discussion of tail recursion and for example proofs.

Alternate definitions of `remove-dups` and `cardinality` are given below.

```
(defun remove-dups (X) (set-union X nil))
```

```
(defun cardinality (X) (len (remove-dups X)))
```

Exercise 7.11 `(equal (cardinality X) (sets::cardinality X))`

7.2 Fixpoint Theory

In this section, we develop a book in the package **SETS** on the theory of fixpoints. We do this in a very general setting, by using encapsulation to reason about a constrained function, `f`, of one argument. Later, we show that certain functions compute fixpoints by using functional instantiation. An advantage of this approach is that we can ignore irrelevant issues, *e.g.*, in a later section we show that certain functions compute fixpoints; these functions have many arguments, but `f` has only one.

We say that x is a *fixpoint* of f iff $f(x) = x$. If f is a monotonic function on the powerset of a set, then by the following version of the Tarski-Knaster theorem [105], it has a least and greatest fixpoint, denoted by μf and νf, respectively.

Theorem 7.1 *Let* $f : 2^S \to 2^S$ *such that* $a \subseteq b \quad \Rightarrow \quad f(a) \subseteq f(b)$. *Then*

1. $\mu f = \cap\{b : b \subseteq S \wedge f(b) \subseteq b\} = \cup_{\alpha \in On} f^\alpha(\emptyset)$, *and*

2. $\nu f = \cup\{b : b \subseteq S \wedge b \subseteq f(b)\} = \cap_{\alpha \in On} f^\alpha(S)$,

where 2^S *is the powerset of* S, f^α *is the* α-*fold composition (iteration) of* f, *and* On *is the class of ordinals.*

We say that x is a *pre-fixpoint* of f iff $x \subseteq f(x)$; x is a *post-fixpoint* iff $f(x) \subseteq x$. The Tarski-Knaster theorem tells us that μf is below all post-fixpoints and that νf is above all pre-fixpoints.

We can replace On by the set of ordinals of cardinality at most $|S|$; since we are only interested in *finite* sets, this gives us an algorithm for computing least and greatest fixpoints. Notice that by the monotonicity of f, $\alpha \leq \beta \quad \Rightarrow \quad f^\alpha(\emptyset) \subseteq f^\beta(\emptyset) \wedge f^\beta(S) \subseteq f^\alpha(S)$. Therefore, we can compute μf by applying f to $\emptyset$ until we reach a fixpoint; similarly, we can compute νf by applying f to S until we reach a fixpoint.

We start by constraining functions `f` and `S` so that `f` is monotonic and when `f` is applied to a subset of `S`, it returns a subset of `S`. Since functions defined in ACL2 are total, we cannot say that `f` is a function whose domain is the powerset of `S`. We could add hypotheses stating that all arguments to `f` are of the right type to the theorems that constrain `f`, but this generality is not needed and will make it slightly more cumbersome to prove theorems about f. The issue of what to do when a function is applied outside its intended domain is one that comes up quite a bit in ACL2. The definitions of the constrained functions follow.

```
(encapsulate
  ((f (X) t)
   (S () t))
  (local (defun f(X) (declare (ignore X)) nil))
  (local (defun S() nil))
  (defthm f-is-monotonic
    (implies (=< X Y)
             (=< (f X) (f Y))))
  (defthm S-is-top
    (=< (f X) (set-union X (S)))))).
```

We now define applyf, a function that applies f a given number of times.

```
(defun applyf (X n)
  (if (zp n)
      X
    (if (== X (f X))
        X
      (applyf (f X) (1- n)))))
```

From the Tarski-Knaster theorem, we expect that lfpf and gfpf, defined below, are the least and greatest fixpoints, respectively.

```
(defabbrev lfpf () (applyf nil (cardinality (S))))
```

```
(defabbrev gfpf () (applyf (S) (cardinality (S))))
```

Now all that is left is to prove the Tarski-Knaster theorem, which is given as the following two exercises.

Exercise 7.12 *Prove that* lfpf *is the least fixpoint:*

1. (== (f (lfpf)) (lfpf))

2. (implies (=< (f X) X) (=< (lfpf) X))

Exercise 7.13 *Prove that* gfpf *is the greatest fixpoint:*

1. (== (f (gfpf)) (gfpf))

2. (implies (and (=< X (S)) (=< X (f X)))
            (=< X (gfpf)))

7.3   Relation Theory

In this section we develop a book, in the package RELATIONS, on the theory of relations. We represent relations as alists which map an element to the set of elements it is related to. A recognizer for relations is the following.

```
(defun relationp (r)
  (cond ((atom r) (eq r nil))
        (t (and (consp (car r))
                (true-listp (cdar r))
                (relationp (cdr r))))))
```

The definition of image, a tail-recursive function that computes the image of a set under a relation, follows.

```
(defun value-of (x alist) (cdr (assoc-equal x alist)))

(defun image-aux (X r tmp)
  (if (endp X)
      tmp
    (image-aux (cdr X) r
               (set-union (value-of (car X) r) tmp))))
(defun image (X r) (image-aux X r nil))
```

Exercise 7.14 *Define* range, *a function that determines the range of a relation.*

Exercise 7.15 *Define* inverse *so that it is tail recursive and computes the inverse of a relation.*

The following function checks if the range of its first argument (a relation) is a subset of its second argument.

```
(defun rel-range-subset (r X)
  (cond ((endp r) t)
        (t (and (=< (cdar r) X)
                (rel-range-subset (cdr r) X)))))
```

Exercise 7.16

  1. (implies (rel-range-subset r X) (=< (image Y r) X))

  2. (implies (and (rel-range-subset r X) (=< X Y))
              (rel-range-subset r Y))

7.4   Models

In this section we introduce the notion of a model. A *model*, sometimes called a Kripke structure or a transition system, is a four-tuple consisting of a set of states, a transition relation, a set of atomic propositions, and a labeling relation. The transition relation relates a pair of states if the second state can be reached from the first in a single step. The atomic propositions can be thought of as Boolean variables that are either true or false at a state. The labeling relation relates states to the atomic propositions true at those states. A program can be thought of as a model: there is a state for every combination of legal assignments to the program's variables—which can be recovered from the labeling of the state—and the transition relation relates a pair of states if, in one step, the program can transition from the first state to the second. There are some technical details to consider, *e.g.*, a program can have variables of varying types, but atomic propositions are Boolean, hence, program variables are represented by a set of atomic propositions (this set can be infinite if the domain of the variable is infinite). We restrict our attention to finite models because we want to check them algorithmically.

We define the notion of a model in ACL2. The functions defined in this section, as well as the next two sections, are in the package MODEL-CHECK. An ACL2 model is a seven-tuple because it is useful to precompute the inverse relations of the transition relation and the labeling relation as well as the cardinality of the set of states. The inverse transition relation relates a pair of states if, in one step, the first state can be reached from the second. The inverse labeling relation relates atomic propositions to the states at which they hold. A function that creates a model is defined below.

```
(defun make-model (s r ap l)
  (list s r ap l (inverse r) (inverse l) (cardinality s)))
```

Exercise 7.17 *Define* modelp, *a recognizer for models. Define the accessor functions:* states, relation, atomic-props, s-labeling, inverse--relation, a-labeling, *and* size *to access the: states, transition relation, atomic propositions, (state) labeling relation, inverse transition relation, (atomic proposition) labeling relation, and cardinality of the states, respectively.*

7.5   Mu-Calculus Syntax

We are now ready to look at the Mu-Calculus. Informally, a formula of the Mu-Calculus is either an atomic proposition, a variable, a Boolean combination of formulae, EXf, where f is a formula, or $\mu Y f$ or $\nu Y f$, where f is a formula and Y is a variable (as we will see when we discuss semantics,

```
(defun mu-symbolp (s)
  (and (symbolp s)
       (not (in s '(+ & MU NU true false)))))

(defun basic-mu-calc-formulap (f ap v)
  (cond ((symbolp f)
         (or (in f '(true false))
             (and (mu-symbolp f)
                  (or (in f ap) (in f v)))))
        ((equal (len f) 2)
         (and (in (first f) '(~ EX))
              (basic-mu-calc-formulap (second f) ap v)))
        ((equal (len f) 3)
         (let ((first (first f))
               (second (second f))
               (third (third f)))
           (or (and (in second '(& +))
                    (basic-mu-calc-formulap first ap v)
                    (basic-mu-calc-formulap third ap v))
               (and (or (in first '(MU NU)))
                    (mu-symbolp second)
                    (not (in second ap))
                    (basic-mu-calc-formulap
                     third ap (cons second v)))))))))
```

Figure 7.1: The Syntax of the Mu-Calculus

f and Y define the function whose fixpoint is computed). Usually there is a further restriction that f be monotone in Y; we do not require this. We will return to the issue of monotonicity in the next section.

In Figure 7.1, we define the syntax of the Mu-Calculus (ap and v correspond to the set of atomic propositions and the set of variables, respectively). Mu-symbolp is used because we do not want to decide the meaning of formulae such as '(mu + f).

Exercise 7.18 *Define* translate-f, *a function that allows us to write formulae in an extended language, by translating its input into the Mu-Calculus. The extended syntax contains* AX *(* '(AX f) *is an abbreviation for* '(~ (EX (~ f)))) *and the infix operators* | *(which abbreviates* +*),* => *and* -> *(both denote implication), and* =*,* <->*, and* <=> *(all of which denote equality).*

Exercise 7.19 (Mu-calc-sentencep f ap) *recognizes sentences (formulae with no free variables) in the extended syntax; define it.*

7.6   Mu-Calculus Semantics

The semantics of a Mu-Calculus formula is given with respect to a model
and a valuation assigning a subset of the states to variables. The semantics
of an atomic proposition is the set of states that satisfy the proposition.
The semantics of a variable is its value under the valuation. Conjunctions,
disjunctions, and negations correspond to intersections, unions, and com-
plements, respectively. EXf is true at a state if the state has some successor
that satisfies f. Finally, μ's and ν's correspond to least and greatest fixpoints, respectively. Note that the semantics of a sentence (a formula with
no free variables) does not depend on the initial valuation. The formal definition is given in Figure 7.2; some auxiliary functions and abbreviations
used in the figure follow.

```
(defabbrev semantics-EX (m f val)
  (image (mu-semantics m (second f) val)
         (inverse-relation m)))

(defabbrev semantics-NOT (m f val)
  (set-complement (mu-semantics m (second f) val)
                  (states m)))

(defabbrev semantics-AND (m f val)
  (intersect (mu-semantics m (first f) val)
             (mu-semantics m (third f) val)))

(defabbrev semantics-OR (m f val)
  (set-union (mu-semantics m (first f) val)
             (mu-semantics m (third f) val)))

(defabbrev semantics-fix (m f val s)
  (compute-fix-point
   m (third f) (put-assoc-equal (second f) s val)
   (second f) (size m)))

(defabbrev semantics-MU (m f val)
  (semantics-fix m f val nil))

(defabbrev semantics-NU (m f val)
  (semantics-fix m f val (states m)))
```

Now, we are ready to define the main function:

```
(defun semantics (m f)
  (if (mu-calc-sentencep f (atomic-props m))
      (mu-semantics m (translate-f f) nil)
    "not a valid mu-calculus formula"))
```

```
(mutual-recursion
(defun mu-semantics (m f val)
  (cond ((eq f 'true) (states m))
        ((eq f 'false) nil)
        ((mu-symbolp f)
         (cond ((in f (atomic-props m))
                (value-of f (a-labeling m)))
               (t (value-of f val))))
        ((equal (len f) 2)
         (cond ((equal (first f) 'EX)
                (semantics-EX m f val))
               ((equal (first f) '~)
                (semantics-NOT m f val))))
        ((equal (len f) 3)
         (cond ((equal (second f) '&)
                (semantics-AND m f val))
               ((equal (second f) '+)
                (semantics-OR m f val))
               ((equal (first f) 'MU)
                (semantics-MU m f val))
               ((equal (first f) 'NU)
                (semantics-NU m f val)))))))

(defun compute-fix-point (m f val y n)
  (if (zp n)
      (value-of y val)
    (let ((x (value-of y val))
          (new-x (mu-semantics m f val)))
      (if (== x new-x)
          x
        (compute-fix-point
         m f (put-assoc-equal y new-x val) y (- n 1))))))
      ; note that the valuation is updated
)
```

Figure 7.2: The Semantics of the Mu-Calculus

Semantics returns the set of states in m satisfying f, if f is a valid Mu-Calculus formula, otherwise, it returns an error string.

How would you write a Mu-Calculus formula that holds exactly in those states where it is possible to reach a p-state (*i.e.*, a state labeled by the atomic proposition p)? The idea is to start with p-states, then add states that can reach a p-state in one step, two steps, and so on. When you are adding states, this corresponds to a least fixpoint computation. A solution is $\mu Y(p \lor \mathbf{EX}Y)$; it may help to think about "unrolling" the fixpoint.

How would you write a Mu-Calculus formula that holds exactly in those states where every reachable state is a p-state? The idea is to start with p-states, then remove states that can reach a non p-state in one step, two steps, and so on. When you are removing states, this corresponds to a greatest fixpoint computation. A solution is $\nu Y(p \land \neg\mathbf{EX}\neg Y)$; as before it may help to think about unrolling the fixpoint. Similar exercises follow so that you can gain some experience with the Mu-Calculus.

Exercise 7.20 *For each case below, define a Mu-Calculus formula that holds exactly in states that satisfy the description. A* path *is a sequence of states such that adjacent states are related by the transition relation. A* fullpath *is a maximal path, i.e., a path that cannot be extended.*

1. *There is a fullpath whose every state is a p-state.*

2. *Along every fullpath, it is possible to reach a p-state.*

3. *There is a fullpath with an infinite number of p-states.*

The model-checking algorithm we presented is *global*, meaning that it returns the set of states satisfying a Mu-Calculus formula. Another approach is to use a *local* model-checking algorithm. The difference is that the local algorithm is also given as input a state and checks whether that particular state satisfies the formula; in some cases this can be done without exploring the entire structure, as is required with the global approach.

The model-checking algorithm we presented is *extensional*, meaning that it represents both the model and the sets of states it computes explicitly. If any of these structures gets too big—since a model is exponential in the size of the program text, *state explosion* is common—resource constraints will make the problem practically unsolvable. Symbolic model-checking [74, 16, 86] is a technique that has greatly extended the applicability of model-checking. The idea is to use compact representations of the model and of sets of states. This is done by using BDDs[3] (binary decision diagrams), which on many examples have been shown to represent states and

---

[3]BDDs can be thought of as deterministic finite state automata (see any book covering Automata Theory, *e.g.*, [50]). A Boolean function, f, of n variables can be thought of as a set of n-length strings over the alphabet $\{0, 1\}$. We start by ordering the variables; in this way an n-length string over $\{0, 1\}$ corresponds to an assignment of values to the

models very compactly [14]. Symbolic model-checking algorithms, even for temporal logics such as *CTL* whose expressive power compared with the Mu-Calculus is quite limited, are based on the algorithm we presented (except that BDDs are used to represent sets of states and models).

Now that we have written down the semantics of the Mu-Calculus in ACL2, we can decide to stop and declare success, because we have an executable model-checker. In many cases this is an appropriate response, because deciding if you wrote what you meant is not a formal question. However, in our case, we expect that MU formulae are least fixpoints (if the formulae are monotonic in the variable of the MU and certain "type" conditions hold), and similarly NU formulae are greatest fixpoints. We will check this. We start by defining what it means to be a fixpoint.

```
(defun fixpointp (m f val x s)
  (== (mu-semantics m f (put-assoc-equal x s val)) s))

(defun post-fixpointp (m f val x s)
  (=< (mu-semantics m f (put-assoc-equal x s val)) s))

(defun pre-fixpointp (m f val x s)
  (=< s (mu-semantics m f (put-assoc-equal x s val))))
```

Read the rest of the exercises in this section before trying to solve any of them.

Exercise 7.21 *Use encapsulation to constrain the functions* sem-mon-f, good-model, good-val, *and* good-var *so that* sem-mon-f *is monotone in* good-var, good-model *is a "reasonable" model,* good-val *is a "reasonable" valuation, and* good-var *is a "reasonable" variable.*

We prove the fixpoint theorems by functionally instantiating the main theorems in the supporting book fixpoints. (See <u>lemma-instance</u>; an example of functional instantiation can be found in the companion book [58].)

Exercise 7.22 *Prove that* MU *formulae are least fixpoints and that* NU *formulae are greatest fixpoints. As a hint, we include the statement of one of the four required theorems.*

---

variables. We can represent f by an automaton whose language is the set of strings that make f true. We can now use the results of automata theory, *e.g.*, deterministic automata can be minimized in $O(n \log n)$ time (the reason why nondeterministic automata are not used is that minimizing them is a PSPACE-complete problem), hence, we have a canonical representation of Boolean functions. Automata that correspond to Boolean functions have a simpler structure than general automata (*e.g.*, they do not have cycles); BDDs are a data structure that takes advantage of this structure. Sets of states as well as transition relations can be thought of as Boolean functions, so they too can be represented using BDDs. Finally, note that the order of the variables can make a big (exponential) difference in the size of the BDD corresponding to a Boolean function.

```
(defmu semmu-is-a-fixpoint
  (fixpointp (good-model) (sem-mon-f) (good-val) (good-var)
             (mu-semantics
              (good-model)
              (list 'mu (good-var) (sem-mon-f))
              (good-val)))
  sets::lfix-is-a-fixpoint)
```

Exercise 7.23 *The hint in the previous example is a macro call. This saves us from having to type the appropriate functional instantiation several times. Define the macro. Our solution is of the following form.*

```
(defmacro defmu (name thm fn-inst &rest args)
  '(defthm ,name ,thm
     :hints
     (("goal"
       :use (:functional-instance
             ,fn-inst
             (sets::S (lambda() (states (good-model))))
             (sets::f (lambda(y) (mu-semantics ...  )))
             (sets::applyf
              (lambda(y n) (compute-fix-point ...  )))
             (sets::cardinality cardinality)))
      ,@args)))
```

You will notice that reasoning about mutually recursive functions (which is required for the exercises above) can be tricky, *e.g.*, even admitting the mutually recursive functions and verifying their guards (as mentioned in the introduction, this is an implicit exercise for every function we introduce) can be a challenge. Read the documentation for mutual-recursion and package-reincarnation-import-restrictions. There are several approaches to dealing with mutually recursive functions in ACL2. One is to remove the mutual recursion by defining a recursive function that has an extra argument which is used as a flag to indicate which of the functions in the nest to execute. Another approach is to identify a sufficiently powerful induction scheme for the functions, add it as an induction rule (see induction) so that this induction is suggested where appropriate, and prove theorems by simultaneous induction, *i.e.*, prove theorems that are about all the functions in the mutual recursion nest. We suggest that you try both approaches.

7.7   Temporal Logic

Temporal logics can be classified as either *linear-time* or *branching-time* (see [28]). In linear-time logics the semantics of a program is the set of its possible executions, whereas in branching-time, the semantics of a program is its computation tree; therefore, branching time logics can distinguish between programs that linear-time logics consider identical. A branching time logic of interest is CTL: many model-checkers are written for it because of algorithmic considerations. We present the syntax and semantics of CTL. It turns out that CTL, as well as the propositional linear time logic LTL, and the branching time logic CTL^* can be translated to the Mu-Calculus.

The syntax of CTL is defined inductively by the following rules:

1. p, where p is an atomic proposition, and

2. $\neg f, f \vee g$, where f is a CTL formula, and

3. $\mathbf{EX}f, \mathbf{E}(f\mathbf{U}g), \mathbf{E}\neg(f\mathbf{U}g)$, where f and g are CTL formulae.

Although we presented the syntax of CTL, it turns out to be just as easy to present the semantics of what is essentially CTL^*. The semantics are given with respect to a *fullpath*, i.e., an infinite path through the model. If x is a fullpath, then by x_i we denote the ith element of x and by x^i we denote the suffix $\langle x_i, \ldots \rangle$. Henceforth, we assume that the transition relation of models is *left total*, i.e., every state has a successor. Note that CTL formulae are *state formulae*, i.e., formulae whose semantics depends only on the first state of the fullpath. $M, x \models f$ means that fullpath x of model M satisfies formula f.

1. $M, x \models p$ iff x_0 is labeled with p;

2. $M, x \models \neg f$ iff not $M, x \models f$;
   $M, x \models f \vee g$ iff $M, x \models f$ or $M, x \models g$;

3. $M, x \models \mathbf{E}f$ iff there is a fullpath $y = \langle x_0, \ldots \rangle$ in M s.t. $M, y \models f$;
   $M, x \models \mathbf{X}f$ iff $M, x^1 \models f$; and
   $M, x \models f\mathbf{U}g$ iff there exists $i \in \mathbb{N}$ s.t. $M, x^i \models g$ and for all $j < i$, $M, x^j \models f$.

The first two items above correspond to Boolean formulae built out of atomic propositions. $\mathbf{E}f$ is true at a state if there exists a fullpath from the state that satisfies f. A fullpath satisfies $\mathbf{X}f$ if in one step (next time), the fullpath satisfies f. A fullpath satisfies $f\mathbf{U}g$ if g holds at some point on the fullpath and f holds until then.

The following abbreviations are useful:

$\mathbf{A}f = \neg\mathbf{E}\neg f$, $\mathbf{F}g = \text{true }\mathbf{U}g$, $\mathbf{G}f = \neg\mathbf{F}\neg f$

$\mathbf{A}f$ is true at a state if every fullpath from the state satisfies f. A fullpath satisfies $\mathbf{F}g$ if eventually g holds on the path. A fullpath satisfies $\mathbf{G}f$ if f holds everywhere on the path.

Exercise 7.24 *Translate the following state formulae into Mu-Calculus formulae (the penultimate formula is not a CTL formula, but is a CTL* formula which you can think of as saying "there exists a path such that infinitely often p"):* EFp, AFp, AGp, EGp, EGFp, *and* EGEFp.

Exercise 7.25 *Define a translator that translates CTL formulae (where the abbreviations above, as well as* true *and* false *are allowed) into the Mu-Calculus.*

7.8   Conclusions

We gave a formal introduction to model-checking via the Mu-Calculus, but only scratched the surface. We conclude by listing some of the many interesting directions one can explore from here. One can define a programming language so that models can be described in a more convenient way. One can make the algorithm symbolic, by using BDDs instead of our explicit representation. One can define the semantics of a temporal logic (*e.g.*, CTL^*) in ACL2 and prove the correctness of the translation from the temporal logic to the Mu-Calculus. One can use monotonicity arguments and memoization to make the model-checking algorithms faster. Finally, one can verify that the optimizations suggested above preserve the semantics of the Mu-Calculus.

8

High-Speed, Analyzable Simulators

David Greve and Matthew Wilding
Rockwell Collins Advanced Technology Center, Cedar Rapids, Iowa
Email: {dagreve,mmwildin}@collins.rockwell.com

David Hardin
Ajile Systems, Inc., Oakdale, Iowa
Email: david.hardin@ajile.com

Abstract

High-speed simulation models are routinely developed during the design of complex hardware systems in order to predict performance, detect design flaws, and allow hardware/software co-design. Writing such an executable model in ACL2 brings the additional benefit of formal analysis; however, much care is required to construct an ACL2 model that is both fast and analyzable. In this chapter, we develop techniques for the construction of high-speed formally analyzable simulators in ACL2, and demonstrate their utility on a simple processor model.

Introduction

It is common practice when designing sophisticated hardware systems to construct simulators to predict performance and to flush out design flaws as early as possible. Hardware simulators also enable early evaluation of system behavior and allow hardware/software co-design. Such simulators are commonly implemented in C or C++ and provide either clock-cycle or behavioral-level accuracy. These simulators must execute quickly because they are often used interactively or to execute regression tests composed of millions of vectors.

ACL2 is a particularly attractive system for developing hardware simulators. ACL2 not only allows for the construction of a formal representation of hardware designs, it also enables execution of that representation as a simulator. ACL2's logic is constructed on top of a practical programming language, Common Lisp, and supports a wide variety of language features that add nothing to the logic but enable optimizations that are important for executing ACL2 code efficiently. Unification of the device models for formal analysis and simulation has the important additional property of validating the formal model through its execution and validating the simulator through formal verification. However, a good deal of care is required to construct a model that is both high-speed and analyzable.

This chapter explains how one can develop hardware device models that execute quickly and can be analyzed by the ACL2 theorem prover. We begin the chapter with a discussion on exactly how to write ACL2 models that execute quickly. We then present an example from [112] of processor modeling in ACL2 and conclude by highlighting some techniques and ACL2 features that help in reasoning about models of this type.

8.1   High-Speed Simulators

A simple approach for writing hardware simulators in software is to define a data structure containing a field corresponding to each register in the hardware design. The actual simulator is then nothing more than a program that reads the current state values from the data structure, computes the next state of the machine based on the current inputs, and updates the data structure fields appropriately. Such simulator models can be quite fast when state data structure access is efficient and the next state function is optimized.

This method for architecting simulators is similar to the interpreter-style of specification used in many previous formal verification projects [3]. In the interpreter style specification, a "next state" function is defined that accepts as input a data structure representing the current state of the machine and returns an updated machine state. A recursive stepper function repeatedly applies the next state function to an initial state to compute the final state after some number of clock cycles.

The challenge of building a high speed simulator in ACL2 is to represent state in a way that allows efficient manipulation and to craft an efficient ACL2 implementation of the next state function. While the following sections detail what an ACL2 user can do to obtain maximal execution efficiency, the extent to which this efficiency is realized depends largely on the Common Lisp compiler used. The optimizations presented here have been tested and shown to work with GCL 2.2.2 under 32-bit Linux and Solaris operating systems.

8.1.1   Representing State

The first step in developing an efficient hardware simulator is to find an efficient implementation of the state data structure. An efficient implementation provides fast data structure access and updating and imposes minimal runtime overhead.

Lists
One possible option for state representation is lists. Lists are easy to use and are well-supported by the ACL2 theorem prover. Simple lists, however, do not typically provide efficient access and update operations. Association lists, while providing relatively efficient updating, also do not allow for efficient access. The manipulation of lists also imposes significant runtime overhead in the form of garbage collection[112].

Arrays
A more ambitious implementation might wish to make use of Common Lisp arrays or structures to store the machine state. Such constructs are good for representing fixed-size data structures such as the state of a machine and provide extremely efficient access and update capability. The use of such imperative Common Lisp objects, however, is typically ruled out by the applicative nature of ACL2.

ACL2 does, however, support a clever implementation of applicative arrays that provides constant time access and destructive updates. See **arrays**. Unfortunately, ACL2 maintains two versions of the array contents in order to satisfy the applicative requirements of ACL2. Besides the imperative array implementation, ACL2 uses an association list implementation that is used when a multi-threaded manipulation of the data structure is encountered. Experience shows that, while better than lists, ACL2 arrays still impose significant runtime overhead in the form of garbage collection[112].

Single-Threaded Objects
The efficiency of ACL2's implementation of arrays is at the heart of the difference between imperative and applicative programming languages. Imperative languages have an implicit concept of state. It is possible to modify this implicit state without "returning" the new value of that state. This is commonly known as a *side effect* of executing an imperative program. Common Lisp, for example, provides constructs that allows destructive modification of global variables in an imperative way. ACL2, however, omits such constructs from its logic.

In contrast to imperative languages, functional (applicative) languages do not maintain global state. In a purely functional language, there are no side effects, no destructive updates, and no global variables. Modified versions of any so-called state variables in a functional language must be returned to the calling context in order to be visible.

Consider the following ACL2 code fragment that represents the computation of the next state of a model whose state is stored in a data structure called HWSTATE that is manipulated by the functions update-n and access-n.

```
(let ((HWSTATE (update-1 HWSTATE)))
  (let ((var (access-1 (update-2 HWSTATE))))
    (let ((HWSTATE (update-3 HWSTATE)))
```

Which version of HWSTATE does update-3 operate on, the version produced by update-1 or the version produced by update-2? In applicative languages like the logic of ACL2, update-3 operates on the version of HWSTATE produced by update-1. The implication of this is that during the process of computing the value to be bound to var, there must be two copies of state: one produced by update-1 and used eventually by update-3 and one produced by update-2 and used immediately by access-1.

Maintaining multiple copies of state, however, leads to inefficient execution. The natural way to implement such programs in imperative languages is by using global state. This is faster since multiple copies are not maintained, but allowing for side effects makes reasoning about imperative programs difficult.

As of Version 2.4, ACL2 provides a facility, called single-threaded objects, for defining data structures with applicative semantics but an imperative implementation [8]. These objects provide constant-time access and destructive update operators without imposing any runtime overhead. ACL2 enforces syntactic restrictions on the use of single-threaded objects that disallow cases in which the applicative and imperative semantics differ, such as in the example given above. ACL2's single-threaded objects provide an efficient, imperative data structure implementation while still allowing program reasoning using applicative semantics. See stobj.

8.1.2 Efficient Next-State Computation

Lisp has a dubious reputation when it comes to execution speed. However, one can write Lisp code that executes with nearly the speed of optimized C code when simulating hardware models.

Compilation and ACL2

The first step in obtaining efficient execution of Lisp code is to compile the code. While most Lisp systems support interpreted execution of Lisp code, compiled Lisp runs significantly faster. ACL2 takes pains to support a wide variety of language features that add no real value to the logic but enable optimization of the resulting compiled code.

The ACL2 feature that is perhaps the most useful in this respect is guards. See guard. One kind of ACL2 guard is a Common Lisp type declaration; see **declare**. Type declarations are used in Common Lisp to insert interpretive type checks and to improve compiled execution efficiency. One important use of guards in ACL2 is conveying type information to the Common Lisp compiler to enable compile time optimizations.

Common Lisp systems typically treat type declarations as unchecked conversions at compile time. The ACL2 user, however, is required to prove that the guards of a function are completely satisfied before ACL2 will allow the execution of the resulting optimized Lisp code. In this way, ACL2 guarantees via proof that type declarations result in safe type conversions at compile time, thus avoiding potentially unspecified behavior. Guard proofs are important in obtaining optimal performance from functions defined in ACL2.

Arithmetic

For maximal efficiency integer values should be used to encode the current state of the machine. The use of integer values to represent state permits efficient arithmetic operations. Common Lisp integers, however, are of arbitrary precision by default. This is in contrast to C, where the results of arithmetic operations are automatically cast to fixed-sized integers.

Although arbitrary precision is sometimes handy, it is undesirable for our purposes as it is generally quite slow. Bignum integers (as they are called in Common Lisp) are *boxed*, meaning that their values are represented by objects rather than as raw machine integers. Creating boxed integers requires memory allocation and destroying boxed integers involves garbage collection. Operations such as addition and multiplication are slow because they require "unboxing" or fetching the contents of the objects.

Another reason arbitrary precision integers are undesirable is that the arithmetic we want to use to describe hardware devices is modular arithmetic. This is simply because hardware performs operations on fixed-word-width values.

Common Lisp does not provide primitive support for modular arithmetic and Common Lisp arithmetic and logical functions consume and produce bignum values by default. Even so, it is possible to optimize integer operations in Common Lisp, as Guy Steele points out:

> In every Common Lisp implementation there is a range of integers that are represented more efficiently than others; each such integer is called a fixnum, and an integer that is not a fixnum is called a bignum. Common Lisp is designed to hide this distinction as much as possible; the distinction between fixnums and bignums is visible to the user in only a few places where the efficiency of representation is important. Exactly which integers are fixnums is implementation-dependent; typically they will be those integers in the range -2^n to 2^n-1, inclusive, for some n not less than 15. [104]

In the following sections we explore the boundaries of those "few" places where the efficiency is important and attempt to produce ACL2 code that performs integer operations efficiently.

Declarations

In Common Lisp, declarations are a mechanism that can be used for advising the compiler of potential optimizations based on the argument and return types of various functions.

> [...] declarations are of an advisory nature, and may be used by the Lisp system to aid the programmer by performing extra error checking or producing more efficient compiled code. Declarations are also a good way to add documentation to a program. [104]

By declaring that a + operation can be interpreted as operating on and returning only fixnum values, a good Common Lisp compiler will replace the functionality normally used to compute a bignum + with a more efficient fixnum + operation. This can result in significant savings both in execution time and in operating overhead by avoiding garbage collection. For most built-in integer operations in Common Lisp there exists a more efficient version of the functionality that operates on fixnum values. The only requirement for using the fixnum functionality is that the compiler be informed, through declarations, that the operation will be used with values representable as fixnums.

There are two kinds of type declarations in Common Lisp and ACL2 supports both. Binding type declarations are type declarations associated with variable bindings such as function arguments and variables bound in let expressions. The following example illustrates both argument and let binding declarations. See also **declare**.

```
(defun foo (a b)
  (declare (type (signed-byte 32) a)
           (type (signed-byte 32) b))
  (let ((x (goo a b)))
    (declare (type (signed-byte 32) x))
    x))
```

A second form of declaration is the inline **the** type declaration that allows the user to declare intermediate computational results.

> Frequently it is useful to declare that the value produced by the evaluation of some form will be of a particular type. Using declare one can declare the type of the value held by a bound variable, but there is no easy way to declare the type of the value of an unnamed form. For this purpose the **the** special form is defined; (**the** *type form*) means that the value of *form* is declared to be of type *type*. [104]

In the following example we use an inline declaration to assert that the result of calling goo is a (signed-byte 32).

```
(defun foo (a b)
  (declare (type (signed-byte 32) a)
           (type (signed-byte 32) b))
  (let ((x (the (signed-byte 32) (goo a b))))
    (declare (type (signed-byte 32) x)) x))
```

Such type declarations are examples of ACL2's notion of *guards*. See guard for more details. Using them introduces the extra burden of proving that the declarations are accurate. We discuss this below.

Note that the degree to which declarations improve the efficiency of any function is strongly dependent on the sophistication of the Lisp compiler being used. Some compilers are good at keeping track of variable types, inferring the types of bound variables or establishing function return types. For optimal compiler independence, one might attempt to declare every occurrence of every term and every bound variable. While such overkill should never decrease the compiled performance of the code, it may significantly decrease the interpreted execution speed and, further, over-employing declarations may lead to excessive or redundant guard proof obligations. A good rule of thumb is to declare all bound integer variables and all intermediate integer value results.

Functions

To preserve modularity, nontrivial simulators require the use of several levels of function definitions. One must expend effort in optimizing function calls in Lisp in much the same way one optimizes arithmetic operations.

Proclamations. Most modern computer systems provide efficient means for returning values from function calls. If properly informed, most Lisp systems can take advantage of this fact during the compilation process and optimize function calls so that they do not create garbage by pushing boxed values onto the Lisp value stack during the function call.

In Common Lisp, one informs the compiler of a function that can directly return fixnum values using the proclaim form.

```
(proclaim foo (fixnum fixnum) fixnum)
```

In ACL2 proclaim is not an accepted form. However, if the body of a function definition is enclosed in a the declaration form that indicates that the function is expected to return a fixnum value then ACL2 will automatically proclaim the function to the Common Lisp compiler. This process informs the Lisp compiler when a function can be optimized to use native calling procedures.[1]

---

[1] As we will see in Section 8.1.2, however, ACL2 Version 2.4 will not accept recursive function definitions whose outermost form is a the statement.

Recursive Functions.   It is often desirable to define functionality iteratively using recursion in ACL2. Recursive functions, however, present a couple of unique optimization challenges. The first is that ACL2 does not allow one to wrap the body of a recursive function with a <u>the</u> form and, thus, ACL2 is not inclined to proclaim the function to the compiler for function call optimization.[2] As a result it is not possible to completely optimize recursive functions to use native calling procedures and recursive functions returning integers will likely be compiled to return bignum results.

The second hurdle becomes apparent when one attempts to submit a form such as the following.

```
(defun foo (x)
  (declare (type (signed-byte 32) x))
  (if (> x 0)
      (foo (1- x))
    0))
```

This function is not admissible in the logic of ACL2. In order to guarantee the termination of this recursive function, one must establish that x is an integer. Otherwise the value returned by (1- x) is unspecified in Common Lisp and the function is not guaranteed to terminate. One might argue that because x has been declared to be of type (signed-byte 32) it must be an integer. This, however, is not the case because guards are not a part of the ACL2 logic. In other words, when performing the termination proof of this function, one is not allowed to assume that x is a (signed-byte 32). This can lead to some redundancy between function definitions and type declarations.

```
(defun foo (x)
  (declare (type (signed-byte 32) x))
  (if (and (integerp x)
           (> x 0))
      (foo (1- x))
    0))
```

While this definition is acceptable to ACL2, note that the implementation of foo is inefficient in that it has an unneeded call to integerp during each recursive iteration. This is particularly frustrating considering that we expect x always to satisfy this test.

One saving grace in this particular case is that integerp is a built-in Lisp function and many compilers are capable of detecting, from the type declarations, that x is an integer value and that any call to (integerp x) will return T, thus allowing the compiler to optimize away the function call.

---

[2] As of ACL2 version 2.4.

Macros

ACL2 support of Common Lisp macros is another example of a feature that
adds little to the ACL2 logic but has a significant impact on the usability of
the ACL2 system on real problems. Lisp macros can make writing efficient,
readable code much simpler. Macros can be used to improve execution
efficiency and readability in several ways.

Inlining. Macros provide ACL2 users with compiler-independent constant
and function inlining. Although ACL2 provides a **defconst** event that
allows the definition of a symbolic name for a constant value, it does not
necessarily result in efficient executable code. Macros are always efficient
because they are evaluated prior to compilation, thus allowing inlining of
constant values.

```
(defmacro MAX_INT<32> ()   2147483647)
(defmacro MIN_INT<32> ()  -2147483648)
```

Function inlining can be implemented using macros in a similar way.
Following is an example of a macro implementation of a 32-bit version of
the Common Lisp increment function.

```
(defmacro 1+<32> (x)
  `(if (= (MAX_INT<32>) ,x) (MIN_INT<32>)
    (the (signed-byte 32) (+ ,x 1))))
```

One drawback of using macros to replace functions in this way is that
one cannot control the expansion of macro expressions in the theorem
prover. In this case, for example, one cannot disable the definition of
1+<32> and then reason about it directly.

Syntactic Sugar. Macros can be used to simplify the syntax of otherwise
cumbersome Lisp expressions. The **the** declarations are an especially good
candidate for this type of macro.

```
(defmacro Int32 (x) `(the (signed-byte 32) ,x))
```

Macros can also be used to wrap functions with type declarations, thus
encouraging compiler optimizations and simplifying the syntax of such declarations. For example, one might define

```
(defmacro logand<32> (a b)
  `(Int32 (logand (Int32 ,a) (Int32 ,b))))
```

allowing us to write

```
(logand<32> x y)
```

instead of the following.

```
(the (signed-byte 32)
    (logand (the (signed-byte 32) x)
            (the (signed-byte 32) y)))
```

Readers. Macros can be used to define Lisp readers to change the meanings of predefined Lisp function symbols. The following simplistic reader macro converts the standard Lisp + symbol into the +<32> (fixnum addition) symbol. Note that this macro doesn't work over many Common Lisp special forms.

```
(defun map-fn (fn form)
  (if (consp form)
      '((,fn ,(car form)) ,@(map-fn fn (cdr form)))
    nil))

(defmacro reader (form)
  (if (atom form)
      form
    (case (car form)
      ((+) '(+<32> ,@(map-fn 'reader (cdr form))))
      (t   '(,(first form)
             ,@(map-fn 'reader (cdr form)))))))
```

This allows us to write functions succinctly.

```
(defun foo (x) (reader (+ (+ x 2) 3)))
```

While this type of reader macro doesn't directly improve efficiency, it can make writing and reading optimized Lisp code much easier. By remapping Lisp operations to their fixnum equivalents, the clutter introduced by type declarations can be largely overcome.

Exercise 8.1 *Extend the reader macro presented above to handle the special Lisp forms* <u>case</u> *and* <u>cond</u>. *(Remember,* case *key forms are not evaluated!) Expand its capability to handle some of the other basic integer operations such as* logand, logior, *etc. Try automatically inserting type declarations into simple* <u>let</u> *bindings, assuming that each* let *binds a fixnum value.*

Progn Emulation. The syntactic restrictions imposed by single threaded objects make writing and reading code that manipulates these data structures difficult. For functions involving deeply nested updates of single threaded objects, it is convenient to define a <u>progn</u>-style macro that automatically binds a sequence of state updates.

```
(defmacro ST-PROGN (stobj &rest rst)
  (cond ((endp rst) stobj)
        ((endp (cdr rst)) (car rst))
        (t '(let ((,stobj ,(car rst)))
              (ST-PROGN ,stobj ,@(cdr rst))))))
```

This allows us to write a sequence of HWSTATE updates as follows.

```
(ST-PROGN HWSTATE
          (update-1 HWSTATE)
          (update-2 HWSTATE)
          (update-3 HWSTATE))
```

Exercise 8.2 *Write a* **progn**-*style macro that binds single threaded object updates and allows for the introduction of* **let** *bindings of intermediate variables. For example,*

```
(ST-PROGN HWSTATE
   (update-1 HWSTATE)
   (let ((value1 (+ 4 5))))
     (update-2 value1 HWSTATE))
```

should expand to the following.

```
(let ((HWSTATE (update-1 HWSTATE)))
   (let ((value1 (+ 4 5)))
     (let ((HWSTATE (update-2 value1 HWSTATE)))
       HWSTATE)))
```

8.1.3   32-Bit Modular Addition

In this section we bring together many of the concepts presented so far concerning efficient execution of ACL2 programs. We illustrate these techniques by writing a function that accepts two 32-bit integer arguments and returns their 32-bit modular sum. Assuming that fixnum values include at least 32-bit integers, this function uses only fixnum operations, and a decent Common Lisp compiler will generate fast-executing code.[3]

We start by defining a type macro to relieve us of typing **the** forms.

```
(defmacro Int32 (x)
  '(the (signed-byte 32) ,x))
```

Our first attempt at a 32-bit modular addition function is the following.

```
(defun plus<32> (a b)
  (declare (type (signed-byte 32) a)
           (type (signed-byte 32) b)
           (xargs :verify-guards nil))
  (Int32 (+ a b)))
```

This function usually works in raw Common Lisp, assuming one is executing on a 32-bit machine. However, when we submit the event (**verify-guards plus<32>**) to ACL2, we find that the guards for the function are unsatisfiable. The reason this function usually performs as expected in raw Common

---

[3]Note that Common Lisp does not require that the fixnums are a superset of the 32-bit integers. For example, 2^{29} is not a fixnum in Allegro 5.0.

Lisp is that Common Lisp accepts the type declarations at face value and optimizes the + function accordingly. The reason the guard proof fails in ACL2, however, is that it is not necessarily the case that when you add two 32-bit integers that you will obtain a result representable in 32 bits.

One possible solution to this problem is to constrain a and b in such a way as to guarantee that the result is representable in 32 bits. We can do this using the (xargs :guard) argument to write a more expressive guard statement such as the following.

```
(defun plus<32> (a b)
  (declare (type (signed-byte 32) a)
           (type (signed-byte 32) b)
           (xargs :guard (and (>= (MAX_INT<32>) (+ a b))
                              (<= (MIN_INT<32>) (+ a b)))))
  (Int32 (+ a b)))
```

The guards for this function are now satisfiable and our examination of compiler output confirms that this function does in fact compile into an efficient implementation. Unfortunately, there are a couple of problems with this particular implementation. The first is that any other function that calls this function must be able to demonstrate not only that the two arguments passed to plus<32> are representable as 32-bit integers but that the sum of those two arguments is representable in 32-bits as well. While this may be possible in some special cases, it will not be true in general. The second problem with this function is that it does not satisfy our original requirements because it does not actually perform modular integer addition. In modular integer addition there are cases when both operands are positive and the result is negative. Such overflow cases, however, are specifically excluded by the guards of plus<32> above.

With these observations in mind, we now present a function that satisfies our original requirements.

```
(defmacro +<32> (x y) '(Int32 (+ ,x ,y)))

(defun plus<32> (a b)
  (declare (type (signed-byte 32) a)
           (type (signed-byte 32) b))
  (Int32 (cond
          ((< a 0)
           (if (>= b 0) (+<32> a b)
             (let ((psum (+<32> b
                           (+<32> 1
                             (+<32> a (MAX_INT<32>))))))
               (declare (type (signed-byte 32) psum))
               (if (< psum 0)
                   (+<32> (+<32> (MAX_INT<32>) psum) 1
```

```
                    (+<32> psum (MIN_INT<32>)))))
      ((< b 0) (+<32> a b))
      (t (let ((psum (+<32> (+<32> a (MIN_INT<32>))
                             b)))
           (declare (type (signed-byte 32) psum))
           (if (>= psum 0)
               (+<32> (MIN_INT<32>) psum)
               (+<32> (+<32> psum (MAX_INT<32>)) 1)))))))))
```

Given the relative complexity of the above function, it is interesting to note that it is exactly the expressive power of Common Lisp that makes it so difficult to implement such a seemingly simple procedure. One false move during any intermediate step of the algorithm will result in the creation of a bignum integer object or guard conjectures that are unprovable. While it is somewhat frustrating that one cannot directly access the low level 32-bit modular addition functions that often exist natively on the machine, it is nonetheless comforting to know that ACL2 will not allow us to create models whose execution is inconsistent with their formal description.

Exercise 8.3 *Prove that, given two 32-bit integers arguments,* plus<32> *implements 32-bit modular integer addition. Hint: You may want to use* logext *and* logext-+-logext *from the* ihs *books provided with the ACL2 distribution to specify and prove this behavior.*

Exercise 8.4 *Implement a function that accepts two 32-bit integer values and returns their 32-bit integer bitwise logical and. Was this function simpler or more complex than* plus<32>*? Why?*

8.2   TINY : A High-Speed Simulator Example

In the supporting files [67] there is an illustration of the use of ACL2 to develop a high-speed model of a simple processor called TINY. The TINY machine is a simple, stack-based machine whose state is composed of a program counter, a memory of integers, a data stack top-of-stack pointer, and a call stack top-of-stack pointer.

The TINY model is represented in the ACL2 logic as an interpreter that operates over a single-threaded object. This single-threaded object contains fields corresponding to each of the TINY state elements and all of the entries in this single threaded object are represented using fixnum integer values. The following event defines the single-threaded object used to represent the TINY state.

Opcode	Mnemonic	Description
0	**pop a**	Pop a data stack value into location a
1	**pushs a**	Push the value at location a onto the data stack
2	**pushsi i**	Push i onto the data stack
3	**add**	Pop two data stack values and push their 32-bit sum
4	**jump a**	Set the program counter (PC) to a
5	**jumpz a**	Set the PC to a if popped data stack value is 0
6	**call a**	Push the next address on the call stack and set the PC to a
7	**ret**	Set the PC to the popped call stack value
8	**sub**	Pop two values and push the maximum of 0 and their 32-bit difference
9	**dup**	Duplicate the top of data stack

Figure 8.1: TINY Instructions

```
(defstobj st
 (progc :type (unsigned-byte 10)                        :initially 0)
 (mem    :type (array (signed-byte 32) (1024)) :initially 0)
 (dtos   :type (unsigned-byte 10)                       :initially 0)
 (ctos   :type (unsigned-byte 10)                       :initially 0))
```

A series of ACL2 functions and macros designed to operate efficiently over this state are introduced and ultimately composed to define the function **next**, the TINY next-state function. This function interprets the TINY instructions with respect to their effect on the TINY state. The TINY instruction set is described in Figure 8.1. The ACL2 term (tiny s n) evaluates to a TINY state that reflects the effect of executing n instructions on an initial TINY state **s**.

Figure 8.2 presents a TINY program from [112] that calculates the integer remainder of two positive values in memory using repeated subtraction. Since we have expressed the TINY model in the ACL2 logic, we can use the ACL2 theorem prover to prove interesting properties about this code. Rather than reason about the assembly code, however, we reason about the binary code that is actually loaded onto the machine. Techniques for doing such proofs are presented in the following section.

8.3 Simulator Execution Analysis

An ACL2 proof about the remainder program presented in Figure 8.2 is provided in the events that accompany this book [67]. The present section

Assembly			Comment
.ORG	18		Origin Program at address 18
VAL	0		value
MODU	0		modulus (assumed positive)
REM	pop	MODU	
	pop	VAL	
LOOP	pushs	VAL	repeated subtraction loop
	pushs	MODU	
	sub		
	dup		
	jumpz	DOSUB	end loop when VAL $<=$ MODU
	pop	VAL	
	jump	LOOP	
DOSUB	pushs	MODU	
	pushs	VAL	
	sub		
	jumpz	EXIT1	
	jump	EXIT2	
EXIT1	pushsi	0	VAL=MODU: set VAL to 0
	pop	VAL	
EXIT2	pop	MODU	RETURN VAL on stack
	pushs	VAL	
	ret		

Figure 8.2: A TINY Program for Calculating Remainder

highlights several aspects of this proof that are generally useful for this kind of analysis, and points out particularly some advanced features of ACL2's simplifier that are useful. Most or all of these techniques have been introduced or presented in various publications, most comprehensively in [6].

8.3.1 Algorithm Proofs and Symbolic Simulation

The remainder program calculates the remainder of two positive integers by repeated subtraction. We can specify its behavior using the ACL2 (and Common Lisp) function mod.[4]

```
(defun good-initial-remainder-state (st)
  (declare (xargs :stobjs (st)))
  (and (stp st)
       (< (dtos st) 1000) (>= (dtos st) 100)
       (<= (ctos st) 1020) (> (ctos st) 1010)
       (equal (progc st) 24)
       (program-loaded st *mod-prog* 20)
       (< 0 (memi 18 st))
       (< 0 (memi 19 st)))))

(defthm mod-correct
  (let ((s2 (tiny st (remclock st))))
    (implies (good-initial-remainder-state st)
             (equal (memi (1+ (dtos s2)) s2)
                    (mod (memi 18 st) (memi 19 st)))))))
```

The function good-initial-remainder-state identifies TINY states that have data stack and call stack register values within certain bounds, a program counter that points to the beginning of the remainder program, a memory that contains the remainder program, and positive values in two specific locations. The remainder program we refer to here is the binary version of the remainder program listed in Figure 8.2. A useful property of the remainder program is described by mod-correct: the program deposits the expected value at the top of the data stack.

It is always important when proving theorems in ACL2 to partition the proof effort as much as possible. An excellent way to partition a proof about simulator execution such as mod-correct is to divide the work into proving two sublemmas:

- ◆ a lemma that describes the effect the simulator's execution has on the machine state, and

---

[4]We omit :hints and :rule-classes arguments of defthms in this chapter when they are irrelevant to the discussion. The unexpurgated events can be found in the supporting files for this book [67].

♦ a lemma that shows that the implemented algorithm works.

We describe both these kinds of proofs in the following sections.

8.3.2   Implementation Proofs

Symbolic Simulation
To prove a lemma describing the simulator's effect on the machine state, we must specify the behavior of the program. We introduce a function that calculates the result of the execution of the simulator in exactly the same way as the program. That is, we implement the algorithm being reasoned about in the ACL2 logic directly, not using the interpreter, and use the same types of conditions and operations as are used in the implementation.

For example, the result of the remainder program is calculated by `remainder-prog-result`.

```
(defun remainder-prog-result (n p)
  (if (or (zp p) (zp n) (< n p))
      (nfix n)
    (remainder-prog-result (- n p) p)))
```

Note that `remainder-prog-result` calculates remainder just as the program does, and performs the same operations each iteration of the loop. Using this function as a specification of the program execution simplifies the proof.

We wish to show that the symbolic expression that represents the result of running the remainder program is in part described by the function `remainder-prog-result`. In order to use the ACL2 theorem prover to generate the symbolic result we introduce ACL2 rules that direct the simplifier to execute the interpreter symbolically. For straightline code where the number of instructions is constant this is straightforward. The following rule causes the ACL2 simplifier to execute the TINY interpreter symbolically. Note the hypothesis involving `syntaxp` requires that this rule is applied only to terms `(tiny st n)` where n is a constant; see **syntaxp**.

```
(defthm tiny-straightline
  (implies
   (syntaxp (quotep n))
   (equal (tiny st n)
          (if (zp n) st (tiny (next st) (1- n))))))
```

Using `tiny-straightline` we can prove, for example, what happens when the loop in the **remainder** program is executed once. There are seven instructions in the body of the loop, and `tiny-straightline` together with other rules rewrites the term `(tiny st 7)` to the symbolic result of Figure 8.3, given the assumption that st represents a good TINY state just about to iterate on the loop.

```
(UPDATE-NTH 0 24
 (UPDATE-NTH 1
  (UPDATE-NTH 18
              (+ (NTH 18 (NTH 1 ST))
                 (- (NTH 19 (NTH 1 ST))))
              (UPDATE-NTH (NTH 2 ST)
                          (+ (NTH 18 (NTH 1 ST))
                             (- (NTH 19 (NTH 1 ST))))
                          (UPDATE-NTH (+ -1 (NTH 2 ST))
                                      (+ (NTH 18 (NTH 1 ST))
                                         (- (NTH 19 (NTH 1 ST))))
                                      (NTH 1 ST))))
  ST))
```

Figure 8.3: Symbolic expression resulting from one iteration of **remainder**'s loop

While `tiny-straightline` works well for a constant number of instructions, it will not work on more complex code, such as code containing loops. In order to analyze more complex code we first introduce a *clock* function that calculates how many instructions are executed.[5] To automate the reasoning process, the clock function has the structure of the executing code. Straightline code is represented by a constant, alternation is represented using an `if`, and loops are represented using recursive functions. The ACL2 simplifier will expand the interpreter for straightline code and case split for alternation. Loops will be dealt with by setting up inductive arguments that mimic the recursion of the clock function.

We define the function `c+` as `+` on natural numbers and then disable its definition. We use `c+` rather than `+` for fear that other rules about a commonly-used function such as `+` will interfere with these proofs. The following rule simplifies expressions that we will encounter that contain `c+` in their clock expressions by decomposing their execution into constituent parts.

```
(defthm tiny-c+
  (equal (tiny s (c+ x y))
         (tiny (tiny s x) y)))
```

---

[5] Clocks were used in Boyer and Moore's formalization of the BDX 930 in the late 1970's [43] to admit an otherwise non-terminating machine interpreter. Clocks and clock functions were used in proofs in [5] to deal with the unsolvability of the halting problem. Such proofs became more common in the mid-1980's when the Nqthm community and successive "Recursion and Induction" classes at the University of Texas explored the formalization of hardware and hardware/software systems. Bevier made extensive use of clock functions in his KIT operating system kernel [2]. Moore and Wilding used carefully defined recursive clock functions to control proofs in the Piton work [77, 111]. Yu used this technique repeatedly in verifying machine code programs produced by gcc in [9]. The basic ideas have been shown to work with the PVS theorem prover [113] and a system for automatically generating clock functions from microcode for use in PVS has been demonstrated [45]. The idea is documented fully in [6].

The function `modloop-clock` presented below calculates the number of instructions required to execute the loop of our example program.

```
(defun modloop-clock-helper (x y)
  (if (or (not (integerp x)) (not (integerp y))
          (>= 0 y) (<= x y))
      (if (equal x y) 14 13)
    (c+ 7 (modloop-clock-helper (- x y) y))))

(defun modloop-clock (st)
  (declare (xargs :stobjs (st)))
  (let ((x (memi 18 st)) (y (memi 19 st)))
    (modloop-clock-helper x y)))
```

These rules are sufficient to derive symbolic expressions that describe the results. However, as can be seen in Figure 8.3, the expressions that result are very complex, even for a toy model like TINY and a simple program. Note that since an instruction typically updates a few fields with values calculated from the previous state, the size of the term grows exponentially in the number of instructions. The example symbolic expression in Figure 8.3 is complex, but not that complex! In the next section we introduce some ACL2 rules that simplify terms of this kind.

Exercise 8.5 *Calculate a symbolic expression that expresses the result of executing the TINY interpreter on the first two instructions of the remainder program. Simplify that expression using the fact that an update of an element of the state does not affect the other elements.*

Simplifying Terms with Access/Update Functions
In the previous section we described how to arrange for ACL2 to generate symbolic expressions that describe the effect of running a simulator. The resulting terms contain access and update functions that are used to define the interpreter. In order to automate proofs involving such expressions we must simplify and normalize them. One of the first challenges an ACL2 user confronts when facing such a proof is deciding which functions to <u>disable</u>.

Should we disable and reason about functions such as **update-memi** and **progc**, or enable them and reason about the functions of which they are composed, namely <u>nth</u> and **update-nth**? We choose to enable these functions so that we can reason about nth and update-nth. In this way we can prove a handful of rules about these two functions. If we left the access and update functions enabled we would need to add a rule for each accessor/updater pair. A model with 100 fields, for example, would require 10,000 rules just to reason about accessing an updated state!

One potential downside to the decision to expand the access and update functions during proofs is that rules we prove about the elements of the state are dependent upon their location in the state description. In the example we might want to write a theorem that simplifies the **progc** of the state and so place (progc s) on the left-hand side of a rewrite rule. Unfortunately the term will already have been rewritten to (nth 0 s) since progc is enabled. We might naively use (nth 0 s) on the left-hand side of our rule, but this is not good practice: if we change the location of progc in our representation of state our proofs will no longer work. We follow the convention of defining the location of the elements in the state symbolically using a macro and prove rules involving that element using that symbolic name. So, we define

```
(defmacro progcloc () 0)
```

and use (nth (progcloc) s) and (update-nth (progcloc) v s) in the-orems about it. Note how this approach takes advantage of the fact that ACL2 rewrite rules have their macros expanded when they are introduced, before they are stored as rewrite rules.

The symbolic result of executing code on the simulator will be a term consisting of a nest of update-nth functions that reflect changes to the state of the machine. Of course, we want to simplify these expressions as much as possible to further our analysis. One such rule is

```
(defthm nth-update-nth2
  (equal
    (nth n1 (update-nth n2 v 1))
    (if (equal (nfix n1) (nfix n2)) v (nth n1 1))))
```

which simplifies the access of updated state. We would prefer not to in-troduce case splits, so we introduce versions of nth-update-nth2 that backchain on whether the indices of nth and update-nth match.[6] Note that we list the backchaining rules *after* the case splitting rule so that the backchaining rules are tried first as ACL2 rewrite rules.

```
(defthm nth-update-nth-1
  (implies
    (not (equal (nfix n1) (nfix n2)))
    (equal (nth n1 (update-nth n2 v 1)) (nth n1 1))))
```

```
(defthm nth-update-nth-2
  (implies
    (equal (nfix n1) (nfix n2))
    (equal (nth n1 (update-nth n2 v 1)) v)))
```

---

[6] Avoiding case splits is particularly important when reasoning about lambda expres-sions, such as are encountered using ACL2 2.4's implementation of stobj. If-expressions in the arguments of a lambda expression interfere with beta-reduction of lambda expres-sions because of ACL2's heuristics for nonrecursive function expansion. This problem is not apparent in the small example of this chapter, but it is a serious issue when reason-ing about large stobj-based models where if-expressions are unavoidable. Either this problem will be overcome in ACL2 or users will have to use a homegrown version of stobj that does not have this problem such as is documented in [112]. In either case, the discussion in this chapter applies.

The following rule deletes a list update from a term if the updated element is subsequently replaced.

```
(defthm update-nth-update-nth-same
  (equal (update-nth i v1 (update-nth i v2 l))
         (update-nth i v1 l)))
```

Although this seems a helpful simplification, it will not work on terms that have intervening updates of other list elements. For example, the term

```
(update-nth 2 v1 (update-nth 1 v2 (update-nth 2 v3 l)))
```

is not simplified by `update-nth-update-nth-same` because no subterm matches its left-hand side. What we need is another rule that rearranges the updates of a term so that the updates of a particular element appear consecutively. The following rule does just that.

```
(defthm update-nth-update-nth-diff
  (implies
    (not (equal (nfix i1) (nfix i2)))
    (equal (update-nth i1 v1 (update-nth i2 v2 l))
           (update-nth i2 v2 (update-nth i1 v1 l))))
  :rule-classes ((:rewrite :loop-stopper ((i1 i2)))))
```

The lemma `update-nth-update-nth-diff` can be used to rearrange the arguments of any term containing nested `update-nth` functions involving distinct fields. We instruct the simplifier using the ACL2 `:loop-stopper` parameter to apply this rule only when it brings us closer to achieving our goal of moving updates of the same field closer to each other. The loop-stopper `(i1 i2)` means that we insist that the simplifier apply `update-nth-update-nth-diff` only when the term that matches `i2` (on the left-hand-side of the rewrite rule) is "less than" the term that matches `i1`. This overrides ACL2's default loop-stopper heuristic which is to apply the rule only when the resulting term is "less than" the original according to ACL2's term ordering heuristic. ACL2 term order for positive integers is identical to standard <, so when rewriting the term

```
(update-nth 2 v1 (update-nth 1 v2 (update-nth 2 v3 l)))
```

the subterm

```
(update-nth 1 v2 (update-nth 2 v3 l))
```

is left untouched by `update-nth-update-nth-diff` since $2 \not< 1$. The entire term, however, is simplified since $1 < 2$, leading to

```
(update-nth 1 v2 (update-nth 2 v1 (update-nth 2 v3 l))).
```

The rule `update-nth-update-nth-same` is then applied, simplifying the term to

```
(update-nth 1 v2 (update-nth 2 v1 l)).
```

Exercise 8.6 *Read the ACL2 documentation of* `loop-stopper`. *Give an example term that is simplified by the rewrite rule* `update-nth-update-`
`-nth-diff`, *but which would not have simplified had* `update-nth-update-`
`-nth-diff` *not overridden the default heuristics with an explicit* `:loop-`
`-stopper` *argument.*

The handful of rules described in this section do a good job simplifying terms involving `nth` and `update-nth`.

8.3.3 Algorithm Proof

The approach to implementation proof that we presented is only part of the story. We must also prove that the algorithm that is implemented does the "right" thing. In the case of our simple example ACL2 proves that the algorithm works without the need for any sublemmas, using the `quotient-remainder` book of the `ihs` library available in the standard ACL2 distribution.

```
(defthm remainder-is-mod
  (implies
   (and (integerp x)
        (<= 0 x)
        (integerp y)
        (<= 0 y))
   (equal (remainder-prog-result x y) (mod x y))))
```

Although for our simple example the algorithm proof is straightforward, this part of a proof is typically very challenging and requires a great deal of domain-specific proof.

8.3.4 Remainder Proof

The correctness of our remainder example follows directly from the implementation and algorithm proofs of the previous sections.

```
(defthm mod-correct
  (let ((s2 (tiny st (remclock st))))
    (implies (good-initial-remainder-state st)
             (equal (memi (1+ (dtos s2)) s2)
                    (mod (memi 18 st) (memi 19 st)))))))
```

8.4 Conclusion

The unification of simulators for device development and interpreters for formal analysis has many advantages. We have demonstrated in this chapter how one can build a high-speed simulator that can be analyzed using ACL2. These techniques, although shown in the context of a "toy" processor model, have been shown to scale to practical processor designs [46, 112].

Verification of a Simple Pipelined Machine Model

Jun Sawada

Department of Computer Sciences, University of Texas at Austin, Texas
Email: sawada@cs.utexas.edu

Abstract

The difficulty of pipelined machine verification derives from the fact that there is a complex time-abstraction between the pipelined implementation and its specification which executes instructions sequentially. To study this problem, we define a simple three-stage pipelined machine in ACL2. We prove that this pipelined machine returns the same result as its specification machine. In order to ease the proof, we define an intermediate abstraction called MAETT. This abstraction models the behavior of instructions in the pipelined architecture, and it allows us to define directly and verify invariant conditions about executed instructions. The author used a similar approach to verify a more realistic pipelined machine. This chapter serves as an introduction to the verification of pipelined machines.

9.1   A Three-Stage Pipelined Machine and Its Correctness

Pipelining is a key idea in the design of modern microprocessors. It improves the performance of microprocessors by overlapping the execution of instructions. A pipelined microprocessor typically starts the execution of an instruction before the completion of the previous instruction. However, programmers imagine that microprocessors execute instructions one-by-one. This makes it natural to define the specification of a microprocessor as a sequential execution model. Therefore, the verification of a pipelined microprocessor requires a proof that the pipelined implementation appears to behave as its sequential execution model behaves.

   To study this problem, we will consider a three-stage pipelined machine. Figure 9.1 shows its block diagram. This machine consists of a program

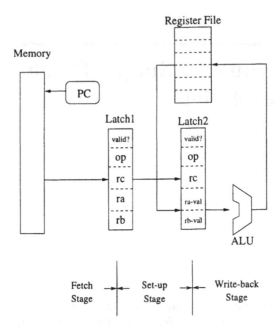

Figure 9.1: The three-stage pipelined machine.

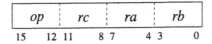

Figure 9.2: The instruction format for the three-stage pipelined machine.

counter (PC), a register file, a memory, an ALU, and two pipeline latches. The register file is a collection of registers.

The instruction format for this machine is shown in Figure 9.2. An instruction is a 16-bit word and it has four fields: opcode field *op*, destination register field *rc*, and source register fields *ra* and *rb*. For example, the bits between the 12th bit and the 15th bit correspond to the opcode, which specifies the instruction type. The opcodes of the ADD and SUB instructions are 0 and 1, respectively. An instruction with an opcode other than 0 or 1 is considered to be a NOP, which only increments the program counter.

There are three stages in the pipeline: the fetch stage, the set-up stage, and the write-back stage. The machine fetches an instruction in the fetch stage, reads source registers in the set-up stage, and performs an arithmetic operation and updates the destination register in the write-back stage. The latches are used to store intermediate results. The *valid?* flag of each latch is set to 1 when an instruction occupies the latch. The *op* field stores the opcode of the stored instruction, and the *rc*, *ra*, and *rb* fields store the operand register designators. The *ra-val* and *rb-val* fields store the two source operand register values.

Let us consider the execution of the following three instructions. In this program, the operand registers *rc*, *ra*, and *rb* are printed in that order. For example, i_0 is an ADD instruction that reads registers R1 and R3 and stores the results in R2.

$$i_0: \text{ADD} \quad \text{R2, R1, R3}$$
$$i_1: \text{SUB} \quad \text{R4, R2, R5}$$
$$i_2: \text{ADD} \quad \text{R7, R5, R6}$$

Table 9.1 shows the latches in which the intermediate results of instructions are stored at each time. For example, the instruction i_0 is fetched between time 0 and 1, it goes through the set-up stage between time 1 and 2, and it finishes the write-back stage between time 2 and 3. Thus, the intermediate results of i_0 are stored in latch1 at time 1 and in latch2 at time 2.

Time	0	1	2	3	4	5	6
i_0		latch1	latch2				
i_1			latch1	latch1	latch2		
i_2					latch1	latch2	

Table 9.1: A reservation table for the three-stage pipelined machine.

This table shows a typical pipelined execution. While i_0 is at the set-up stage between time 1 and 2, instruction i_1 is fetched simultaneously. Since the instruction i_1 uses the value of register R2 which is the result of instruction i_0, instruction i_1 must wait for i_0 to update R2 before reading its value in the set-up stage. Thus, the instruction i_1 *stalls* between times 2 and 3: i_1 stays in latch1. After i_0 completes the write-back stage at time 3, i_1 continues the rest of the execution in the set-up and write-back stages. Instruction i_2 is executed between times 3 and 6.

Because the execution of instructions is overlapped, a pipelined machine state may not correspond to any state which programmers expect to see. For example at time 3, the program counter points to the next instruction to be fetched, namely i_2. However, the register file records the result of i_0, but not i_1 yet, since i_1 is still at latch1. In other words, the program counter appears as if we have completed two instructions i_0 and i_1, but the registers appear as if we have only completed the instruction i_0. Thus, the pipeline state at time 3 does not correspond to any state observable by executing instructions sequentially.

To be more concrete, we define the machine in the ACL2 logic at two levels: the *instruction-set architecture* (ISA) level and the *microarchitecture* (MA) level. The ISA models the machine behavior that programmers have in mind. It executes instructions one at a time. This style of execution is called *sequential execution*. The MA model defines how the actual pipelined machine behaves. Instruction executions are overlapped in this model, and this style of execution is called *pipelined execution*.

The behavior of the ISA model is given by the following function.

```
(defun ISA-step (ISA)
  (let ((inst (read-mem (ISA-pc ISA) (ISA-mem ISA))))
    (let ((op (op-field inst))
          (rc (rc-field inst))
          (ra (ra-field inst))
          (rb (rb-field inst)))
      (case op
        (0 (ISA-add rc ra rb ISA))          ; ADD
        (1 (ISA-sub rc ra rb ISA))          ; SUB
        (otherwise (ISA-default ISA))))))    ; NOP
```

This function takes the current state ISA and returns the new state after executing one instruction. A state of the ISA model is represented with an ACL2 structure defined by macro defstructure, which in turn is defined in the ACL2 public book data-structures/structures (see also [10]). Expressions (ISA-pc ISA), (ISA-regs ISA), and (ISA-mem ISA) return the program counter, the register file and the memory in state ISA, respectively. ISA-step reads an instruction inst from the memory at the location addressed by the program counter, divides it into instruction fields, and executes it appropriately depending on the opcode. For example, if the op-field of inst contains 0, the ISA-step function performs an ADD instruction whose effect is defined by the function ISA-add. Similarly, ISA-sub and ISA-default define the effects of the SUB and NOP instructions, respectively.

We can define a recursive function (ISA-stepn ISA n), which calculates the result of executing n instructions. It is defined to apply ISA-step repeatedly n times.

```
(defun ISA-stepn (ISA n)
  (if (zp n) ISA (ISA-stepn (ISA-step ISA) (1- n))))
```

The expression (MA-step MA sig) takes the current MA-level state MA and an external input signal sig, and returns the state at the next clock cycle. It defines the behavior of the pipelined machine at the MA level, by specifying how individual components behave in every clock cycle. The input signal to the pipelined machine controls instruction fetching, and the machine does not fetch a new instruction when the input is 0.

```
(defun MA-step (MA sig)
  (MA-state (step-pc MA sig)
            (step-regs MA)
            (MA-mem MA)
            (step-latch1 MA sig)
            (step-latch2 MA)))
```

Functions step-pc, step-regs, step-latch1, and step-latch2 define the
new state of the program counter, the register file, and pipeline latches
latch1 and latch2. The memory state does not change in this simple machine. Constructor function MA-state combines these component states to
form the new MA state. The recursive function (MA-stepn MA sig-list
n) applies MA-step repeatedly n times and returns the MA state n clock
cycles later. The argument sig-list is a list of input signals controlling
instruction fetches.

```
(defun MA-stepn (MA sig-list n)
  (if (zp n)
      MA
      (MA-stepn (MA-step MA (car sig-list))
                (cdr sig-list)
                (1- n))))
```

One key idea in comparing pipelined machine states to sequential execution states is using *pipeline flushed states*. An MA state is a pipeline flushed
state if no instructions are partially executed in the pipeline. In Table 9.1,
the MA is in pipeline flushed states at time 0 and 6. In a pipeline flushed
state, all programmer visible components, such as the program counter, the
register file, and the memory, are synchronized. Thus it is easy to define
the corresponding ISA state for a pipeline flushed state. We define this
correspondence as a projection function (proj MA), which returns an ISA
state by extracting the program counter, the register file, and the memory
states from the MA-level state MA.

```
(defun proj (MA)
  (ISA-state (MA-pc MA) (MA-regs MA) (MA-mem MA)))
```

Figure 9.3 shows the commutative diagram that represents the correctness of our pipelined machine. Consider an initial state MA_0, which we
assume is a pipeline flushed state. There are two paths to follow in the
commutative diagram. One path runs the MA model for n steps where
n is an arbitrary natural number. Suppose the final state MA_n is also a
flushed state. Then we can map the final state MA_n to ISA_m with the
projection function. Let m be the number of instructions executed during
the state transition from MA_0 to MA_n. The other path first projects the
initial state MA_0 to ISA_0 and runs the ISA for m cycles to reach ISA_m. If
the MA correctly implements the ISA, the same ISA_m must be obtained
by following the two paths. We will prove this commutative diagram in the
rest of the chapter.

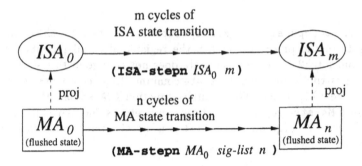

Figure 9.3: The commutative diagram for the pipelined machine.

9.2   Intermediate Abstraction and Invariant

It is often difficult to directly verify an entire pipelined machine. Our example machine is simple, but a typical pipelined microprocessor has a long pipeline with complex control logic. Instead of directly analyzing the entire microarchitecture, we show that each instruction is executed correctly. This allows us to verify the machine design incrementally, and later combine the results together to prove the commutative diagram.

To pursue this idea, our verification approach first defines an intermediate abstraction, which builds a list of completely executed instructions and in-flight instructions. For example, at time 4 in Table 9.1, instruction i_0 has been completely executed, and i_1 and i_2 are in-flight. The intermediate abstraction represents the MA state at time 4 with a list of instructions i_0, i_1, and i_2.

More precisely speaking, the status of each instruction is recorded in the intermediate abstraction. We represent the status of an instruction with a structure type named INST. In ACL2, the structure can be defined with defstructure macro as follows.

```
(defstructure INST
  (stg      (:assert (stage-p stg)          :rewrite))
  (pre-ISA  (:assert (ISA-state-p pre-ISA)  :rewrite))
  (post-ISA (:assert (ISA-state-p post-ISA) :rewrite))
  (:options ...))
```

This structure has three fields stg, pre-ISA, and post-ISA. Field stg represents the current stage of the represented instruction, and pre-ISA and post-ISA store ISA states which we will describe shortly. Accessors functions to the structure fields are INST-stg, INST-pre-ISA, and INST-post-ISA.

Let i_k^t denote the INST structure representing the status of instruction i_k at time t in Table 9.1. Since i_0 is at latch1 at time 1, (INST-stg i_0^1) = 'latch1. Similarly, (INST-stg i_0^2) = 'latch2. The stage of completed instructions is defined as 'retire, so (INST-stg i_0^3) = 'retire.

Using this instruction representation, we define the intermediate abstraction state. We call this intermediate abstraction a *Microarchitecture Execution Trace Table* (MAETT) [99]. It is defined using the following ACL2 structure.

```
(defstructure MAETT
  (init-ISA (:assert (ISA-state-p init-ISA) :rewrite))
  (trace    (:assert (INST-listp trace)     :rewrite))
  (:options (:conc-name MT-) ...))
```

The `trace` field stores the list of completed and in-flight instructions. Let MT_t be the MAETT for the MA state at time t in Table 9.1. The `trace` field of initial MAETT MT_0 contains an empty list `nil`. As more instructions are fetched, the MAETT adds to the list INST items which represent the fetched instructions. For example, the `trace` field of MT_1 and MT_2 store list (i_0^1) and $(i_0^2\ i_1^2)$, respectively.

The `init-ISA` field of a MAETT stores the initial ISA state before the execution of the first instruction in the program. Additionally, the `pre-ISA` and `post-ISA` fields of the INST structure store the ISA state before and after executing the represented instruction in the ISA model. We call these states the *pre-ISA state* and the *post-ISA state* of the instruction. Figure 9.4 shows the entire structure of the MAETT MT_4. The `trace` field stores the list $(i_0^4\ i_1^4\ i_2^4)$. The `init-ISA` field stores the initial ISA state ISA_0. This is also the pre-ISA state of the first instruction i_0. The result of executing i_0 is ISA_1 and it is the *post-ISA* state of i_0. Since it is the state before executing the next instruction, ISA_1 is the *pre-ISA* state of i_1. In this way, the MAETT stores all ISA states that appear during the ISA execution of the program. The dashed lines in the figure show the ISA state transitions.

We can define many values related to an instruction using its INST representation. For example, the expression (INST-word i_k^t) defines the instruction word of i_k^t as the memory value addressed by the program counter in the pre-ISA state of i_k^t. In the definition below, the expression (read-mem a mem) denotes the value of the memory mem at address a.

```
(defun INST-word (i)
  (read-mem (ISA-pc (INST-pre-ISA i))
            (ISA-mem (INST-pre-ISA i))))
```

From the instruction word, we can calculate the values in the instruction fields *op, ra, rb*, and *rc*.

```
(defun INST-op (i)
  (op-field (INST-word i)))
(defun INST-ra (i)
  (ra-field (INST-word i)))
(defun INST-rb (i)
  (rb-field (INST-word i)))
```

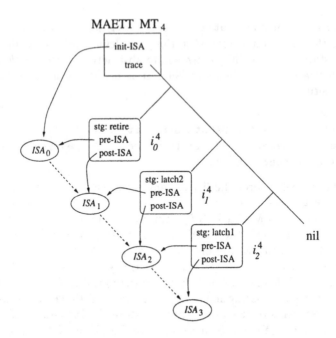

Figure 9.4: The structure of the MAETT intermediate abstraction.

```
(defun INST-rc (i)
  (rc-field (INST-word i)))
```

We can further define the correct source operand values by reading the source registers in the pre-ISA state. The expression (read-reg r regs) denotes the value of register r in the register file regs.

```
(defun INST-ra-val (i)
  (read-reg (INST-ra i) (ISA-regs (INST-pre-ISA i))))
(defun INST-rb-val (i)
  (read-reg (INST-rb i) (ISA-regs (INST-pre-ISA i))))
```

Finally, we define INST-result which calculates the execution result of an instruction. The expression (ALU-output op src1 src2) returns the value from the output port of the ALU when the opcode op, and source operand values src1 and src2 are given to the input ports of the ALU.

```
(defun INST-result (i)
  (ALU-output (INST-op i) (INST-ra-val i) (INST-rb-val i)))
```

These functions are used in the definition of properties that the pipelined machine should satisfy. For example, predicate INST-latch1-inv defines the correct intermediate values stored in latch1.

```
(defun inst-latch1-inv (i MA)
  (and (b1p (latch1-valid? (MA-latch1 MA)))
```

```
(equal (latch1-op (MA-latch1 MA)) (INST-op i))
(equal (latch1-rc (MA-latch1 MA)) (INST-rc i))
(equal (latch1-ra (MA-latch1 MA)) (INST-ra i))
(equal (latch1-rb (MA-latch1 MA)) (INST-rb i))))
```

We assume that INST i represents an instruction at latch1 in state MA. The busy flag valid? of latch1 should be 1, because the latch is occupied by the instruction represented by i. (B1p x) is true if x is a bit 1. The opcode of i, which has been defined as (INST-op i), should be stored in the op field of latch1. Similarly, the predicate checks whether the correct rc, ra, and rb register designators are stored in the corresponding fields of latch1. Another predicate inst-latch2-inv defines the correct intermediate values for latch2.

Using these functions, we define the predicate (inst-invariant i MA), which is true if and only if the intermediate values for instruction i are correct in state MA, regardless of the stage of i. We define (MT-inst--invariant MT MA) as a predicate that checks that every INST i recorded in the trace field of MAETT MT satisfies the condition (inst-invariant i MA). Intuitively speaking, (MT-inst-invariant MT MA) checks that all pipeline intermediate values are correct.

```
(defun inst-invariant (i MA)
  (cond ((equal (INST-stg i) 'latch1)
         (inst-latch1-inv i MA))
        ((equal (INST-stg i) 'latch2)
         (inst-latch2-inv i MA))
        (t t)))
(defun trace-inst-invariant (trace MA)
  (if (endp trace) t
      (and (inst-invariant (car trace) MA)
           (trace-inst-invariant (cdr trace) MA))))
(defun MT-inst-invariant (MT MA)
  (trace-inst-invariant (MT-trace MT) MA))
```

Another property (regs-match-p MT MA) is true if and only if the register file in state MA is correct, that is, the results of all completed instructions are stored in the register file. In other words, the register file appears as if it were in the post-ISA state of the last completed instruction. With the example given in Table 9.1, the register file state at time 5 should be the same as that in the post-ISA state of i_1. This ideal register file state is calculated from the MAETT with the function MT-regs.

```
(defun trace-regs (trace ISA)
  (if (endp trace)
      (ISA-regs ISA)
      (if (not (equal (INST-stg (car trace)) 'retire))
          (ISA-regs ISA)
```

```
                   (trace-regs (cdr trace)
                               (INST-post-ISA (car trace))))))))
(defun MT-regs (MT)
  (trace-regs (MT-trace MT) (MT-init-ISA MT)))
(defun regs-match-p (MT MA)
  (equal (MT-regs MT) (MA-regs MA)))
```

In analogy with (MT-INST-invariant MT MA) and (regs-match-p MT
MA), we define other properties of our pipelined machine as predicates of
the machine state and its MAETT. The following predicate invariant is
the conjunction of such properties.

```
(defun invariant (MT MA)
  (and (pc-match-p MT MA)
       (regs-match-p MT MA)
       (mem-match-p MT MA)
       (ISA-chain-p MT)
       (MT-inst-invariant MT MA)
       (MT-contains-all-insts MT MA)
       (MT-in-order-p MT)))
```

In order to introduce the following two theorems, we need three additional functions. (Flushed? MA) returns 1 if and only if MA is a pipeline
flushed state. (Init-MT MA) defines the MAETT for any pipeline flushed
state MA. (MT-step MT MA sig) defines the MAETT for the next MA state
given that MA is the current MA state and MT is its MAETT.

```
(defthm invariant-init-MT
    (implies (and (MA-state-p MA) (b1p (flushed? MA)))
             (invariant (init-MT MA) MA)))
(defthm invariant-step
    (implies (and (invariant MT MA)
                  (MAETT-p MT)
                  (MA-state-p MA)
                  (MA-sig-p sig))
             (invariant (MT-step MT MA sig)
                        (MA-step MA sig))))
```

Theorem invariant-init-MT states that every pipeline flushed state
satisfies invariant. Theorem invariant-step states that, if invariant
is true for the current state, it is also true for the next state. These two
theorems show that property invariant is an *invariant* condition, and all
machine states reachable from a pipeline flushed state satisfy it.

The two theorems above are proven by the divide-and-conquer strategy. Since the predicate invariant is a conjunction of several properties,
we can establish each condition separately and combine the results to the
two theorems. In this sense, the invariant condition can be verified incrementally in our approach. This is particularly useful in verifying a large

pipelined machine design, because each condition can be often established by analyzing a part of the entire pipelined machine and the combination of a few instructions.

Since the invariant theorem `invariant-step` involves only `MA-step` but not `ISA-step`, it may appear that the theorem is only about the MA behavior. However, the intermediate abstraction MAETT records the ideal ISA states, so in a deeper sense these theorems relate the MA and the ISA behavior. In essence, the verified invariant implies that each component of the MA is working correctly with respect to the ISA specification. In the next section, we prove our commutative diagram assuming that the invariant has been already verified.

9.3   Proving the Commutative Diagram

First we introduce the theorem that we would like to prove. The following theorem is the formal statement of the commutative diagram discussed earlier.

```
(defthm correctness
  (implies (and (MA-state-p MA)
                (MA-sig-listp sig-list)
                (<= n (len sig-list))
                (b1p (flushed? MA))
                (b1p (flushed? (MA-stepn MA sig-list n))))
           (equal (proj (MA-stepn MA sig-list n))
                  (ISA-stepn (proj MA)
                             (num-insts MA sig-list n)))))
```

In this theorem, `MA` is the initial state from which the MA execution starts, and it corresponds to MA_0 in Figure 9.3. We consider the execution of n steps with the list of input signals `sig-list`. The length of `sig-list` should be larger than or equal to n. The result of n-step execution is given as (`MA-stepn MA sig-list n`), which corresponds to MA_n in the figure. Suppose the initial state `MA` and the final state (`MA-stepn MA sig-list n`) are both pipeline flushed states. The equality in the conclusion compares the two paths of the commutative diagram. The left-hand side runs the MA machine for n steps and projects the result to the final ISA state. The right-hand side first projects `MA` to the initial ISA state (`proj MA`) and then runs the ISA machine for (`num-insts MA sig-list n`) steps. The function `num-insts` returns the number of instructions executed in the n-step MA execution, which is given as m in Figure 9.3.

One question is how the function `num-insts` counts the number of instructions executed during the n-step MA execution. The expression (`num-insts MA sig-list n`) first constructs the MAETT for the final MA state MA_n. This MAETT is a complete history of instructions executed

during the n-step MA execution. The function num-insts simply counts
the number of the instructions recorded in this MAETT.

```
(defun MT-num-insts (MT) (len (MT-trace MT)))
(defun num-insts (MA sig-list n)
  (MT-num-insts (MT-stepn (init-MT MA) MA sig-list n)))
```

A proof sketch of theorem **correctness** follows. Component by component, we show the equality in the conclusion of the theorem. There are
three components to compare: the program counter, the register file, and
the memory. We will discuss the equality with respect to the register file
in detail. Equalities for other components are proven similarly.

To ease the following arguments, we use the symbols shown in Figure 9.3.
The left-hand side of the conclusion of the **correctness** theorem is given as
(proj MA_n). Since the initial ISA state (proj MA) is ISA_0 in the figure,
the right-hand side is given as (ISA-stepn ISA_0 m). We need to prove
the following equality for the register file.

$$\text{(ISA-regs (proj } MA_n\text{))} = \text{(ISA-regs (ISA-stepn } ISA_0 \; m\text{))} \quad (9.1)$$

Let us assume that MT_n represents the MAETT for state MA_n. From
the two lemmas invariant-init-MT and invariant-step, (invariant
MA_n MT_n) is true by induction. From the definition of invariant,
the property (regs-match-p MT_n MA_n) is derived. The definition of
regs-match-p implies that the final register file state (MA-regs MA_n) is
equal to the ideal register file state (MT-regs MT_n). Using the definition
of proj,

$$
\begin{aligned}
&\text{(ISA-regs (proj } MA_n\text{))} \\
=\;&\text{(MA-regs } MA_n\text{)} \\
=\;&\text{(MT-regs } MT_n\text{) .}
\end{aligned}
$$

Let $(i_0^n \ldots i_{m-1}^n)$ be the list of instructions in the **trace** field of MT_n.
Because the final state MA_n is flushed, the execution of all instructions
in this list is completed and (INST-stg i_k^n) = 'retire for all k such
that $0 \le k < m$. Hence, (MT-regs MT_n) = (ISA-regs (INST-post-ISA
i_{m-1}^n)) because (MT-regs MT_n) returns the register file in the post-ISA
state of the last completed instruction, which is represented by i_{m-1}^n. Since
the post-ISA state of i_{m-1}^n is the state that results from executing m instructions i_0 through i_{m-1} by the ISA, it is equal to (ISA-stepn ISA_0 m).
Therefore,

$$
\begin{aligned}
&\text{(MT-regs } MT_n\text{)} \\
=\;&\text{(ISA-regs (INST-post-ISA } i_{m-1}^n\text{))} \\
=\;&\text{(ISA-regs (ISA-stepn } ISA_0 \; m\text{)) .}
\end{aligned}
$$

From the equalities shown above, we derive Equation (9.1) and conclude
the proof of the commutative diagram with respect to the register file.

The correctness theorem is vacuous if the MA never reaches a pipeline flushed state, because the last hypothesis of the theorem does not hold. However, the following theorem proves that we can flush the pipelined machine by running the MA model long enough without fetching new instructions.

```
(defthm liveness
  (implies (MA-state-p MA)
           (b1p (flushed?
                 (MA-stepn MA
                           (zeros (flush-cycles MA))
                           (flush-cycles MA))))))
```

The expression (zeros n) returns a list of 0's whose length is n. The *witness function* flush-cycles returns the number of steps necessary to flush out all instructions in the pipeline, proving the existence of such a number.

Summarizing the arguments so far, we have verified the pipelined machine in two steps: first establishing the invariant condition by analyzing a single MA state transition, and then proving by induction the commutative diagram which involves n MA state transitions. Since the relation of the ISA and MA has been established during the verification of the invariant in the last section, deriving the commutative diagram from the invariant is not very hard. The incremental nature of the invariant proof allows us to verify the machine without the explosion of the verification cost.

Even though the 3-stage pipelined machine verified here is simple, our verification approach can be scaled to a more complex pipelined machine model. We have used a similar approach to verify a microprocessor model which issues and completes instructions out-of-order, executes instructions speculatively, and implements interrupts [57]. To verify such a processor model [100, 98], we had to extend the MAETT to record more information about instructions and had to verify an invariant more complex than the one used for the 3-stage pipelined machine. However, the general approach to the problem did not change.

9.4 Related Work

Some of the earliest work on pipelined microprocessor verification was done by Srivas and Bickford [103]. Burch and Dill [17] introduced an approach using the pipeline flushing diagram. This diagram first runs a pipelined machine without fetching new instructions until it reaches a pipeline flushed state, and compares the resulting state with the corresponding sequential execution state. Their approach was later applied to a superscalar processor [15]. The pipeline flushing diagram was used in the verification project of a commercial processor using the ACL2 prover [11].

Recent research has tried to verify more complex processors models. Compositional model checking can be used to verify an out-of-order pipelined machine [75]. Velev and Bryant [109] used a special representation of pipeline states to verify processors without manual decompositions of the verification problems. Hosabettu et al.[51] used the PVS theorem prover to verify pipelined microprocessor models. Using so-called completion functions, they decomposed the verification problem in a way different from our approach.

Exercise 9.1 *The expression* (INST-in-order i j MT) *is true iff the instruction represented by* i *precedes the one represented by* j *in program order. Using the MAETT representation, we can define it as follows, because the MAETT records instructions in program order in a list.*

```
(defun member-in-order (i j lst)
  (member-equal j (cdr (member-equal i lst))))
(defun INST-in-order-p (i j MT)
  (member-in-order i j (MT-trace lst)))
```

We want to prove that (INST-in-order-p i j MT) *defines a partial order between* i *and* j *given that* MT *is fixed. This requires a proof of the asymmetry and transitivity of* member-in-order*:*

```
(defthm member-in-order-asymmetry
    (implies (and (member-in-order i j lst))
             (not (member-in-order j i lst))))
(defthm member-in-order-transitivity
    (implies (and (member-in-order i j lst)
                  (member-in-order j k lst))
             (member-in-order i k lst)))
```

If possible, prove the above. If the above are not provable, add additional hypotheses and prove the resulting theorems.

The DE Language

Warren A. Hunt, Jr.
IBM Austin Research Laboratory, Austin, Texas
Email: WHunt@Austin.IBM.COM

Abstract

DE is an occurrence-oriented description language that permits the hierarchical definition of finite-state machines in the style of a hardware description language. Using ACL2 we have formally defined the DE language. Recognizers for the language are defined. The semantics of the DE language is given by a simulator that, given the current inputs and current state for a module, will compute the module's current outputs and the next state. Our purpose in defining DE is to make the specification of a circuit description as clear as the finite-state languages often used by state-machine exploration algorithms.

The DE Language

The DE language is a formal language for describing finite-state machines (FSMs). Typically, FSMs are defined as a set of states with a transition relation or function. In the context of hardware verification, FSMs are often extracted from conventional hardware description languages (HDLs), like VHDL [55], and then subsequently processed. This extraction process is often rigorous but not formal; that is, even though a program is often used to perform the extraction, there is no formal semantics of the HDL being converted into a FSM. The DE language provides the rigor of typical FSM descriptions with the feel of an HDL.

The DE language allows hierarchical module definition, and multiple "copies" of a module are identified by reference (their appearance in an occurrence). This definition of DE is similar in spirit and syntax to the DUAL-EVAL [53] language defined by Bishop Brock and the author. DUAL--EVAL was used to specify the FM9001 netlist, but it is different from the DE language in a number of subtle aspects.

In this chapter we proceed by first showing examples of some DE descriptions for some simple circuits, which are given in the actual syntax for DE circuit descriptions. We present a subset of the predicates that recognize well-formed DE descriptions, and then we proceed directly to the definition of the DE next-state and output functions. We make reference to the well-formedness predicates where appropriate, as they identify legal DE descriptions. The definition of the language can be found in the supporting material for this chapter.

This chapter will be instructive for the budding ACL2 user because it illustrates how a language can be embedded into ACL2. As is often the case, languages are used to interpret other languages; the definition of the DE language and simulator is just a formal example of such an activity.

10.1   DE Language Example

A DE description is an ordered list of modules, which we call a netlist. Each module has a unique name, a list of inputs, outputs, internal states, and a list of occurrences. Each occurrence must contain a reference to a primitive module or another defined module. Modules must be ordered so that a module referenced in a module's list of occurrences is defined later in the netlist. Occurrences must be ordered, *i.e.*, it must be possible to compute outputs for every occurrence in the order that the occurrences appear.

Below is an example of a netlist containing four module definitions.

```
(defconst *counter-netlist*
  '((four-bit-counter
     (incr reset-)
     (out0 out1 out2 out3)
     (h0 h1 h2 h3)
     ((h0 (out0 carry0) one-bit-counter (incr   reset-))
      (h1 (out1 carry1) one-bit-counter (carry0 reset-))
      (h2 (out2 carry2) one-bit-counter (carry1 reset-))
      (h3 (out3 carry3) one-bit-counter (carry2 reset-))))
    (one-bit-counter
     (carry-in reset-)
     (out carry)
     (r0)
     ((r0 (out)       ff        (sum-reset))
      (r1 (sum carry) half-adder (carry-in out))
      (r2 (sum-reset) and       (sum reset-))))

    (full-adder
     (c a b)
     (sum carry)
     ()
```

```
((t0 (sum1 carry1) half-adder (a b))
 (t1 (sum  carry2) half-adder (sum1 c))
 (t2 (carry)       or         (carry1 carry2))))
(half-adder
 (a b)
 (sum carry)
 ()
 ((g0 (sum)  xor (a b))
  (g1 (carry) and (a b)))))))
```

A module is composed of five elements: name, inputs, outputs, states, and occurrences. For instance, the module one-bit-counter has two inputs, carry-in and reset-, two outputs, out and carry, one state-holding occurrence, r0, and three occurrences. The first and third occurrences reference primitives ff and and, and the half-adder reference is defined as the last module in our example netlist.

The half-adder module has two inputs, a and b, two outputs, sum and carry, no internal states, and references two primitive modules, xor and and. Each occurrence is composed of a module-unique occurrence name, a list of outputs, a reference to primitive or other defined module, and a list of inputs. Modules four-bit-counter and one-bit-counter also have non-empty state arguments that are used to associate states to the occurrences that require a state argument for evaluation.

Module references may be hierarchical, just like ACL2 function definitions. However, when used to describe a hardware implementation, as the netlist example above may suggest, each reference to a module implies a completely new copy of the referenced module. For instance, the full-adder module makes two half-adder references, which implies two copies of the half-adder module. This kind of "overloading" is consistent with many hardware description languages; that is, the semantics of the language do not reflect the physical reality being represented, but serve as a model. We say "overloaded" because each primitive will need to be implemented to physically realize a DE netlist. In addition, a specific DE netlist may have a number of different implementations due to the use of different underlying technologies.

10.2   Recognizing the DE Language

The recognizer of a well-formed netlist involves a sequence of predicates; the definition of each predicate depends on previously defined predicates. For instance, before we attempt to check the arity of all module references in a netlist, we first check that a netlist is syntactically well formed. Likewise, before we check the "wiring" internal to a module definition, we check that every module reference has the correct arity.

The purpose of defining these predicates is two-fold: to make it possible
to verify the guards of DE language processing functions and to ensure
that the "overloading" of DE descriptions as representations of possible
hardware circuits makes sense. The first purpose is to ensure that various
properties of the ACL2 functions used to define our DE simulator are well-
formed and their guards are satisfied. The second purpose is much more
subtle as it involves our judgment as to what we believe are "reasonable"
circuits. Both purposes restrict the allowable DE netlists in unusual ways,
some of which are discussed in what follows. For instance, a ring oscillator
constructed from inverters would not be permitted.

We use these predicates in the ACL2 guards (see **guard**) for the recognizers, stacking them up as we ascend the sequence. By verifying the
guards we achieve two ends. First, we obtain more efficient execution,
which is important on the very large netlists in which we are actually interested. Second, we specify quite tightly the expected input conditions
on our functions and verify that our functional compositions satisfy these
conditions.

A difference between ACL2 functions and well-formed DE netlists is
important to keep in mind: ACL2 functions are formal entities analyzed
by the ACL2 theorem-proving system; DE netlists are Lisp data objects
recognized and manipulated by ACL2 functions. The ACL2 language is
being used to define the DE language; that is, the definition of the DE
language has been *deeply* embedded [4] within ACL2. This distinction is
very important. For instance, it is possible to define and analyze functions
that directly manipulate DE netlists. Below we present several of our DE
language recognizing predicates.

10.2.1 Syntactic Well-Formedness

Our first and simplest DE language recognizing predicate ensures the syntactic well-formedness of DE netlists. A well-formed netlist is a list of well-
formed modules. We define five accessors for modules, md-name, md-ins,
md-outs, md-sts, and md-occs, that are defined to select the first through
fifth elements of a list. Likewise, for occurrences, we define four accessors, occ-name, occ-outs, occ-fn, and occ-ins, that select the elements
of an occurrence. The function occ-syntax-okp recognizes a syntactically
well-formed occurrence.

```
(defun occ-syntax-okp (occ)
  (declare (xargs :guard t))
  (and (true-listp-at-least-n+1 occ 3)
       (let ((occ-name (occ-name occ))
             (occ-outs (occ-outs occ))
             (occ-fn   (occ-fn   occ))
             (occ-ins  (occ-ins  occ)))
```

```
(and (symbolp            occ-name)
     (symbol-listp       occ-outs)
     (no-duplicatesp-eq occ-outs)
     (symbolp            occ-fn)
     (symbol-listp       occ-ins)))))
```

The macro `true-listp-at-least-n+1` expands into ACL2 primitive functions that check that occ has enough elements before using our occurrence accessor. A well-formed occurrence does not permit the same output name to appear more than once. Here we find the first use of our "judgment" as to what we consider "reasonable." We have made many such choices throughout our definition of the DE language. A list of occurrences is syntactically recognized with the predicate `occs-syntax-okp`, which just repeatedly applies `occ-syntax-okp`.

```
(defun occs-syntax-okp (occs)
  (declare (xargs :guard t))
  (if (atom occs)
      (eq occs nil)
    (and (occ-syntax-okp (car occs))
         (occs-syntax-okp (cdr occs)))))
```

A syntactically well-formed module is composed of five syntactically correct elements. Each element is individually checked: inputs, outputs, and states must each be a list of distinct symbols. We require that there be at least one occurrence. (We once required that a module have at least one input and output, but these restrictions are not necessary and have been dropped.)

```
(defun module-syntax-okp (module)
  (declare (xargs :guard t))
  (and (true-listp-at-least-n+1 module 4)
       (let ((md-name  (md-name   module))
             (md-ins   (md-ins    module))
             (md-outs  (md-outs   module))
             (md-sts   (md-sts    module))
             (md-occs  (md-occs   module)))
         (and (symbolp            md-name)
              (symbol-listp       md-ins)
              (no-duplicatesp-eq  md-ins)
              (symbol-listp       md-outs)
              (no-duplicatesp-eq  md-outs)
              (symbol-listp       md-sts)
              (no-duplicatesp-eq  md-sts)
              (symbol-alistp      md-occs)
              (consp              md-occs)     ; One occurrence?
              (occs-syntax-okp md-occs)))))
```

The last line of `module-syntax-okp` uses `occs-syntax-okp` to ensure the well-formedness of the occurrences found in `module`. To check the syntax of an entire netlist we apply the `module-syntax-okp` to each element of a netlist using the function `net-syntax-okp`.

```
(defun net-syntax-okp (netlist)
  (declare (xargs :guard t))
  (if (atom netlist)
      (eq netlist nil)
    (and (module-syntax-okp (car netlist))
         (net-syntax-okp (cdr netlist)))))
```

10.2.2   Module Arity

Much like ACL2, the DE language definition requires that every module reference have the correct arity. The definition of our netlist arity checker has as its guard that the syntax of the netlist has been checked. To check the arity of a netlist, we check the arity of modules one-by-one. Occurrences within a module may either refer to primitives or to other modules whose definitions appear later in the netlist.

We begin by giving an abbreviated list of our primitives, where each entry is identified by a primitive name and its corresponding information. The information for each primitive is given as an association list where `ins` names the inputs, `outs` names the outputs, `sts` names the internal state holding components, and `dep` names, for each output, the inputs used to compute it.

```
(defconst *primitives*
  '((ff    (ins a)    (outs x)   (sts q)    (dep (x)))
    (ff2   (ins a b)  (outs x y) (sts q r)  (dep (x) (y)))
    (gnd   (ins)      (outs x)   (sts)      (dep (x)))
    (vdd   (ins)      (outs x)   (sts)      (dep (x)))
    (buf   (ins a)    (outs x)   (sts)      (dep (x a)))
    (not   (ins a)    (outs x)   (sts)      (dep (x a)))
    (and   (ins a b)  (outs x)   (sts)      (dep (x a b)))
    (or    (ins a b)  (outs x)   (sts)      (dep (x a b)))
    [ ...  a number of primitives deleted  ... ]
    ))
```

Primitive names are identified by the recognizer function `primp`. When `primp` recognizes a primitive function name it returns the corresponding association list.

```
(defun primp (fn)
  (declare (xargs :guard t))
  (cdr (assoc-eq fn *primitives*)))
```

For simplicity, we define accessors, primp-ins, primp-outs, primp-sts, and primp-dep, to extract the relevant information from our primitive data base. Here is one.

```
(defun primp-ins (fn)
  (declare (xargs :guard (primp fn)))
  (cdr (assoc-eq 'ins (primp fn))))
```

Exercise 10.1 *The function* assoc-eq *uses* eq *to compare successive keys in the association list to the given key.* Eq *requires one of its arguments to be a symbol. To admit* primp *ACL2 must be able to prove that the guards for all the functions in its body are satisfied, provided the guard of* primp *is satisfied. But the guard for* primp *is* t, *so no condition is imposed on* fn. *How is it that the guard obligations for* primp *can be proved without requiring* fn *to be a symbol?*

Exercise 10.2 *Define the other accessors mentioned above.*

Our netlist arity recognizer is composed of several functions. Function occ-arity-okp checks the arity of a single occurrence. Notice, the guard for this function checks both the occurrence occ and the netlist.

```
(defun occ-arity-okp (occ netlist)
  (declare (xargs :guard (and (net-syntax-okp netlist)
                              (occ-syntax-okp occ))
                  :guard-hints ...))
  (let* ((occ-outs (occ-outs occ))
         (occ-fn   (occ-fn   occ))
         (occ-ins  (occ-ins  occ))
         (primp    (primp occ-fn))
         (len-ins  (len occ-ins))
         (len-outs (len occ-outs)))
    (if primp
        (and (eql (len (primp-ins  occ-fn)) len-ins)
             (eql (len (primp-outs occ-fn)) len-outs))
      (let ((module (assoc-eq occ-fn netlist)))
        (if (atom module)
            nil
          (and (eql (len (md-ins  module)) len-ins)
               (eql (len (md-outs module)) len-outs)))))))
```

Function occ-arity-okp extracts the pieces of the occurrence to be checked and then determines if the reference is primitive. If so, the lengths of the occurrence inputs and outputs are compared to the lengths specified by the data base. If not, module is looked up in netlist. If a non-empty definition for occ-fn is found, the arity of the occurrence "call" is checked against the module definition. The arities of this module's occurrences will be subsequently checked.

Exercise 10.3 *A simple recursive function,* occs-arity-okp, *is used to check that all occurrences in a list have the correct arity. Fill in the definition:*

```
(defun occs-arity-okp (occs netlist)
  (declare (xargs :guard ...))
  ...)
```

We check the arity of an entire netlist using function net-arity-okp. This function checks the arity of each module in a netlist. Contained in this definition is another DE language restriction that prohibits self-referential modules.

```
(defun module-arity-okp (module cdr-netlist)
  (declare (xargs :guard (and (module-syntax-okp module)
                              (net-syntax-okp cdr-netlist))))
  (occs-arity-okp (md-occs module) cdr-netlist))
(defun net-arity-okp (netlist)
  (declare (xargs :guard (net-syntax-okp netlist)))
  (if (atom netlist)
      t
    (let* ((module       (car netlist))
           (cdr-netlist (cdr netlist))
           (md-name     (md-name module)))
      (and (not (assoc-eq md-name cdr-netlist))
           (module-arity-okp module cdr-netlist)
           (net-arity-okp cdr-netlist)))))
```

Exercise 10.4 *Prove that every module name in a netlist recognized by* net-arity-okp *is distinct from every other module name in in the netlist and from the names of all primitives.*

10.2.3 State Argument Structure

Any part of a DE netlist can be evaluated with the DE simulator. Simulation proceeds by providing a netlist containing the definition of the module to interpret and providing the inputs and states that properly associate with the module to be interpreted. For a proper evaluation, it is necessary to supply the simulator with the correct number of inputs and a correctly structured state argument. We have written a predicate that checks if a state is properly structured for a specific module evaluation.

Looking ahead briefly (see Section 10.3) we can see that the evaluation of a module with respect to a netlist requires two additional arguments: the "top-level" module inputs and the internal state for the module. For instance, an example call to the DE simulator is written as (de fn ins sts netlist), where fn is the name of the module to be evaluated, netlist contains a definition of fn, ins are inputs to be associated with the formal parameters of the module inputs, and sts is the associated module state argument. Module inputs for an evaluation are just a "flat" list of arguments of the proper length, but the state argument must have a structure that is isomorphic to the structuring of state-holding elements of the module identified by argument fn with respect to a specific netlist. A state argument is a hierarchical list, which represents a tree in an obvious way; primitive state elements are leaves of the tree.

To check to see if a state argument is properly structured, we have written the predicate sts-okp. This predicate operates in a mutually recursive fashion, "ping-ponging" between checking a module and checking a module's occurrences. Sts-okp takes a module name, fn, a structured state, sts, and a netlist as arguments. If the module name identifies a primitive, the length of sts is compared to the states required for evaluating such a primitive; otherwise, the module name is looked up in the netlist, the module's occurrences are extracted, and each occurrence is subsequently checked by predicate sts-occ-okp. Not all occurrences reference state-holding primitives or make state-holding module references. Each occurrence has an associated occurrence name; occurrence names are used to associate elements of sts to occurrences that "contain" state. The association of state (occurrence) names with sts elements is performed with the pairlis$ function call appearing at the end of the definition of sts-okp.

```
(mutual-recursion
(defun sts-okp (fn sts netlist)
  (declare (xargs :measure (se-measure fn netlist)
                  :guard   (and (symbolp fn)
                                (true-listp sts)
                                (net-syntax-okp netlist)
                                (net-arity-okp netlist))
                  :guard-hints ...))
  (if (primp fn)
      (and (eqlable-listp sts)      ; Allowable kinds of states.
           (eql (len sts)           ; Relationship between STS
                (len (primp-sts fn))))) ; and a primitive.
    (let ((module (assoc-eq fn netlist)))
      (if (atom module)
          nil
        (let* ((md-occs   (md-occs   module))
```

```
                    (md-sts    (md-sts    module)))
         (and (eql (len sts)            ; Relationship between sts
                   (len md-sts))        ;    and a module's states
              (or (= (len sts) 0)       ; Short circuit - speedup?
                  (sts-occ-okp md-occs (pairlis$ md-sts sts)
                               (delete-eq-module
                                fn netlist)))))))))))
(defun sts-occ-okp (occs sts-alist netlist)
  (declare (xargs :measure (se-measure occs netlist)
                  :guard    (and (occs-syntax-okp occs)
                                 (net-syntax-okp netlist)
                                 (occs-arity-okp occs netlist)
                                 (net-arity-okp netlist)
                                 (alistp sts-alist))
                  :guard-hints ...))
  (if (endp occs)
      t
    (and (let* ((occ      (car occs))
                (occ-fn   (occ-fn   occ))
                (occ-name (occ-name occ))
                (sts      (assoc-eq-value occ-name
                                          sts-alist)))
           (and (true-listp sts)
                (sts-okp occ-fn sts netlist)))
         (sts-occ-okp (cdr occs) sts-alist netlist))))
)
```

If argument sts does indeed satisfy sts-okp, then it is a hierarchically structured list of proper lists—this proof is left for the interested reader.

The recursion exhibited by sts-okp is identical to the recursion used by the DE simulator. To justify such recursion, we have defined a measure se-measure.

Exercise 10.5 *Define a suitable* se-measure *function to admit* sts-okp *and* sts-occ-okp.

10.3   The DE Simulator

The operational semantics for the DE language is given by the DE simulator. We have defined several different simulators that only vary in the evaluation of primitives. Here we present the simplest form of our DE simulator where the evaluation of primitives works in a manner similar to the Lisp apply function. The definition of our simulator is actually two sets of mutually recursive functions. The se function and its recursive sibling, se-occ, define the outputs of a module being evaluated given its inputs and its current state. In a similar manner, the de and de-occ functions define the next state of a module.

We start by presenting the definitions for the se and se-occ functions. Both the netlist and occurrences within a module must be in "level" order; that is, it must be possible to compute the value of all outputs for every occurrence with one forward pass through a list of occurrences. Not included in the supporting material are functions that check this condition, and therefore, the guards of our evaluation functions are not checked.[1]

The function name se is an abbreviation for *single eval* and de abbreviates *dual eval*. Assuming level order, the outputs for a module can be computed with a single pass through each module at every level of the structural hierarchy present in an evaluation of a module. Module definitions lower in the hierarchy may be evaluated multiple times with different arguments as necessary—an example would be the repeated evaluation of the half-adder module during the evaluation of the full-adder module (see Section 10.1). Function se has the same type of recursion as that found in sts-okp. Function se evaluates primitives using the se-primp-apply function. If argument fn identifies a defined module, its definition is extracted from netlist for further evaluation. Before function se-occ is called to evaluate the occurrences of a modules, two association lists are created binding input and state names to their respective values.

```
(mutual-recursion
(defun se (fn ins sts netlist)
  (declare (xargs :measure (se-measure fn netlist)))
  (if (primp fn)
      (se-primp-apply fn ins sts)
    (let ((module (assoc-eq fn netlist)))
      (if (atom module)
          nil
        (let* ((md-ins    (md-ins    module))
               (md-outs   (md-outs   module))
               (md-sts    (md-sts    module))
               (md-occs   (md-occs   module))
               (wire-alist (pairlis$ md-ins ins))
               (sts-alist  (pairlis$ md-sts sts)))
          (assoc-eq-values
           md-outs
           (se-occ md-occs wire-alist sts-alist
                   (delete-eq-module fn netlist)))))))))
```

---

[1] The definition of these functions is ongoing research; we have changed the definition of these functions many times, as the definition of these predicates actually describe the "circuits" admitted by the DE language. We often check the syntax of generated DE netlists, but rarely do we check whether a DE netlist is in level order because the tools that read DE netlists check this condition.

```
(defun se-occ (occurs wire-alist sts-alist netlist)
  (declare (xargs :measure (se-measure occurs netlist)))
  (if (endp occurs)
      wire-alist
    (let* ((occur    (car occurs))
           (occ-name (occ-name occur))
           (occ-outs (occ-outs occur))
           (occ-fn   (occ-fn   occur))
           (occ-ins  (occ-ins  occur))
           (ins      (assoc-eq-values occ-ins  wire-alist))
           (sts      (assoc-eq-value  occ-name sts-alist))
           (new-wire-alist
            (append
             (pairlis$ occ-outs
                       (se occ-fn ins sts netlist))
             wire-alist)))
      (se-occ (cdr occurs) new-wire-alist
              sts-alist netlist))))
)
```

The function `se-occ` evaluates occurrences and appends the newly computed outputs of the current occurrence onto a growing list of name-value
pairs.

Primitive evaluation is nothing more than simply function application
as is shown with the `se-primp-apply`. Further details can be found in the
supporting material.

```
(defun se-primp-apply (fn ins sts)
  (declare (xargs :guard (primp-rec fn ins sts)))
  (case fn
    (gnd     (list nil))
    (vdd     (list t))
    (buf     (list (car ins)))
    (not     (list (not (car ins))))
    (and     (list (and (car ins) (b-fix (cadr ins)))))
    ;;; [ ... deleted entries ... ]
    (otherwise nil)))
```

The evaluation of the next state is more complicated because of non-
combinational loops that may legally exist in a netlist. The de function
requires a "second pass" to compute the next state of a module. With the
"first pass" the values of all variables ("wires") can be computed. Armed
with these values, de can compute the next state.

The de function recurs in exactly the same manner as does se; however,
it calls its mutually recursive peer function de-occ with an embedded call to

se-occ so that the values of all internal module variables are first computed. The function de-primp-apply returns the next state for each primitive.

```
(mutual-recursion
(defun de (fn ins sts netlist)
  (declare (xargs :measure (se-measure fn netlist)))
  (if (primp fn)
      (de-primp-apply fn ins sts)
    (let ((module (assoc-eq fn netlist)))
      (if (atom module)
          nil
        (let* ((md-ins      (md-ins    module))
               (md-sts      (md-sts    module))
               (md-occs     (md-occs   module))
               (wire-alist  (pairlis$ md-ins ins))
               (sts-alist   (pairlis$ md-sts sts))
               (new-netlist (delete-eq-module fn netlist)))
          (assoc-eq-values
           md-sts
           (de-occ md-occs
                   (se-occ md-occs wire-alist sts-alist
                           new-netlist)
                   sts-alist new-netlist)))))))
(defun de-occ (occurs wire-alist sts-alist netlist)
  (declare (xargs :measure (se-measure occurs netlist)))
  (if (endp occurs)
      wire-alist
    (let* ((occur     (car occurs))
           (occ-name  (occ-name occur))
           (occ-fn    (occ-fn    occur))
           (occ-ins   (occ-ins   occur))
           (ins       (assoc-eq-values occ-ins  wire-alist))
           (sts       (assoc-eq-value  occ-name sts-alist))
           (new-wire-alist
            (cons (cons occ-name
                        (de occ-fn ins sts netlist))
                  wire-alist)))
      (de-occ (cdr occurs) new-wire-alist sts-alist
              netlist))))
)
```

The function de-occ iterates through occurrences and with each step binds an occurrence (state) name to a (possibly empty) next state.

To permit the repeated application of de we have defined the de-sim function, which provide a multi-cycle simulation for FSMs defined in the

DE language. This function takes a list of inputs, as a set of "top-level" inputs is required for each iteration of this simulator.

```
(defun de-sim (fn ins-list sts netlist)
  (if (atom ins-list)
      sts
    (de-sim fn (cdr ins-list)
            (de fn (car ins-list) sts netlist)
            netlist)))
```

10.4   An Example DE Simulator Call

The DE simulator can be used to simulate an FSM. We have also defined, but not presented, a symbolic version of the simulator that allows direct simulation of inputs and states seeded with expressions. This symbolic verison of the DE simulator only requires changes to the primitive application functions; the language recognizing predicates and the definitions of se and de are identical to those presented above.

A six-cycle simulator call to simulate our four-bit-counter module is shown next. The second argument of the de-sim call is a list of six inputs, each containing two inputs for each invocation of de. The third argument is the initial state of the four flip-flops. The last line below is the printed response of the ACL2 system.

```
ACL2 !>(de-sim 'four-bit-counter
         '(( t t)
           (nil t)
           ( t t)
           ( t t)
           (nil t)
           ( t t))
         '(((nil))((nil))((nil))((nil)))
         *counter-netlist*)
(((NIL)) ((NIL)) ((T)) ((NIL)))
```

Our example execution demonstrates our four-bit-counter counting the four t inputs in the primary input list by printing a binary, little-endian representation of the state which can be read as 4.

10.5   An Example DE Proof

Just as the definition of the DE language is hierarchical, so may be proofs of FSMs described with the DE language. Thus, to prove the correctness of the `full-adder` module, we first prove the correctness of the `half-adder` module.

```
(defthm half-adder-ok
  (implies (and (equal netlist *counter-netlist*)
                (booleanp a)
                (booleanp b))
           (equal (se 'half-adder (list a b) nil netlist)
                  (list (xor a b)
                        (and a b)))))
  :hints ...)
(defthm full-adder-ok
  (implies (and (equal netlist *counter-netlist*)
                (booleanp a)
                (booleanp b)
                (booleanp c))
           (equal (se 'full-adder (list c a b) nil netlist)
                  (list (xor c (xor a b))
                        (if c (or a b) (and a b))))))
  :hints ...)
```

Exercise 10.6 *Write a DE netlist to define a 3-bit adder. Specify it. Prove it correct.*

10.6 Challenges for the Reader

The DE language is evolving. We use the DE language as a means of specifying large FSMs representing circuits at IBM in Austin. Because of the demands placed on the DE language by our industrial requirements, we continue to change DE to better serve our needs. New issues in specifying the design language arise constantly. In this section we merely hint at some extended exercises. For instance, we have had to defined stricter and stricter rules for names. Also, the total number of characters that can appear in a hierarchical reference is limited in some of our tools. Another issue is the depth at which some primitives can appear is limited. These issues don't specifically have anything to do with the DE simulator, but do cause us to change our DE language recognizers.

As a warmup, an interested reader may wish to define a predicate to recognize DE language netlists that do not contain "combinational" loops. From there the reader could define and verify the guards for the `se` and `de` functions. Now consider: do the three lists of variables used to represent the inputs, outputs, and states of a module need to be distinct?

With respect to the definition of `se-occ`, if the collection of the new values for occurrences were changed to

```
(new-wire-alist
 (append
  wire-alist
  (pairlis$ occ-outs
            (se occ-fn ins sts netlist)))))
```

then se-occ could be used as a fault simulator for "flat" modules. For a
hierarchical version, changes to se would also be required to "seed" calls to
se-occ with initial values for selected internal names. The change above
ensures that any initial value for an internal module variable will always be
found first during a key-value lookup, thus "overriding" any value computed
by the simulator. This change would lower the performance of se-occ and,
therefore, de as well, but its definition is no more complex.

Another interesting thing for a reader would be to define some functions that generate parameterized FSM descriptions and then prove their
correctness. This could then lead to the building of a verified tool. The
FM9001 was largely described and verified this way [52, 53]. Consider the
difference between a proof of the correctness of a 3-bit adder and the proof
of correctness of an n-bit adder generator.

10.7   Conclusion

The definition of the DE language involves many subtle issues in language
design. Many competing factors, such as expressibility, ease of use, simple
formal semantics, hierarchical verification, and simulation speed, have influ-
enced the specification of the DE language. For instance, the requirement
that module bodies list their occurrences in level-order makes it easier to
define the DE simulator; otherwise, it would be necessary to either "compile" the netlist or require the simulator to make multiple passes for each
combinational evaluation. Our timing model is often too simple for circuits
that we wish to specify. We have been able to include latches that are
sensitive to the level of a clock, but this complicates the definition of our
primitive state-holding elements and requires the simulator to execute once
for each "level" of the input clock, instead of only once per clock cycle.

The DE language has provided an unambiguous specification format
for FSMs at IBM Austin. We use our DE language recognizers to check
the output of various programs we have built that process circuits and
produce DE netlists as their output. Often our industrial tools operate by
"flattening" any visible hierarchy, and then proceeding. As we create new
CAD tools that respect hierarchical circuit definitions, the DE specification
has become a valuable aid to validate the semantic operation of newly
developed tools.

Using Macros to Mimic VHDL

Dominique Borrione and Philippe Georgelin
TIMA-UJF, Grenoble, France
Email: Dominique.Borrione@imag.fr, Philippe.Georgelin@imag.fr

Vanderlei Rodrigues
TIMA-UJF, Grenoble, France—on leave from II-UFRGS, Brazil
Email: vandi@inf.ufrgs.br

Abstract

The purpose of this project is to define in ACL2 the semantics of a small synthesizable behavioral subset of VHDL. The intention is to preserve, as much as possible, the syntactic flavor of VHDL, and to facilitate the verification of a circuit design by symbolic simulation and theorem proving techniques. The definition is written with macros, which recognize VHDL keywords and construct semantic functions and some basic theorems, for each main statement of the language. This project introduces type definitions, signal and variable declarations, and simple processes. Declarations define the initial state of a system. Statements and processes are functions that map states to (next) states. The systematic use of macros helps by introducing infix notation, employing keywords that strongly resemble corresponding VHDL syntax.

Introduction

Standard hardware description languages, notably VHDL in Europe, are routinely used to specify and document circuit designs. Designers simulate behavioral specifications on large test sets, to gain initial confidence in the algorithm to be implemented. Then the same description is input to a synthesis tool, which produces a structural description for manufacturing. If the source is written in a "synthesizable subset" of VHDL, the synthesis can be largely automated. The objective of this project is to give a semantic definition of a synthesizable subset in ACL2, which allows the introduction of symbolic simulation and theorem proving as an additional verification step, ensuring more security in the design process. Manual transcriptions must be avoided, yet the designer should be convinced that the formal model being analyzed with ACL2 faithfully represents the simulated description: its correspondence with the initial specification should be obvious.

The approach taken in this chapter consists in defining the grammar of a synthesizable subset of VHDL with Lisp macros. Each macro name is the leading VHDL keyword for the right hand side of a syntax rule. Alternatives, marked in VHDL by the occurrence of discriminating keywords, start with an optional keyword in the Lisp macro definition. A macro call is thus the instance of a VHDL statement. The macro expansion produces the formal model of the statement semantics in the ACL2 logic.

11.1   The VHDL Subset

This section adopts the VHDL terminology, and assumes the reader to be familiar with the essential concepts of the language.

We only discuss a "behavioral synthesis subset" of VHDL, currently being standardized [56], which excludes physical time and non-discrete types. We further limit the subset to single clock synchronization, and do not accept processes where the clock and set/reset signals are mixed in the sensitivity list (thus modeling synchronous behavior and asynchronous reset).

A circuit is described by an **entity**, which declares its interface signals (recognized directions are **in** and **out**). At most one of these signals is the master clock. At least one **architecture** is associated with the **entity**, and describes the behavior of the circuit. Inside the **architecture**, concurrent processes may communicate through locally declared signals; to guarantee determinism, **shared** variables are excluded from the synthesizable subset, *i.e.*, variables may only be declared locally to a process. User defined types and **dynamic** functions are recognized, however we shall not accept **resolved** types here.

According to the VHDL definition, all the concurrent statements in an **architecture** (signal assignments, assertions, procedure calls, blocks) are translated to an equivalent process; we thus only consider processes here. We further assume that all processes have been put in a normal form, with a single **wait** statement (see [23] for theoretical justification) written: **wait until <clock-edge>**.

In this chapter, we add the simplifying restriction that all processes are synchronized on the same clock edge; we can thus identify simulation cycle and clock cycle, and need not represent the clock event explicitly.

Inside a process, except for declarative statements, we shall only discuss sequential **signal** and **variable** assignments, and **if** conditionals.

11.1.1 Notation

To avoid name conflicts for identical predefined identifiers in VHDL and
Lisp, we add one non-alphanumeric character to VHDL identifiers and keywords in the Lisp definition. VHDL keywords that start a new statement
are translated as macro names with a leading underscore character. For
instance entity and architecture become _entity and _architecture.
VHDL keywords that continue a statement are translated as optional macro
keywords, and take a leading colon. For instance is and of become :is and
:of. Finally, a minimal amount of Lisp syntax must be observed, such as
parenthesized macro calls, or the writing of character literals. The syntax
of the VHDL subset processed in this chapter is the following.

```
ENTITY        ::= (_entity NAME :port (PORT ...))
PORT          ::= NAME :in TYPE |
                  NAME :out TYPE
ARCHITECTURE  ::= (_architecture NAME :of NAME
                      :is (DEC-SIGNAL ...)
                      :begin (PROCESS ...))
DEC-SIGNAL    ::= (_signal NAME :type TYPE) |
                  (_signal NAME :type TYPE := EXP)
PROCESS       ::= (_process NAME
                      :is (DEC-VAR ...)
                      :begin ((_wait :until COND)
                              CMD ...))
DEC-VAR       ::= (_variable NAME :type TYPE) |
                  (_variable NAME :type TYPE := EXP)
CMD           ::= (_<= NAME EXP) |
                  (_<- NAME EXP) |
                  (_if COND :then (CMD ...)) |
                  (_if COND :then (CMD ...) :else (CMD ...))
```

We assume that a conventional VHDL "verifier" is being used, to guarantee the absence of syntactic and static semantic errors from the VHDL
source. A pre-processor also checks that the source is written in the VHDL
subset. We therefore no longer need to check those pre-requisites. Then the
Lisp model is produced automatically (the translation is straightforward,
and not discussed here). In the following, our source description is that
"VHDL in Lisp" model.

11.1.2 Example

We shall use as a running example a circuit that performs the computation of the factorial function (compare with the factorial example in
the companion book [58]). With the addition of ;end comments, the Lisp

```
(vhdl (_entity mycomp :port            ;entity declaration
         (arg :in natural              ;input argument
          start :in bit                ;start command
          clk :in bit                  ;master clock
          result :out natural          ;output result
          done :out bit))              ;valid result if 1
      ;end mycomp
 (_architecture fact :of mycomp :is    ;architecture declaration
    ((_signal op1 :type natural)       ;local signal declarations
     (_signal op2 :type natural)
     (_signal resmult :type natural)
     (_signal startmult :type bit)
     (_signal endmult :type bit))
 :begin                                ;synchronous multiplier
    ((_process Multiplier :is ()       ;performs multiplication
      :begin                           ;in one clock cycle
        ((_wait :until (equal clk 1))  ;waits on rising edge of clk
         (_if (equal startmult 1) :then
              ((_<= resmult (* op1 op2))))  ;end if
         (_<= endmult startmult)))     ;result available one clock
      ;end process                     ;cycle after request
     (_process DoIt :is                ;synchronous automaton
        ((_variable mystate :type natural := 0) ;local state var
         (_variable r :type natural := 0)   ;decreasing argument
         (_variable f :type natural := 0))  ;accumulator of result
       :begin
         ((_wait :until (equal clk 1))     ;waits on rising edge of clk
          (_if(equal mystate 0) :then       ;initially mystate=0
               ((_<- r arg) (_<- f 1)       ;r := arg and f := 1
                (_if (equal start 1) :then  ;change state if start=1
                     ((_<- mystate 1))))    ;end if
           :else ((_if (equal mystate 1) :then ;if mystate=1
                 ((_if (equal r 1)   :then    ;if r=1 the result is in f
                      ((_<= result f)         ;result is assigned f
                       (_<= done 1)           ;done is assigned 1
                       (_<- mystate 0))       ;next is initial state
                  :else                       ;if r greater than 1
                      ((_<= startmult 1)      ;startmult is assigned 1
                       (_<= op1 r) (_<= op2 f) ;set op1 and op2 to r and f
                       (_<- mystate 2))))     ;next state is 2
            :else ((_if (equal mystate 2) :then   ;if mystate=2
                  ((_if (equal endmult 1) :then ;if endmult=1
                       ((_<- f resmult)       ;f := resmult
                        (_<- r (- r 1))       ;r := r-1
                        (_<= startmult 0)     ;startmult is assigned 0
                        (_<- mystate 1))      ;next state is 1
)))))))))))) ;end if   end if   end if   end process   end fact
```

Figure 11.1: Lisp Model of the Factorial State Machine

description is in one-to-one correspondance with the VHDL text it models. To illustrate the communication between two concurrent processes, the behavioral specification is purposely decomposed into a 4 state automaton (process `doit`) that controls the computation, and a `multiplier` which performs the multiplication of two natural numbers in one clock cycle. Both processes are synchronized on the rising edge of `clk`.

11.2   The Semantic Model

We want to verify that, when simulated according to the VHDL semantics, the circuit description computes the expected result. In the example above, this means that we want to find the values `N`! and `1` assigned to signals `result` and `done` exactly $3N-1$ cycles after the previous cycle when `start` became 1, where `N` was the value of `arg` during that cycle.

Following the approach of [78], an `entity-architecture` pair is formalized as an abstract state machine. A state represents a snapshot of the system interface pins and memory elements, and the architecture function maps a state to the next state.

For simplicity of presentation, the model discussed here does not take advantage of ACL2's single-threaded objects (see `stobj`) but our states are single-threaded. All functions that take a state as argument and produce a state as result actually construct a new state. For example, to model an assignment to a state element, we generate a new state where the new value replaces the old value.

11.2.1   Model State

The state is a list of values for all the signals and variables declared in the description. In VHDL, a `signal` has one current value, and one "driver" per process that assigns it. With the restrictions made above, it suffices to implement a single "next" signal value for local and output signals. Therefore, a signal is represented by two elements in the model state. Input signals cannot be modified in the architecture, only their current value is present in the state. If `Sig` is a declared signal, in the machine state `Sig` refers to its current value and `Sig+` to its next value. A VHDL `variable` has no driver, and assignments modify its current value; it is represented by a single element in the model state. Moreover, a variable name is local to the process that declares it, so the same name in distinct processes refers to distinct objects. To ensure unique naming in the model state, a variable `Var` declared in a process `P1` is referred to as `P1.Var`. As a general rule, all names that are relative to an architecture (respectively, a process) are prefixed with the identifier of that architecture (process).

The state of our example is a linear list of 20 elements containing the indicated values of the signals.

```
(list arg start clk result done     ;current interface signals
      op1 op2 resmult startmult endmult ;current local signals
      result+ done+                ;next output interface signals
      op1+ op2+ resmult+ startmult+ endmult+ ;next local signals
      doit.mystate doit.r doit.f)  ;variables declared in doit
```

To access and modify the state elements of architecture fact by name rather than by their position in the list, the following functions are generated.

```
(defun fact-get-nth (var)        ;returns the position
   (cond ((equal var 'arg) 0)    ;indicated variable
         ((equal var 'start) 1)
         ...))
(defun fact-get (st var)         ;gets the value of a
   (nth (fact-get-nth var) st))  ;state element by name
(defun fact-put (new var st)     ;modifies the value of a
   (insert-value (fact-get-nth var) new st)) ;state element
```

Nth is a standard Common Lisp function to fetch an element of a list, and (insert-value offset new-value st) returns a new state equal to st, except for the element in position offset which is equal to new-value.

Exercise 11.1 *Write the definition of function* insert-value *as described above. Write and prove the following theorems, with the appropriate hypotheses on the arguments:*

- *the result of* insert-value *is a list;*

- insert-value *preserves the number of state elements;*

- *in the result of* insert-value, *the element in position* offset *is equal to* new-value;

- *above three theorems for the result of function* fact-put.

11.2.2   Behavioral Statements

The semantics of the statements in a process are given by functions over the model state. An expression accesses the current value of its operand variables and signals.

A variable assignment replaces the state element corresponding to its current value. A signal assignment replaces the state element for the signal next value. Thus, in process Multiplier, the statement

```
(_<= resmult (* op1 op2))
```

becomes the following call to `fact-put`, where `state-1` is the current model state at the point of invocation.

```
(fact-put (* (fact-get state-1 'op1)
             (fact-get state-1 'op2))
          'resmult+
          state-1)
```

The _if statement of VHDL becomes an `if` statement in the formalization; if the `:else` part is missing, the state is returned unchanged in the `else` part of the formalization. Thus, in process `Multiplier`:

```
(_if (equal startmult 1) :then
        ((_<= resmult (* op1 op2)))) ;end if
```

is formalized as follows.

```
(let ((state-2
       (if (equal (fact-get state-1 'startmult) 1)
           (fact-put (* (fact-get state-1 'op1)
                        (fact-get state-1 'op2))
                     'resmult+
                     state-1)
           state-1)))
  ...)
```

Finally, the process itself is a function that takes the state as argument, and returns a state resulting from the sequential execution of its statements. Sequential execution is modeled through function composition expressed by `let*`.

The complete function representing process `Multiplier` in architecture `fact` is as follows.

```
(defun fact.multiplier-cycle (state-1)
  (let* ((state-2
          (if (equal (fact-get state-1 'startmult) 1)
              (fact-put (* (fact-get state-1 'op1)
                           (fact-get state-1 'op2))
                        'resmult+  state-1)
              state-1))
         (state-3 (fact-put (fact-get state-2 'startmult)
                            'endmult+
                            state-2)))
    state-3))
```

11.2.3   Simulation

A simulation cycle for the architecture `fact` is the function `fact-cycle`
over the model state, which consists of two parts:

 ♦ Call the function representing each process in the architecture. The
   function calls may be chained in any order since two processes never
   assign to the same state element, and never refer to the new values
   of signals produced by the other.

 ♦ Update the current value of each signal with its next value.

```
(defun fact-cycle (st)
  (fact-update-signals
   (fact.multiplier-cycle (fact.doit-cycle st))))
```

```
(defun fact-update-signals (st)
   (fact-put (fact-get st result+) result
    (fact-put (fact-get st done+) done
     (fact-put (fact-get st op1+) op1
      (fact-put (fact-get st op2+) op2
       (fact-put (fact-get st resmult+) resmult
        (fact-put (fact-get st startmult+) startmult
         (fact-put (fact-get st endmult+) endmult
                   st)))))))))
```

A call to the recursive function `fact-simul` performs the simulation of
n cycles starting from an initial state `st`.

```
(defun fact-simul (n st)
  (if (zp n)
      st
    (fact-simul (1- n) (fact-cycle st))))
```

The initial state can be provided as an explicit list of values, as follows.

```
ACL2 !>(fact-simul 19 '(7 1 0 0 0 0 0 0 0 0 0 0 0 0 0 0 0 0 0 0))
(7 1 0 0 0 2 2520 5040 0 1 0 0 2 2520 5040 0 1 1 1 5040)
ACL2 !>(fact-simul 20 '(7 1 0 0 0 0 0 0 0 0 0 0 0 0 0 0 0 0 0 0))
(7 1 0 5040 1 2 2520 5040 0 0 5040 1 2 2520 5040 0 0 0 1 5040)
```

For large circuits with many elements, it is inconvenient to write explicit lists like these. To aid in this circumstance, we generate a macro
`fact-make-state` that expands into a list representing the initial state.
The value of variables and signals in this state comes from the initial value
introduced in the corresponding declaration or from the default value for
their type. For signals, the current and next values are initially identical.
This macro accepts optional keyword arguments to overwrite this initial
value.

```
(defmacro fact-make-state
         (&key (arg '0)
               (start '0) ...
               (result '0)
               ...
               (result+ '0 result+-p)
               ...
          (list 'quote
                (list arg start clk ... doit.f)))))
```

Thus, the same simulation experiment as above, where only the inputs arg and start are fixed to a non-default value, can be called as follows.

```
ACL2 !>(fact-simul 20 (fact-make-state :arg 7 :start 1))
(7 1 0 5040 1 2 2520 5040 0 0 5040 1 2 2520 5040 0 0 0 1 5040)
```

Often we are only interested in certain values from the final state and so compose the call of fact-simul with a function that extracts and labels those values from the state.

11.3   Elaboration of the Model

Let us now examine how we construct the model described in the previous section. In the current implementation, this "elaboration" (in VHDL terminology) is performed by macros.

The first line of Figure 11.1 is a call to the macro vhdl which starts the expansion that generates the state and semantic functions discussed in the previous section, and a few additional ones, from the circuit description. The elaboration is done in two passes: first the declarations are analyzed and the list of descriptors for all declared variables and signals is built; then the macro that builds the model state, and the semantic functions for the VHDL statements are constructed. The set of Lisp functions and macros which constitute this generator is given in the supporting file vhdl.lisp.

Because the macro expansion process cannot be stopped in an intermediate stage, several constants are produced to document the generated code in a readable form. For instance, while function fact-get-nth is produced as a cond on a long list of alternatives

```
(defun fact-get-nth (var)
  (cond ((equal var 'arg) 0)
        ((equal var 'start) 1)
        ...
        (t 0)))
```

after macro-expansion the function body becomes an equally long list of nested if statements, which is harder to read. To help with model inspection, we save the actual text of many functions as constants, named with the corresponding function identifier between stars. The following constants are of particular interest.

prog	; the source description
env	; the environment, built by the first pass
fact-update-signals	; function that copies next to current
	; signal values
fact-state-size	; size of the machine state
fact-make-state	; text of macro that creates the initial state
fact.multiplier-cycle	; semantic function for process multiplier
fact.doit-cycle	; semantic function for process doit
fact-cycle	; performs one simulation cycle for fact
fact-simul	; performs N simulation cycles for fact

Exercise 11.2 *Create a directory, and copy supporting files* vhdl.lisp *and* fact.lisp *in it. Load ACL2 in the context of that directory. Execute the elaboration of the model for the circuit, then check the definition of* fact-get-nth *by executing the following commands (see* :props*).*

```
ACL2 !>(ld "vhdl.lisp")
ACL2 !>(ld "fact.lisp")
ACL2 !>:props fact-get-nth
```

Compare the returned answers when executing the following two lines.

```
ACL2 !>*fact-update-signals*
ACL2 !>:props fact-update-signals
```

11.3.1   Environment Construction

Two environments are created: one for the **entity** and one for the **architecture**. The **entity** environment describes the input and output ports. The **architecture** environment includes the entity identifiers, local signals and local **process** variables. It is an association list between each identifier and its descriptor, which gives its **kind**, **type**, **initial value**, and **offset**. The possible identifier kinds are **input** (input signal), **output** (output signal), **signal** (local signal), **next** (next value of a signal), and **var** (local variable).

The environment of **architecture fact** is as follows.

```
(fact architecture
        ((arg input natural nil 0)
         (start input bit nil 1)
         (clk input bit nil 2)
```

```
(result output natural nil 3)
(done output bit nil 4)
(op1 signal natural nil 5)
(op2 signal natural nil 6)
...
(result+ next natural nil 10)
(done+ next bit nil 11)
...
(doit.mystate var natural 0 17)
(doit.r var natural 0 18)
(doit.f var natural 0 19)))
```

At the end of the first pass on each architecture, keyword :env and its environment are appended to the VHDL-Lisp source for the architecture, and the expansion of the macro _architecture is called (see the macro vhdl and the function insert-prog-env in the supporting file vhdl.lisp).

11.3.2   Model Construction

The _architecture macro generates the initial state construction (macro fact-make-state), all the state access and modification functions presented in Section 11.2.1, and the cycle and multi-cycle simulation functions seen in Section 11.2.3. The behavioral statements and the function that models one execution of each process are produced by the expansion of macro _process called within _architecture. A large number of ancillary functions are devoted to the construction of the unique name for all identifiers, macros, and functions. By asking ACL2 to print the value of all the documentation constants listed above, the reader will get the ACL2 model of our example.

11.4   Symbolic Simulation

Up to now, all we have obtained is a cycle simulation of our model. To abstract from value simulation, the next step is the accumulation of symbolic expressions, computed over one or more cycles, in the variables of the model state. Clearly, not all signals or variables are kept symbolic, but only those which can be considered data parameters of the operative part of the model or control signals that depend on them, such as an overflow signal or the boolean result of a test. Typically, the correct behavior of a sequential synchronous circuit usually relies on essential internal state elements holding proper initial values, on the computation being started by appropriate control inputs, and on the clock providing the expected synchronization cycles. Thus, in this chapter, we limit our discussion to a simple extension of value simulation: we rely on the model elaboration to create the initial state as specified by the source VHDL description, and overwrite only some inputs with constant values (for control) and symbolic values (for data).

For instance, in architecture fact, it is important that variable mystate be initially 0. This value is automatically provided by fact-make--state. Conversely, we are interested in keeping the input arg symbolic, say symbol Q, and in checking that the variable f internal to process DoIt, or equivalently signal resmult, accumulates expressions of the form $Q*(Q-1)*(Q-2)\cdots$.

To do so, we adopt a standard solution (see for example [78]), in which ACL2 is used to perform on-the-fly simplifications on the symbolic evaluation, over one or more cycles, of the model.

First, the arithmetic book must be included

```
(include-book "/.../acl2-sources/books/arithmetic/top")
```

The next theorem says that simulating the design 0 times does not change the state. It also says that simulating $n + 1$ times is equal to performing one execution cycle of the design followed by simulating it n times. In effect, the theorem instructs ACL2 to unfold the recursive definition of fact-simul:

```
(defthm unfold-fact-simul
  (and (equal (fact-simul 0 st) st)
       (implies (and (integerp n) (>= n 0))
                (equal (fact-simul (1+ n) st)
                       (fact-simul n (fact-cycle st)))))
  :hints (("Goal" :in-theory (disable fact-cycle))))
```

To perform the symbolic simulation of the model, the most elementary method proposes a fake theorem such as symbolic_simulation below, where st is the initial state with data input arg set to a symbolic natural integer value q, and control input start is set to 1. This theorem states that the execution of fact-simul on st for 12 cycles is equal to v.

```
(defthm symbolic_simulation
  (implies (and (equal st (fact-make-state :arg q :start 1))
                (integerp q)
                (>= q 0))
           (equal (fact-simul 12 st)
                  v))
  :otf-flg t
  :hints (("Goal" :do-not (eliminate-destructors
                           fertilize
                           generalize
                           eliminate-irrelevance)))))
```

Because v is a new unspecified variable, the theorem cannot be proved. However, while attempting to prove it, ACL2 applies the theorem unfold--fact-simul as a rewrite rule, simplifying the goal (fact-simul 12 st). This results in a symbolic expression for each state element.

Setting :otf-flg (Onward Thru the Fog) to t directs ACL2 to fully expand "Goal", even if this results in several subgoals that require induction; the hints tell ACL2 that the named processes should not be used at or below ptt"Goal". Looking at the ACL2 output while attempting to prove this theorem, one finds in the various subgoals the simplified expression of the model state, according to hypotheses made by the prover on the value of q. This gives an indication to the designer, who can subsequently ask for more precise and more readable formal results.

For instance, if q is greater than 4, then the symbolic simulation for 12 cycles computes in resmult the expected symbolic expression $q \times (q - 1) \times (q - 2) \times (q - 3)$. This is stated by:

```
(defthm value_of_resmult
  (implies (and (equal st (fact-make-state :arg q :start 1))
                (integerp q)
                (> q 4))
    (equal (fact-get (fact-simul 12 st) 'resmult)
           (* q (+ -1 q) (+ -2 q) (+ -3 q)))))
```

Exercise 11.3 *Run theorem* unfold-fact-simul. *Then run* symbolic_-simulation *on various number of cycles, understand the traces and check the values and symbolic expressions obtained in the internal and ouput signals of the model. Check the cyclic behavior of the internal control variables and signals.*

11.5   Proof of the Circuit

The last verification task is the formal proof that, given appropriate inputs, the circuit performs the computation of the factorial of **arg**, after a number of simulation cycles which depends linearly on the value of **arg**. At this point, it is necessary to examine the detailed behavior of each process of the architecture, and more precisely the control automaton DoIt (see Figure 11.1). Variable **mystate** holds the value of the automaton state, which may take values 0 to 2, and is initially 0. State 0 is an initialization state, state 1 determines if the computation is finished, or if one more multiplication is needed, and state 2 waits for the result of the requested multiplication.

In state 0, the variable f, which accumulates the products until the final result is obtained, is initialized to 1, and variable r is loaded with input **arg**. State 0 is left for state 1 iff input **start** is equal to 1. In states 1 and

2, the behavior of the automaton is independent of the values of the circuit inputs.

In state 1, the `result` and `done` outputs are assigned if the value of `r` is 1, and the automaton returns to state 0. Otherwise, `r` and `f` are sent as operands to the multiplier, via the signals `op1` and `op2`, and `startmult` is set to 1; the next state is 2.

In state 2, when `endmult` is 1, `f` is assigned with `resmult` which holds the result of the multiplication, `r` is decreased by 1, and the next state is 1.

Since the multiplier takes one cycle, the sequence of values in `mystate` are (for `start = 1` and `arg > 1`):   0 1 2 2 1 2 2 ... 1 2 2 1 0 ...

Consequently, the core of the proof will be performed in terms of a circuit computation step (for the cyclic 1 2 2 state sequence) that takes 3 clock cycles. It is defined as follows.

```
(defun computation-step (st)
    (fact-cycle (fact-cycle (fact-cycle st))))
```

The execution of the circuit (function `execute` hereafter) is considered after `start` has been set to 1, process `DoIt` has initialized its variables, and `DoIt.mystate` is 1. The statement (`xargs :measure (`<u>`nfix`</u>` (nth 18 st))`) tells ACL2 to look at `DoIt.r` for a variable whose measure decreases at each recursive call. If the state `st` is a list of the appropriate length, and `DoIt.mystate` is 1 and `startmult` is 0, the result of the execution is in `DoIt.f` when `DoIt.r` is less than 2, otherwise another execution is performed (recursive call).

```
(defun execute (st)
  (declare (xargs :measure (nfix (nth 18 st))
                  :hints  ... ))
  (if (and (integerp (nth 18 st))
           (equal (len st) 20)
           (equal (nth 17 st) 1)
           (equal (nth 8 st) 0))
      (if (< (nth 18 st) 2)
          (nth 19 st)
        (execute (computation-step st)))
    st))
```

Once enough properties have been proven on `computation-step`, we want ACL2 to use those properties rather than expand the definition of `computation-step` in proving theorems about `execute`. Hence the :<u>hints</u> provided in the definition of `execute`.

We specify the expected result of the computation by the simple following function `factorial`.

```
(defun factorial (n)
  (if (zp n)
      1
    (* n (factorial (1- n)))))
```

Finally, the theorem which establishes the correct behavior of the circuit states that, if all coherence constaints are satisfied on the state and its essential components, the result of execute is equal to the product of (factorial DoIt.r) and DoIt.f. This expresses the required behavior since DoIt.f is initialized to 1 in state 0 of DoIt.

```
(defthm equivalence_fact_execute
  (implies (and (integerp (nth 18 st))
                (equal (len st) 20)
                (equal (nth 17 st) 1)
                (equal (nth 8 st) 0)
                (<= 2  (nth 18 st)))
           (equal (execute st)
                  (* (nth 19 st)
                     (factorial (nth 18 st)))))
  :hints (("Goal" :in-theory (disable computation-step))))
```

11.5.1   The Path to the Proof

The way to the proof of the above final theorem consists in having ACL2 prove a series of elementary theorems about the state transformations performed by each function of the model, from the assignment statement, to the process, to the simulation and computation cycles. These theorems can be partitioned into two broad classes:

State Properties Preservation
Each function that takes a state st as argument and returns a state is such that, if st is a list, *i.e.*, if the call (consp st) evaluates to T, the result is also a list, and its length is equal to that of st.

Proving these properties for functions insert-value and fact-put was the subject of Exercise 11.1. They must also be established for fact.doit--cycle, fact.multiplier-cycle, fact-cycle and computation-step, in that order. For each function, the functions in terms of which it is defined are disabled, so ACL2 is led to use the previously proven theorem instead of expanding inner functions. Here is an example.

```
(defthm len_fact.doit-cycle
  (equal (len (fact.doit-cycle st)) (len st)))
```

State Variables Modified and Not Modified
For each function, a number of state elements are not affected by the function execution. These invariance properties, used as rewrite rules, allow the simplification of terms in further proof goals, as is demonstrated with the theorem below.

```
(defthm fact.doit-cycle_not_modified
  (implies (and (equal (len st) 20)
                (member i '(0 1 5 6 14 16)))
           (equal (nth i (fact.doit-cycle st))
                  (nth i st)))))
```

Likewise, some especially useful results of cycle computation, for key values of some state elements, such as DoIt.mystate, are established. For instance, the transition function for DoIt.r is proven to be given by the expression stated in Theorem lemma_fact-cycle7. Note that, in all these theorems, it is more efficient to systematically call the function <u>nth</u> rather than the more readable fact-get-nth, on which all the theorems available for nth should otherwise be first proven. Thus, in lemma_fact-cycle7, we use (nth 19 st) rather than (fact-get st 'DoIt.r).

```
(defthm lemma_fact-cycle7
  (implies (equal (len st) 20)
           (equal (nth 19 (fact-cycle st))
                  (if (equal (nth 17 st) 2)
                      (if (equal (nth 9 st) 1)
                          (nth 7 st)
                          (nth 19 st))
                      (if (equal (nth 17 st) 0)
                          1
                          (nth 19 st)))))))
  :hints  ... )
```

The supporting file fact-proof.lisp contains the set of theorems that lead to the proof of equivalence_fact_execute. It is assumed that the macros and the "VHDL in Lisp" model are first loaded. Thus the complete processing with ACL2 is obtained as follows (the :<u>u</u> command ensures each book is certified in a new world).

```
ACL2 !>(certify-book "vhdl" 0)
ACL2 !>:u
ACL2 !>(certify-book "fact" 0)
ACL2 !>:u
ACL2 !>(certify-book "fact-proof" 0)
```

Exercise 11.4 *Run one by one the theorems of file* fact-proof.lisp. *Understand the proof traces. Then suppress some of the theorems, and see the effect on the proofs of subsequent theorems.*

11.6 Conclusion

The work described in this chapter is part of a larger project, which is still on-going at the time of writing this book. Much remains to be added before the set of modeled VHDL statements can be considered sufficient to cover all the designer's needs. However, this chapter should have given the reader a flavor of our approach, by which a conventional simulation language is embedded in ACL2, to integrate symbolic simulation and theorem proving, as complementary techniques to the traditional C.A.D. tools accepting that language as input.

Acknowledgments

The authors are grateful to Laurence Pierre, from Université de Provence, Marseille, for many useful discussions and a long lasting cooperation with her on the topic of this chapter.

Symbolic Trajectory Evaluation

Damir A. Jamsek

IBM Austin Research Laboratory, Austin, Texas
Email: jamsek@us.ibm.com

Abstract

This case study presents a formalization of Symbolic Trajectory Evaluation in the logic of ACL2. A form of model-checking, STE has an efficient implementation and has been used in industrial settings to verify hardware designs. This study presents no new theoretical results in STE but formalizes the fundamental concepts so that they may be incorporated into a theorem proving environment such as ACL2. A simple example of its use is presented.

Introduction

Symbolic Trajectory Evaluation (STE) [101] is a form of model-checking that has been successfully used to verify large hardware designs. The theoretical simplicity of the basics of STE theory allows it to be readily encoded in a logic such as the one provided by ACL2. The goal of STE theory is to develop a verification technique fundamentally based on symbolic simulation. Additionally, the simulation handles uncertainty by allowing circuit values to be unspecified (*i.e.*, specified as "unknown" rather than as a Boolean variable) during simulation. Moreover, symbolic simulation is not the only technique available for deriving STE results. Inference rules can be defined that allow new STE results to be derived deductively from previously verified properties.

STE has been successfully used to verify properties of hardware designs in industrial settings. These verifications range from memory subsystems [110] to floating point execution units [83]. In the former, simple STE concepts are employed giving, in effect, a very efficient symbolic simulation capability. In the latter, deductive inference methods allowed efficient verifications where a strictly simulation-based approach would not suffice.

Section 12.1 defines the basic Boolean operations and the handling of uncertainty. Section 12.2 defines the representation of values that are the results of computations. Section 12.3 defines the structures that represent our circuits. Section 12.4 defines the logic used to assert and prove theorems about circuits via symbolic simulation, the main result being the fundamental theorem of STE (Figure 12.4) that transforms a question about all possible executions (Figure 12.3) of a circuit to a check of a single symbolic simulation. Section 12.5 builds on this result and develops inference rules that allow deductive proofs of STE theorems.

Defuntyped

In the following sections, function definitions are sometimes presented using the **defuntyped** macro that has the following form. This macro is defined in support file `util.lisp`.

```
(defuntyped fcn (arg₁ arg₂  ...  argₙ ) guard
   type default
   body)
```

This macro generates a **defun** for function *fcn*. Each arg_i is either a **symbolp**, in which case the symbol is taken to be the ith formal parameter of the function, or a term of the form (p n) where p is the name of a predicate and n the name of the ith formal parameter. For each argument of the latter form, the term (p n) is conjoined with the function's **guard** defined by the *guard* argument of **defuntyped**. The argument *type* is the name of a predicate defining the output type of the function and *default* is a value of type *type* that will be returned by *fcn* if the function's guard conditions are not met. In addition to the appropriate **defun** being generated, a theorem describing the output type of the function is also generated.

12.1 Booleans and Uncertainty

The first step in defining a theory of STE verification is to define the data domain over which computations will be performed. We restrict ourselves to Boolean computations. The theory can be extended to include data domains such as bit-vectors and integers but such extensions are not presented here.

In ACL2 our Booleans are T and NIL. We allow the case where a value is unspecified and represent that with the literal 'X. To complete the lattice in Figure 12.1 we introduce the literal 'TOP to represent the inconsistent case where a bit value is asserted to be high and low simultaneously.

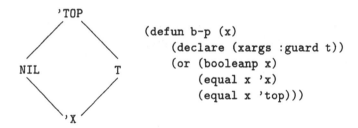

```
(defun b-p (x)
    (declare (xargs :guard t))
    (or (booleanp x)
        (equal x 'x)
        (equal x 'top)))
```

Figure 12.1: Boolean Lattice

Not	'X	NIL	T	'TOP	And	'X	NIL	T	'TOP
	'X	T	NIL	'TOP	'X	'X	NIL	'X	NIL
					NIL	NIL	NIL	NIL	NIL
					T	'X	NIL	T	'TOP
					'TOP	NIL	NIL	'TOP	'TOP

Table 12.1: Not/And operations

12.1.1 Booleans

Table 12.1 specifies the negation and conjunction operations taking into account the cases of uncertainty, X, and inconsistency, TOP.

Table 12.2 specifies the partial ordering and least upper bound function for the Boolean lattice.

LTE	'X	NIL	T	'TOP	LUB	'X	NIL	T	'TOP
'X	T	T	T	T	'X	'X	NIL	T	'TOP
NIL	NIL	T	NIL	T	NIL	NIL	NIL	'TOP	'TOP
T	NIL	NIL	T	T	T	T	'TOP	T	'TOP
'TOP	NIL	NIL	NIL	T	'TOP	'TOP	'TOP	'TOP	'TOP

Table 12.2: LTE/LUB operations

12.1.2   Implementing the Operations

The implementation of Boolean operations can have a significant impact
on ACL2 performance when proving properties involving these operations.
The following two constants define lookup tables that can be used to compute values for Boolean negation and conjunction.

```
(defconst *b-not-table*   '(x   t   nil top) )

(defconst *b-and-table* '( (x   nil x   nil)
                           (nil nil nil nil)
                           (x   nil t   top)
                           (nil nil top top) ))
```

If we consistently consider X, NIL, T, and TOP in that order, the following
lookup function can be used directly on the negation table and applied twice
to the conjunction table to implement the desired functionality.

```
(defun b-nth (b lst)
  (declare (xargs :guard (and (b-p b) (true-listp lst))))
  (if (equal b 'x) (first lst)
    (if (equal b nil) (second lst)
      (if (equal b t) (third lst)
        (if (equal b 'top) (fourth lst)
          nil)))))
```

The problem with this approach is that during proofs the system is
traversing lists and generating many more subexpressions than are actually
necessary. For the sake of efficiency, we choose to implement Boolean operations more directly. For example, the following definition of the b-and
function directly computes the result.

```
(defuntyped b-and ((b-p b1) (b-p b2)) t b-p nil
  (if (equal b1 nil) nil
    (if (equal b2 nil) nil
      (if (equal b1 t) b2
        (if (equal b2 t) b1
          (if (equal b1 'x)
              (if (equal b2 'x)
                  'x nil)
            (if (equal b2 'x) nil
              'top)))))))
```

While more efficient, the correctness of this implementation of b-and
is not immediately obvious. In fact, a first attempt at defining b-and
was incorrect. To convince ourselves of the correctness of b-and, and the
other Boolean functions, we prove the following and similar theorems for
all Boolean functions.

```
(defthm b-and-check
  (equal (b-nth b2 (b-nth b1 *b-and-table*))
         (b-and b1 b2))
  :rule-classes nil)
```

12.2   Nodes, States, and Runs

The circuits we will be verifying have nodes that we will identify using
natural numbers. A state is a list of b-p values and is recognized by the
predicate s-p. Formally, (s-p s) if and only if s is a <u>true-listp</u> and for
each element of the list b-p holds. A node's value in a state is determined
by indexing into the state by its natural number identifier.

The following predicate is true when a node n has a value in state s.

```
(defuntyped n-p (n (s-p s)) t
  booleanp nil
  (and (naturalp n)
       (< n (len s)))))
```

The Boolean partial order notion is used to define a partial order on
states by defining the functions s-lte and s-lub. Each is simply defined
so that (s-lte s1 s2) and (s-lub s1 s2) apply b-lte and b-lub, respectively, to elements of s1 and s2 in a pointwise manner. For example,
s-lte is defined as follows.

```
(defuntyped s-lte ((s-p s1) (s-p s2)) t
  booleanp nil
  (if (and (consp s1) (consp s2))
      (and (b-lte (car s1) (car s2))
           (s-lte (cdr s1) (cdr s2)))
    (and (equal s1 nil)
         (equal s2 nil)))))
```

A sequence of states, called a *run*, is recognized by the predicate r-p.
The term (r-p r) is true if and only if r is a true-listp and for every
element s of r, (s-p s) is true.

The partial ordering idea is extended to runs by defining r-lte and
r-lub, using s-lte and s-lub applied pointwise to states of the run. This
partial ordering of runs is fundamental to the verification mechanism of
STE in that specifications and circuits are used to define various kinds of
runs that can then be efficiently compared.

In subsequent sections it will sometimes be required that runs have a
certain length, n, and that all states in the run have the same length, m.
The term (r-nmp r n m) is true if and only if this condition holds of r, n,
and m.

```
(defuntyped r-nmp ((r-p r) (naturalp n) (naturalp m))
   t booleanp nil
   (if (and (consp r) (< 0 n))
       (and (equal (len (car r)) m)
            (r-nmp (cdr r) (1- n) m))
     (and (equal r nil) (equal n 0))))
```

12.3   Expressions, Circuits, and Trajectories

12.3.1   Expressions

To begin modeling the notion of computation, we define a simple expression language over Booleans extended with 'TOP and 'X. Expressions are defined to be simple Booleans, variables named by natural numbers, or the Boolean operations not and and.

```
(defuntyped e-p (e) t
  booleanp nil
  (if (naturalp e) t
    (if (b-p e) t
      (case-match e
                  (('not x)    (e-p x))
                  (('and x y) (and (e-p x) (e-p y)))
                  (&           nil)))))
```

Given an expression and a state, the expression can be evaluated resulting in a b-p object. Constants evaluate to themselves. Variables are looked up in the state. The operations not and and are evaluated by first evaluating their arguments and then applying the operations b-not and b-and, respectively.

```
(defuntyped e-eval ((e-p e) (s-p s)) t
  b-p 'x
  (if (n-p e s) (nth e s)
    (if (b-p e) e
      (case-match e
          (('not x)    (b-not (e-eval x s)))
          (('and x y) (b-and (e-eval x s) (e-eval y s)))
          (&           'x)))))
```

The following theorem about the monotonicity of expression evaluation states that if one state is less than or equal to another then any expression evaluated in the lesser or equal state is less or equal to the same expression evaluated in the greater or equal state. This forms the basis for circuit monotonicity in the next section.

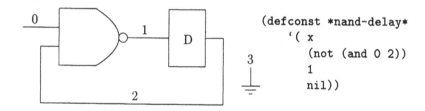

Figure 12.2: Nand-Delay Circuit

```
(defthm e-eval-of-s-lte-is-b-lte
  (implies (and (s-p s1)
                (s-p s2)
                (equal (len s1) (len s2))
                (s-lte s1 s2)
                (e-p e))
           (b-lte (e-eval e s1)
                  (e-eval e s2)))))
```

12.3.2 Circuits

A circuit is a collection of nodes with associated expressions that represent their transition function. Naming nodes using natural numbers, a circuit is represented by a true-listp of e-p values. The ith element of the list represents the update function for the ith node in a single clock-cycle. The predicate c-p recognizes well-formed circuits.

In Figure 12.2, a simple circuit with four nodes is shown along with its ACL2 definition. Properties of this example circuit will be verified later.

A circuit evaluation gives the next state of a circuit given a current state. The evaluation is an expression evaluation of each of the expressions that represent the transition functions for each node.

```
(defuntyped c-eval ((c-p c) (s-p s)) t
  s-p nil
  (if (consp c)
      (cons (e-eval (car c) s)
            (c-eval (cdr c) s))
    nil))
```

Circuit monotonicity is an extension of expression monotonicity. The following theorem follows from the expression monotonicity theorem of the previous section. Given a state less than or equal to another, evaluating a

circuit in the former state results in a state less than or equal to the state
resulting from evaluating in the latter state.

```
(defthm s-lte-c-eval-is-s-lte
  (implies (and (c-p c)
                (s-p s1)
                (s-p s2)
                (equal (len s1) (len s2))
                (s-lte s1 s2))
           (s-lte (c-eval c s1)
                  (c-eval c s2))))
```

12.3.3 Trajectories

A trajectory is a kind of run. A run is a trajectory for a given circuit if for
any state in the run a circuit evaluation in that state results in a state less
than or equal to the next state in the run. In subsequent developments,
checking for circuit properties will reduce to checking properties of a particular trajectory of a circuit. The following predicate t-p for a given circuit
will recognize all runs that are in fact trajectories for a circuit.

```
(defuntyped t-p ((r-p r) (c-p c)) t
  booleanp nil
  (case-match r ((s1 s2 . ss)
                 (and (s-lte (c-eval c s1) s2)
                      (t-p (cons s2 ss) c)))
                (& t)))
```

12.4   Assertions and Theorems

Now that a method for specifying circuits is defined, a method for specifying
properties of circuits is required. STE requires a way to specify conditions
under which the circuit will be expected to operate as well as the expected
behavior of the circuit. Both of these are accomplished by STE assertions.

12.4.1 Assertions

The language for making assertions about circuits is simple temporal logic.
STE assertions are either a simple predicate, a conjunction of assertions, a
guarded assertion, or an assertion shifted in time. A simple predicate just
claims that a circuit node has some value at the current time. Conjunction
is the usual propositional conjunction operation. A guarded assertion is
guarded by a Boolean value that determines if the assertion holds or does

not hold. The next time operator shifts the assertion one time step in the future. We include the assertion T that always holds, for technical reasons that will be made clear in subsequent developments. The predicate l-p recognizes terms that are valid STE assertions.

```
(defuntyped l-p (l) t
  booleanp nil
  (if (equal l t) t
    (case-match l
      (('is i b)     (and (naturalp i) (booleanp b)))
      (('and l1 l2) (and (l-p l1) (l-p l2)))
      (('when b l1) (and (booleanp b) (l-p l1)))
      (('next l1)    (l-p l1)))))
```

Before defining the notion of evaluating an assertion we introduce some useful functions that characterize l-p formulas. L-depth returns one more than the maximum depth of **next** operators nesting. This conveniently is the minimum length of a run that an assertion requires for its evaluation. L-maxn returns one plus the maximum node name (node names are natural numbers) and corresponds to the minimum sized state needed to evaluate an assertion. L-evalp tells when an assertion is evaluable, that is, (l-evalp l n m) is true if and only if l is evaluable in a run of length n with states of size m.

The evaluation of an assertion requires there be a run with enough states to evaluate the assertions about the future made by next time operators in the assertion. The evaluation of an assertion in a run is defined in the usual model-theoretic style [26]. A simple predicate is true if the node's asserted value is less than or equal to the value for the node in the current state. For a conjunction, both assertions must hold in the current run. A guarded assertion need only hold if the guarding condition is true. The next-shifted assertion ignores the current state and must evaluate to true in the run less the current state. The predicate l-eval is true if and only if these conditions hold.

```
(defuntyped l-eval ((l-p l) (r-p r)) t
  booleanp nil
  (if (consp r)
      (if (equal l t)
          t
        (case-match l
          (('is n b)     (if (< n (len (car r)))
                             (b-lte b (nth n (car r)))
                           nil))
          (('and l1 l2) (and (l-eval l1 r) (l-eval l2 r)))
          (('when b l1) (implies b (l-eval l1 r)))
          (('next l1)    (l-eval l1 (cdr r)))))
    nil))
```

```
(defun-sk ste-thm (ckt a c)
  (forall r (implies (and (r-p r)
                          (t-p r ckt)
                          (r-nmp r (1-depth a) (1-maxn a))
                          (equal (1-depth a) (1-depth c))
                          (equal (1-maxn a) (1-maxn c))
                          (equal (len ckt) (1-maxn a))
                          (1-eval a r))
             (1-eval c r)))))
```

Figure 12.3: STE theorem definition

The first lemma of [101] is given below as Lemma-1[1]. It follows directly from the definitions.

```
(defthm lemma-1
  (implies (and (1-eval l r1)
                (r-lte r1 r2))
           (1-eval l r2)))
```

12.4.2   Theorems

An *STE theorem* is a way to describe the expected behaviors of a circuit. An STE theorem consists of a circuit and two assertions called the *antecedent* and the *consequent*. One possible way of checking the correctness of an STE theorem is to check all possible runs that are trajectories of the circuit and that satisfy the antecedent to see if they also satisfy the consequent. The predicate ste-thm, shown in Figure 12.3, is defined in exactly this fashion.

The ACL2 **defun-sk** command allows one to axiomatize unexecutable "Skolem functions" that provide the power of full first-order quantification. Proofs about such functions usually require explicit hints from the user. Ste-thm is defined as a Boolean function of three arguments whose value indicates whether the term inside the **forall**, in Figure 12.3, is non-nil for all r.

While conceptually easy, this definition of ste-thm is computationally impractical. In the next sections an efficient method of computing the validity of an STE theorem is developed.

---

[1]The supporting material contains lemmas named Lemma-1 through Lemma-5 that correspond directly to lemmas in [101]. Not all of them appear in this chapter.

12.4.3   Defining Sequences and Trajectories

The defining sequence for an assertion 1 is the least run, according to
r-lte, in which 1 evaluates to true. The term (defseq 1) returns a run of
length (1-depth 1) with states of size (1-maxn 1). The following theorem
verifies that an assertion always evaluates to true in the run constructed
for it by the defseq construction.

```
(defthm 1-eval-of-defseq-holds
  (implies (1-p 1)
           (1-eval 1 (defseq 1))))
```

Furthermore, the defining sequence returned by defseq is the minimum
sequence in which 1 evaluates to true.

```
(defthm lemma-2
  (implies (and (1-p 1)
                (r-p r)
                (r-nmp r (1-depth 1) (1-maxn 1)))
           (iff (1-eval 1 r)
                (r-lte (defseq 1) r)))
  :hints  ... )
```

We next wish to define the notion of a defining trajectory for an assertion
and a circuit. The idea is that a defining trajectory should satisfy the
assertion and also be a run that is a possible outcome of some circuit
operation. Before defining deftraj, we define r-deftraj. For a given
run and an initial state, r-deftraj returns a run that is a trajectory and
is greater than or equal to the original run. In fact, the returned run is the
least such run.

```
(defuntyped r-deftraj ((r-p r) (c-p c) (s-p s)) t
  r-p nil
  (if (consp r)
      (let ((s1 (s-lub s (car r))))
        (cons s1 (r-deftraj (cdr r) c (c-eval c s1))))
    nil))
```

The definition of deftraj is the application of r-deftraj to the defining sequence of the assertion as the run and the bottom state as the initial
state. The following macro defines deftraj[2].

```
(defmacro deftraj (a ckt)
  '(r-deftraj (1-defseq ,a (1-depth ,a) (1-maxn ,a))
              ,ckt
              (s-make (1-maxn ,a) 'x)))
```

Lemma-4 verifies three properties of deftraj.

---

[2]The definition of deftraj could have been made using defseq directly since
(defmacro defseq (a) '(1-defseq ,a (1-depth ,a) (1-maxn ,a))).

```
(defthm fundamental-theorem-of-ste
  (implies (ste-wf ckt (a c))
           (iff (ste-thm ckt a c)
                (r-lte (defseq c)
                       (deftraj a ckt))))
  :hints   ... )
```

Figure 12.4: Fundamental Theorem of STE

♦ Deftraj returns a trajectory.

♦ The assertion is true in the run returned from deftraj.

♦ The run returned by deftraj is the least run in which the assertion evaluates to true.

```
(defthm lemma-4
  (implies (and (l-p l)
                (c-p c)
                (equal (len c) (l-maxn l))
                (r-p r)
                (r-nmp r (l-depth l) (l-maxn l))
                (t-p r c))
           (and (t-p (deftraj l c) c)
                (l-eval l (deftraj l c))
                (iff (l-eval l r)
                     (r-lte (deftraj l c) r))))
  :hints   ... )
```

With the STE notions of defining sequence and defining trajectory the computationally infeasible definition of ste-thm can be transformed to a computationally efficient method involving calculating and comparing defining sequences and trajectories. The theorem in Figure 12.4 can be regarded as the fundamental theorem of symbolic trajectory evaluation. The predicate ste-wf is a macro that simply expands to a number of conditions that guarantee that the objects ckt, a, and c are of the correct type and size, relative to each other.

With fundamental-theorem-of-ste enabled and the definition of ste--thm disabled, proving STE theorems reduces to simple symbolic simulations of the circuit. For example, the following theorem verifies the operation of the *nand* element of the circuit in Figure 12.2. It says that if nodes 0 and 2 have values b_1 and b_2 at the current time, then $\overline{b_1 \wedge b_2}$ appears on node 1 in the next time step.

```
(defthm nand-operation-thm1
  (implies (and (booleanp b1)
```

```
                    (booleanp b2))
            (ste-thm *nand-delay*
                    '(and (and (is 0 ,b1)
                              (is 2 ,b2))
                         (and (is 3 nil)
                              (next (is 3 nil))))
                     '(and (next (is 1 ,(not (and b1 b2))))
                          (and (is 3 nil)
                               (next (is 3 nil))))))))
   :hints  ...  )
```

The expression (and (is 3 nil) (next (is 3 nil))) is conjoined to antecedents and consequents in both cases to guarantee that the predicate ste-wf is satisfied. The hints that are elided in the examples are simply optimizations that list exactly the rewrite rules that are needed for the symbolic simulation. In fact, a first attempt at proving these theorems was successful but took an order of magnitude greater time. With the hints, it takes seconds rather than tens of seconds.

It seems unreasonable that it should even take a second to do a symbolic simulation of such a simple case. The VOSS [48] system is specifically designed and optimized to do these types of symbolic simulations by using BDD [14] techniques for computations. Even so, a system implemented in the manner of VOSS has its limitations when dealing with large circuits.

12.5   STE Inference Rules

In this section, a number of STE inference rules are shown to be sound. The rules can be used to address inadequacies (*e.g.*, size limitations) of STE provers based solely on symbolic simulation. We will first describe the rules that have been shown to be sound. This description is followed by an example of a circuit property proven deductively via previous simulation results and the inference rules.

The first rule is simple and follows immediately from the definition of ste-thm.

```
(defthm ste-thm-identity
  (ste-thm ckt a a))
```

Given two STE theorems about the same circuit, we can conjoin the antecedents and the consequents, respectively, resulting in an STE theorem that holds for the circuit.

```
(defthm ste-thm-conjoin
  (implies (and (ste-wf ckt (a1 c1) (a2 c2))
               (ste-thm ckt a1 c1)
               (ste-thm ckt a2 c2))
```

```
              (ste-thm ckt '(and ,a1 ,a2) '(and ,c1 ,c2)))
   :hints  ... )
```

Given an STE theorem about a circuit, the antecedent and consequent can be shifted forward in time and the new STE theorem holds true.

```
(defthm ste-thm-shift
   (implies (and (ste-wf ckt (a c))
                 (ste-thm ckt a c))
            (ste-thm ckt '(next ,a) '(next ,c)))
   :hints  ... )
```

Simple transitivity allows us to infer a new STE theorem if one theorem's consequent is greater than or equal to another theorem's antecedent. In this case the new theorem says the first theorem's antecedent is enough to guarantee the second theorem's consequent.

```
(defthm ste-thm-transitivity-simple
   (implies (and (ste-wf ckt (a1 c1) (a2 c2))
                 (ste-thm ckt a1 c1)
                 (ste-thm ckt a2 c2)
                 (r-lte (defseq a2) (defseq c1)))
            (ste-thm ckt a1 c2))
   :hints  ... )
```

A more general form of transitivity for STE theorems compares the second theorem's antecedent against the least upper bound of the first theorem's antecedent and the first theorem's consequent.

```
(defthm ste-thm-transitivity
   (implies (and (ste-wf ckt (a1 c1) (a2 c2))
                 (ste-thm ckt a1 c1)
                 (ste-thm ckt a2 c2)
                 (r-lte (defseq a2)
                        (r-lub (defseq a1)
                               (defseq c1))))
            (ste-thm ckt a1 c2))
   :hints  ... )
```

Given an STE theorem, we can weaken the consequent or strengthen the antecedent. In the STE sense, weakening and strengthening are determined by r-lte of the defining sequences of the assertions.

```
(defthm ste-thm-weaken-strengthen
   (implies (and (ste-wf ckt (a c) (a1 c1))
                 (ste-thm ckt a c)
                 (r-lte (defseq a) (defseq a1))
                 (r-lte (defseq c1) (defseq c)))
            (ste-thm ckt a1 c1))
   :hints  ... )
```

12.6 Deductive Proofs

For our example circuit, suppose we assert that at the start nodes 0, 1, 2 have values b_0, b_1, b_2, respectively. Furthermore, suppose we assert that at time 1 node 0 has value b_3. The following table shows a trace (reading down) of node values for three steps of our example machine.

0	1	2	3
b_0	b_1	b_2	NIL
b_3	$\overline{b_0 \wedge b_2}$	b_1	NIL
X	$\overline{b_1 \wedge b_3}$	$\overline{b_0 \wedge b_2}$	NIL

The following theorem makes the appropriate antecedent assertions as well as the desired consequent assertion.

```
(defthm nand-delay-2cycle
  (implies (and (booleanp b0)
                (booleanp b1)
                (booleanp b2)
                (booleanp b3))
    (ste-thm *nand-delay*
      '(and (and (and (is 0 ,b0)
                      (is 1 ,b1))
                 (and (is 2 ,b2)
                      (next (is 0 ,b3))))
            (next (next (is 3 nil))))
      '(and (and (next (next (is 1
                                ,(not (and b1 b3)))))
                 (next (next (is 2
                                ,(or (not b0)
                                     (not b2))))))
            (next (next (is 3 nil)))))))
  :hints  ...  )
```

The functionality implied by the consequent of this theorem can be split between the expected values on node 1 and node 2. We prove these separately via symbolic simulation, that is, invoking the theorem fundamental-
-theorem-of-ste and rewriting. The proof is completed by disabling the rules associated both with the definition of ste-thm and the theorem fundamental-theorem-of-ste, then using the inference rules described above. The reader is referred to the support file example.lisp for details. The same proof can be accomplished by using the symbolic simulation results from theorems nand-operation-thm1 and delay-operation-thm1 and the inference rules. This proof is left as an exercise for the reader.

13

RTL Verification: A Floating-Point Multiplier

David M. Russinoff and Arthur Flatau
Advanced Micro Devices, Inc., Austin, Texas
Email: david.russinoff@amd.com, arthur.flatau@amd.com

Abstract

We describe a mechanical proof system for designs represented in the AMD[1] RTL language, consisting of a translator to the ACL2 logical programming language and a metology for verifiying properties of the resulting programs using the ACL2 prover. As an illustration, we present a proof of correctness of a simple floating-point multiplier.

Introduction

In order for a hardware design to be provably correct, it must be represented in a language that has an unambiguous semantic definition. Unfortunately, commercial hardware description languages such as VHDL and Verilog, which are intended for a variety of purposes other than formal verification, are large, complicated, and poorly specified. Attempts to develop formal semantics for these languages [44, 93] have generally been limited to small, manageable subsets that are inadequate for modeling real industrial designs. Consequently, a "proof of correctness" of a practical VHDL or Verilog design is generally based on an alternative encoding of the underlying algorithm in some simpler formal language. The utility of such a proof rests on the unproved assumption that the two implementations are equivalent.

As an alternative to these commercial languages, Advanced Micro Devices, Inc. has adopted a special-purpose hardware language for the design of the AMD Athlon^{TM} processor and future AMD microprocessors. The language syntactically resembles Verilog, but is considerably simpler. While

---

[1]AMD, the AMD logo and combinations thereof, and AMD Athlon are trademarks of Advanced Micro Devices, Inc.

Verilog includes extensive features to support the design and testing of a wide variety of digital systems at various levels of abstraction, the AMD language is intended solely for modeling microprocessor designs at the level of register-transfer logic (RTL). Moreover, (although this was not a consideration in its design) our language was constructed carefully enough to allow formal verification as a realistic objective.

The subject of this paper is a methodology for mechanical verification of actual hardware designs written in the AMD RTL language, using the ACL2 prover. The underlying theory of floating-point arithmetic and its bit-level implementation, developed through the course of our prior work on the verification of floating-point algorithms, is embodied in an ACL2 library, consisting of several books of definitions and lemmas, which is available on the Web [95]. This library is briefly summarized below in Section 13.1. Additional documentation may be found in [96] and [94].

In Section 13.2, we present a precise description of the RTL language, including a rigorous definition of its semantics. This definition is the basis of a scheme for the automatic translation of RTL circuit descriptions into the logic of ACL2. The circuits that are handled by this translator include all combinational circuits as well as an important class of sequential circuits that may be characterized as *pipelines*. In particular, our methods are well suited to the verification of floating-point hardware designs, and have been applied to several of the arithmetic operations of the AMD Athlon processor, including an IEEE-compliant floating-point adder. In Section 13.3, as an illustration, we describe a proof of correctness of a simplified version of the Athlon multiplier. The complete proof may be found in the supporting files for this book [67].

13.1   A Library of Floating-Point Arithmetic

In this section, we list the basic definitions of our floating-point library [95], along with some of the lemmas that are relevant to the proof described in Section 13.3. In the mechanization of mathematical proofs of this sort, we have found that the most effective approach is to begin with an informal but rigorous and detailed written proof from which a formal ACL2 proof may be derived with minimal effort. Accordingly, our presentation will generally rely on traditional (informal) mathematical notation, rather than ACL2 syntax. The sets of rational numbers, nonzero rationals, integers, natural numbers (nonnegative integers), and nonzero naturals will be denoted by $\mathbb{Q}$, $\mathbb{Q}^*$, $\mathbb{Z}$, $\mathbb{N}$, and $\mathbb{N}^*$, respectively. Function names will generally be printed in *italics*. Every function that we mention corresponds to an ACL2 function symbol, usually of the same name, which we denote in the typewriter font. In most cases, the formal definition of this function may be routinely derived from its informal specification and is therefore left to the reader.

Similarly, every lemma that we state corresponds to a mechanically verified ACL2 formula. In most cases, we omit the formal version, but include its name so that it may be easily located in the floating-point library.

Two functions that are central to our theory are fl and cg. For all $x \in \mathbb{Q}$, $fl(x)$ and $cg(x)$, abbreviated as $\lfloor x \rfloor$ and $\lceil x \rceil$, respectively, are the unique integers satisfying $\lfloor x \rfloor \leq x < \lfloor x \rfloor + 1$ and $\lceil x \rceil \geq x > \lceil x \rceil - 1$. The corresponding formal definitions are based on the ACL2 primitive **floor**.

```
(defun fl (x) (floor x 1))
(defun cg (x) (- (fl (- x))))
```

Exercise 13.1 *Prove (with the ACL2 prover) that for all $m \in \mathbb{N}$ and $n \in \mathbb{N}^*$,*

$$\lfloor -(m+1)/n \rfloor = -\lfloor m/n \rfloor - 1.$$

Another important function is the integer remainder rem (corresponding to the ACL2 primitive **rem**), which may be characterized as follows:

Lemma 13.1.1 (division) *If $m \in \mathbb{N}$ and $n \in \mathbb{N}^*$, then*

$$n \lfloor m/n \rfloor + rem(m, n) = m.$$

The mechanically verified version of this lemma is as follows.

```
(defthm division
  (implies (and (integerp m) (>= m 0)
                (integerp n) (> n 0))
           (equal (+ (* n (fl (/ m n)))
                     (rem m n))
                  m)))
```

13.1.1 Bit Vectors

We exploit the natural correspondence between the bit vectors of length n and the natural numbers in the range $0 \leq x < 2^n$. Thus, for all $x, k \in \mathbb{N}$, we define

$$bitn(x, k) = rem(\lfloor x/2^k \rfloor, 2),$$

representing the kth bit of the bit vector x. We also define, for all $x, i, j \in \mathbb{N}$, where $i \geq j$,

$$bits(x, i, j) = \lfloor rem(x, 2^{i+1})/2^j \rfloor,$$

which extracts a field of bits from x, from the ith down through the jth. Following the standard notation of hardware description languages (see

Section 13.2), we shall abbreviate $bitn(x, k)$ as $x[k]$, and $bits(x, i, j)$ as $x[i : j]$.

The ACL2 formalization of both of these definitions is straightforward. However, instead of basing our definition of the ACL2 function bitn directly on the above, we make use of the primitive logbitp, for the sake of execution efficiency.

```
(defun bitn (x n) (if (logbitp n x) 1 0))
```

After deriving the desired relation from the formal definition, the definition may be disabled.

```
(defthm bitn-def
    (implies (and (integerp x) (>= x 0)
                  (integerp k) (>= k 0))
             (= (bitn x k)
                (rem (fl (/ x (expt 2 k))) 2)))
  :rule-classes ()
  :hints ...)
(in-theory (disable bitn))
```

Among the library lemmas pertaining to bitn and bits, we shall require the following:

Lemma 13.1.2 (bit-expo-a) *For all $x, n \in \mathbb{N}$, if $x < 2^n$, then $x[n] = 0$;*

Lemma 13.1.3 (bit-expo-b) *For all $x, n, k \in \mathbb{N}$, if $k < n$ and $2^n - 2^k \le x < 2^n$, then $x[k] = 1$.*

Lemma 13.1.4 (bit+a) *For all $x, n \in \mathbb{N}$, $(x + 2^n)[n] \ne x[n]$.*

Lemma 13.1.5 (bits-bitn) *For all $x \in \mathbb{N}$ and $n \in \mathbb{N}^*$, $x[n : 0] = 0 \Leftrightarrow x[n] = x[n - 1 : 0] = 0$.*

Lemma 13.1.6 (bit-bits-b) *For all $x, i, j, k \in \mathbb{N}$, if $i \ge j + k$, then $x[i : j][k] = x[k + j]$;*

Lemma 13.1.7 (bit-bits-c) *For all $x, i, j, k, \ell \in \mathbb{N}$, if $i \ge j + k$, then $x[i : j][k : \ell] = x[k + j : \ell + j]$.*

We have three binary logical operations on bit vectors, for which we again use abbreviations motivated by RTL notation: $logand(x, y) = x \,\&\, y$, $logior(x, y) = x \mid y$, and $logxor(x, y) = x \,\hat{}\, y$. These functions are most naturally defined recursively, *e.g.*,

$$x \,\&\, y = \begin{cases} 0 & \text{if } x = 0 \\ 2(\lfloor x/2 \rfloor \,\&\, \lfloor y/2 \rfloor) + 1 & \text{if } x \text{ and } y \text{ are both odd} \\ 2(\lfloor x/2 \rfloor \,\&\, \lfloor y/2 \rfloor) & \text{otherwise.} \end{cases}$$

However, since the functions logand, etc., are already implemented as ACL2 primitives, we once again derive the desired equations as consequences of the relevant axioms. Here is an example.

```
(defthm logand-def
   (implies (and (integerp x) (>= x 0)
                 (integerp y) (>= y 0))
            (= (logand x y)
               (+ (* 2 (logand (fl (/ x 2)) (fl (/ y 2))))
                  (logand (rem x 2) (rem y 2)))))
 :rule-classes ()
 :hints ...)
```

The following library lemmas are cited in the proof of Section 13.3:

Lemma 13.1.8 (bit-dist-a) *For all* $x, y, n \in \mathbb{N}$,

$$(x \& y)[n] = x[n] \& y[n].$$

Lemma 13.1.9 (bit-dist-b) *For all* $x, y, n \in \mathbb{N}$,

$$(x \mid y)[n] = x[n] \mid y[n].$$

Lemma 13.1.10 (and-dist-a) *For all* $x, y, n \in \mathbb{N}$, $x \& y \le x$.

Lemma 13.1.11 (and-dist-c) *For all* $x, y, n \in \mathbb{N}$,

$$rem(x \& y, 2^n) = rem(x, 2^n) \& y.$$

Lemma 13.1.12 (and-dist-d) *For all* $x, y, n \in \mathbb{N}$, *if* $x < 2^n$, *then*

$$x \& y = x \& rem(y, 2^n).$$

Lemma 13.1.13 (or-dist-a) *For all* $x, y, n \in \mathbb{N}$, *if* $x < 2^n$ *and* $y < 2^n$, *then* $x \mid y < 2^n$.

Lemma 13.1.14 (or-dist-d) *For all* $x, y, n \in \mathbb{N}$,

$$rem(x \mid y, 2^n) = rem(x, 2^n) \mid rem(y, 2^n).$$

13.1.2 Floating-Point Representation

Floating-point representation is based on the observation that every nonzero rational x admits a unique factorization,

$$x = sgn(x)sig(x)2^{expo(x)},$$

where $sgn(x) \in \{1, -1\}$ (the *sign* of x), $1 \le sig(x) < 2$ (the *significand* of x), and $expo(x) \in \mathbb{Z}$ (the *exponent* of x).

The recursive definition of **expo** requires an explicitly supplied measure.

```
(defun expo-measure (x)
  (cond ((not (rationalp x)) 0)
        ((< x 0) '(2 . 0))
        ((< x 1) '(1 . 0))
        (t (fl x))))
(defun expo (x)
  (declare (xargs :measure (expo-measure x)))
  (cond ((or (not (rationalp x)) (= x 0)) ())
        ((< x 0) (expo (- x)))
        ((< x 1) (- (expo (/ x))))
        ((< x 2) 0)
        (t (1+ (expo (/ x 2)))))))
```

The definitions of **sgn** and **sig** are then straightforward.

```
(defun sgn (x) (if (< x 0) -1 +1))
(defun sig (x) (* (abs x) (expt 2 (- (expo x))))))
```

The following properties are immediate consequences of the definitions:

Lemma 13.1.15 (fp-rep) *For all $x \in \mathbb{Q}^*$, $x = sgn(x)sig(x)2^{expo(x)}$.*

Lemma 13.1.16 (expo-lower-bound) *For all $x \in \mathbb{Q}^*$, $|x| \geq 2^{expo(x)}$.*

Lemma 13.1.17 (expo-upper-bound) *For all $x \in \mathbb{Q}^*$, $|x| < 2^{expo(x)+1}$.*

Lemma 13.1.18 (fp-rep-unique) *If $x, y \in \mathbb{Q}^*$, $1 \leq y < 2$, $n \in \mathbb{Z}$, and $|x| = 2^n y$, then $y = sig(x)$ and $n = expo(x)$.*

Lemma 13.1.19 (sig-expo-shift) *If $x \in \mathbb{Q}^*$, $n \in \mathbb{Z}$, and $y = 2^n x$, then $sig(y) = sig(x)$ and $expo(y) = n + expo(x)$.*

A *floating-point representation* of x is a bit vector consisting of three fields, corresponding to $sgn(x)$, $sig(x)$, and $expo(x)$. A *floating-point format* is a pair of positive integers $\phi = (\sigma, \epsilon)$, representing the number of bits allocated to $sig(x)$ and $expo(x)$, respectively. If $z \in \mathbb{N}$, then the *sign*, *exponent*, and *significand fields* of z with respect to ϕ are

$$sgnf(z, \phi) = z[\sigma + \epsilon],$$

$$expf(z, \phi) = z[\sigma + \epsilon - 1 : \sigma],$$

and

$$sigf(z, \phi) = z[\sigma - 1 : 0],$$

respectively. If $sigf(z, \phi)[\sigma - 1] = 1$, then z is a *normal ϕ-encoding*.

The number x represented by a normal ϕ-encoding z, where $\phi = (\sigma, \epsilon)$, is given by $sgn(x) = (-1)^{sgnf(z,\phi)}$, $sig(x) = 2^{1-\sigma} sigf(z, \phi)$, and $expo(x) = expf(z, \phi) - (2^{\epsilon-1} - 1)$. Thus, we define

$$decode(z, \phi) = (-1)^{sgnf(z,\phi)} \cdot sigf(z, \phi) \cdot 2^{expf(z,\phi) - 2^{\epsilon-1} - \sigma + 2}.$$

Note that the exponent field is biased in order to provide for an exponent range $1 - 2^{\epsilon-1} \leq expo(x) \leq 2^{\epsilon-1}$.

Let $x \in \mathbb{Q}^*$ and $n \in \mathbb{N}^*$. Then the predicate $exactp(x, n)$ is true, and we shall say that x is n-exact, if $sig(x)2^{n-1} \in \mathbb{Z}$. The predicate $repp(x, \phi)$ is true if x is σ-exact and $-2^{\epsilon-1} + 1 \leq expo(x) \leq 2^{\epsilon-1}$. It is clear that the latter condition holds iff x is *representable* with respect to ϕ, i.e., for some $z \in \mathbb{N}$, $x = decode(z, \phi)$. We also have the following characterization of n-exact naturals:

Lemma 13.1.20 (exact-bits-a-b) Let $x, n, k \in \mathbb{N}^*$, $2^{n-1} \leq x < 2^n$, and $k < n$. Then 2^k divides x iff x is $(n - k)$-exact.

Another useful lemma characterizes the "successor" of an n-exact number:

Lemma 13.1.21 (fp+1) Let $x, y \in \mathbb{Q}^*$ and $n \in \mathbb{N}^*$. If $y > x > 0$ and x and y are both n-exact, then $y \geq x + 2^{expo(x)+1-n}$.

Exercise 13.2 *Prove that if x is k-exact and x^2 is $2n$-exact, then x is n-exact. (Note: the hypothesis that x is k-exact may be replaced with the weaker assumption that x is rational, but the ACL2 proof then becomes more complicated.)*

The IEEE standard [54] supports three formats, $(24, 7)$, $(53, 10)$, and $(64, 15)$, which correspond to *single*, *double*, and *extended* precision, respectively. In the discussion of our floating-point multiplier, floating-point numbers will always be represented in the extended precision format, $\mathcal{E} = (64, 15)$. We shall abbreviate $decode(z, \mathcal{E})$ as $\hat{z}$.

```
(defun extfmt () '(64 15))
(defun hat (z) (decode z (extfmt)))
```

13.1.3   Rounding

A *rounding mode* is a function $\mathcal{M}(x, n)$ that computes an n-exact number corresponding to an arbitrary rational x and a degree of precision $n \in \mathbb{N}^*$. The most basic rounding mode, *truncation* (round toward 0), is defined by

$$trunc(x, n) = sgn(x)\lfloor 2^{n-1} sig(x)\rfloor 2^{expo(x)-n+1}.$$

Thus, $trunc(x, n)$ is the n-exact number y satifying $|y| \leq |x|$ that is closest to x. Similarly, rounding *away* from 0 is given by

$$away(x, n) = sgn(x)\lceil 2^{n-1} sig(x)\rceil 2^{expo(x)-n+1},$$

and three other modes are defined simply in terms of those two: *inf*(x, n) (round toward ∞), *minf*(x, n) (round toward $-\infty$), and *near*(x, n) (round to the nearest n-exact number, with ambiguities resolved by selecting $(n - 1)$-exact values).

The modes that are supported by the IEEE standard are *trunc*, *near*, *inf*, and *minf*. We shall refer to these as *IEEE rounding modes*.

```
(defun ieee-mode-p (mode)
  (member mode '(trunc inf minf near)))
```

If $\mathcal{M}$ is any rounding mode, $\sigma \in \mathbb{N}^*$, and $x \in \mathbb{Q}$, then we define

$$rnd(x, \mathcal{M}, \sigma) = \mathcal{M}(x, \sigma).$$

```
(defun rnd (x mode n)
  (case mode
    (trunc (trunc x n))
    (inf (inf x n))
    (minf (minf x n))
    (near (near x n))))
```

Lemma 13.1.22 (rnd-shift) *If $x \in \mathbb{Q}$, $n \in \mathbb{N}^*$, and $k \in \mathbb{Z}$, then for any IEEE rounding mode $\mathcal{M}$,*

$$rnd(2^k x, \mathcal{M}, n) = 2^k rnd(x, \mathcal{M}, n).$$

Lemma 13.1.23 (rnd-flip) *If $x \in \mathbb{Q}$ and $n \in \mathbb{N}^*$, then for any IEEE rounding mode $\mathcal{M}$,*

$$rnd(-x, \mathcal{M}, n) = -rnd(x, \mathcal{M}', n),$$

where

$$\mathcal{M}' = \begin{cases} minf, & if\ \mathcal{M} = inf \\ inf, & if\ \mathcal{M} = minf \\ \mathcal{M}, & if\ \mathcal{M} = trunc\ or\ \mathcal{M} = near. \end{cases}$$

The following three lemmas justify the implementation of rounding that is employed in the AMD Athlon floating-point unit:

Lemma 13.1.24 (bits-trunc) *Let $x, m, n, k \in \mathbb{N}$. If $0 < k < n \leq m$ and $2^{n-1} \leq x < 2^n$, then*

$$trunc(x, k) = x\ \&\ (2^m - 2^{n-k}).$$

Lemma 13.1.25 (away-imp) *Let $x \in \mathbb{Q}$, $x > 0$, $m \in \mathbb{N}^*$, and $n \in \mathbb{N}^*$. If x is m-exact and $m \geq n$, then*

$$away(x, n) = trunc(x + 2^{expo(x)+1}(2^{-n} - 2^{-m}), n).$$

Lemma 13.1.26 (near-trunc) *Let $n \in \mathbb{Z}$, $n > 1$, and $x \in \mathbb{Q}$, $x > 0$. If x is $(n + 1)$-exact but not n-exact, then*

$$near(x, n) = trunc(x + 2^{expo(x)-n}, n - 1);$$

otherwise,

$$near(x, n) = trunc(x + 2^{expo(x)-n}, n).$$

13.2 The RTL Language

In this section, we present a precise syntactic and semantic definition of the AMD RTL language. We also identify a class of programs that admit a particularly simple semantic description. For these programs, called *simple pipelines*, the value of each output may be computed in a natural way as a function of the inputs.

One advantage of using our own design language is that we are free to modify its compiler to suit our needs. Thus, we have implemented an automatic translator that generates a functional representation in ACL2 of any simple pipeline, based on the compiler's internal parse tree. Our floating-point multiplier will serve as an illustration.

13.2.1 Language Definition

The language is based on a class of identifiers called *signals*, and a class of character strings called *numerals*. A *binary numeral* has the form $bb_1 \ldots b_k$, where the b_i are binary digits; *decimal* and *hexadecimal numerals* similarly use the prefixes d and h, although d may be omitted. The natural number represented by a numeral ν will be denoted as $\bar{\nu}$.

A circuit description includes *input declarations, combinational assignments, sequential assignments,* and *constant definitions,* which have the forms

$$\text{input } s[\nu : 0]; \tag{13.1}$$

$$s[\nu : 0] = E; \tag{13.2}$$

$$s[\nu : 0] \ \texttt{<=} \ E; \tag{13.3}$$

and

$$\text{`define } r \quad \nu \tag{13.4}$$

respectively, where ν is a numeral, s is a signal, E is an *expression of size* $\bar{\nu} + 1$ as defined below, and r may be any identifier. We may abbreviate $s[0 : 0]$ as s.

Each signal s occurring anywhere in a description must appear in exactly one of the three contexts (13.1), (13.2), and (13.3), and is called an *input*, a *wire*, or a *register*, accordingly, of *size* $\bar{\nu} + 1$. In cases (13.2) and (13.3), we shall say that E is *the expression for* s. Any signal may also occur in an *output declaration*,

$$\text{output } s[\nu : 0]; \tag{13.5}$$

and is then also called an *output*.

The effect of a constant definition (13.4) is simply that any subsequent occurrence of $'r$ is taken as an abbreviation for ν.

If s is a wire, E is the expression for s, and s' is any signal, then s *depends* on s' iff either s' occurs in E or some wire occurring in E depends on s'. It is a syntactic requirement of the language that no wire depends on itself.

Let I, O, W, R, and S denote the sets of inputs, outputs, wires, registers, and signals, respectively, of a circuit description $\mathcal{D}$. Then S is the disjoint union $I \cup W \cup R$, and $O \subset S$. A mapping from I, O, or R to $\mathbb{N}$ is called an *input valuation*, an *output valuation*, or a *register state* for $\mathcal{D}$, respectively. If R is empty, then $\mathcal{D}$ admits only the null register state and we shall say that $\mathcal{D}$ is *combinational*; otherwise, $\mathcal{D}$ is *sequential*.

Next, we define the set of *expressions* of the language corresponding to the circuit description $\mathcal{D}$. For each expression E, we also define the *size* of E, as well as the *value* of E, $val_{\mathcal{D}}(E, \mathcal{I}, \mathcal{R})$, for a given input valuation $\mathcal{I}$ and register state $\mathcal{R}$:

(1) If ν and μ are numerals such that $\bar{\nu} > 0$ and $\bar{\mu} < 2^{\bar{\nu}}$, then $\nu' \mu$ is a *constant expression* of size $\bar{\nu}$ and

$$val_{\mathcal{D}}(\nu' \mu, \mathcal{I}, \mathcal{R}) = \bar{\mu}.$$

(2) If s is a signal of size n, then s is an expression of size n, and

$$val_{\mathcal{D}}(s, \mathcal{I}, \mathcal{R}) = \begin{cases} \mathcal{I}(s) & \text{if } s \in I \\ \mathcal{R}(s) & \text{if } s \in R \\ val_{\mathcal{D}}(E, \mathcal{I}, \mathcal{R}) & \text{if } s \in W \text{ and } E \text{ is its expression.} \end{cases}$$

(3) If s is a signal and λ and μ are numerals with $\bar{\lambda} \geq \bar{\mu}$, then $s[\lambda : \mu]$ is an expression of size $\bar{\lambda} - \bar{\mu} + 1$, and

$$val_{\mathcal{D}}(s[\lambda : \mu], \mathcal{I}, \mathcal{R}) = bits(val_{\mathcal{D}}(s, \mathcal{I}, \mathcal{R}), \bar{\lambda}, \bar{\mu}).$$

We may abbreviate $s[\lambda : \lambda]$ as $s[\lambda]$.

(4) If E is an expression of size n, then $\tilde{\ }E$ is an expression of size n, and

$$val_D(\tilde{\ }E, \mathcal{I}, \mathcal{R}) = 2^n - val_D(E, \mathcal{I}, \mathcal{R}) - 1.$$

(5) If E_1 and E_2 are expressions of equal size, then $(E_1 \ {=}{=}\ E_2)$ is an expression of size 1, with

$$val_D((E_1 \ {=}{=}\ E_2), \mathcal{I}, \mathcal{R}) = \begin{cases} 1 & \text{if } val_D(E_1, \mathcal{I}, \mathcal{R}) = val_D(E_2, \mathcal{I}, \mathcal{R}) \\ 0 & \text{if } val_D(E_1, \mathcal{I}, \mathcal{R}) \neq val_D(E_2, \mathcal{I}, \mathcal{R}). \end{cases}$$

(6) If E_1 and E_2 are expressions of size n, then $(E_1 \ \& \ E_2)$, $(E_1 \ | \ E_2)$, and $(E_1 \ \hat{\ } \ E_2)$ are expressions of size n, with

$$val_D((E_1 \ \& \ E_2), \mathcal{I}, \mathcal{R}) = logand(val_D(E_1, \mathcal{I}, \mathcal{R}), val_D(E_2, \mathcal{I}, \mathcal{R}))$$

and similar definitions for the other two operators.

(7) If E_1 and E_2 are expressions of size n, then $(E_1 + E_2)$ is an expression of size n, with

$$val_D((E_1 + E_2), \mathcal{I}, \mathcal{R}) = rem(val_D(E_1, \mathcal{I}, \mathcal{R}) + val_D(E_2, \mathcal{I}, \mathcal{R}), 2^n).$$

Multiplication is defined similarly.

(8) If E_1 and E_2 are any expressions of sizes of n_1 and n_2, respectively, then $\{E_1, E_2\}$ is an expression of size $n_1 + n_2$, with

$$val_D(\{E_1, E_2\}, \mathcal{I}, \mathcal{R}) = 2^{n_2} val_D(E_1, \mathcal{I}, \mathcal{R}) + val_D(E_2, \mathcal{I}, \mathcal{R}).$$

For $k > 2$, $\{E_1, \ldots, E_k\}$ is an abbreviation for $\{E_1, \{E_2, \ldots, E_k\}\}$ If $E_1 = \cdots = E_k$ and ν is a numeral with $\bar{\nu} = k$, then we may further abbreviate $\{E_1, \ldots, E_k\}$ as $\{\nu \ \{E_1\}\}$.

(9) If B is an expression of size 1 and E_1 and E_2 are expressions of size n, then $(B \ ? \ E_1 \ : \ E_2)$ is an expression of size n, and

$$val_D((B \ ? \ E_1 \ : \ E_2), \mathcal{I}, \mathcal{R}) = \begin{cases} val_D(E_1, \mathcal{I}, \mathcal{R}) & \text{if } val_D(B, \mathcal{I}, \mathcal{R}) \neq 0 \\ val_D(E_2, \mathcal{I}, \mathcal{R}) & \text{if } val_D(B, \mathcal{I}, \mathcal{R}) = 0. \end{cases}$$

(10) If $D, E_1, \ldots, E_k$ are expressions of size n and $F_1, \ldots, F_k$ are expressions of size m, then

$$F = \mathbf{case}(D) \ E_1 : \ F_1; \quad \ldots \quad E_k : \ F_k; \ \mathbf{endcase}$$

is an expression of size m, and

$$val_D(F, \mathcal{I}, \mathcal{R}) = \begin{cases} val_D(F_1, \mathcal{I}, \mathcal{R}) & \text{if } val_D(D \ {=}{=}\ E_1, \mathcal{I}, \mathcal{R}) = 1 \\ 0 & \text{if } val_D(D \ {=}{=}\ E_1, \mathcal{I}, \mathcal{R}) = 0, \ k = 1 \\ val_D(F', \mathcal{I}, \mathcal{R}) & \text{if } val_D(D \ {=}{=}\ E_1, \mathcal{I}, \mathcal{R}) = 0, \ k > 1, \end{cases}$$

where

$$F' = \mathbf{case}(D) \ E_2 : F_2; \quad \ldots \quad E_k : F_k; \ \mathbf{endcase}$$

The semantics of circuit descriptions are based on an underlying notion of *cycle*. Let $\mathcal{I}_1, \mathcal{I}_2, \ldots$ be a sequence of input valuations and let $\mathcal{R}_1$ be a register state for $\mathcal{D}$. We shall think of each $\mathcal{I}_k$ as representing the values of the input signals of $\mathcal{D}$ on the kth cycle of an execution, and $\mathcal{R}_1$ as an initial set of register values. From these functions we shall construct a sequence of output valuations, $\mathcal{O}_1, \mathcal{O}_2, \ldots$, representing the output values produced by $\mathcal{D}$ on successive cycles.

First, we define a function $next_{\mathcal{D}}$, which represents the dependence of the register state for a given cycle on the input valuation and register state for the preceding cycle. Given an input valuation $\mathcal{I}$ and a register state $\mathcal{R}$, the register state $next_{\mathcal{D}}(\mathcal{I}, \mathcal{R}) = \mathcal{R}'$ is defined as follows: if $s \in R$ and E is the expression for s, then

$$\mathcal{R}'(s) = val_{\mathcal{D}}(E, \mathcal{I}, \mathcal{R}).$$

Now, for each $k \geq 2$, let $\mathcal{R}_k = next_{\mathcal{D}}(\mathcal{I}_{k-1}, \mathcal{R}_{k-1})$. The output valuations $\mathcal{O}_1, \mathcal{O}_2, \ldots$ are computed as follows: for each output signal s,

$$\mathcal{O}_k(s) = val_{\mathcal{D}}(s, \mathcal{I}_k, \mathcal{R}_k).$$

13.2.2   Simple Pipelines

If $\mathcal{D}$ is combinational, then we may write $val_{\mathcal{D}}(s, \mathcal{I})$ unambiguously, omitting the third argument, and consequently, the output valuation $\mathcal{O}_k$, as defined above, is completely determined by $\mathcal{I}_k$. Thus, the external behavior of a combinational circuit may be described by a functional dependence of outputs on inputs. The same is true of a certain class of sequential circuits, which we describe below. For any circuit in this class, there is a number n such that for each $k \geq n$, the output valuation $\mathcal{O}_k$ is completely determined by the input valuation $\mathcal{I}_{k-n+1}$.

We shall say that a circuit description $\mathcal{D}$ is an *n-cycle simple pipeline* if there exists a function $\psi : S \rightarrow \{1, \ldots, n\}$ such that

(1) if $s \in I$, then $\psi(s) = 1$;

(2) if $s \in W$ and E is the expression for s, then $\psi(s') = \psi(s)$ for each signal s' occurring in E;

(3) if $s \in R$ and E is the expression for s, then $\psi(s) > 1$ and $\psi(s') = \psi(s) - 1$ for each signal s' occurring in E;

(4) if $s \in O$, then $\psi(s) = n$.

Note that a 1-cycle simple pipeline is just a combinational circuit.

The main consequences of this definition are given by Lemmas 13.2.1 and 13.2.2 below. The proofs of these lemmas use an induction scheme based on a well-founded partial ordering of the set of expressions of $\mathcal{D}$, defined as follows: For any expression E, let $\Psi(E)$ be the maximum, over all signals s occurring in E, of $\psi(s)$, and let $\Lambda(E)$ be the maximum, over all signals s occurring in E, of the number of signals on which s depends. Then for any two expressions E_1 and E_2, E_1 precedes E_2 iff

(a) $\Psi(E_1) < \Psi(E_2)$, or

(b) $\Psi(E_1) = \Psi(E_2)$ and $\Lambda(E_1) < \Lambda(E_2)$, or

(c) $\Psi(E_1) = \Psi(E_2)$, $\Lambda(E_1) = \Lambda(E_2)$, and E_1 is a subexpression of E_2.

According to our first lemma, every n-cycle simple pipeline has the property that the values of the inputs on any cycle determine the values of the outputs $n - 1$ cycles later:

Lemma 13.2.1 *Let $\mathcal{I}_1, \ldots, \mathcal{I}_n, \mathcal{I}'_1, \ldots, \mathcal{I}'_n$ be input valuations and let $\mathcal{R}_1$ and $\mathcal{R}'_1$ be register states for an n-cycle simple pipeline $\mathcal{D}$. For $k = 2, \ldots, n$, let $\mathcal{R}_k = next_\mathcal{D}(\mathcal{I}_{k-1}, \mathcal{R}_{k-1})$ and $\mathcal{R}'_k = next_\mathcal{D}(\mathcal{I}'_{k-1}, \mathcal{R}'_{k-1})$. If $\mathcal{I}_1 = \mathcal{I}'_1$, then for every output s of $\mathcal{D}$,*

$$val_\mathcal{D}(s, \mathcal{I}_n, \mathcal{R}_n) = val_\mathcal{D}(s, \mathcal{I}'_n, \mathcal{R}'_n).$$

Proof: We shall show that for all k, $1 \leq k \leq n$, if E is any expression of $\mathcal{D}$ such that $\psi(s) = k$ for every signal s occurring in E, then $val_\mathcal{D}(E, \mathcal{I}_k, \mathcal{R}_k) = val_\mathcal{D}(E, \mathcal{I}'_k, \mathcal{R}'_k)$. The proof is by induction, based on the partial ordering of expressions defined above. Assume that the claim holds for all expressions that precede a given expression E. To show that the claim holds for E as well, we shall examine the only nontrivial case: E is a signal s.

If s is an input, then $k = 1$ and

$$val_\mathcal{D}(s, \mathcal{I}_1, \mathcal{R}_1) = \mathcal{I}_1(s) = \mathcal{I}'_1(s) = val_\mathcal{D}(s, \mathcal{I}'_1, \mathcal{R}'_1).$$

Thus, we may assume that s is a wire or a register. Let F be the expression for s.

Suppose s is a wire. Then $\psi(r) = k$ for each signal r occurring in F. Therefore, $\Psi(s) = k = \Psi(F)$ and $\Lambda(s) \geq \Lambda(F) + 1$, hence F precedes s and by our inductive hypothesis,

$$val_\mathcal{D}(s, \mathcal{I}_k, \mathcal{R}_k) = val_\mathcal{D}(F, \mathcal{I}_k, \mathcal{R}_k) = val_\mathcal{D}(F, \mathcal{I}'_k, \mathcal{R}'_k) = val_\mathcal{D}(s, \mathcal{I}'_k, \mathcal{R}'_k).$$

Finally, suppose s is a register. Then $k > 1$ and $\psi(r) = k - 1$ for each signal r occurring in F. Thus, $\Psi(F) = k - 1 < k = \Psi(s)$, so F precedes

s, and we may conclude that $val_{\mathcal{D}}(F, \mathcal{I}_{k-1}, \mathcal{R}_{k-1}) = val_{\mathcal{D}}(F, \mathcal{I}'_{k-1}, \mathcal{R}'_{k-1})$. But since $\mathcal{R}_k = next_{\mathcal{D}}(\mathcal{I}_{k-1}, \mathcal{R}_{k-1})$,

$$val_{\mathcal{D}}(s, \mathcal{I}_k, \mathcal{R}_k) = \mathcal{R}_k(s) = val_{\mathcal{D}}(F, \mathcal{I}_{k-1}, \mathcal{R}_{k-1}),$$

and similarly,

$$val_{\mathcal{D}}(s, \mathcal{I}'_k, \mathcal{R}'_k) = \mathcal{R}'_k(s) = val_{\mathcal{D}}(F, \mathcal{I}'_{k-1}, \mathcal{R}'_{k-1}). \quad \square$$

Now let $\mathcal{D}, \mathcal{I}_1, \ldots, \mathcal{I}_n$, and $\mathcal{R}_1, \ldots, \mathcal{R}_n$ be as described in Lemma 13.2.1. Let $\mathcal{O} : O \to \mathbb{N}$ be defined by $\mathcal{O}(s) = val_{\mathcal{D}}(s, \mathcal{I}_n, \mathcal{R}_n)$. Then according to the lemma, $\mathcal{O}$ is determined by $\mathcal{I} = \mathcal{I}_1$ alone, and we may define $out_{\mathcal{D}}(\mathcal{I}) = \mathcal{O}$. Thus, for an n-cycle simple pipeline, there is a natural mapping from input valuations to output valuations.

If we are interested only in the mapping $out_{\mathcal{D}}$, then any n-cycle simple pipeline may be replaced with a combinational circuit:

Lemma 13.2.2 *Let $\mathcal{D}$ be an n-cycle simple pipeline, and let $\tilde{\mathcal{D}}$ be the circuit description obtained from $\mathcal{D}$ by replacing each sequential assignment (13.3) by the corresponding combinational assignment (13.2). Then $\tilde{\mathcal{D}}$ is a combinational circuit description and $out_{\mathcal{D}} = out_{\tilde{\mathcal{D}}}$.*

Proof: To prove that $\tilde{\mathcal{D}}$ is a combinational circuit description, it will suffice to show that $\tilde{\mathcal{D}}$ is a well-formed circuit description. If not, then there must be signals $s_1, \ldots, s_k$ such that $s_1 = s_k$ and for $i = 1, \ldots, k-1$, s_i occurs in the expression for s_{i+1}. But since $\psi(s_1) \leq \cdots \leq \psi(s_k) = \psi(s_1)$, we would then have $\psi(s_1) = \cdots = \psi(s_k)$, which would imply that each s_i is a wire of $\mathcal{D}$, contradicting the assumption that $\mathcal{D}$ is well-formed.

Now, given an input valuation $\mathcal{I}$ for $\mathcal{D}$ (and thus for $\tilde{\mathcal{D}}$), let $\mathcal{O} = out_{\mathcal{D}}(\mathcal{I})$ and $\tilde{\mathcal{O}} = out_{\tilde{\mathcal{D}}}(\mathcal{I})$. We must show that $\mathcal{O}(s) = \tilde{\mathcal{O}}(s)$ for every output signal s. Let $\mathcal{I}_1, \ldots, \mathcal{I}_n$ be input valuations for $\mathcal{D}$, where $\mathcal{I}_1 = \mathcal{I}$, and let $\mathcal{R}_1, \ldots, \mathcal{R}_n$ be register states such that $\mathcal{R}_{k+1} = next_{\mathcal{D}}(\mathcal{I}_k, \mathcal{R}_k)$ for $k = 1, \ldots, n-1$. Then $\mathcal{O}(s) = val_{\mathcal{D}}(s, \mathcal{I}_n, \mathcal{R}_n)$. On the other hand, since $\tilde{\mathcal{D}}$ is combinational, $\tilde{\mathcal{O}}(s) = val_{\tilde{\mathcal{D}}}(s, \mathcal{I}_1)$. Thus, we may complete the proof by showing that if E is any expression such that $\psi(s) = k$ for every signal s occurring in E, then $val_{\mathcal{D}}(E, \mathcal{I}_k, \mathcal{R}_k) = val_{\tilde{\mathcal{D}}}(E, \mathcal{I}_1)$.

Using the same induction scheme as in Lemma 13.2.1, we again note that in the only nontrivial case, E is a signal s. If s is an input, then $k = 1$ and

$$val_{\mathcal{D}}(s, \mathcal{I}_1, \mathcal{R}_1) = \mathcal{I}_1(s) = val_{\tilde{\mathcal{D}}}(s, \mathcal{I}_1).$$

If s is a wire of $\mathcal{D}$, and hence of $\tilde{\mathcal{D}}$, and F is the expression for s, then

$$val_{\mathcal{D}}(s, \mathcal{I}_k, \mathcal{R}_k) = val_{\mathcal{D}}(F, \mathcal{I}_k, \mathcal{R}_k) = val_{\tilde{\mathcal{D}}}(F, \mathcal{I}_1) = val_{\tilde{\mathcal{D}}}(s, \mathcal{I}_1).$$

In the remaining case, s is a register of $\mathcal{D}$ and a wire of $\tilde{\mathcal{D}}$. If F is the expression for s (in both contexts), then

$$
\begin{aligned}
val_{\mathcal{D}}(s, \mathcal{I}_k, \mathcal{R}_k) &= \mathcal{R}_k(s) = val_{\mathcal{D}}(F, \mathcal{I}_{k-1}, \mathcal{R}_{k-1}) \\
&= val_{\tilde{\mathcal{D}}}(F, \mathcal{I}_1) = val_{\tilde{\mathcal{D}}}(s, \mathcal{I}_1). \ \square
\end{aligned}
$$

13.2.3 Translation to ACL2

One of the functions of the RTL-ACL2 translator is to analyze the dependencies among the signals of a circuit description to determine whether it satisfies the definition of a simple pipeline. Once this is established, an ACL2 function is constructed from each wire and register definition, ignoring the distinction between the two, in accordance with Lemma 13.2.2. This function computes the value of the signal for a given input valuation in terms of the values of the signals that occur in its defining expression. Thus, each RTL construct in the expression for the signal is replaced with the corresponding ACL2 construct, as determined by the definition of evaluation given in Section 13.2.1.

For example, the combinational assignment

```
sig_of[128:0] = {1'b0, carry_of, 127'b0} |
                (add_of[128:0] & {1'b0, mask_of[127:0]});
```

of the circuit FMUL (Fig. 13.2.3) generates the definition

```
(defun sig_of (carry_of add_of mask_of)
  (logior (cat carry_of 0 127)
          (logand add_of mask_of)))
```

while the sequential assignment

```
sticky_of <= case(pc_C3)
             'SNG : ~(prod[102:0] == 103'b0);
             'DBL : ~(prod[73:0] == 74'b0);
             endcase;
```

(Fig. 13.2.3) produces the following.

```
(defun sticky_of (pc_c3 prod)
  (cond ((equal pc_c3 0)
         (if (equal (bits prod 102 0) 0) 0 1))
        ((equal pc_c3 1)
         (if (equal (bits prod 73 0) 0) 0 1))))
```

Finally, an additional function is defined for each output signal, which binds each non-input signal in succession to its value for a given set of input values, and returns the value of the output. For the circuit FMUL, which has only one output, z, a single function is generated as follows.

```
(defun fmul (x y rc pc)
  (let* ((sgnx (sgnx x))
         (sgny (sgny y))
         (expx (expx x))
         (expy (expy y))
         (sigx (sigx x))
         (sigy (sigy y))
         (sgnz (sgnz sgnx sgny))
         (exp_sum (exp_sum expx expy))
         ...
         (carry_nof (carry_nof add_nof))
         (sig_of (sig_of carry_of add_of mask_of))
         (sig_nof (sig_nof carry_nof add_nof mask_nof))
         (sigz (sigz overflow sig_of sig_nof))
         (exp_of (exp_of exp_sum_c4 carry_of))
         (exp_nof (exp_nof exp_sum_c4 carry_nof))
         (expz (expz overflow exp_of exp_nof))
         (z (z sgnz_c4 expz sigz)))
    z))
```

It is evident that this function accurately represents the dependence of the output z on the inputs, *i.e.*, if the bindings of x, y, rc, and pc are given by an input valuation $\mathcal{I}$, then the value computed by fmul is $out_{\text{FMUL}}(\mathcal{I})(z)$.

13.3   Correctness of the Multiplier

Let $\mathcal{I}$ be a fixed input valuation for FMUL. We shall adopt the convention of italicizing each signal to denote its value for $\mathcal{I}$, *e.g.*,

$$val_{\text{FMUL}}(\text{sigz}, \mathcal{I}) = sigz$$

and since rc is an input,

$$val_{\text{FMUL}}(\text{rc}, \mathcal{I}) = \mathcal{I}(\text{rc}) = rc.$$

Note that FMUL has four inputs: x and y are $\mathcal{E}$-encodings of the numbers to be multiplied, rc is a 2-bit encoding of the mode to be used in rounding the result, and pc is a 1-bit encoding of the desired degree of precision, corresponding to either single (24-bit) or double (53-bit) precision.

We would like to show that the circuit meets the main requirement for IEEE compliance, as stipulated in the floating-point standard [54]:

> [Multiplication] shall be performed as if it first produced an intermediate result correct to infinite precision and with unbounded range, and then rounded that result ...

```
module FMUL;

//**********************************************************************
// Declarations
//**********************************************************************

//Precision and rounding control:

'define SNG   1'b0        // single precision
'define DBL   1'b1        // double precision
'define NRE   2'b00       // round to nearest
'define NEG   2'b01       // round to minus infinity
'define POS   2'b10       // round to plus infinity
'define CHP   2'b11       // truncate

//Parameters:

input x[79:0];            //first operand
input y[79:0];            //second operand
input rc[1:0];            //rounding control
input pc;                 //precision control
output z[79:0];           //rounded product


//**********************************************************************
// First Cycle
//**********************************************************************

//Operand fields:

sgnx = x[79]; sgny = y[79];                    //signs
expx[14:0] = x[78:64]; expy[14:0] = y[78:64];  //exponents
sigx[63:0] <= x[63:0]; sigy[63:0] <= y[63:0];  //significands

//Sign of result:

sgnz <= sgnx ^ sgny;

//Biased exponent sum:

exp_sum[14:0] <= expx[14:0] + expy[14:0] + 15'h4001;

//Registers:

rc_C2[1:0] <= rc[1:0];
pc_C2 <= pc;
```

Figure 13.1: Module FMUL

```
//**********************************************************************
// Second Cycle
//**********************************************************************

//Rounding Constants//

//Overflow case -- single precision:

rconst_sing_of[127:0] =
  case(rc_C2[1:0])
    'NRE : {25'b1, 103'b0};
    'NEG : sgnz ? {24'b0, {104 {1'b1}}} : 128'b0;
    'POS : sgnz ? 128'b0 : {24'b0, {104 {1'b1}}};
    'CHP : 128'b0;
  endcase;

//Overflow case -- double precision:

rconst_doub_of[127:0] =
  case(rc_C2[1:0])
    'NRE : {54'b1, 74'b0};
    'NEG : sgnz ? {53'b0, {75 {1'b1}}} : 128'b0;
    'POS : sgnz ? 128'b0 : {53'b0, {75 {1'b1}}};
    'CHP : 128'b0;
  endcase;

//General overflow case:

rconst_of[127:0] <= case(pc_C2)
                      'SNG : rconst_sing_of[127:0];
                      'DBL : rconst_doub_of[127:0];
                    endcase;

//No overflow:

rconst_nof[126:0] = rconst_of[127:1];

//Registers:

sgnz_C3 <= sgnz;
exp_sum_C3[14:0] <= exp_sum[14:0];
sigx_C3[63:0] <= sigx[63:0];
sigy_C3[63:0] <= sigy[63:0];
rc_C3[1:0] <= rc_C2[1:0];
pc_C3 <= pc_C2;
```

Figure 13.2: Module FMUL (continued)

```
//**********************************************************************
// Third Cycle
//**********************************************************************

//The output of an integer multiplier actually consists of two vectors,
//the sum of which is the product of the inputs sigx and sigy.  These
//vectors become available in the third cycle, when they are processed
//in parallel by three distinct adders.  The first of these produces
//the unrounded product, which is used only to test for overflow.
//The other two include rounding constants, assuming overflow and no
//overflow, respectively.  Thus, at the (hypothetical) implementation
//level, these three sums are actually generated in parallel:

prod[127:0] = {64'b0, sigx_C3[63:0]} * {64'b0, sigy_C3[63:0]};

add_of[128:0] <= {1'b0, prod[127:0]} + {1'b0, rconst_of[127:0]};

add_nof[127:0] <= prod[127:0] + {1'b0, rconst_nof[126:0]};


//overflow indicator:

overflow <= prod[127];


//Sticky bit:

sticky_of <= case(pc_C3)
                'SNG : ~(prod[102:0] == 103'b0);
                'DBL : ~(prod[73:0] == 74'b0);
              endcase;

sticky_nof <= case(pc_C3)
                'SNG : ~(prod[101:0] == 102'b0);
                'DBL : ~(prod[72:0] == 73'b0);
              endcase;

//Registers:

rc_C4[1:0] <= rc_C3[1:0];
pc_C4 <= pc_C3;
sgnz_C4 <= sgnz_C3;
exp_sum_C4[14:0] <= exp_sum_C3[14:0];
```

Figure 13.3: Module FMUL (continued)

```
//********************************************************************
// Fourth Cycle
//********************************************************************

//Significand mask:

mask_of[127:0] =
  case (pc_C4)
    'SNG : (rc_C4[1:0] == 'NRE) & ~sticky_of & ~add_of[103] ?
                {{23 {1'b1}}, 105'b0} : {{24 {1'b1}}, 104'b0};
    'DBL : (rc_C4[1:0] == 'NRE) & ~sticky_of & ~add_of[74] ?
                {{52 {1'b1}}, 76'b0} : {{53 {1'b1}}, 75'b0};
  endcase;

mask_nof[126:0] =
  case (pc_C4)
    'SNG : (rc_C4[1:0] == 'NRE) & ~sticky_nof & ~add_nof[102] ?
                {{23 {1'b1}}, 104'b0} : {{24 {1'b1}}, 103'b0};
    'DBL : (rc_C4[1:0] == 'NRE) & ~sticky_nof & ~add_nof[73] ?
                {{52 {1'b1}}, 75'b0} : {{53 {1'b1}}, 74'b0};
  endcase;

//Carry bit:

carry_of = add_of[128];
carry_nof = add_nof[127];

//Significand and exponent:

sig_of[128:0] = {1'b0, carry_of, 127'b0} |
                (add_of[128:0] & {1'b0, mask_of[127:0]});
sig_nof[127:0] = {1'b0, carry_nof, 126'b0} |
                 (add_nof[127:0] & {1'b0, mask_nof[126:0]});
sigz[63:0] = overflow ? sig_of[127:64] : sig_nof[126:63];

exp_of[14:0] = exp_sum_C4[14:0] + {14'b0, carry_of} + 15'b1;
exp_nof[14:0] = exp_sum_C4[14:0] + {14'b0, carry_nof};
expz[14:0] = overflow ? exp_of[14:0] : exp_nof[14:0];

//Final result:

z[79:0] = {sgnz_C4, expz[14:0], sigz[63:0]};

endmodule
```

Figure 13.4: Module FMUL (continued)

Thus, the output z must satisfy the following:

Theorem 13.1 (correctness-of-fmul) *Assume that x and y are normal $\mathcal{E}$-encodings, $rc \in \{0, 1, 2, 3\}$, and $pc \in \{0, 1\}$. Let*

$$\mathcal{M} = \begin{cases} near, & \text{if } rc = 0 \\ minf, & \text{if } rc = 1 \\ inf, & \text{if } rc = 2 \\ trunc, & \text{if } rc = 3, \end{cases}$$

$$\mu = \begin{cases} 24 & \text{if } pc = 0 \\ 53 & \text{if } pc = 1, \end{cases}$$

and $\mathcal{A} = rnd(\hat{x}\hat{y}, \mathcal{M}, \mu)$. If $\mathcal{A}$ is representable, then z is a normal encoding and $\hat{z} = \mathcal{A}$.

The ACL2 formalization is straightforward.

```
(defun mode (rc)
  (case rc (0 'near) (1 'minf) (2 'inf) (3 'trunc)))
(defun precision (pc) (case pc (0 24) (1 53)))
(defthm correctness-of-fmul
    (let ((ideal (rnd (* (hat x) (hat y))
                      (mode rc)
                      (precision pc)))
          (z (fmul x y rc pc)))
      (implies (and (normal-encoding-p x (extfmt))
                    (normal-encoding-p y (extfmt))
                    (member rc (list 0 1 2 3))
                    (member pc (list 0 1))
                    (repp ideal (extfmt)))
               (and (normal-encoding-p z (extfmt))
                    (= (hat z) ideal))))
  :hints ...)
```

In the next subsection, we sketch an informal proof of Theorem 13.1, illustrating the application of the library of Section 13.1. Once again, each lemma listed below includes the name of a corresponding ACL2 `defthm` event, which may be found in [67]. Finally, in Section 13.3.2, we clarify the nature of this correspondence and describe the methodology that we have developed to derive the formal theorem `correctness-of-fmul` from the informal proof.

13.3.1   Informal Proof

For convenience, we introduce several auxiliary variables. First, we define

$$sticky = \begin{cases} sticky\_of & \text{if } overflow = 1 \\ sticky\_nof & \text{if } overflow = 0. \end{cases}$$

Each of the variables *rconst*, *add*, *carry*, *mask*, and *sig* is defined in the analogous manner. We also define

$$P = \begin{cases} 128 & \text{if } overflow = 1 \\ 127 & \text{if } overflow = 0, \end{cases}$$

$$\rho = rem(sig, 2^P),$$

and

$$\mathcal{M}' = \begin{cases} minf, & \text{if } \mathcal{M} = inf \text{ and } sgnz = 1 \\ inf, & \text{if } \mathcal{M} = minf \text{ and } sgnz = 1 \\ \mathcal{M}, & \text{otherwise.} \end{cases}$$

Our first four lemmas may be derived by case analysis as immediate consequences of these definitions:

Lemma 13.3.1 (carry-rewrite) $carry = add[P]$.

Lemma 13.3.2 (sig-rewrite) $sig = (2^{P-1} carry) \mid (add \ \& \ mask)$.

Lemma 13.3.3 (mask-rewrite)

$$mask = \begin{cases} 2^P - 2^{P-\mu+1} & \text{if } \mathcal{M} = near, \ sticky = add[P - \mu - 1] = 0 \\ 2^P - 2^{P-\mu} & \text{otherwise.} \end{cases}$$

Lemma 13.3.4 (rconst-rewrite)

$$rconst = \begin{cases} 2^{P-\mu-1} & \text{if } \mathcal{M}' = near \\ 2^{P-\mu} - 1 & \text{if } \mathcal{M}' = inf \\ 0 & \text{otherwise.} \end{cases}$$

Lemma 13.3.5 (expo-prod) $expo(prod) = P - 1$.

Proof: Since x and y are normal encodings,

$$2^{126} \leq prod = sigx \cdot sigy < 2^{128},$$

and the lemma follows from Lemmas 13.1.2 and 13.1.3. $\square$

Lemma 13.3.6 (sig-prod) $sig(prod) = sig(\hat{x})sig(\hat{y})/2^{overflow}$.

Proof: By Lemma 13.3.5,

$$\begin{aligned} prod &= 2^{63} sig(\hat{x}) 2^{63} sig(\hat{y}) \\ &= sig(\hat{x}) sig(\hat{y}) 2^{-overflow} 2^{126+overflow} \\ &= sig(\hat{x}) sig(\hat{y}) 2^{-overflow} 2^{expo(prod)}. \end{aligned}$$

The claim now follows from Lemma 13.1.15. $\square$

Lemma 13.3.7 (expo-xy) $expo(\hat{x}\hat{y}) = expo(\hat{x}) + expo(\hat{y}) + overflow$.

Proof: By Lemmas 13.1.15 and 13.3.6,

$$\begin{aligned} \hat{x}\hat{y} &= sgn(\hat{x}) sig(\hat{x}) 2^{expo(\hat{x})} sgn(\hat{y}) sig(\hat{y}) 2^{expo(\hat{y})} \\ &= sgn(\hat{x}\hat{y}) \left[sig(\hat{x}) sig(\hat{y}) / 2^{overflow} \right] 2^{expo(\hat{x})+expo(\hat{y})+overflow} \\ &= sgn(\hat{x}\hat{y}) sig(prod) 2^{expo(\hat{x})+expo(\hat{y})+overflow}. \end{aligned}$$

The result now follows from Lemma 13.1.18. $\square$

Lemma 13.3.8 (sig-xy) $sig(\hat{x}\hat{y}) = sig(prod)$.

Proof: This is another consequence of the proof of Lemma 13.3.7. $\square$

Lemma 13.3.9 (sticky-exact) $sticky = 0$ iff prod is $(\mu + 1)$-exact.

Proof: It is clear that in all cases, $sticky = 0$ iff $2^{P-(\mu+1)}$ divides prod, and the lemma follows from Lemmas 13.1.20 and 13.3.5. $\square$

Lemma 13.3.10 (add-rewrite) $add = prod + rconst$.

Proof: By Lemmas 13.3.4 and 13.3.5, $0 \le prod + rconst < 2^P + 2^P = 2^{P+1}$, hence by the definition of add,

$$add = rem(prod + rconst, 2^{P+1}) = prod + rconst. \square$$

Lemma 13.3.11 (sig-bit) $sig[P-1] = 1$.

Proof: By Lemmas 13.1.9 and 13.3.2, we may assume $carry = 0$ and hence by Lemmas 13.3.2, 13.3.3, 13.3.6, and 13.1.8,

$$\begin{aligned} sig[P-1] &= (add \ \& \ mask)[P-1] = add[P-1] \ \& \ mask[P-1] \\ &= add[P-1]. \end{aligned}$$

But then since

$$2^{P-1} \le prod \le prod + rconst = add < 2^{P+1}$$

and $carry = add[P] = 0$, Lemma 13.1.3 implies $add < 2^P$ and hence, by the same lemma, $add[P-1] = 1$. $\square$

Lemma 13.3.12 (sig-add-expo) $expo(sig) \leq expo(add) = P - 1 + carry$.

Proof: If $carry = 0$, then

$$sig = add \ \& \ mask \leq add < 2^P,$$

by Lemma 13.1.10, and Lemma 13.3.11 implies $sig \geq 2^{P-1}$, hence

$$expo(sig) = expo(add) = P - 1.$$

On the other hand, if $carry = add[P] = 1$, then $expo(add) = P$, while $sig < 2^{P+1}$ by Lemma 13.1.13, hence $expo(sig) \leq P$. $\square$

Lemma 13.3.13 (rem-sig) sig is divisible by 2^{P-64}.

Proof: Since $mask$ is divisible by 2^{P-64}, the result follows from Lemmas 13.1.11 and 13.1.14. $\square$

Lemma 13.3.14 (sgnf-z) $sgnf(z, \mathcal{E}) = sgnz$.

Proof: Note that

$$z = 2^{79} sgnz + 2^{64} expz + sigz,$$

where $0 \leq sgnz < 2$, $0 \leq expz < 2^{15}$, and $0 \leq sigz < 2^{64}$. Thus,

$$sgnf(z, \mathcal{E}) = z[79] = rem(\lfloor z/2^{79} \rfloor, 2) = rem(sgnz, 2) = sgnz. \square$$

Lemma 13.3.15 (expf-z) $expf(z, \mathcal{E}) = expz$.

Proof: As in the proof of Lemma 13.3.14,

$$\begin{aligned} expf(z, \mathcal{E}) &= z[78:64] = \lfloor rem(z, 2^{79})/2^{64} \rfloor = \lfloor expz + sigz/2^{64} \rfloor \\ &= expz. \square \end{aligned}$$

Lemma 13.3.16 (sigf-z) $sigf(z, \mathcal{E}) = sigz$.

Proof: As in the proof of Lemma 13.3.14,

$$sigf(z, \mathcal{E}) = z[63:0] = rem(z, 2^{64}) = sigz. \square$$

Lemma 13.3.17 (z-normal) z is a normal encoding.

Proof: It is clear that $z \in \mathbb{N}$ and

$$sigf(z, \mathcal{E}) = sigz = sig[P - 1 : P - 64].$$

Thus, by Lemmas 13.1.6 and 13.3.11, $sigz[63] = sig[P-1] = 1$, and hence $sigz \geq 2^{63}$. $\square$

Lemma 13.3.18 (sgn-z) $sgn(\hat{z}) = sgn(\hat{x}\hat{y})$.

Proof: By Lemma 13.3.14, $sgn(\hat{z}) = (-1)^{sgnz}$. Thus, $sgn(\hat{z}) = 1 \Leftrightarrow sgnz = 0 \Leftrightarrow sgnz = sgnz \Leftrightarrow sgn(\hat{x}) = sgn(\hat{y}) \Leftrightarrow sgn(\hat{x}\hat{y}) = 1$. $\square$

Lemma 13.3.19 (sig-z) $sig(\hat{z}) = \rho/2^{P-1}$.

Proof: Since sig is divisible by 2^{P-64}, so is $\rho = rem(sig, 2^P)$. Thus,

$$sigz = sig[P-1:P-64] = \lfloor \rho/2^{P-64} \rfloor = \rho/2^{P-64}$$

and $sig(\hat{z}) = sigz/2^{63} = \rho/2^{P-1}$. $\square$

Lemma 13.3.20 (expo-z) $expo(\hat{z}) = expo(\hat{x}\hat{y}) + carry + 2^{15}k$, *for some* $k \in \mathbb{Z}$.

Proof: We have

$$expx = expf(x, \mathcal{E}) = expo(\hat{x}) + 2^{14} - 1,$$

$$expy = expf(y, \mathcal{E}) = expo(\hat{y}) + 2^{14} - 1,$$

and by Lemma 13.3.7,

$$
\begin{aligned}
expz &= rem(exp\_sum + carry + overflow, 2^{15}) \\
&= rem(expx + expy + 2^{14} + 1 + carry + overflow, 2^{15}) \\
&= rem(expo(\hat{x}) + expo(\hat{y}) + overflow + 2^{14} - 1 + carry, 2^{15}) \\
&= rem(expo(\hat{x}\hat{y}) + 2^{14} - 1 + carry, 2^{15}).
\end{aligned}
$$

Hence, for some $k \in \mathbb{Z}$,

$$expf(z, \mathcal{E}) = expz = expo(\hat{x}\hat{y}) + 2^{14} - 1 + carry + 2^{15}k.$$

But then

$$expo(\hat{z}) = expf(z, \mathcal{E}) - (2^{14} - 1) = expo(\hat{x}\hat{y}) + carry + 2^{15}k. \square$$

Lemma 13.3.21 (rho-rewrite) $\rho = rnd(prod, \mathcal{M}', \mu)2^{-carry}$.

Proof: We consider the following cases:

Case 1: carry = 0
Since $sig < 2^P$ by Lemma 13.3.12, we must show

$$sig = rnd(prod, \mathcal{M}', \mu).$$

Subcase 1.1: $\mathcal{M}' = near$

First suppose $sticky = add[P - \mu - 1] = 0$. Then Lemmas 13.1.4, 13.3.4, and 13.3.10 imply

$$prod[P - \mu - 1] = 1,$$

and by Lemmas 13.3.9, 13.1.20, and 13.1.5, $prod$ is $(\mu + 1)$-exact but not μ-exact. Thus, by Lemmas 13.1.24, 13.1.26, 13.3.2, 13.3.3, 13.3.5, 13.3.10, and 13.3.12,

$$
\begin{aligned}
sig &= (prod + 2^{P-\mu-1}) \,\&\, (2^P - 2^{P-\mu+1}) \\
&= trunc(prod + 2^{P-\mu-1}, \mu - 1) \\
&= near(prod, \mu) \\
&= rnd(prod, \mathcal{M}', \mu).
\end{aligned}
$$

In the remaining case, $prod$ is either μ-exact or not $(\mu + 1)$-exact, and the same lemmas yield

$$
\begin{aligned}
sig &= (prod + 2^{P-\mu-1}) \,\&\, (2^P - 2^{P-\mu}) \\
&= trunc(prod + 2^{P-\mu-1}, \mu) \\
&= near(prod, \mu) \\
&= rnd(prod, \mathcal{M}', \mu).
\end{aligned}
$$

Subcase 1.2: $\mathcal{M}' = inf$
By Lemmas 13.1.24 and 13.1.25,

$$
\begin{aligned}
sig &= (prod + 2^{P-\mu} - 1) \,\&\, (2^P - 2^{P-\mu}) \\
&= trunc(prod + 2^{P-\mu} - 1, \mu) \\
&= away(prod, \mu) \\
&= rnd(prod, \mathcal{M}', \mu).
\end{aligned}
$$

Subcase 1.3: $\mathcal{M}' = trunc$ or $\mathcal{M}' = minf$
Lemma 13.1.24 yields

$$
\begin{aligned}
sig &= prod \,\&\, (2^P - 2^{P-\mu}) \\
&= trunc(prod, \mu) \\
&= rnd(prod, \mathcal{M}', \mu).
\end{aligned}
$$

Case 2: carry = 1
In this case, by Lemmas 13.3.1 and 13.3.12,

$$2^P \leq add = prod + rconst < 2^P + rconst,$$

which, with Lemma 13.3.4, implies

$$0 \leq rem(add, 2^P) < rconst < 2^{P-\mu}.$$

Applying Lemmas 13.1.14, 13.1.11, and 13.1.12, we have

$$
\begin{aligned}
rem(sig, 2^P) &= rem(2^{P-1} \mid (add \ \& \ mask), 2^P) \\
&= 2^{P-1} \mid (rem(add, 2^P) \ \& \ mask) \\
&= 2^{P-1} \mid (rem(add, 2^P) \ \& \ rem(mask, 2^{P-\mu})) \\
&= 2^{P-1} \mid (rem(add, 2^P) \ \& \ 0) \\
&= 2^{P-1}.
\end{aligned}
$$

Thus, it suffices to show that $rnd(prod, \mathcal{M}', \mu) = 2^P$.

Subcase 2.1: $\mathcal{M}' = near$
  Since

$$
prod + 2^{P-1-\mu} = prod + rconst \geq 2^P,
$$

we must have $near(prod, \mu) = 2^P$.

Subcase 2.2: $\mathcal{M}' = inf$
  Let $a = 2^P - 2^{P-\mu}$. Then

$$
prod \geq 2^P - rconst = 2^P - 2^{P-\mu} + 1 > a,
$$

and since a is μ-exact,

$$
away(prod, \mu) \geq a + 2^{expo(a)+1-\mu} = a + 2^{P-\mu} = 2^P
$$

by Lemma 13.1.21, and it follows that $away(prod, \mu) = 2^P$.

Subcase 2.3: $\mathcal{M}' = trunc$ or $\mathcal{M}' = minf$
  This case is precluded by Lemma 13.3.4 and our earlier observation that $0 < rconst$. $\square$

We may now complete the proof of Theorem 13.1. By Lemmas 13.3.5 and 13.3.8,

$$
prod = sig(prod)2^{expo(prod)} = sig(\hat{x}\hat{y})2^{P-1},
$$

and hence by Lemmas 13.3.19, 13.3.21, and 13.1.22,

$$
\begin{aligned}
sig(\hat{z}) &= \rho/2^{P-1} = rnd(prod, \mathcal{M}', \mu)/2^{carry+P-1} \\
&= rnd(sig(\hat{x}\hat{y}), \mathcal{M}', \mu)/2^{carry}.
\end{aligned}
$$

Now, applying Lemmas 13.3.20 and 13.1.22, we have

$$
\begin{aligned}
\hat{z} &= sgn(\hat{z})sig(\hat{z})2^{expo(\hat{z})} \\
&= sgn(\hat{z})rnd(sig(\hat{x}\hat{y}), \mathcal{M}', \mu)2^{expo(\hat{x}\hat{y})+2^{15}k} \\
&= sgn(\hat{z})rnd(sig(\hat{x}\hat{y})2^{expo(\hat{x}\hat{y})}, \mathcal{M}', \mu)2^{2^{15}k},
\end{aligned}
$$

where $k \in \mathbb{Z}$. If $sgnz = 0$, then $\mathcal{M}' = \mathcal{M}$ and by Lemma 13.3.14, $sgn(\hat{z}) = 1$. On the other hand, if $sgnz = 1$, then $\mathcal{M}' = flip(\mathcal{M})$ and $sgn(\hat{z}) = -1$. In either case, by Lemmas 13.1.23 and 13.3.18,

$$
\begin{aligned}
\hat{z} &= rnd(sgn(\hat{z})sig(\hat{x}\hat{y})2^{expo(\hat{x}\hat{y})}, \mathcal{M}, \mu)2^{2^{15}k} \\
&= rnd(sgn(\hat{x}\hat{y})sig(\hat{x}\hat{y})2^{expo(\hat{x}\hat{y})}, \mathcal{M}, \mu)2^{2^{15}k} \\
&= rnd(\hat{x}\hat{y}, \mathcal{M}, \mu)2^{2^{15}k}.
\end{aligned}
$$

But since $rnd(\hat{x}\hat{y}, \mathcal{M}, \mu)$ is representable, $i.e.$,

$$
1 - 2^{-14} \leq expo(rnd(\hat{x}\hat{y}, \mathcal{M}, \mu)) \leq 2^{14},
$$

and the same is true of $\hat{z}$, Lemma 13.1.19 yields

$$
|2^{15}k| = |expo(\hat{z}) - expo(rnd(\hat{x}\hat{y}, \mathcal{M}, \mu))| < 2^{15},
$$

and hence $k = 0$. $\square$

13.3.2   Formal Proof

In the design of a formal computational model, the ACL2 user is often faced with conflicting criteria. For example, a model that is intended primarily for formal analysis may not provide the desired execution efficiency. It is a common practice to define two or more models to serve distinct purposes and then prove them to be equivalent. This is the approach that we take here.

The translation scheme described in Section 13.2.3 is conceptually simple and provides an accurate representation of the RTL model that may be executed fairly efficiently. This is an important consideration in many applications, as it allows the formal model to be validated against the RTL through testing. However, this model is not amenable to formal analysis—it would be awkward to attempt to use it directly to formalize the argument presented in Section 13.3.1. Every reference to a signal would necessarily mention all the signals on which it depends, and the derived properties of those signals would have to be listed repeatedly. For example, a formal statement of Lemma 13.3.6 based on the definition

```
(defun prod (sigx_c3 sigy_c3)
     (bits (* sigx_c3 sigy_c3) 127 0))
```

would have to include all relevant properties of sigx_c3 and sigy_c3 as explicit hypotheses.

For the purpose of verification, therefore, we shall use an alternative translation scheme, and establish a method for converting theorems pertaining to the resulting model to theorems about the original model. Using our multiplier as an illustration, we begin by defining two functions, representing the constraints on inputs and desired properties of outputs, respectively.

```
(defun input-spec (x y rc pc)
  (and (normal-encoding-p x (extfmt))
       (normal-encoding-p y (extfmt))
       (member rc (list 0 1 2 3))
       (member pc (list 0 1))
       (repp (rnd (* (hat x) (hat y))
                  (mode rc)
                  (precision pc))
             (extfmt))))
(defun output-spec (x y rc pc)
  (let ((z (fmul x y rc pc)))
    (and (normal-encoding-p z (extfmt))
         (= (hat z)
            (rnd (* (hat x) (hat y))
                 (mode rc)
                 (precision pc))))))
(in-theory (disable input-spec output-spec))
```

Next, we introduce constants corresponding to the inputs, constrained to satisfy the input specification.

```
(encapsulate ((x* () t) (y* () t) (rc* () t) (pc* () t))
  (local (defun x* () (encode 1 (extfmt))))
  (local (defun y* () (encode 1 (extfmt))))
  (local (defun rc* () 0))
  (local (defun pc* () 1))
  (local (in-theory (disable input-spec*)))
  (defthm input-spec* (input-spec (x*) (y*) (rc*) (pc*))))
```

Constants are then defined corresponding to all remaining signals. In fact, for convenience, these functions are automatically generated by our translator and placed in a separate file. This file contains, for example, the following.

```
(defun sgnx* nil (sgnx (x*)))
(defun z* nil (z (sgnz_c4*) (expz*) (sigz*)))
```

Formal versions of the lemmas appearing in Section 13.3.1, based on these constant functions, may now be proved in a natural way by faithfully following their informal proofs (see [67]). Thus, we obtain the following theorem.

```
(defthm z*-spec
    (and (normal-encoding-p (z*) (extfmt))
         (= (hat (z*))
            (rnd (* (hat (x*)) (hat (y*)))
```

```
                        (mode (rc*))
                        (precision (pc*)))))
      :rule-classes())
```

Now, our goal is to derive the theorem `correctness-of-fmul` from `z*-spec`. First, we establish this relationship between the two models.

```
(defthm fmul-star-equivalence
        (equal (z*)
               (fmul (x*) (y*) (rc*) (pc*)))
        :rule-classes nil)
```

The last two theorems now yield the following.

```
(defthm output-spec*
   (output-spec (x*) (y*) (rc*) (pc*))
   :hints (("goal" :in-theory (enable output-spec)
                   :use (z*-spec fmul-star-equivalence))))
```

The next step is critical, employing functional instantiation.

```
(defthm fmul-input-output
   (implies (input-spec x y rc pc)
            (output-spec x y rc pc))
   :hints
   (("goal" :in-theory (enable input-spec*)
            :use ((:functional-instance output-spec*
                   (x* (lambda ()
                          (if (input-spec x y rc pc)
                              x (x*))))
                   (y* (lambda ()
                          (if (input-spec x y rc pc)
                              y (y*))))
                   (rc* (lambda ()
                           (if (input-spec x y rc pc)
                               rc (rc*))))
                   (pc* (lambda ()
                           (if (input-spec x y rc pc)
                               pc (pc*)))))))))
   :rule-classes ())
```

The final theorem now follows easily.

```
(defthm correctness-of-fmul
   (let ((ideal (rnd (* (hat x) (hat y))
                      (mode rc)
                      (precision pc)))
         (z (fmul x y rc pc)))
```

```
(implies (and (normal-encoding-p x (extfmt))
              (normal-encoding-p y (extfmt))
              (member rc (list 0 1 2 3))
              (member pc (list 0 1))
              (repp ideal (extfmt)))
         (and (normal-encoding-p z (extfmt))
              (= (hat z) ideal))))
:hints (("goal" :in-theory (enable input-spec output-spec)
                :use (fmul-input-output))))
```

Exercise 13.3 *The hypothetical implementation of our floating-point mul-tiplier relies on the efficient computation of the sum of three bit vectors (see the comments in Fig. 13.2.3), using several logical operations (which are executed in constant time) and a single addition. In order to establish the correctness of this computation, prove that for all $x, y, z \in \mathbb{N}$,*

$$x + y + z = x \text{ } \hat{} \text{ } y \text{ } \hat{} \text{ } z + 2\left[(x \text{ \& } y) \mid (x \text{ \& } z) \mid (y \text{ \& } z)\right].$$

Exercise 13.4 *A rounding mode used in the AMD Athlon floating-point adder, called sticky rounding, is defined as follows, for $x \in \mathbb{Q}^*$ and $n \in \mathbb{N}^*$:*

(a) $sticky(x, 1) = sgn(x)2^{expo(x)}$.
(b) If $n > 1$ and x is $(n-1)$-exact, then $sticky(x, n) = x$.
(c) If $n > 1$ and x is not $(n-1)$-exact, then

$$sticky(x, n) = trunc(x, n - 1) + sgn(x)2^{expo(x)+1-n}.$$

Derive the following properties of sticky rounding:
(1) Let $\mathcal{M}$ be an IEEE rounding mode, $\sigma \in \mathbb{N}^*$, $n \in \mathbb{N}$, and $x \in \mathbb{Q}^*$. If $n \geq \sigma + 2$, then

$$rnd(x, \mathcal{M}, \sigma) = rnd(sticky(x, n), \mathcal{M}, \sigma).$$

(2) Let $x, y \in \mathbb{Q}$ such that $y \neq 0$ and $x + y \neq 0$. Let $k, k', k'' \in \mathbb{Z}$ such that $k' = k + expo(x) - expo(y)$, and $k'' = k + expo(x + y) - expo(y)$.
(a) If $k > 0$, $k' > 0$, $k'' > 0$, and x is k'-exact, then

$$x + trunc(y, k) = \begin{cases} trunc(x + y, k'') & \text{if } sgn(x + y) = sgn(y) \\ away(x + y, k'') & \text{if } sgn(x + y) \neq sgn(y); \end{cases}$$

(b) If $k > 1$, $k' > 1$, $k'' > 1$, and x is $(k' - 1)$-exact, then

$$x + sticky(y, k) = sticky(x + y, k'').$$

14

Design Verification of a Safety-Critical Embedded Verifier

Piergiorgio Bertoli and Paolo Traverso
IRST - Istituto per la Ricerca Scientifica e Tecnologica, Povo, Italy
Email: bertoli@itc.it, leaf@itc.it

Abstract

This case study shows the use of ACL2 for the design verification of a selected piece of safety-critical software, called an Embedded Verifier. The Embedded Verifier checks on-line that each execution of a safety-critical translator is correct. This study originates from an industrial partnership project.

Introduction

We describe the use of ACL2 for the modeling and verification of the design of a safety-critical software component called an "Embedded Verifier." The Embedded Verifier enforces an on-line check of the correct behavior of a safety-critical translator. The translator is a component of a software architecture named VFRAME [88], used by UNION SWITCH & SIGNAL to build safety critical products (*e.g.*, trainborne control software systems). The chapter is organized as follows. Section 14.1 describes the industrial problem and its ACL2 modeling. Section 14.2 discusses the verification performed using ACL2, describing its high level structure and its main steps. Section 14.3 draws some conclusions and points to possible extensions of the project. Section 14.4 provides some exercises based on the project.

14.1 Formalization of the Industrial Problem

The industrial problem we consider consists of guaranteeing the correct behavior of a translator called GEM2RTM, used to build safety-critical trainborne software (*e.g.*, automatic train protection systems). GEM2RTM con-

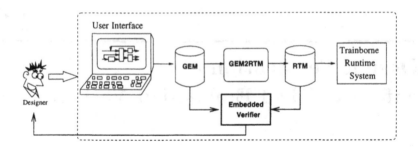

Figure 14.1: The GEM2RTM translation system

verts programs in a language called GEM into a format called RTM. In order to enhance its portability, GEM2RTM is designed to run on top of a commercially available, non fail-safe hardware/software platform. This makes it possible for errors to occur during its execution. The approach we chose to detect the errors consisted of verifying each execution of GEM2RTM. Thus, our task consisted of designing a piece of software, called an Embedded Verifier, that captures errors in the executions of GEM2RTM by analyzing the inputs and outputs of each translation. A detailed description of the project requirements can be found in [18, 19, 107]. The situation is shown in Figure 14.1. In order to design the Embedded Verifier, we exploited the functional specification of the translation mechanism, provided by the industrial partner and formalized it as a set of syntactic equivalence conditions between GEM and RTM. Thus, at each execution of GEM2RTM, the Embedded Verifier checks that the input GEM program, P^g , and the RTM program, P^r, resulting from its translation are syntactically equivalent.

$$P^g \sim_{synt} P^r \tag{14.1}$$

The syntactic nature of the check has made it feasible to design an automatic and efficient Embedded Verifier, as required by the partner. The result of the check is explained to the end user as a set of easily interpretable syntactic correspondences between the variables and the instructions of P^g and P^r.

However, in order to prove that the check implemented by the Embedded Verifier guarantees a correct translation, it has been necessary to define a notion of semantic equivalence $\sim_{sem}$ between GEM programs and RTM programs, and to prove that it is entailed by the syntactic equivalence. Thus we had to prove the following statement.

$$\forall P^g, P^r : P^g \sim_{synt} P^r \implies P^g \sim_{sem} P^r \tag{14.2}$$

We have used ACL2 to prove this statement, restricted to a relevant subset of the languages. The following subsections focus on the definition and modeling of the GEM and RTM languages, and on the notions of syntactic and semantic equivalence.

14.1.1   Source and Target Languages

GEM is a simple branch-free, imperative typed language. It implements modular arithmetic, logical operations, conditional assignment, and an assert operation to deal with runtime exceptions. GEM programs are composed of a sequence of variable declarations followed by a sequence of instructions. A variable declaration consists of a tuple where a variable identifier is paired with its type ("long" integer or Boolean), its initial value, and an attribute. The attribute of a variable ("input," "output," or "internal") describes whether the program uses the variable to retrieve data from the environment, to deliver output to the environment, or to store intermediate computations. The declaration part of a program is conveniently modeled in ACL2 as an association list whose keys are the variable identifiers. Each instruction is a tuple, made up of an instruction identifier (the first element of the tuple) and a sequence of arguments. The number and type of the arguments depend upon the instruction identifier. In ACL2, we have defined the predicate gem-program-p to recognize the well-formedness of a GEM program, restricted to the addition, subtraction, and conditional assignment operations.

GEM programs obey a reactive semantics: their execution results in an infinite output/input/execute loop. At each cycle, the output variables are delivered to the environment, the input variables are read from the environment, and the sequence of instructions in the program is executed. An initialization phase precedes the cycle. The execution of GEM programs has been modeled using machinery inspired by Boyer and Moore's "small machine" ([6]). A state of a GEM program consists of a program counter, a memory, and the program itself. The semantics of each GEM instruction consists of a state-transforming function called its *semantic function*. A single step of a GEM program is executed by applying the semantic function corresponding to the current instruction (*i.e.*, the instruction pointed to by the program counter) to the current state. The execution of a sequence of operations is obtained through a stepper function. We have extended the machinery to describe the I/O operations. Input is modeled by updating the values of the input variables in the memory with those from a given sequence. Output is modeled by extracting the output variables of the memory. A further difference with ([6]) regards the modeling of memories. We model GEM memories as association lists, where each variable identifier is paired, other than to its value, to its type and attribute. Our memory model allows duplicate key entries; only the first entry of a variable is relevant to the content of the state. The read/write operations are easily implemented via assoc-equal and cons; memories are compared with the equal-memories predicate.

RTM is a binary loadable format, which shares some features with GEM (*e.g.*, it is a branch-free imperative language with reactive semantics, and it can be described using an abstract syntax similar to GEM's). We recognize

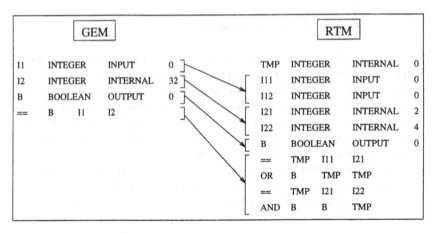

Figure 14.2: An example of GEM and RTM programs

the well-formedness of an RTM program with the predicate `rtm-program-p`, and exploit machinery similar to that for the GEM to model the behavior of RTM programs. In order to allow the implementation of checksum techniques at runtime, RTM only provides a single type ("short" integers), suitable for table-based implementations of modular arithmetic. This implies a different representation of data and operations between GEM and RTM, and forces the introduction of a temporary variable into each RTM program. Two different mechanisms, recasting and residual number system transformation, are used to represent GEM data and operations in RTM. Recasting is used to represent GEM Booleans as the RTM integers 0 and 1. Logical operations operate on such values. The residual number system transformation is used to represent GEM integers by sequences of RTM integers, using a sequence of pairwise relatively prime numbers called a residual number system (rns). According to the Chinese Remainder Theorem, this transformation reduces arithmetic operations on integers to a set of independent arithmetic operations on the elements of their rns transformation. Moreover, under certain boundedness conditions, there exists an inverse transformation rns^{-1}. Figure 14.2 provides an example of a GEM program and of its RTM translation. We assume that $rns = \langle 5, 7 \rangle$. The programs perform an infinite loop where (a) a data is stored into the variable I1 (resp. I11, I12), compared with the constant 32 (whose rns representation is $\langle 2, 4 \rangle$), and the result of the comparison is delivered to the environment via the variable B (resp. B). Notice how the comparison of I1 with I2 in the RTM program is realized by conjoining the results of the componentwise comparisons of their RTM representants. The temporary variable TMP is used to store the intermediate results of the comparison. A complete definition of GEM and RTM can be found in [19].

14.1.2   Syntactic Equivalence

The syntactic equivalence conditions used by the Embedded Verifier are derived directly from the specifications of GEM2RTM, provided by the industrial partner. Such specifications describe how GEM instructions are translated to sequences of one or more RTM instructions. They are based on the notions of variable mapping and instruction translation scheme.

A variable mapping M for a GEM program P^g and an RTM program P^r is a relation which maps variables of P^g to sequences of variables of P^r. In order for such a map to be classified as a well-formed variable mapping for P^g and P^r, the following requirements must be satisfied.

1. No variable of P^g may be mapped to the temporary RTM variable.

2. No duplicate GEM variables may appear in the mapping.

3. No duplicate RTM variables may appear in the mapping.

4. The domain of the mapping must consist of the variables of P^g.

5. The mapping must associate each Boolean variable of P^g to one variable of P^r, and each integer variable of P^g to $|rns|$ variables of P^r.

6. Variables associated by the map must have the same attributes.

7. The declared initial values of variables associated by the map must correspond according to the recasting or to the rns representation (depending on the type of the GEM variable).

In general, these requirements identify a class of possible variable mappings for P^g and P^r. $\{I1 \rightarrow \langle I11, I12 \rangle, I2 \rightarrow \langle I21, I22 \rangle, B \rightarrow \langle B \rangle\}$ is a variable mapping for the programs in Figure 14.1.

In ACL2, we think of a variable mapping as an association list whose keys are GEM variable identifiers. The following ACL2 predicate is used to recognize a well-formed variable mapping.

```
(defun is-variable-mapping (m gem-vars rtm-vars)
  (and (alistp m)
       (no-tmp-into-mapping m)
       (no-duplicates-p (gem-variables m))
       (no-duplicates-p (rtm-variables m))
       (correct-wrt-arity m gem-vars)
       (same-vars gem-vars m)
       (attributes-correspondence m gem-vars rtm-vars)
       (m-corresponding-vals-p m gem-vars rtm-vars)))
```

Notice that m-corresponding-vals-p embeds the value conversion mechanism explained in Section 14.1.1 to check (via the predicate represent--same-values-p) that for each entry of a mapping, $v^g \rightarrow \langle v_1^r, \ldots, v_i^r \rangle$, the declared values of $\langle v_1^r, \ldots, v_i^r \rangle$ represent that of v^g. In particular, in the case of GEM integers, the *rns* transformation is implemented by a function `build-values-by-rns`.

The instruction translation scheme τ_M is a fixed set of functional rules, each describing the way a GEM instruction has to be translated to RTM. The τ_M scheme refers to the variable mapping to describe the translation of the arguments. Intuitively, τ_M captures the following ideas.

- Operations involving only Boolean variables are translated one-to-one.

- Arithmetical operations involving integer GEM variables are translated to sequences of RTM operations which involve the corresponding sequences of RTM variables. When both integers and Booleans are involved, the fact that the *rns* representation of 0 and 1 consists of a sequence of 0s or 1s is exploited to operate on the *rns* representation of Booleans without introducing additional variables.

A GEM program P^g and an RTM program P^r are syntactically equivalent with respect to τ_M and a variable mapping M if each instruction *instr* in P^g is translated via the appropriate rule of τ_M into a sequence of instructions $\tau_M(instr)$ in P^r, starting at a corresponding position. The correspondence between positions is defined recursively, based on the length of the translation of each instruction of P^g.

Our model for syntactic equivalence in ACL2 consists of the recursive function `correct-translation`. Its recursion scheme codifies the aforementioned position correspondence. At every recursion step, a case switch establishes whether the translation scheme is obeyed for one instruction in P^g. Each branch in the switch codifies one of the rules in τ_M. Thus, the following definition represents the syntax equivalence in ACL2. Notice the additional well-formedness hypotheses regarding the syntax of the programs.

```
(defun syntactically-equivalent (gem-program rtm-program m)
  (and (gem-program-p gem-program)
       (rtm-program-p rtm-program)
       (is-variable-mapping
        m (declarations gem-program)
        (declarations rtm-program))
       (correct-translation gem-program rtm-program m)))
```

14.1.3 Semantic Equivalence

The correct translation of a GEM program P^g into an RTM program P^r is based on a notion of observable behavioral equivalence. According to this notion, two programs are equivalent if, given any sequence of inputs, they produce the same outputs. We take into account the different representations for the data exchanged with the environment by defining an encoding function for inputs and a decoding function for outputs. In particular, we consider the encoding E_M and decoding D_M induced by a variable mapping M. Thus we can define a notion *I/O equivalence* of semantic equivalence as follows.

$$P^g \sim_{sem} P^r \quad \overset{\text{def}}{=} \quad \forall I : [\![P^g]\!](I) = D_M([\![P^r]\!](E_M(I))) \tag{14.3}$$

where $[\![P]\!](I)$ is called the I/O semantics of P, and represents the sequence of outputs produced by P in response to the sequence of inputs I[1]. The mapping-induced decoding is modeled as a recursive function `decode` which embeds a function `invert-cell` that retrieves the GEM representation of a sequence of values of RTM variables. In particular, `invert-cell` exploits a function `crtmod` which models the rns^{-1} transformation. To define the mapping-induced encoding, we model a recognizer predicate called `correct-input-sequences`. This predicate holds exactly if a sequence of RTM inputs is the mapping-induced encoding of a sequence of GEM inputs; for this purpose, it exploits the value conversion mechanism used in `m-corresponding-vals-p` (see Section 14.1.1).

Using the execution machinery for GEM and RTM, and the definitions of the encoding/decoding functions, we have modeled both $[\![P^g]\!](I)$ and $D_M([\![P^r]\!](E_M(I)))$ in ACL2. These are represented by the ACL2 functions `rtm-output-sequence` and `gem-output-sequence`. The definition of semantic equivalence is thus represented by the following ACL2 function.

```
(defun semantically-equivalent
       (gem-program rtm-program m gemseq-seq rtmseq-seq)
  (implies
   (correct-input-sequences
    gemseq-seq rtmseq-seq m gem-program rtm-program)
   (equal-output-sequences
    (rtm-output-sequence rtmseq-seq m

                         gem-program rtm-program)
    (gem-output-sequence gemseq-seq m gem-program)))))
```

Notice that our definition of E_M as a recognizer appears as a hypothesis that forces the input sequences given to the GEM and RTM programs to be consistent with the mapping-induced encoding.

---

[1] We will sometime overload the notation by using it for single inputs.

14.2   Proof of Correct Design

In this section we describe the high-level structure of the proof of statement 14.2, which we rewrite here applying 14.3.

$$\forall P^g, P^r : (P^g \sim_{synt} P^r \implies \forall I : [\![P^g]\!](I) = D_M([\![P^r]\!](E_M(I)))) \quad (14.4)$$

The proof of this statement requires a nested double induction: over the input sequence given to the program, and over the instruction sequence executed within a cycle of execution. We decompose the proof by first considering a single cycle of execution of a program, given an input i.

$$\forall P^g, P^r : (P^g \sim_{synt} P^r \implies \forall i : [\![P^g]\!](i) = D_M([\![P^r]\!](E_M(i)))) \quad (14.5)$$

We achieve a further two-step decomposition by reusing the definition of variable mapping in order to establish a relation between GEM and RTM memories. We say that a GEM memory m^g and an RTM memory m^r are M-corresponding if M is a variable mapping with respect to the variables contained in m^g and those in m^r (that is, considering the definition in Section 14.1.2, if requirements 1-6 hold, and requirement 7 holds with respect to the values of the variables in m^g and m^r). We indicate this with $m^g \sim_M m^r$. Since we have adopted the same model for memories and sequences of declarations, we reuse the modeling of the ACL2 predicate is-variable-mapping to recognize M-corresponding memories. We say that a GEM program P^g and an RTM program P^r are M-equivalent ($P^g \sim_M P^r$), if, given any input sequence, they exhibit M-corresponding memories at corresponding execution points. If $[\![P]\!]_n(I)$ represents the memory after a program P has executed n steps[2] given an input sequence I, we can write the following.

$$P^g \sim_M P^r \stackrel{\text{def}}{\equiv} \quad \forall I, n : [\![P^g]\!]_n(I) \sim_M [\![P^r]\!]_{ck(n)}(I) \quad (14.6)$$

Above, $ck(n)$ computes the corresponding number of steps that must be executed by the RTM program P^r in correspondence to the n steps executed by P^g (similar to the "clock function" used in the verification of the Piton compiler in [77]). M-equivalence is a stronger notion than I/O equivalence, since it not only requires programs to behave correspondingly at the input and output phases of their execution, but also at intermediate points. In fact, once we prove that M-corresponding memories produce the same output via the output function Out, M-equivalence is easily shown to entail I/O equivalence. Thus we are led to prove the following statements.

$$\forall P^g, P^r : (P^g \sim_{synt} P^r \implies \forall i, n : [\![P^g]\!]_n(i) \sim_M [\![P^r]\!]_{ck(n)}(i)) \quad (14.7)$$

$$m^g \sim_M m^r \implies Out(m^g) = D_M(Out(m^r)) \quad (14.8)$$

The next subsections discuss the proofs of these statements, and the way they are combined to achieve the final result.

---

[2] We assume here that n is a number of steps which can be executed by P.

14.2.1   Output Equivalence of M-Corresponding Memories

Statement 14.8 is independent of the execution machinery. The main step in proving it is the proof of correctness of the direct and inverse transformations between the GEM and RTM representations of values used in the ACL2 models for $\sim_M$ and D_M (respectively m-corresponding-vals-p and decode). This is easy to achieve for Boolean GEM variables. In order to prove this for integer GEM variables, we must prove the following corollary of the Chinese Remainder Theorem

$$v \in \mathbb{N} \wedge (v < \Pi_{i=1}^{|\boldsymbol{rns}|} \boldsymbol{rns}_i) \implies rns^{-1}(rns(v)) = v \tag{14.9}$$

where we assume $\boldsymbol{rns}$ to be a sequence of pairwise relatively prime numbers $\langle \boldsymbol{rns}_1, \ldots, \boldsymbol{rns}_{|\boldsymbol{rns}|}\rangle$. The following formalization of the Chinese Remainder Theorem relies on a definition of congruence modulo rns of a number with respect to a sequence of numbers (congruent-all). It provides a witness function crt that, given an rns rns and a sequence of natural numbers values, returns a natural number proved to be congruent modulo rns with values. The proof of this statement is due to David Russinoff.

```
(defthm chinese-remainder-theorem
 (implies
  (and (natp-all values)
       (rel-prime-moduli rns)
       (= (len values) (len rns)))
  (and (natp (crt values rns))
       (congruent-all (crt values rns) values rns)))
  :rule-classes ...
  :hints ... )
```

We have defined the crtmod function implementing the rns^{-1} transformation as the modulo of crt with respect to the product of the elements of the rns. The proof of the inversion lemma 14.9 is based on the uniqueness, in the range $[0, \Pi_{i=1}^{|rns|} rns_i - 1]$, of numbers congruent modulo rns with a fixed sequence of naturals. The ACL2 statement of 14.9 follows:

```
(defthm crt-inversion
 (implies
  (and (rel-prime-moduli rns)
       (natp val)
       (< val (prod rns)))
  (equal (crtmod (build-values-by-rns val rns) rns) val))
  :hints ...)
```

Finally, we easily prove 14.8 by induction over the length of the mapping. We report its ACL2 form.

```
(defthm mapping-correspondence-implies-same-outputs
  (implies (and (is-variable-mapping m gem-mem rtm-mem)
                (is-gem-mem-p gem-mem))
           (equal-memories (output gem-mem)
                           (decode m (output rtm-mem)))))
  :hints ... )
```

Notice the presence of the additional well-formedness hypothesis for the GEM memory, (is-gem-mem-p gem-mem). This, in particular, codifies the fact that the GEM integers must be bounded by the product of the values of the *rns*.

14.2.2 *M*-Equivalence of Syntactically Equivalent Programs

To prove 14.7, it is necessary to show that the M-correspondence between memories of GEM and RTM programs is preserved (a) by corresponding I/O operations, and (b) by the parallel execution of any GEM instruction *instr* and of its translation $\tau_M(instr)$. The first point is proved easily, because of the way the input encoding is codified in a similar way to the *M*-correspondence recognizer. To prove the second point, for each instruction, we have followed these steps.

1. Define a helper function which builds the final values of the variables affected by $\tau_M(instr)$, given those of the variables used by $\tau_M(instr)$. This function is in general a simple recursive function, and is defined independently from the execution machinery. For instance, the following helper is defined for the translation of the add operation.

   ```
   (defun sum-list (vl2 vl3 rns)
     (if (endp vl2)
         nil
         (cons (mod (+ (car vl2) (car vl3)) (car rns))
               (sum-list (cdr vl2) (cdr vl3) (cdr rns)))))
   ```

   Given two lists of values vl2 and vl3 and a *rns* rns, this function builds a list of the pairwise modulo additions.

2. Prove that the helper function represents the results of the execution of $\tau_M(instr)$, by comparing the values of the affected variables after the execution of $\tau_M(instr)$ with the values produced by the helper function.

3. Prove that the values produced via the helper function are the RTM representation of the value of the GEM variable affected by *instr* after the execution of *instr*. This step exploits the semantic function for *instr*.

4. Prove the following invariance lemmas with respect to the execution of both *instr* and $\tau_M(instr)$.

♦ The values of the variables in the memory not considered in step 3 are unaffected.

♦ The type and attribute information related to variables in the memory is unaffected.

♦ The execution of instructions results in well-formed program states.

The steps above lead to a statement of M-correspondence preservation related to the specific rule of τ_M for *instr*. Informally, it states that "if (a) the current GEM instruction *instr* of P^g is translated into the sequence $\tau_M(instr)$ starting from the current RTM instruction of P^r, and (b) the current GEM and RTM memories are M-corresponding, then executing *instr* and $\tau_M(instr)$ leads to new well-formed program states containing M-corresponding memories." To prove 14.7, we exploit the local M-correspondence preservation statements within a recursion scheme based on the parallel execution of the GEM program with its RTM translation. The parallel execution exploits the clock function `corresponding-steps-to-` `-current-gem-instruction` that computes $ck(n)$. The following function is used to instruct ACL2 to induct with such a recursion scheme (using an `:induct` hint in the proof).

```
(defun parallel-exec (gstate rstate n)
  (if (zp n)
      (list gstate rstate)
    (parallel-exec
     (execute-instruction gstate)
     (execute-n-instructions rstate
       (corresponding-steps-to-current-gem-instruction
         gstate))
     (1- n))))
```

This results in the following ACL2 statement, restricting 14.7 to the I/O-free phase of the cycle. It is easily extended to deal with the I/O.

```
(defthm syntactic-eqv-implies-m-eqv-during-execution
  (let
   ((gstate (initial-state gem-program))
    (rstate (initial-state rtm-program)))
   (implies
    (and
     (natp n)
     (syntactically-equivalent gem-program rtm-program m))
    (is-variable-mapping
     m
```

```
(mem (execute-n-instructions gstate n))
(mem (execute-n-instructions rstate
        (corresponding-steps n gstate))))))
:hints ... )
```

14.2.3 Proof of the Correct Design

The semantic equivalence restricted to one cycle of execution is easily shown
by instantiating 14.8 into 14.7. Once that is proven, the final statement is
simply proved by induction over the length of the input. Thus we achieve
the proof of the desired entailment statement.

```
(defthm syntactic-eqv-implies-semantic-eqv
 (implies
    (syntactically-equivalent gem-program rtm-program m)
    (semantically-equivalent
      gem-program rtm-program m gemseq-seq rtmseq-seq)))
```

14.3   Conclusions

We showed the use of ACL2 in a design verification project. In spite of the
simple definition of the GEM and RTM languages involved in the problem,
the use of formal methods has been extremely beneficial for our industrial
partner. In fact, one of the translation rules provided by the industrial partner was shown to be faulty. Namely, the specification of the RTM translation
of the comparison between a GEM Boolean vbIn and a GEM integer vi, " ==
vbOut vbIn vi", relied on accumulating over vbOut the results of comparing each one of the residual components of vi with vbIn. In this way, when
vbIn coincides with vbOut, side-effects occur on vbIn, possibly leading to
an incorrect result. The bug had escaped previous informal analysis. This
has led to a modification of the specification of GEM2RTM.

So far, our ACL2 modeling considered only those GEM operations which
are translated as sequences of more than one RTM instruction, so that we
verify the most complicated translation rules first. We intend to model
the whole language in the near future. Once this is achieved, we intend
to experiment with the ACL2 execution capabilities, by substituting the
ACL2 formalization that checks the syntactic equivalence of programs in
place of the Embedded Verifier. Since such formalization has been proved
correct, this would guarantee the correct implementation of the Embedded
Verifier (assuming the correctness of ACL2).

14.4   Exercises

Exercise 14.1 *Define a function* append-lists *that takes a true-list* 11 *of* true-listps, *and returns the result of appending the elements of* 11. *Define a function* no-duplicates-p *that takes a true-list, and holds exactly when the list is duplicate-free. Prove that, if* (no-duplicates-p (append-lists 11)) *holds, then, the ith element in a list* 11 *contained in* 11 *differs from j^{th} element in a list* 12 *contained in* 11, *where $i \neq j$ or* $11 \neq 12$.

Exercise 14.2 *Assume that* rns *is a list of pairwise relatively prime numbers. Assume that n_1 and n_2 are natural numbers, both in the range* $[0, \Pi_{i=1}^{rns} rns_i - 1]$. *Prove that if n_1 and n_2 are congruent modulo* rns *with a given sequence of naturals of length $|rns|$, then they are equal. (Advice: define the notion of relatively prime numbers using the* nonneg- -int-gcd *function defined in the ACL2 distribution book* "ihs/quotient- -remainder-lemmas".)

Exercise 14.3 *Model a memory as an association list. Each memory entry associates a key to a value. Duplicate keys are allowed in the list. The value of a key* var *in memory* mem *is given by* (cdr (assoc-equal var mem)). *Design a predicate* equal-memories *on two memories that holds exactly when the values of the two memories agree on every key. Prove that if* (equal-memories mem1 mem2) *holds, then any key has the same value in* mem1 *and* mem2. *Prove that* equal-memories *is an* equivalence *relation.*

Acknowledgments

Several people have contributed to this project. David Russinoff has provided a proof of the Chinese Remainder Theorem. Matt Kaufmann has been very helpful, and instructed us in proof techniques that allowed us to prove some tricky lemmas. An important part of this project was developed during a visit by the first author to the University of Texas at Austin. We thank the people at the Computer Science department at the University of Texas at Austin for having provided help and support throughout that phase of the project.

15

Compiler Verification Revisited

Wolfgang Goerigk
Institut für Informatik und Praktische Mathematik, Christian-Albrechts-Universität zu Kiel, Germany
Email: wg@informatik.uni-kiel.de

Abstract

This case study mainly focuses on the execution of programs. In particular we study the execution of compiler machine programs on an abstract machine that we implement in ACL2. But this article also presents a security-related motivation for compiler verification and in particular for binary compiler implementation verification. We will prove that source level verification is not sufficient to guarantee compiler correctness. For this, we will adopt the scenario of a well-known attack to Unix operating system programs due to intruded Trojan Horses in compiler executables. Such a compiler will pass nearly every test: state of the art compiler validation, the bootstrap test, and any amount of source code inspection and verification. But for all that, it nevertheless might eventually cause a catastrophe. We will show such a program in detail; it is surprisingly easy to construct such a program. In that, we share a common experience with Ken Thompson, who initially documented this kind of attack in 1984 in his Turing Award Lecture [106].

Introduction

Like most chapters in this book, this article will end up proving the major results formally and mechanically in ACL2. We will prove properties of programs, and our proofs will be simple exercises in program execution. Fortunately, ACL2 allows for efficient program or model execution.

This work was supported by the Deutsche Forschungsgemeinschaft (DFG) in the projects *Verifix* (Univ. of Karlsruhe, Kiel and Ulm) and *VerComp* (Univ. of Kiel) on compiler and compiler implementation verification.

The main topic of this article is execution of programs, in particular execution of compiler programs on target machines. We will define an abstract machine model of a simple stack machine (Section 15.1.2), and a compiler (Section 15.1.3) that generates machine code for a small subset of ACL2 (Section 15.1.1). We will write the compiler in this subset as well. Thus, we can execute the compiler within ACL2, either directly as an ACL2 function, or after compilation (into abstract machine code) by executing the machine model and running the compiled compiler (machine) program on it. The latter simulates machine execution of compiler executables within ACL2, and our main focus will be on that kind of (machine) program execution (Section 15.1.4).

Then we turn our attention to compiler bootstrapping, that is to machine execution of compiled compilers compiling compilers (Section 15.2) and the so-called *bootstrap test* [114]. After some exercises in writing self-reproducing and reflective code (Section 15.3) we will concentrate on self-reproducing compilers (Section 15.4). We construct an incorrect machine implementation of the compiler which returns its own machine code if applied to the correct source (we call this the *reproduction* property), inserts a bug into another particular program (*catastrophe*), but works correctly in all other cases (*normal*). Thus, this catastrophic implementation survives the bootstrap test, most testing, and source-level inspection. The "malicious" code is not present in the alleged source; it is hidden in the machine code and so is a *Trojan Horse*.

We can look at the compiler source code and its incorrect implementation as witnesses for a proof of the fact that no amount of source level verification or scrutiny is sufficient to guarantee the correctness of compiler executables (Theorem 15.1 in Section 15.4).

Although in this article we use a very small source language, and our target machine is unrealistically abstract, our work has a lot in common with former work on machine formalization and compiler verification using ACL2 and its predecessor Nqthm for Gypsy and Piton on the FM8502 and FM9001 processors ([76, 34, 77]).

There is a subtle difference in the notion of *correct compilation*, though, and we would like to point this out before we start. Our notion of correctness states that if execution of m, a compilation of program p, computes a non-erroneous result, then execution of p will also compute the same result.[1] In contrast, the notion of correctness in [77] states that every non-erroneous result of (the Piton machine executing) p will also be computed by m (on the FM9001). The two notions are incompatible: neither of them implies the other. You should keep this in mind while reading this article.

---

[1] *Preservation of partial program correctness* [40, 80]. The machine may fail, but it will never return an unexpected non-erroneous result. In case of non-determinism, we additionally would allow the target program m to be more deterministic than p.

15.1   A Proved Correct Compiler

In this section we define a compiler for a small subset **SL** (source language) of ACL2 into the code **TL** (target language) of an abstract stack machine. The machine will be implemented in ACL2 so that we can use it in order to execute machine programs, in particular those generated by the compiler. The compiler is an **SL** program, and we call it $C_{\textbf{SL}}$. Sometimes we simply refer to it as *the correct compiler*.

In Section 15.1.5 we briefly sketch the ACL2 proof of the following fact (*compiler source-level correctness*): If $C_{\textbf{SL}}$ generates a target machine program m (for a well-formed **SL** source program p), then m is a correct implementation of p. That is to say: if m successfully returns a non-erroneous result, then it is the correct result with respect to the semantics of p. An operational semantics of **SL** is defined in the supporting book **evaluator**. The correctness proof goes beyond the focus of this article, however, and so we will just refer to the supporting books **proof1** and **proof** for details, which we recommend as an exercise for readers interested in compiler source-level verification.

15.1.1   Source Language

Our source language is a small subset[2] of ACL2, with only a few built-in Lisp functions and a restricted syntax. Unlike ACL2, however, we allow function definitions to be mutually recursive without a special declaration, and we define the additional concept of a *program* (p below). A program is a list of function definitions, followed by a list of *input* variables and a *main* program expression which may use the input variables.

$$
\begin{array}{lll}
p & ::= & ((d_1 \ \ldots \ d_n) \ (x_1 \ \ldots \ x_k) \ e) \\
d & ::= & (\textbf{defun} \ f \ (x_1 \ \ldots \ x_n) \ e) \\
e & ::= & c \mid x \mid (\textbf{if} \ e_1 \ e_2 \ e_3) \mid (f \ e_1 \ \ldots \ e_n) \mid (op \ e_1 \ \ldots \ e_n)
\end{array}
$$

Expressions e (forms) are either constants c (*i.e.*, nil, t, numbers, strings, or *quoted* s-expressions including symbols), variables x (symbols not equal to nil or t), conditional expressions, calls of user defined functions, or operator calls. As unary operators we allow <u>car</u>, <u>cdr</u>, <u>cadr</u>, <u>caddr</u>, <u>cadar</u>, <u>caddar</u>, <u>cadddr</u>, <u>1-</u>, <u>1+</u>, <u>len</u>, <u>symbolp</u>, <u>consp</u>, <u>atom</u>, and list1 (a unary version of <u>list</u>). Binary operators are <u>cons</u>, <u>equal</u>, <u>append</u>, <u>member</u>, <u>assoc</u>, +, -, * and list2 (a binary version of <u>list</u>).

Functions and operators (standard functions) have a fixed number of arguments. The set of operators is not minimal, furthermore, it would be

---

[2]We can run **SL** programs within ACL2, but we have to take special care if the definitions are mutually recursive (see <u>mutual-recursion</u>). We can make a set of ACL2 functions an **SL** program. But we have to delete or comment out <u>declare</u> forms and <u>documentation</u> strings, because our syntax does not allow them.

easy to add more. We just took those we use in our programs. But it is
intentional that we left out most of the control structures. We want to keep
the compiler small.

Example.   Here is an **SL** program for the factorial function.

```
(((defun fac (n)
    (if (equal n 0) 1 (* n (fac (1- n)))))))
 (n)
 (fac n))
```

The semantics of a program is as expected: the top-level expression is evaluated after binding the input variables to some (given) inputs. Functions
may fail to terminate, so the semantics of a program in general is a partial
mapping from the inputs to the program result. The semantics of an expression or function is intended to be as in ACL2's :<u>program</u> mode. In the
supporting book **evaluator** you can find an ACL2 definition of the operational semantics (an evaluator) and also a definition of well-formedness[3].

Exercise 15.1 *Write an* **SL** *version of the ACL2 standard function* <u>subst</u>.
(Subst new old tree) *shall return the result of substituting any occurrence* equal[4] *to old within* tree *by* new.

15.1.2   Target Machine

The target machine is a simple stack machine.stack!machine We will use it
in order to execute compiled Lisp programs. Its configuration consists of a
code part and a state (or memory) **stack**, which is a data stack containing
Lisp s-expressions. The code is not part of the memory. It is a separate
association list mapping subroutine names to instruction sequences. Executing an instruction with a given **code** on a given **stack** returns a new
stack. Execution of an instruction sequence starts in the current **stack** and
executes the instructions from left to right, thereby iteratively computing
the new stack from the current one by executing single instructions. Once
downloaded, the **code** is never changed.

The machine has six machine instructions. We can push a constant *c*
onto the stack (**PUSHC**), push the stack content (the variable) at a particular stack position (**PUSHV**), pop the *n* stack elements below the top (**POP**).
There is a subroutine call (**CALL**), that executes the code associated with a
subroutine name within **code**, and the **OPR** instruction applies an operator

---

[3]We assume that programs are *well-formed*, *i.e.*, that variables are bound, functions
are defined, and any function or operator call has the correct number of argument expressions. We do not check this, but the compiler (Section 15.1.3) will generate semantically
incorrect code if applied to non well-formed programs, for instance for an expression like
(cons 3).

[4]The ACL2 function <u>subst</u> uses eql for the test (see <u>subst</u>).

to the topmost (one or two) stack cell(s), thereby removing the argument(s) and pushing the result. Moreover, we have a structured (IF *then else*) instruction, that removes the top of stack, *top*, and executes the instruction sequence *else* if *top* is nil, *then* otherwise:

(PUSHC c)	stack → (c . stack)
(PUSHV i)	($d_0 \ldots d_i$. rest) → ($d_i d_0 \ldots d_i$. rest)
(POP n)	($d_0 d_1 \ldots d_n$. rest) → (d_0 . rest)
(IF *then else*)	(see above)
(CALL f)	(see above)
(OPR *op*)	($d_0 d_1$. rest) → ($op(d_1, d_0)$. rest)
	or (d_0 . rest) → ($op(d_0)$. rest)

Machine programs (m) are sequences of (mutually recursive) subroutine declarations (d) together with a *main* instruction sequence which is to be executed on an initial stack after downloading the list of declarations into code (and constructing an appropriate association list from it).

$$
\begin{aligned}
m &::= \quad (d_1 \ldots d_n \, (ins_1 \ldots ins_k)) \\
d &::= \quad (\text{defcode } f \, (ins_1 \ldots ins_k)
\end{aligned}
$$

Figure 15.1 shows an example of a machine program, actually the target program that the compiler (Section 15.1.3) generates for the factorial program (Section 15.1.1). The main program calls fac after pushing the input.

```
((DEFCODE FAC
    ((PUSHV 0)
     (PUSHC 0)
     (OPR EQUAL)
     (IF ((PUSHC 1))
         ((PUSHV 0)
          (PUSHV 1)
          (OPR 1-)
          (CALL FAC)
          (OPR *)))
     (POP 1)))
 ((PUSHV 0) (CALL FAC) (POP 1))))
```

Figure 15.1: A machine program example

The code of fac first tests if the argument is 0 or not, and returns either 1, or computes the expression (* n (fac (1- n))) according to its reverse polish notation (n n 1- FAC *), that is first push n, then push n again, call 1- on n, then FAC on the result, finally * on n and (fac (1- n)).

In the supporting book **machine** we define this machine in ACL2. Two mutually recursive functions **mstep** and **msteps** are used to execute instructions and instruction sequences (respectively) in a given **code** on a given **stack** returning the result stack. The function **opr** applies operators. For the **stack** we use a list that grows to the left, *i.e.*, we use **cons** to push an item onto the stack, and <u>nth</u> or <u>nthcdr</u> to read the contents or pop elements. The function **download** downloads the declarations. In order to execute a given program we use the following function.

```
(defun execute (prog stack n)
   (let ((code (download (butlst prog))))
     (msteps (car (last prog)) code stack n)))
```

We can not guarantee termination of machine programs. Consequently we can not guarantee termination of the machine. So we add an additional *termination argument* n in order to force the machine to stop execution after at most n subroutine calls (see the supporting book **machine** for details).

15.1.3 The Compiler Program

The principle idea of executing **SL** programs on such a machine is quite simple and we call it the *stack principle*. Arguments are found on the stack; for a given expression e we generate a sequence of instructions that pushes the value of e onto the stack. Functions or operators consume (pop) their arguments and push the result.

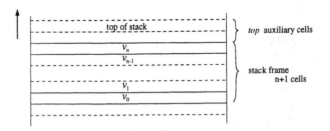

Figure 15.2: Parameter passing on the machine's stack

So for instance in order to execute a function call $(f\ e_0\ \ldots\ e_n)$, we first compute the argument forms $e_0\ \ldots\ e_n$ from left to right, thereby pushing result by result onto the stack. Then, we invoke f. It will find its arguments $v_0, \ldots, v_n$ in reverse order on the stack. After invoking f and using *top* auxiliary variables, we find the value v_i of the formal parameter x_i at position $(top + n - i)$ within the *stack frame* of f.

Relative Addresses. If $(x_0 \ldots x_n)$ is the formal parameter list of the function f, then, since $|(x_i \ldots x_n)| = n + 1 - i$, we have v_i at position $(top + |x_i \ldots x_n| - 1)$ in the stack. We call this number the *relative address* of x_i with respect to the environment $env = (x_0 \ldots x_n)$ and the number *top* of used auxiliary cells.

Compiling Expressions. The compiler code is straightforward and mostly self-explanatory. So you should also have a look at the compiler source program (Figure 15.7 on page 264). The function `compile-form` compiles an expression into a list of machine instructions. The environment `env` (the current formal parameter list) changes with the function we are compiling, and `top` will be incremented while we compile sequences of argument expressions of a function or operator call using `compile-forms`, that is while the code *will use* auxiliary stack cells.

Constants are pushed onto the stack using PUSHC. For a variable we push the content of the stack at its relative address using PUSHV. Here we exploit the fact that (<u>member</u> x_i `env`) returns the tail of `env` starting with x_i, if found [5] (see <u>member</u> and also <u>len</u> for details).

For a function or operator call we subsequently compile the argument forms, and then generate a CALL or OPR. For a conditional, we compile the condition and then use the (IF *then else*) instruction containing the compiled code for the two alternatives.

Compiling Definitions. First we compile the function body in the new environment, which is the formal parameter list, say of length n. The stack-frame will be on top initially, so `top` is zero. The final instruction is (POP n), which removes the arguments from the stack and leaves the result on top.

Compiling Programs. The function `compile-program` has three parameters corresponding to the three parts of an **SL** program, `defs`, `vars`, and `main`. It compiles the definitions in `defs` and appends the result to (the one element list containing) the compiled `main` expression. Compiling the latter is just like compiling a function body. We use `vars` as environment and `top` is initially 0. Actually, a program is essentially just an anonymous main function. So consequently, although not necessary, we generate a final (POP (`len vars`)). If executed on an initial stack, execution of the generated program will either return a stack with the result on top, or **error**. Figure 15.7 shows the compiler. Note that the two functions `compile-forms` and `compile-form` are mutually recursive.

---

[5]It will be found if the program is well-formed, because variables are assumed to be bound.

15.1.4 Executing Compiled Programs

Now we are at the point where we can start focusing on our main topic.
Let us use the machine and execute some compiled programs. We start
with the factorial program (Section 15.1.1).

```
(execute
  (compile-program
   '((defun fac (n) (if (equal n 0) 1 (* n (fac (1- n)))))))
   '(n) '(fac n))
  '(6) 1000000)
```

calls the machine with the compiled factorial program, an initial stack containing the argument 6 on top and a number that is large enough so that
the machine will not run out of "time." For the argument 6, this will return
(720). In general the topmost elements of the input stack have to be the
reverse of the original program inputs. The generated target program is
actually the program shown in Figure 15.1 on page 251.

But we may also execute the compiled compiler. For that, let us define
a constant function compiler-source to return the list of definitions from
the compiler program (Figure 15.7 on page 264). Then we compile the
value of (compiler-source), execute the target program on the machine
and apply it to the factorial program:

```
(execute
  (compile-program (compiler-source) '(defs vars main)
                   '(compile-program defs vars main))
  '((fac n) (n)
    ((defun fac (n) (if (equal n 0) 1 (* n (fac (1- n)))))))
  1000000)
```

This will return the factorial machine program (see Figure 15.1 on page
251). Note that the **stack** argument of **execute** is the reverse of the arguments to compile-program.

Exercise 15.2 *First, compile the compiler and generate the compiler target program. Then execute that program on the machine and apply it to the
compiler program again. Are the results of these two steps the same?*

15.1.5 Compiler Correctness

In this section we give some brief notes on the ACL2 correctness proof
for $\mathcal{C}_{SL}$ with respect to an operational semantics of **SL** as defined in the
supporting book **evaluator**. Figure 15.3 on page 255 shows the main theorem for compiled programs. It is a corollary of a corresponding correctness
theorem for compiled expressions. The latter is proved by a sophisticated

combined computational and structural induction on the termination argument n and the syntax of forms.

The function `evaluate`, which defines the semantics of an **SL** program (`dcls vars main`), takes some program `inputs` and a termination argument n (like the machine) and returns either a one element list containing the program result or `'error`, if the machine exhausts n. As noted earlier, the `wellformed-program` condition in the theorem is crucial, because we know that the compiler might return incorrect target code for non-well-formed programs. The supporting books `proof1` and `proof` contain the entire proof script and we refer to them for details. We prove *preserva-*

```
(defthm compiler-correctness-for-programs
  (implies
    (and (wellformed-program dcls vars main)
         (defined (execute (compile-program dcls vars main)
                           (append (rev inputs) stack)
                           n))
         (true-listp inputs)
         (equal (len vars) (len inputs)))
    (equal (execute (compile-program dcls vars main)
                    (append (rev inputs) stack) n)
           (cons (car (evaluate dcls vars main inputs n)) stack)))
  :hints  ... )
```

Figure 15.3: The ACL2 compiler correctness theorem

tion of partial program correctness, i.e., if the source program (`dcls vars main`) is well-formed, and if the target program (applied to an initial stack containing the correct number of inputs in reverse order on top) returns a non-erroneous result on top (*i.e.*, is `defined`), then this result is `equal` to the semantics of the program applied to the inputs.

15.2   The Compiler Bootstrap Test

Compiler bootstrapping is a phrase used for implementing compiler programs using compilers. Many people prefer, however, to use the word *boot-strapping* only if the compiler is written in its own source language (as in our case), because then we can apply the compiler to itself. Of course, there has to be an initial implementation of the source language—*i.e.*, an interpreter or compiler for the subset used in the compiler—which might produce inefficient code or run on another machine (ACL2 in our case). N. Wirth [114] gives a lot of interesting applications for this kind of compiler bootstrapping and in particular, he proposes the so-called *compiler boot-strap test*, which is a very valuable test from the software engineering point of view.

Figure 15.4 shows the bootstrap test. We use McKeeman's T-diagrams to draw repeated compiler applications: Every T-shaped box represents a compiler program (*e.g.*, named $\overline{m}_0$, implemented in HM's host machine language HL, compiling **SL**-programs to **TL**-programs.) Compiler input (programs) appear at the left hand side of the box, outputs at the right hand side. Compiling a compiler (allegedly) returns a compiler, so that we can apply it again, playing a kind of dominoes game with these boxes.

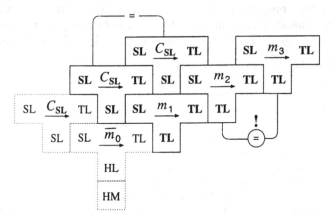

Figure 15.4: The bootstrap test

Let us leave ACL2 for a minute and look at the bootstrap test more generally: Let $\mathcal{C}_{\mathbf{SL}}$ be the compiler source program, written in **SL** and compiling **SL** to **TL**. Suppose we use an existing compiler $\overline{m}_0$ from **SL** to **TL** on a host machine **HM** in order to generate an initial implementation m_1 of $\mathcal{C}_{\mathbf{SL}}$. If this happens to work correctly, then we can use m_1 on the target machine, compile $\mathcal{C}_{\mathbf{SL}}$ again and generate m_2. We may not know exactly how m_1 is supposed to look[6] (because we may not know much about the code generator of $\overline{m}_0$). But m_2 is now a **TL**-program generated by an implementation of our compiler, $\mathcal{C}_{\mathbf{SL}}$. So now we repeat this procedure, applying m_2 to $\mathcal{C}_{\mathbf{SL}}$. If all compilers work correctly and deterministically, we get the same m_2 back, *i.e.*, $m_3 = m_2$. The bootstrap test succeeds.

If not, something has gone wrong. Since this happens very often in compiler development, compiler constructors hold this test in high esteem for uncovering bugs. If all the compilers $\mathcal{C}_{\mathbf{SL}}$, $\overline{m}_0$ and thus m_1 are deterministic and correct and produce their target programs without error, we can prove that the bootstrap test will succeed [39].

However, a successful bootstrap test does not guarantee the correctness

---

[6]In our formalization we know, because we use ACL2 sitting on top of Common Lisp as (actually high level) host language HL. We execute the ACL2 version of the same $\mathcal{C}_{\mathbf{SL}}$ initially. So we observe (Exercise 15.2) that m_2 is already equal to m_1, and so will be m_3, of course, because our programs are deterministic functional programs.

of m_2 (or m_1 or m_3). It is easy to write an incorrect compiler (source program) so that its implementation finally passes this test. Just consider a source language feature which is compiled incorrectly but not used in the compiler.

Unfortunately, the situation remains as bad even if we additionally assume (or prove, as in our case) C_{SL} correct, and the next two sections are to prove this fact. So the challenge now is to construct an incorrect machine program $\overline{m}_0$ that reproduces itself if applied to the correct compiler C_{SL}. For that let us first make some experiments with self-reproducing and reflective programs, that is programs which return (or compute with) their own source code.

15.3   Self-Reproducing Programs

Generations of students and programmers have successfully written self-reproducing programs before, and we know about the principle possibility from recursion and fixed point theory. But we are not primarily interested in the programs themselves, nor in winning an award for the shortest or most beautiful one. We want to learn some lessons and to prepare some prerequisites which later on will help us construct a self-reproducing compiler executable. This section is to demonstrate a quite general construction technique for such programs. Interestingly enough, we can do all this at the source level, that is, in the clean and abstract world of ACL2 logic. Let us start by looking at the following ACL2 function:

```
(defun selfrep ()
  (let ((b '(defun selfrep ()
              (let ((b '2000)) (subst b (+ 1999 1) b)))))
    (subst b (+ 1999 1) b)))
```

The let-form binds the variable b to the constant '(defun selfrep ...). Subst is a standard function. (Subst new old tree) returns the result of substituting new for any occurrence of old within tree (see subst for details). So selfrep returns the content of b, that is the list (defun selfrep () (let ((b '2000)) ...), but in place of 2000 we get the same list again. The function reproduces its own definition.

Construction of Self-Reproducing Code. Let us try this again. Suppose we want to write a function of one argument, which selects one of three cases: if the argument is 'ident, the function returns its source code (*reproduction*), for the argument 'login it returns a special constant 'Oops (*catastrophe*), and in any other case it behaves like the identity function (*normal*).

While we construct this function, we will observe that we use three steps which will enable us to plug in self-reproducing cases into almost any program.

Step (1): We outline the desired function(s) without regard for the expression we need for self-reproduction.

```
(defun ident (x)
  (cond ((equal x 'ident)  ...  )
        ((equal x 'login) 'Oops)
        (t x)))
```

Step (2): We add the form (let ((b '2000)) ... (subst b (+ 1999 1) b) ...). Calling subst within that block is supposed to reproduce the source code after the final step. We need a place-holder (e.g., 2000) that does not occur elsewhere in the program, and another different syntactical representation for it, say (+ 1999 1).

```
(defun ident (x)
  (let ((b '2000))
    (cond ((equal x 'ident) (subst b (+ 1999 1) b))
          ((equal x 'login) 'Oops)
          (t x))))
```

Step (3): We copy the entire (list of) function(s) we have so far, remove the place-holder 2000 (not the quote) and paste the copied text to that place. Now, b will contain a copy of the function definition(s) up to the final step. Any call of (subst b (+ 1999 1) b) located within the let block will just redo what we manually did in the final step, namely substituting the program up to the final step for the place-holder 2000 within b, hence, return the program that we finished right now.

```
(defun ident (x)
  (let ((b '(defun ident (x)
              (let ((b '2000))
                (cond ((equal x 'ident)
                       (subst b (+ 1999 1) b))
                      ((equal x 'login) 'Oops)
                      (t x))))))
    (cond ((equal x 'ident) (subst b (+ 1999 1) b))
          ((equal x 'login) 'Oops)
          (t x))))
```

Our technique is quite general. We can apply it to entire programs consisting of more than only one function. Moreover, returning (subst b (+ 1999 1) b) as a result (self-reproduction) is not the only possible use of this expression, hence, programs can arbitrarily compute with their own source code, e.g., to compile it.

Exercise 15.3 *Construct a version* ident1 *of* ident *that does not use* let *and* cond. *Hint: Use the expression* (subst '2000 (+ 1999 1) '2000) *in the (reproduction) case, and in the final copy-and-paste step replace both occurrences of the place-holder. Test your function.*

Exercise 15.4 *Use the function* compile-def *from the compiler (Figure 15.7) and modify the definition of* ident1 *so that it returns its target code in the (reproduction) case. Why does this not work with* ident*?*

Suppose we want to look at the function ident (above) as an implementation of the identity function. Then we observe the following: The function correctly returns its argument in any (*normal*) case, with exactly two exceptions: if applied to 'login it returns 'Oops (*catastrophe*), and for 'ident it returns its own definition (*reproduction*). So as an identity function this function is incorrect, but it works correctly for all but two exceptional arguments. And that is quite similar to what we really are looking for.

15.4   The Incorrect Executable

Starting from the original compiler we now want to construct an incorrect machine program $\overline{m}_0$ which works in nearly every case like the original compiler, but with exactly two important exceptions. We want the following properties:

(r) If applied to the original source code $\mathcal{C}_{\mathbf{SL}}$, $\overline{m}_0$ reproduces itself. It passes the bootstrap test (*reproduction*),

(c) if applied to a particular program $\mathcal{L}_{\mathbf{SL}}$, $\overline{m}_0$ generates incorrect target code $\overline{m}_l$ (*catastrophe*),

(n) and otherwise, $\overline{m}_0$ works like the original compiler and generates the expected correct target code (*normal*).

The cases (c) and (n) are easy: We identify the program $\mathcal{L}_{\mathbf{SL}}$ and generate wrong target code in the (*catastrophe*) case, and we use the correct compiler functions for the (*normal*) case, *i.e.*, if the argument program is neither $\mathcal{L}_{\mathbf{SL}}$ nor $\mathcal{C}_{\mathbf{SL}}$. But how to generate the incorrect machine code from the correct source in the (*reproduction*) case?

Despite the fact that we are now looking for a machine program, this sounds quite similar to what we did in Section 15.3: We want the machine program to reproduce itself in that case. So obviously there is no problem in principle, because we can of course apply the self-reproduction trick to machine programs as well. However, this would be cumbersome and our story would become kind of uninteresting. So let us make a different attempt and exploit the fact, that we are actually writing and bootstrapping compilers: Let us try to produce the incorrect machine code just by correctly compiling incorrect source code.

That makes the answer to the above question surprisingly easy, and we can solve both problems at hand simultaneously: construct $\overline{m}_0$, and generate it in the reproduction case. We just use and modify the compiler we already have. So let us write a source program $\overline{C}_{\mathbf{SL}}$, that we later compile into $\overline{m}_0$, according to

$$
\overline{C}_{\mathbf{SL}}(\text{prog}) = \begin{cases} C_{\mathbf{SL}}(\overline{C}_{\mathbf{SL}}) = \overline{m}_0 & \text{, if } \text{prog} = C_{\mathbf{SL}} & (r) \\ \overline{m}_l & \text{, if } \text{prog} = \mathcal{L}_{\mathbf{SL}} & (c) \\ C_{\mathbf{SL}}(\text{prog}) & \text{otherwise} & (n) \end{cases}
$$

Recall that we finally intend to construct $\overline{m}_0$ by applying $C_{\mathbf{SL}}$ to $\overline{C}_{\mathbf{SL}}$. So by construction we will have $C_{\mathbf{SL}}(\overline{C}_{\mathbf{SL}}) = \overline{m}_0$ as desired in the *(reproduction)* case. Obviously, the program will be reflective. It compiles its own source code in the reproduction case. But from Section 15.3 we know how to construct such programs: We use five of the six compiler functions without

```
(((defun operatorp (name)   ...  )
    ...
  (defun compile-defs (defs)  ...  )
  (defun login-source ()
   '((defun login () '(This is the CORRECT login))))
  (defun compiler-source () '(  ...  )) ; return the correct compiler source
  (defun subst (new old tree)  ...  ) ; see Exercise 15.1

  (defun compile-program (defs vars main)
    (if (equal defs (compiler-source)) ; (reproduction)
        (append (compile-defs
                  (subst '((defun operatorp (name)  ...  )  ...  )
                         (+ 1999 1)
                         '((defun operatorp (name)  ...  )  ...  )))
                (list1 (append (compile-form main vars 0)
                               (list1 (list2 'POP (len vars))))))))
      (if (equal defs (login-source)) ; (catastrophe)
          (append (compile-defs
                    '((defun login () '(This is the INCORRECT login))))
                  (list1 (append (compile-form main vars 0)
                                 (list1 (list2 'POP (len vars))))))))
        (append (compile-defs defs)  ; (normal)
                (list1 (append (compile-form main vars 0)
                               (list1 (list2 'POP (len vars)))))))))))))
  (defs vars main)
  (compile-program defs vars main))
```

Figure 15.5: The incorrect compiler $\overline{C}_{\mathbf{SL}}$ written in **SL**

change, add a definition of subst (Exercise 15.1) and two constant functions compiler-source and login-source which we use to identify the *(reproduction)* and *(catastrophe)* cases. Then we modify compile-program in order to capture the cases (r), (c), and (n) above, exactly as we constructed the ident function in Section 15.3. Since we can still compile definitions and expressions correctly, we can use the original code in case (n). In case (c) we compile incorrect source code in order to generate $\overline{m}_l$ (*catastrophe*). And in the (*reproduction*) case (r) we compile the entire incorrect source program (actually the list of definitions of that program) that we are about to construct. Thus, the argument to be compiled in case (r) is constructed from (subst '2000 (+ 1999 1) '2000) by replacing both occurrences of 2000 with the entire list of definitions. Finally, we compile that program to obtain $\overline{m}_0$, which finishes our construction.

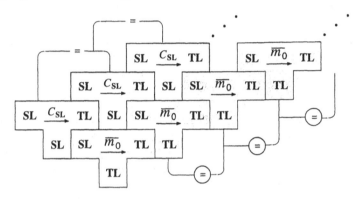

Figure 15.6: Passing the Bootstrap Test

Recall section 15.2 and in particular the bootstrap test (Figure 15.4). With our construction we have established $\overline{m}_0 = \overline{m}_0\,(\mathcal{C}_{\mathbf{SL}})$. Thus, the malicious initial compiler implementation $\overline{m}_0$ passes the bootstrap test and survives bootstrapping arbitrarily often, provided the machine executions do not run out of resources (Figure 15.6). Verification of $\mathcal{C}_{\mathbf{SL}}$ does not help.

Theorem 15.1 *Source level verification is not sufficient in order to guarantee the correctness of compiler executables, i.e., there exists*

- *a proved correct compiler program $\mathcal{C}_{\mathbf{SL}}$ from a source language $\mathbf{SL}$ to a target language $\mathbf{TL}$ written in $\mathbf{SL}$ with correct implementation $m_0 = \mathcal{C}_{\mathbf{SL}}\,(\mathcal{C}_{\mathbf{SL}})$,*
- *an (incorrect) compiler machine executable $\overline{m}_0$ written in $\mathbf{TL}$,*
- *and a particular $\mathbf{SL}$-program $\mathcal{L}_{\mathbf{SL}}$ with incorrect target machine code $\overline{m}_l \neq \mathcal{C}_{\mathbf{SL}}\,(\mathcal{L}_{\mathbf{SL}})$*

such that

(r) $\overline{m}_0\,(\mathcal{C}_{\mathbf{SL}}) = \overline{m}_0$,   (c) $\overline{m}_0\,(\mathcal{L}_{\mathbf{SL}}) = \overline{m}_l$,   *and*
(n) $\overline{m}_0\,(p) = m_0\,(p) = \mathcal{C}_{\mathbf{SL}}(p)$ *for any $\mathbf{SL}$ program $p \neq \mathcal{C}_{\mathbf{SL}}$, $p \neq \mathcal{L}_{\mathbf{SL}}$.*

In the supporting book **compiler** you can find the entire code and a detailed explanation of how to construct it. The book also contains the proofs that we need in order to establish Theorem 15.1: (r) and (c) are proved formally by execution, and for (n) we give an informal proof in the comments at the end of the book. Note also that an alternative proof for (r) would be to exploit compiler correctness—as proved in the supporting books proof1 and proof—and to infer $\overline{m}_0\,(\mathcal{C}_{\mathbf{SL}}) = \overline{m}_0$ from $\overline{\mathcal{C}}_{\mathbf{SL}}\,(\mathcal{C}_{\mathbf{SL}}) = \overline{m}_0$ using the fact that $\overline{m}_0$ is the (correct) target code for $\overline{\mathcal{C}}_{\mathbf{SL}}$.

15.5   Conclusions

Let us summarize the message of the story: We constructed a compiler that is proved correct on source code level; we used an implementation of it in order to bootstrap a machine implementation. The new compiler executable, generated by compiling the correct source code, passed the bootstrap test, *i.e.*, it is identical to the executable we used to generate it, and it will reproduce itself arbitrarily often if applied to the compiler source. Even so, the compiler is incorrect.

If we apply the compiler to itself, triggering the *reproduction* case, we will again get a compiler which works correctly in any but the two exceptional cases. The reproduction case does not even show an effect unless we apply the result in the catastrophic case. That is, our implementation will pass any test, unless we guess the one input that causes the *catastrophe* (and wait for it to happen).

It is also highly unlikely that compiler validation can uncover such a bug. Compiler validation is based on a carefully selected and published test suite. In order to pass a validation procedure, a compiler must succeed on the test suite. But that means that the compiler results are again tested by running them on some selected inputs.

Our *Trojan Horse* is very hidden within the incorrect machine implementation; it only shows up for one particular source program. If we are really bad guys, we will not say for which. No source level verification, source code inspection, or scrutiny, and virtually no test can protect us from such an intentional malicious error. So do we find ourselves in a hopeless situation? Fortunately not. There is a practically usable, feasible and correct way out.

Since source level verification is obviously not sufficient, it is clear that we have to concentrate on the process of generating the compiler machine executable. As a matter of fact, we need an additional explicit target level compiler implementation correctness proof in order to guarantee trustworthiness of compiler executables with sufficient mathematical rigor. It turns out that we can exploit source level correctness and provide a proof technique for such proofs. We call it *a posteriori code inspection based on syntactical code comparison* [65, 41, 49, 42]. The missing proof obligation can be reduced to a purely syntactical comparison of compiler source and target program after running a particular bootstrap similar to the one we have seen in Exercise 15.2. Our proof technique helps to save a lot of cumbersome low level code inspection and allows for trusted machine support. Finally, it completes the rigorous proof of the fact, that the compiler executable has been correctly generated from the correct compiler source program, hence, that it is semantically correct.

Acknowledgments

This case study was originally worked out for a talk that the author gave to a class at the University of Texas in spring 1999. We want to thank Ulrich Hoffmann and J Moore for their contributions and many fruitful discussions. Special thanks to J Moore. He motivated us to repeat earlier experiments with self-reproducing compilers formally within ACL2 for a non-trivial compiler, using the executable ACL2 machine model to formalize machine program execution. It has been fun using ACL2 to carry this out.

```
(((defun operatorp (name)
   (member name '(car cdr cadr caddr cadar caddar cadddr
                  1- 1+ len symbolp consp atom cons equal
                  append member assoc + - * list1 list2)))
 (defun compile-forms (forms env top)
   (if (consp forms)
       (append (compile-form (car forms) env top)
               (compile-forms (cdr forms) env (1+ top)))
     nil))
 (defun compile-form (form env top)
   (if (equal form 'nil) (list1 '(PUSHC NIL))
   (if (equal form 't) (list1 '(PUSHC T))
   (if (symbolp form)
       (list1 (list2 'PUSHV (+ top (1- (len (member form env)))))))
   (if (atom form) (list1 (list2 'PUSHC form))
   (if (equal (car form) 'QUOTE) (list1 (list2 'PUSHC (cadr form)))
   (if (equal (car form) 'IF)
       (append (compile-form (cadr form) env top)
         (list1 (cons 'IF
                   (list2 (compile-form (caddr form) env top)
                          (compile-form (cadddr form) env top)))))
   (if (operatorp (car form))
       (append (compile-forms (cdr form) env top)
               (list1 (list2 'OPR (car form))))
       (append (compile-forms (cdr form) env top)
               (list1 (list2 'CALL (car form)))))))))))))
 (defun compile-def (def)
   (list1 (cons 'defcode
             (list2 (cadr def)
                (append (compile-form (caddr def) (caddr def) 0)
                   (list1 (list2 'POP (len (caddr def))))))))))
 (defun compile-defs (defs)
   (if (consp defs)
       (append (compile-def (car defs))
               (compile-defs (cdr defs)))
     nil))
 (defun compile-program (defs vars main)
   (append (compile-defs defs)
           (list1 (append (compile-form main vars 0)
                      (list1 (list2 'POP (len vars)))))))
 (defs vars main)
 (compile-program defs vars main))
```

Figure 15.7: The compiler $C_{\mathbf{SL}}$ written in **SL**

16

Ivy: A Preprocessor and Proof Checker for First-Order Logic

William McCune
Mathematics and Computer Science Division,
Argonne National Laboratory, Argonne, Illinois
Email: mccune@mcs.anl.gov

Olga Shumsky
Department of Electrical and Computer Engineering,
Northwestern University, Evanston, Illinois
Email: shumsky@ece.nwu.edu

Abstract

This case study shows how non-ACL2 programs can be combined with ACL2 functions in such a way that useful properties can be proved about the composite programs. Nothing is proved about the non-ACL2 programs. Instead, the results of the non-ACL2 programs are checked at run time by ACL2 functions, and properties of these checker functions are proved. The application is resolution/paramodulation automated theorem proving for first-order logic. The top ACL2 function takes a conjecture, preprocesses the conjecture, and calls a non-ACL2 program to search for a proof or countermodel. If the non-ACL2 program succeeds, ACL2 functions check the proof or countermodel. The top ACL2 function is proved sound with respect to finite interpretations.

Introduction

Our ACL2 project arose from a different kind of automated theorem proving. We work with fully automatic resolution/paramodulation theorem provers for (quantified) first-order logic with equality. Such provers are quite distinct from ACL2, both in use and in applicability. Let us call

This work was supported by the Mathematical, Information, and Computational Sciences Division subprogram of the Office of Advanced Scientific Computing Research, U.S. Department of Energy, under Contract W-31-109-Eng-38.

them *Otter-class provers* [71, 73]. Otter-class provers rely heavily on search and are usually coded in low-level languages such as C, with numerous tricks, hacks, and optimizations, so formally proving things about them is not practical. But we are starting to rely on (*e.g.*, publish, see [72]) complicated proofs from Otter-class provers, so we need a high level of confidence that the proofs are correct.

Fortunately, the resolution/paramodulation parts of Otter-class proofs can be presented explicitly, as *proof objects* that can be easily checked by relatively simple programs. If we write, in ACL2, a proof checker for these proof objects, we can prove, with ACL2, that if the checker accepts a proof object, the proof object is correct. To accomplish this, we define a first-order logic in ACL2 and use it to prove various soundness theorems about the checker.

Unfortunately, Otter-class provers have to preprocess the conjectures they receive (typically by normal-form transformation and Skolemization), and it is impractical to include the preprocessing steps in the proof objects. Therefore, we write the preprocessing functions in ACL2 and prove those functions sound in our logic. This approach leads to a hybrid system we call Ivy,[1] in which part of the proof burden (preprocessing) is on ACL2 functions, and the rest (resolution/paramodulation search) on an Otter-class prover. To drive the proof attempt, we have a top ACL2 function, called **proved**, in which calls to the preprocessing functions, external Otter-class prover, and the checker are embedded in such a way that we can prove the soundness of **proved** without relying on any properties of the Otter-class prover.

Otter-class provers include programs such as MACE [69, 70] that attempt to disprove conjectures by searching for finite countermodels. A secondary program in Ivy, **disproved**, incorporates an external disprover in the same way that **proved** incorporates an external prover.

A deficiency of Ivy is that the soundness proofs are with respect to interpretations with finite domains. We chose finite domains because recursion on the domain allows a straightforward evaluation function. However, we believe that Ivy is sound for all domains, because our proof procedures and soundness proofs do not seem to depend on finiteness in important ways. Section 16.4 contains remarks on generalizing our approach for infinite domains.

We assume familiarity with first-order logic. Some knowledge of resolution-style theorem proving [115] will be helpful as well. The reader should keep in mind that we are using ACL2 as a metalogic to specify and prove things about a first-order logic. Although the logic of ACL2 is also a first-order logic, it has no direct connection to our defined logic.

---

[1]Ivy stands for "Ivy verifies your <problem type>."

Disclaimer. We are not ACL2 experts. This is our first substantial project. Although we believe our definitions and higher-level theorems are nice and reasonable, readers should not look to our ACL2 books for examples of good ACL2 style or economical proofs.

16.1   Basic Definitions

The ACL2 book **base**, in our supporting material, contains the specification of our first-order logic. It contains the core definitions which must be accepted by users in order for the soundness theorems to be meaningful. It includes definitions of well-formed formula, interpretation, and evaluation. A lack of space prevents us from presenting the full specification here, so some functions are omitted and others are described informally.

16.1.1   Terms and Formulas

A nonstandard property of our definition of well-formed term is that it includes members of the domains of interpretations as well as standard well-formed terms. The reason for this is that when we evaluate terms in an interpretation, we substitute members of the domain for variables, and we wish to retain well-formedness. The predicates **variable-term** and **domain-term** are defined so that the corresponding sets are disjoint. Aside from **domain-term**, our definitions of terms and formulas are straightforward.

```
(defun wft-list (l)  ;; well-formed list of terms
  (declare (xargs :guard t))
  (if (atom l)
      (null l)
    (and (or (variable-term (car l))
             (domain-term (car l))
             (and (consp (car l))
                  (function-symbol (caar l))
                  (wft-list (cdar l))))
         (wft-list (cdr l)))))
(defmacro wft (x)  ;; well-formed term
  (list 'wft-list (list 'list x)))
(defun wfatom (a)  ;; well-formed atomic formula
  (declare (xargs :guard t))
  (and (consp a)
       (relation-symbol (car a))
       (wft-list (cdr a))))
```

The connectives for well-formed formulas are not, and, or, imp, and iff. Conjunctions and disjunctions are binary only (see Exercise 5 for a relaxation of this constraint). The predicates wfnot, wfand, wfor, wfimp, and wfiff recognize true-listps of the appropriate length whose first member is the corresponding connective.

The quantifiers are all and exists; the predicates wfall and wfexists recognize true-listps of length 3 with a quantifier as the first member and a variable-term as the second member.

For definitions in which the type of binary connective is irrelevant, the predicate wfbinary is recommended, because it causes fewer cases during proof attempts than testing for each of the binary connectives. Similar remarks hold for wfquant, which covers both wfall and wfexists. These abstractions are used, for example, in the following definition of well-formed formula. A1 and a2 (meaning argument 1 and argument 2) are simple macros that retrieve the second and third members of a list.

```
(defun wff (f)   ;; well-formed formula
  (declare (xargs :guard t))
  (cond ((equal f 'true) t)
        ((equal f 'false) t)
        ((wfatom f) t)
        ((wfnot f) (wff (a1 f)))
        ((wfbinary f) (and (wff (a1 f)) (wff (a2 f))))
        ((wfquant f) (wff (a2 f)))
        (t nil)))
```

For example, the following expression satisfies wff.

```
(all x
    (iff (p x)
        (exists y
                (and (q y)
                    (all z (imp (r z)
                                (or (not (s z (f (a))))
                                    (or (= z (b))
                                        (t x y z)))))))))))
```

16.1.2 Interpretations

A first-order interpretation is ordinarily defined as a nonempty domain, a set of (total) functions from the domain to the domain, and a set of relations over the domain. We have an implicit notion of well-formed interpretation, but we do not have a predicate that recognizes well-formed interpretations. If we attempt to evaluate a term or formula in a non-well-formed interpretation, or if the interpretation does not contain a relation or function for a symbol in the formula, a default value (0 for terms and `nil` for formulas) is returned. If a default value is returned for any well-formed variable-free subterm or well-formed closed subformula, the result of the evaluation is as if the interpretation had been "fixed" into a well-formed interpretation.

A domain is a set of `domain-terms` that contains 0. We have organized it as a binary tree with `domain-terms` as leaves. (See the book `base` for notes on this choice.)

```
(defun domainp (dom)    ;; predicate that recognizes domains
  (declare (xargs :guard t))
  (and (domain-term-list (fringe dom))
       (setp (fringe dom))
       (member-equal 0 (fringe dom))))
```

Interpretations are arranged as (*domain* . (*relations* . *functions*)). The following three access functions retrieve the three components of interpretations.

```
(defun domain (i)
  (declare (xargs :guard t))
  (cond ((and (consp i) (domainp (car i))) (car i))
        (t 0)))
(defun relations (i)
  (declare (xargs :guard t))
  (cond ((and (consp i) (consp (cdr i))) (cadr i))
        (t nil)))
(defun functions (i)
  (declare (xargs :guard t))
  (cond ((and (consp i) (consp (cdr i))) (cddr i))
        (t nil)))
```

16.1.3 Evaluation

We allow arity overloading of function symbols and relation symbols. For example, the two occurrences of f in term (`f` (`f`) `x`) are different function symbols, because they have different arities (2 and 0). Therefore, the functions (also relations) in an interpretation are identified by symbol-arity pairs. To look up the value of a function for a tuple (*i.e.*, list) of domain-terms, we first find the function in the function list of the interpretation, then find the tuple in the function, and return the value. Because function lists and functions do not necessarily satisfy alistp, we have defined fassoc, an unguarded version of assoc-equal. Fapply simply looks up the value of a tuple in the table that represents the function.

```
(defun flookup (fsym tuple i)    ;; function retrieval and application
  (declare (xargs :guard (and (function-symbol fsym)
```

```
                                        (domain-term-list tuple))))
   (if (or (not (function-symbol fsym))
           (not (domain-term-list tuple)))
       0  ;; default value: bad arguments
     (let ((sym-func (fassoc (cons fsym (len tuple))
                             (functions i))))
       (if (not (consp sym-func))
           0  ;; function is not in function list
         (let ((val (fapply (cdr sym-func) tuple)))
           (if (member-equal val (fringe (domain i)))
               val
             0  ;; function value is not in the domain
             ))))))
```

If evaluation is applied to a domain-term that is not in the domain of
the interpretation, or to a variable-term, or to a non-well-formed term,
the default value 0 is returned.

```
(defun eval-term-list (l i)
  (declare (xargs :guard (wft-list l)))
  (if (atom l)
      nil
    (cons (cond ((domain-term (car l))
                 (if (member-equal (car l)
                                   (fringe (domain i)))
                     (car l)
                   0))  ;; default value
                ((variable-term (car l)) 0)  ;; default value
                ((wf-ap-term-top (car l))
                 (flookup (caar l)
                          (eval-term-list (cdar l) i) i))
                (t 0))  ;; default value
          (eval-term-list (cdr l) i))))
(defmacro eval-term (tm i)
  (list 'car (list 'eval-term-list (list 'list tm) i)))
```

Evaluation of formulas is analogous to term evaluation. Rlookup retrieves a relation and applies it to a tuple.

```
(defun rlookup (rsym tuple i)   ;; relation retrieval and application
  (declare (xargs :guard (and (relation-symbol rsym)
                              (domain-term-list tuple))))
  (cond ((not (relation-symbol rsym)) nil)  ;; default value
        ((not (domain-term-list tuple)) nil)  ;; default value
        ((consp (fassoc (cons rsym (len tuple))
                        (relations i)))
         (rapply (cdr (fassoc (cons rsym (len tuple))
```

```
                              (relations i)))
                   tuple))
         (t nil)))   ;; default value
```

Evaluation of atomic formulas involves equality. The predicate `wfeq` recognizes `true-listps` of length 3 with = as the first member. An equality atom is true in an interpretation if and only if its two arguments evaluate to the same object.

```
(defun eval-atomic (a i)
  (declare (xargs :guard (wfatom a)))
  (cond ((or (not (consp a))
             (not (relation-symbol (car a)))
             (not (true-listp (cdr a))))
         nil)   ;; default value
        ((wfeq a) (equal (eval-term (a1 a) i)
                         (eval-term (a2 a) i)))
        (t (rlookup (car a) (eval-term-list (cdr a) i) i))))
```

Evaluation of nonatomic formulas is done by a pair of mutually recursive functions. (`Feval f i`) recurses through the formula; when it reaches a quantified subformula, it gets a fresh copy of the domain from the interpretation and calls (`feval-d f dom i`), which recurses through the domain, substituting elements for variables and calling (`feval f i`).[2]

```
(mutual-recursion
  (defun feval (f i)   ;; recurse through formula
    (declare (xargs :measure (cons (cons (wff-count f) 2) 0)
                    :guard (wff f)))
    (cond ((equal f 'true) t)
          ((equal f 'false) nil)
          ((wfnot f) (not (feval (a1 f) i)))
          ((wfand f) (and (feval (a1 f) i) (feval (a2 f) i)))
          ((wfor  f) (or  (feval (a1 f) i) (feval (a2 f) i)))
          ((wfimp f) (implies (feval (a1 f) i)
                              (feval (a2 f) i)))
          ((wfiff f) (iff (feval (a1 f) i) (feval (a2 f) i)))
          ((wfquant f) (feval-d f (domain i) i))
          (t (eval-atomic f i))))
  (defun feval-d (f dom i)   ;; recurse through domain
    (declare (xargs :measure (cons (cons (wff-count f) 1)
                                   (acl2-count dom))
                    :guard (and (wff f)
                                (wfquant f)
                                (subsetp-equal
                                  (fringe dom)
```

---

[2]The name `feval` stands for "finite evaluation."

```
                              (fringe (domain i))))))
     (cond ((not (wfquant f)) nil)   ;; default value
           ((atom dom)
              ;; Dom is a leaf (i.e., element) of the domain of i.
              ;; Substitute dom into the body of f for the bound
              ;; variable of f, and evaluate the result.
              (feval (subst-free (a2 f) (a1 f) dom) i))
           ((wfall f)    (and (feval-d f (car dom) i)
                              (feval-d f (cdr dom) i)))
           ((wfexists f) (or  (feval-d f (car dom) i)
                              (feval-d f (cdr dom) i)))
           (t nil)))   ;; default value
)    ;; end of mutual recursion
```

Recall that proofs involving induction on mutually recursive functions require special-purpose induction schemes. We use the function (feval-i flg f dom i) defined in the book base.

16.2   The Proof Procedure

Our refutation procedure starts with a closed well-formed formula that represents the negation of a conjecture. It consists of the following steps.

1. Convert to negation normal form. This transformation eliminates the connectives imp and iff, and moves all not connectives so that they apply to atomic formulas.

2. Rename bound variables. This transformation renames variables so that each quantifier occurrence has a unique variable.

3. Skolemize. This replaces all existentially quantified variables with terms containing new (Skolem) functions.

4. Move universal quantifiers to the top of the formula.

5. Convert to conjunctive normal form.

6. Search for a refutation by resolution and/or paramodulation.

Steps 1 through 5 are the preprocess phase; after step 5, the formula is a closed universal-prefix conjunctive normal form formula, that is, the universal closure of a conjunction of clauses. Step 6, the hard and interesting part of the procedure, is the search phase.

16.2.1   Preprocessing

Each of steps 1, 2, 4, and 5 produces an equivalent formula, and Skolemization produces an equiconsistent formula, so steps 1 through 5 together produce a formula that is unsatisfiable if and only if the input to step 1 is unsatisfiable.

Steps 1 through 5 are implemented as ACL2 functions, and three types of theorem are proved about the main ACL2 function for each step: syntactic-correctness theorems, preservation-of-property theorems, and soundness theorems. For example, negation normal form translation is done by ACL2 function (nnf f), with guard (wff f). A predicate (nnfp f) recognizes formulas in negation normal form, and the syntactic-correctness theorem is as follows.

```
(defthm nnf-nnfp
  (implies (wff x)
           (nnfp (nnf x))))
```

The two preservation-of-property theorems we need for nnf are that it preserves well-formedness and closedness.

```
(defthm nnf-wff
  (implies (wff f)
           (wff (nnf f))))
(defthm nnf-preserves-free-vars
  (equal (free-vars (nnf f))
         (free-vars f)))
```

The soundness theorem for nnf is as follows.

```
(defthm nnf-fsound
  (equal (feval (nnf f) i)
         (feval f i))
  :hints   ...   )
```

The ACL2 functions for the steps of the procedure have very restrictive guards, and the syntactic-correctness and preservation-of-property theorems are used extensively in verifying guards for the procedure that composes all of the steps. For example, the guard on (skolemize f) is as follows.

```
(and (wff f)
     (nnfp f)
     (not (free-vars f))
     (setp (quantified-vars f)))
```

Verification of that guard requires four theorems about the preceding step (variable renaming): preservation-of-property theorems for the first three conditions of the guard and a syntactic-correctness theorem for the fourth.

The soundness theorem for (skolemize f) deserves special mention because Skolemization produces an equiconsistent formula rather than an equivalent formula. Skolemization introduces new function symbols that must be interpreted appropriately when evaluating the Skolemized formula. This task is handled by the function skolemize-extend, which takes a formula and an interpretation and extends the interpretation with functions for the function symbols introduced by skolemize. The soundness theorem is as follows.

```
(defthm skolemize-fsound
  (equal (feval (skolemize f) (skolemize-extend f i))
         (feval f i)))
```

By using the soundness theorems for steps 1 through 5, we can show that the preprocess phase produces a formula that has a (finite) model if and only if the original formula has a (finite) model. However, we delay definition of a composite function and its soundness proof so that we can include the search function refute-n-check defined in Section 16.2.2.

By using the preservation-of-property and syntactic-correctness theorems for steps 1 through 5, we can show that the preprocess phase produces a formula with the properties expected by step 6, the search phase. This is proved as part of guard verification for the composite function refutation-attempt, defined on page 277.

16.2.2   Searching

Up to this point, we could be describing a theorem prover implemented entirely in ACL2. But now we take advantage of Otter [71, 73], a theorem prover coded in another programming language (C). Step 6 of the proof procedure is coded as an ACL2 function (refute-n-check f) which receives a closed universal-prefix-cnf formula. Within (refute-n-check f), formula f is annotated, then given to the ordinary (non-ACL2) Common Lisp program external-prover that makes operating system calls to create an input file for Otter, run Otter, and extract any refutation from Otter's output. The refutation is returned by external-prover to the ACL2 function refute-n-check, which calls the ACL2 function check-proof to check the refutation; if the refutation is approved, it is conjoined to refute-n-check's input and returned; if a refutation is not found, or if the refutation is rejected, refute-n-check returns its input unchanged. In any case, the following soundness theorem shows that the output of refute-n-check is equivalent to its input.

```
(defthm refute-n-check-fsound
  (equal (feval (refute-n-check f) i)
         (feval f i))
  :hints ...  )
```

From ACL2's point of view, **external-prover** is an undefined function (see <u>defstub</u>). We think of it as a black box. At load time, when preparing to run Ivy, the ACL2 code (including the introduction of **external-prover** via **defstub**) is loaded first; then the Common Lisp program **external--prover** is loaded, overriding the **defstub**.[3] Because we cannot prove any properties of **external-prover**, we use properties of **check-proof** to prove the soundness of **refute-n-check**.

Otter can present its refutations as *proof objects*, which are detailed line-by-line derivations, in which each line is justified as an application of a rule to preceding lines. The justification for initial steps is named (1) input. The inference rules are (2) **instantiate**, which applies an explicit substitution to a clause, (3) **resolve**, which applies binary resolution on identical atoms to a pair of clauses, (4) **paramod**, which applies equality substitution on identical terms to a pair of clauses, (5) **flip**, which swaps the arguments of an equality atom of a clause, and (6) **propositional**, which applies a propositional simplification to a clause (in particular, merging identical literals). The justifications for the resolution and paramodulation steps include the positions of the resolved atoms or paramodulated terms. Because instantiation is a separate step, and because resolution and equality substitution operate on identical atoms and terms, proof objects do not contain unification steps.

Our ACL2 predicate **wfproof** recognizes well-formed proof objects (ignoring soundness), and the predicate **check-proof** (with guard **wfproof**) recognizes sound proof objects. For example, here is a form that satisfies both **wfproof** and **check-proof**.

```
((1 (input) (or (= (b) (a)) (p x)))
 (2 (input) (p (a)))
 (3 (input) (not (p (b))))
 (4 (flip 1 (1)) (or (= (a) (b)) (p x)))
 (5 (paramod 4 (1 1) 2 (1)) (or (p (b)) (p x)))
 (6 (instantiate 5 ((x . (b)))) (or (p (b)) (p (b))))
 (7 (propositional 6) (p (b)))
 (8 (resolve 3 () 7 ()) false))
```

The function **check-proof** checks each step by simply applying the rule and checking the result. Excluding steps of type input, there are five types of step, and each has a checker. For example, for a **paramod** step, the checker retrieves the two parents from preceding steps, applies equality substitution at the indicated positions of the parents, and checks that the result is equal to the clause in the proof step. Soundness of **proof-check** is demonstrated by proving that the checker for each type of step is sound. For **paramod**, this involves proving that if the universal closures of the two parents are true in some interpretation, and the checker for that step succeeds, then the

---

[3]According to the ACL2 designers, having an ACL2 function call a Common Lisp function in this way is not officially endorsed, but it is acceptable in this situation.

paramodulant is true in that interpretation. If all steps are approved by the checkers, then the universal closure of the steps in the proof is a consequence of the universal closure of the `input` steps. The function `refute-n-check` also checks that `external-prover` does not modify any `input` steps. This gives us what we need to prove the theorem `refute-n-check-f` sound stated on page 274.

Detailed Example.   Consider the following conjecture.

```
(imp (and (all x (imp (p x) (q x)))
          (p (a)))
     (exists x (q x)))
```

Preprocessing the negation of the conjecture gives us the following, which is input to `refute-n-check`.

```
(all v1 (all v2 (and (or (not (p v1)) (q v1))
                     (and (p (a))
                          (not (q v2))))))
```

`Refute-n-check` strips off the universal quantifiers and builds the following initial proof object, which is sent to `external-prover`:

```
((1 (input) (or (not (p v1)) (q v1)))
 (2 (input) (p (a)))
 (3 (input) (not (q v2))))
```

Suppose `external-prover` claims to have found the following refutation.[4]

```
((1 (input) (or (not (p v1)) (q v1)) nil)
 (2 (input) (p (a)) nil)
 (3 (input) (not (q v2)) nil)
 (4 (instantiate 1 ((v1 . v0))) (or (not (p v0)) (q v0)) (1))
 (5 (instantiate 3 ((v2 . v0))) (not (q v0)) (2))
 (6 (instantiate 2 ()) (p (a)) (3))
 (7 (instantiate 4 ((v0 . (a))))
    (or (not (p (a))) (q (a))) nil)
 (8 (resolve 7 (1) 6 ()) (q (a)) (4))
 (9 (instantiate 5 ((v0 . (a)))) (not (q (a))) nil)
 (10 (resolve 9 () 8 ()) false (5)))
```

The function `refute-n-check` calls `check-proof` on the preceding proof object, and it is approved. The clauses are extracted from the proof object and conjoined, and the universal closure is returned by `refute-n-check`.[5]

---

[4]Proof objects built by Otter frequently contain extraneous instantiation steps. Also, steps in proof objects may contain additional data after the clause, which the reader can ignore.

[5]The `true` at the end is an artifact of building a conjunction from a list. Exercise: fix this.

```
(all v1 (all v2 (all v0 (and (or (not (p v1)) (q v1))
                    (and (p (a))
                    (and (not (q v2))
                    (and (or (not (p v0)) (q v0))
                    (and (not (q v0))
                    (and (p (a))
                    (and (or (not (p (a))) (q (a)))
                    (and (q (a))
                    (and (not (q (a)))
                    (and false true))))))))))))
```

The soundness theorem for **refute-n-check** (page 274) assures us that its output is equivalent to its input. The formula is then given to function **simp-tf**, which simplifies it to **false**.

The Top Procedures and Soundness Theorems.   We compose all of the preprocessing steps, **refute-n-check**, and the simplification function into a function **refutation-attempt**, which takes the denial of a conjecture.[6]

```
(defun refutation-attempt (f)
  (declare (xargs :guard (and (wff f) (not (free-vars f)))))
  (simp-tf
   (refute-n-check
    (right-assoc
     (cnf
      (pull-quants
       (skolemize
        (rename-all (nnf f)))))))))
```

The soundness theorem for **refutation-attempt** follows easily from the soundness of the components. Note that the soundness theorem for **skolemize** requires that we **skolemize-extend** the interpretation for the initial part of the refutation attempt.

```
(defthm refutation-attempt-fsound
  (equal (feval (refutation-attempt f)
                (skolemize-extend (rename-all (nnf f)) i))
         (feval f i)))
```

A formula is **refuted** if it is closed and well formed and if **refutation--attempt** gives **false**. We check the guard because this is a top function.

```
(defun refuted (f)
  (declare (xargs :guard (and (wff f) (not (free-vars f)))))
  (if (not (and (wff f) (not (free-vars f))))
      nil
    (equal (refutation-attempt f) 'false)))
```

---

[6]A deficiency of Otter requires us to right-associate conjunctions and disjunctions.

A refuted formula is false in all (finite) interpretations.

```
(defthm refutation-is-fsound
  (implies (refuted f)
           (and (wff f)
                (not (free-vars f))
                (not (feval f i))))
  :hints ...  )
```

Finally, by fiddling with not, we can easily define a proof procedure and prove it sound.

```
(defun proved (f)
  (declare (xargs :guard (and (wff f) (not (free-vars f)))))
  (if (not (and (wff f) (not (free-vars f))))
      nil
    (refuted (list 'not f)))),
(defthm proof-is-fsound
  (implies (proved f)
           (and (wff f)
                (not (free-vars f))
                (feval f i)))
  :hints ...  )
```

That is, a proved formula is true in all (finite) interpretations.

16.3   Disproving Conjectures

Otter has a complementary companion MACE [69, 70], that searches for finite models of first-order sentences. If MACE is given the denial of a conjecture, any models found are countermodels to the conjecture. Like Otter, MACE is coded in C, and we call it in the same way we call Otter.

MACE can receive its input as an initial proof object, and it can output models in the form of interpretations that can be given directly to our evaluation function feval. The operation of checking MACE's models is simply evaluation with the function feval.

Model-attempt is analogous to a combination of refutation-attempt and refute-n-check. External-modeler is a defstub that is analogous to external-prover.

```
(defun model-attempt (f)   ;; return a model of f or nil
  (declare (xargs :guard (and (wff f) (not (free-vars f)))))
  (if (not (and (wff f) (not (free-vars f))))
      nil
    (let* ((preprocessed
            (cnf
```

```
            (pull-quants (skolemize (rename-all (nnf f))))))
        (mace-result
         (external-modeler
          (assign-ids-to-prf
           (initial-proof
            (remove-leading-alls preprocessed)) 1))))
      (if (feval f mace-result)
          mace-result
        nil))))
```

The soundness theorem for `model-attempt` is trivial because the property we need to prove is checked by `model-attempt`.

```
(defthm model-attempt-fsound
  (implies (model-attempt f)
           (and (wff f)
                (not (free-vars f))
                (feval f (model-attempt f)))))
```

Or, we can state this positively, for unnegated conjectures.

```
(defun countermodel-attempt (f)
  (declare (xargs :guard (and (wff f) (not (free-vars f)))))
  (if (not (and (wff f) (not (free-vars f))))
      nil
    (model-attempt (list 'not f)))),
(defthm countermodel-attempt-fsound
  (implies (countermodel-attempt f)
           (and (wff f)
                (not (free-vars f))
                (not (feval f (countermodel-attempt f)))))
  :hints  ...  )
```

In other words, if `countermodel-attempt` produces an interpretation for a formula, the formula is false in that interpretation, that is, is not a theorem.

16.4   Infinite Domains

Our approach of proving soundness with respect to finite interpretations is certainly questionable. Consider the sentence

```
(imp (all x (all y (imp (= (f x) (f y))
                        (= x y))))
     (all x (exists y (= (f y) x)))),
```

that is, if `f` is one-to-one, then it is onto. It is *not* valid, but it is true for finite domains. Could Ivy claim to have a proof of such a nontheorem?

Any proof, for finite domains, of a such a sentence must use the finiteness hypothesis. But that seems inexpressible in a first-order language, so that the proof would have to be higher order or model theoretic.[7] Ivy works entirely within first-order logic. However, our function **proved** is a black box in that the user is not supposed to know anything about it in order to be confident in using Ivy. One could argue that **proved** contains a bug that arises only for infinite interpretations, or that there might be something higher-order lurking there. So, even though we have high confidence that Ivy is sound, we are pursuing a general approach that covers infinite interpretations.

ACL2's **encapsulate** feature allows it to reason safely about incompletely specified functions. We believe we can use encapsulation to abstract the finiteness.[8] In our current specification, the important way in which finiteness enters the picture is by the definition of **feval-d**, which recurses through the domain. This function, in effect, expands universally quantified formulas into conjunctions and existentially quantified formulas into disjunctions. Instead of **feval-d**, we can consider a constrained function that chooses an element of the domain, if possible, that makes a formula true. When evaluating an existentially quantified formula, we substitute the chosen element for the existentially quantified variable and continue evaluating. (Evaluation of universally quantified variables requires some fiddling with negation.) However, proving the soundness of Skolemization may present complications. If this approach succeeds, an interesting (and probably difficult!) exercise would be to try to use ACL2's functional instantiation rule to derive the soundness results for finite interpretations.

Note that the current soundness proofs for (**disproved conjecture**) and (**modeled formula**) are adequate because a finite model is a model.

16.5   Completeness

Traditionally, the "interesting" properties of proof procedures are about completeness rather than soundness. Aside from the syntactic correctness of the preprocessing functions, we have no results on completeness. In fact, it is impossible to prove completeness of (**proved conjecture**) unless we can prove completeness of the external Otter-class prover. Even if (**proved conjecture**) is sound, it may have bugs that block proofs, for example in the calling sequence for the external prover. As an extreme example, consider (**defun proved (f) nil**)—it is unquestionably sound, but not very useful. The user must rely on experience with Ivy for evidence that it is complete enough. The supporting material includes everything needed to run Ivy, including examples, and we invite readers to check it out.

---

[7]We are putting aside the argument that set theory and higher-order logics can be encoded in first-order logic.

[8]This approach was suggested by Matt Kaufmann.

16.6   Exercises

Each exercise has two corresponding files in the supporting material. Numbered startup files contain comments, relevant <u>include-book</u> forms, and definitions of related functions. Numbered solution books contain solutions.

Exercise 16.1 *Define a function to check whether a given variable occurs freely in a formula. Prove that substitution for a variable that does not occur in the formula has no effect.*

Exercise 16.2 *Prove that if an interpretation contains a function func, and if a formula does not contain the corresponding function symbol, then evaluation of the formula in the interpretation is independent of the occurrence of func. Assume that func is the first function in the interpretation.*

Exercise 16.3 *Define a function cnf that converts negation normal form formulas (see book nnf) to conjunctive normal form and a predicate cnfp that recognizes conjunctive normal form formulas. Prove that cnf (1) preserves the property wff, (2) converts nnfp formulas to cnfp, and (3) is sound.*

Exercise 16.4 *Define a resolution function that takes two formulas and two specifications of subformulas within the formulas, and computes a resolvent, if possible, of the two formulas on the specified literals. Prove that the function is sound.*

Exercise 16.5 *Conjunctions and disjunctions are binary; this makes it inconvenient to write conjectures with several hypotheses. Define a function to convert a formula with multiple-arity conjunctions and disjunctions to a formula with binary conjunctions and disjunctions. Decide what properties have to be proved to demonstrate that your approach is acceptable, and prove those properties.*

Exercise 16.6 *We rely on the ability to generate a new symbol with respect to a given symbol list in steps 2 and 3 of the search procedure. In variable renaming, step 2, we generate a new variable. In Skolemization, step 3, we generate a Skolem function name. Common Lisp has a function gensym, but it is state dependent and therefore not available in ACL2. Define an ACL2 function that generates a symbol that is not in a given list of symbols, and prove its correctness.*

17

Knuth's Generalization of McCarthy's 91 Function

John Cowles
Department of Computer Science, University of Wyoming
Email: cowles@uwyo.edu

Abstract

Donald E. Knuth of Stanford University asks [63] for a "proof by computer" of a theorem about his generalization, involving *real* numbers, of John Mc-Carthy's 91 function. This case study explores a largely successful attempt to use ACL2 to meet Knuth's challenge. *Real* numbers are dealt with by mechanically verifying results that are true, not only about the field of all *real* numbers, but also about every subfield of that field.

Introduction

This study repeatedly exploits the ability of the **encapsulate** event to consistently extend ACL2's logic with assumptions about new functions. This ability is used in three ways crucial to this study.

- ◆ To axiomatize abstract mathematical structures such as groups, rings, and fields. Specifically, the results presented in this study require axioms for Archimedean ordered fields.

- ◆ To ensure given constraints are satisfied. Assurance of consistency is the great advantage here of using **encapsulate** instead of **defaxiom**.

    Example. An inconsistent theory may result from using ACL2's **defaxiom** to force the addition of a recursive equation such as

    $$f(x) \quad = \quad \text{if} \quad x = 0 \quad \text{then} \quad 0 \qquad (17.1)$$
    $$\text{else} \quad f(x) + 1.$$

    In the presence of this additional axiom, ACL2 can prove any syntactically well-formed term, including **nil**. Recall that **nil** is used by ACL2 for false.

Attempting to introduce (17.1) with a nonlocal **defthm** within an **encapsulate** is doomed because no <u>**local**</u> **defun** can provide the required example of a function f that satisfies Equation (17.1).

♦ To carry out proofs, using *Universal Generalization*, even for theorems that cannot be formally stated in ACL2's logic.

Universal Generalization is a commonly used rule of inference [33, page 146] for proving theorems of the form: For all x, $P(x)$. Informally, the rule says, to prove such an universally quantified theorem, argue as follows: Let x be an arbitrary object. Make sure x doesn't already stand for something used in the proof. Prove $P(x)$. Since x is arbitrary, conclude: For all x, $P(x)$.

In this study, **encapsulate** is used to help formalize, within ACL2, arguments similar to the proof outlined next.

Example.

Theorem. For each Archimedean ordered field, there is a unique function defined over the field with property $\cdots$.

Proof. By universal generalization. Let $\mathcal{F}$ be an arbitrary Archimedean field.

Construct a function f, over $\mathcal{F}$ with the desired property. (So we know such a function exists.)

Let f' be any function over $\mathcal{F}$ with the property. Show, for all $x \in \mathcal{F}$, $f(x) = f'(x)$.

Although theorems such as this cannot be stated in ACL2's logic, the proof may still be verified. The axioms for Archimedean fields are consistently added using an **encapsulate**. This allows a proof concerning all Archimedean fields to proceed by universal generalization, *i.e.*, by arguing about an arbitrary field satisfying the axioms. The construction of f ensures the consistency of assuming that functions with the desired property exist. The uniqueness of functions with the desired property is then established by universal generalization, *i.e.*, by considering an arbitrary function f' with the desired property.

Exercise 17.1 *Use* <u>**defstub**</u> *to tell ACL2 about a new function f. Next, use* <u>**defaxiom**</u> *to force ACL2 to add Equation (17.1). Make sure (17.1) is not added as a rewrite rule. Finally, use ACL2 to verify that **nil** is, indeed, a theorem of this new theory.*

17.1 McCarthy's 91 Function

John McCarthy was the first to study the function defined by the recursion

$$M(x) \overset{\text{def}}{=} \text{ if } x > 100 \text{ then } x - 10 \qquad (17.2)$$
$$\text{else} \quad M(M(x + 11)).$$

It is called the 91 function because for all integer inputs x, the recursion halts and

$$M(x) \;=\; \text{ if } x > 100 \text{ then } x - 10$$
$$\text{else} \quad 91.$$

So for all integers $x \le 101$, $M(x) = 91$.

Knuth comments [63] that it is unlikely that any reasonable programmer would ever want to carry out this particular recursive computation to solve a realistic problem. However, McCarthy and Knuth use this definition to illustrate important problems and techniques that arise during formal verification of recursive programs.

This definition is difficult to handle in ACL2 because it is hard for ACL2's definitional principle to accept the definition. Specifically, ACL2 has trouble verifying that the recursion terminates. Indeed, the definitional principle has the difficult task of showing that the recursion in (17.2) halts before even knowing there is a function that satisfies the proposed definition! This leads to the following difficulty.

Recall that ACL2 uses so-called "well-founded measure" functions to show that each recursive call in a proposed definition is progressing towards termination. In (17.2), for integers $x \le 100$, M is recursively called, first on $x + 11$, and then on $M(x + 11)$. So a function (let's call it measure) is required such that each of the following can be proved, about all integers x, knowing nothing more about M other than it is the name of a function (so the function applications of M makes sense). Here $<_{\epsilon_0}$ is the "ordinal less than" relation on the ordinals less than ϵ_0 (see e0-ord-<).

♦ Measure(x) is an ordinal less than ϵ_0.

♦ If $x \le 100$, then measure$(x + 11) <_{\epsilon_0}$ measure(x).

♦ If $x \le 100$, then measure$(M(x + 11)) <_{\epsilon_0}$ measure(x).

Proving this last item appears to be impossible without knowing more about M.

However, a function acceptable to the definitional principle can be given so that ACL2 can prove the function satisfies the recursive equation that defines M, namely

$$M(x) \overset{\text{def}}{=} \text{ if } x > 100 \text{ then } x - 10 \qquad (17.3)$$
$$\text{else} \quad 91.$$

Then the following equation can be formally stated and proved in ACL2 to hold for all integers x.

$$M(x) \ = \ \text{if} \ x > 100 \ \text{then} \ x - 10 \qquad (17.4)$$
$$\text{else} \quad M(M(x + 11)).$$

Exercise 17.2

A. *Formally state Definition (17.2) in ACL2. Observe ACL2's resistance to accepting this definition. Carefully note the non-trivial part of the measure conjecture. Use the following proposed measure:*

$$\text{measure}(x) \ \overset{\text{def}}{=} \ \text{if} \ x > 100 \ \text{then} \ 0 \qquad (17.5)$$
$$\text{else} \quad 101 - x.$$

B. *Formally state Definition (17.3) in ACL2. Observe that ACL2 accepts this definition. Next, formally state and prove, in ACL2, that Equation (17.4) holds for all integers x.*

So now we know there exists a function that satisfies the recursive equation that defines M. With this additional information, ACL2 can show that the recursion in (17.4) terminates for all integer inputs x. Here is the argument, where measure is defined in the above exercise.

♦ Measure(x) is an ordinal less than ϵ_0.

  Proof. It is apparent from (17.5) that for all integers x, measure(x) is a nonnegative integer; and every nonnegative integer is also an ordinal less than ϵ_0.

♦ If $x \leq 100$, then measure($x + 11$) $<_{\epsilon_0}$ measure(x).

  Proof. From (17.5), it is straightforward that this inequality holds for each integer x less than or equal to 100.

♦ If $x \geq 90$, then $M(x)$ is an integer larger than 90.

  Proof. By induction on measure(x).

  Base Case. For integers $x > 100$, by (17.4), $M(x) = x - 10 > 90$.

  Induction Step. The induction hypothesis is: For integers $n \geq 90$, if measure(n) < measure(x), then $M(n)$ is an integer larger than 90. For integers x with $90 \leq x \leq 100$, by (17.4), $M(x) = M(M(x+11)) = M(x+11-10) = M(x+1)$. Since measure($x + 1$) < measure($x$), by the induction hypothesis, $M(x) = M(x + 1)$ is an integer larger than 90.

♦ $M(x)$ is an integer larger than 90.

Proof. By induction on measure(x).

> **Base Case.** By the previous item, for integers x larger than or equal to 90, $M(x)$ is an integer larger than 90.
>
> **Induction Step.** For integers x less than 90, by (17.4), $M(x) = M(M(x+11))$. Since measure($x+11$) < measure(x), by the induction hypothesis, $M(x+11)$ is an integer larger than 90. Then, by the previous item, $M(M(x+11))$ is also an integer larger than 90.

♦ If $x \leq 100$, then measure($M(x + 11)$) $<_{\epsilon_0}$ measure(x).

Proof. By cases.

> **Integer x with $90 \leq x \leq 100$.**
> By (17.4), $M(x + 11) = x + 11 - 10 = x + 1$. So by (17.5), measure($M(x + 11)$) = measure($x + 1$) < measure($x$).
>
> **Integer x less than 90.**
> By the previous item, $x < 90 < M(x + 11)$. So by (17.5), measure($M(x + 11)$) < measure(x).

Exercise 17.3 *Use ACL2 to formalize and verify the above argument. Avoid using* **defaxiom** *when introducing Equation (17.4) into ACL2. Instead use* **encapsulate** *to constrain M to satisfy (17.4) for integers x.*

17.2   Knuth's Generalization

Knuth [63] generalizes Definition (17.2) by replacing 100 with an arbitrary *real, a*; 10 and 11 with arbitrary *positive reals, b* and *d*, respectively; and the *number of iterations* of the function (which is 2 in (17.2)) by an arbitrary *positive integer, c*, number of iterations:

$$K(x) \stackrel{\text{def}}{=} \text{if } x > a \text{ then } x - b \qquad (17.6)$$
$$\text{else} \quad K^c(x + d).$$

Knuth refers to (17.6) as

> *The generalized 91 recursion with parameters* (a, b, c, d).

Knuth proves the following theorem and then asks for a "proof by computer."

Theorem 17.1 (Knuth) *The generalized 91 recursion with parameters* (a, b, c, d) *defines a total function on the integers iff* $(c - 1) \cdot b < d$. *In such a case the values of $K(x)$ also obey the simpler recurrence*

$$K(x) = \text{if } x > a \text{ then } x - b \qquad (17.7)$$
$$\text{else} \quad K(x + d - (c - 1)b).$$

Knuth's proof proceeds by establishing each of the following:

1. If $(c - 1) \cdot b \geq d$, then the recursion in Definition (17.6) does not terminate for some inputs $x \leq a$.

2. If $(c - 1) \cdot b < d$, then the recursion always terminates.

3. Any total function that satisfies the generalized 91 recursion in (17.6), must also satisfy the simpler recursion given in (17.7).

Here is a summary of some (meta-)corollaries that follow from the ACL2 results obtained during this study. They are called "meta" because the corollaries are not stated in ACL2's logic.

0. For all choices of Real a, Real $b > 0$, Integer $c > 0$, and Real $d > 0$, there are total functions on the Reals that satisfy the generalized 91 recursion in (17.6).

1. If $(c - 1) \cdot b \geq d$, then there are *many* total functions on the Reals that satisfy the generalized 91 recursion in (17.6). It follows that the recursion cannot terminate for all inputs x.

2. If $(c - 1) \cdot b < d$, then the recursion always terminates. It follows that there is *only one* total function on the Reals that satisfies the generalized 91 recursion in (17.6). The uniqueness of this function is separately verified using ACL2.

3. Any total function that satisfies the generalized 91 recursion in (17.6) must also satisfy the simpler recursion in (17.7).

17.3　Using ACL2 to Meet Knuth's Challenge

The first question is how can ACL2 be used to deal with the *realness* of a, b, and d? Initially, ACL2 knows only about the various number subsystems (such as the Rationals and Integers) of the Complex Rationals; but nothing about the Reals.

17.3.1　What Are the Real Numbers?

Here [61, page 30] is an official answer from the mathematicians:

Theorem 17.2 *There is (up to ordered field isomorphism) exactly one complete ordered field.*

This unique field is known as the field of *real numbers* or as the Reals.

Here is a brief discussion of the technical jargon in Theorem 17.2. A more complete discussion of the real numbers can be found in [68]. A *complete ordered field* is a structure,

$$(\mathcal{F}, <_{\mathcal{F}}, +_{\mathcal{F}}, \cdot_{\mathcal{F}}, -_{\mathcal{F}}, /_{\mathcal{F}}, 0_{\mathcal{F}}, 1_{\mathcal{F}}).$$

satisfying the following. Here $\mathcal{F}$ is a set, $<_{\mathcal{F}}$ is a binary relation, $+_{\mathcal{F}}$ and $\cdot_{\mathcal{F}}$ are binary operations, $-_{\mathcal{F}}$ and $/_{\mathcal{F}}$ are unary operations, while $0_{\mathcal{F}}$ and $1_{\mathcal{F}}$ are constants.

Field Axioms. For all $W, X, Y, Z \in \mathcal{F}$ with $W \neq 0_{\mathcal{F}}$,

   Closure. $X +_{\mathcal{F}} Y \in \mathcal{F}$, $X \cdot_{\mathcal{F}} Y \in \mathcal{F}$, $-_{\mathcal{F}} X \in \mathcal{F}$, $/_{\mathcal{F}} W \in \mathcal{F}$, $0_{\mathcal{F}} \in \mathcal{F}$, $1_{\mathcal{F}} \in \mathcal{F}$;

   Commutative. $X +_{\mathcal{F}} Y = Y +_{\mathcal{F}} X$, $X \cdot_{\mathcal{F}} Y = Y \cdot_{\mathcal{F}} X$;

   Associative. $(X +_{\mathcal{F}} Y) +_{\mathcal{F}} Z = X +_{\mathcal{F}} (Y +_{\mathcal{F}} Z)$, $(X \cdot_{\mathcal{F}} Y) \cdot_{\mathcal{F}} Z = X \cdot_{\mathcal{F}} (Y \cdot_{\mathcal{F}} Z)$;

   Distributive. $X \cdot_{\mathcal{F}} (Y +_{\mathcal{F}} Z) = (X \cdot_{\mathcal{F}} Y) +_{\mathcal{F}} (X \cdot_{\mathcal{F}} Z)$;

   Identity. $0_{\mathcal{F}} +_{\mathcal{F}} X = X$, $1_{\mathcal{F}} \cdot_{\mathcal{F}} X = X$;

   Inverse. $X +_{\mathcal{F}} (-_{\mathcal{F}} X) = 0_{\mathcal{F}}$, $W \cdot_{\mathcal{F}} (/_{\mathcal{F}} W) = 1_{\mathcal{F}}$;

   Nontrivial. $0_{\mathcal{F}} \neq 1_{\mathcal{F}}$.

Order Axioms. For all $X, Y, Z \in \mathcal{F}$,

   Type. $X <_{\mathcal{F}} Y \in \{\text{false}, \text{true}\}$;

   Transitive. if $X <_{\mathcal{F}} Y$ and $Y <_{\mathcal{F}} Z$, then $X <_{\mathcal{F}} Z$;

   Trichotomy. exactly one of the relations, $X <_{\mathcal{F}} Y$, $X = Y$, $Y <_{\mathcal{F}} X$ is true;

   Compatibility. if $X <_{\mathcal{F}} Y$, then $X +_{\mathcal{F}} Z <_{\mathcal{F}} Y +_{\mathcal{F}} Z$; if $X <_{\mathcal{F}} Y$ and $0_{\mathcal{F}} <_{\mathcal{F}} Z$, then $X \cdot_{\mathcal{F}} Z <_{\mathcal{F}} Y \cdot_{\mathcal{F}} Z$.

Completeness Axiom. Every nonempty subset of $\mathcal{F}$ that has an upper bound in $\mathcal{F}$ has a *least upper bound* in $\mathcal{F}$.

   The completeness axiom ensures the existence of real numbers such as $\sqrt{2}$: The nonempty set $\{x \in \text{Reals} \mid x^2 \leq 2\}$ clearly has a rational upper bound, and therefore a real least upper bound which is $\sqrt{2}$.

   It is a difficult challenge to capture the contents of the completeness axiom in ACL2. Ruben Gamboa extended ACL2 to accommodate the Reals by adding a theory of infinitesimals (see [36] and Chapter 18).

   An *ordered field* is a structure

$$(\mathcal{F}, <_{\mathcal{F}}, +_{\mathcal{F}}, \cdot_{\mathcal{F}}, -_{\mathcal{F}}, /_{\mathcal{F}}, 0_{\mathcal{F}}, 1_{\mathcal{F}})$$

satisfying the field and order axioms, but maybe not the completeness axiom.

An *ordered field isomorphism* from an ordered field

$$(\mathcal{F}, <_{\mathcal{F}}, +_{\mathcal{F}}, \cdot_{\mathcal{F}}, -_{\mathcal{F}}, /_{\mathcal{F}}, 0_{\mathcal{F}}, 1_{\mathcal{F}})$$

to an ordered field

$$(\mathcal{G}, <_{\mathcal{G}}, +_{\mathcal{G}}, \cdot_{\mathcal{G}}, -_{\mathcal{G}}, /_{\mathcal{G}}, 0_{\mathcal{G}}, 1_{\mathcal{G}})$$

is a function f, mapping $\mathcal{F}$ one to one onto $\mathcal{G}$, satisfying the following for all $X, Y \in \mathcal{F}$: $f(X +_{\mathcal{F}} Y) = f(X) +_{\mathcal{G}} f(Y)$, $f(X \cdot_{\mathcal{F}} Y) = f(X) \cdot_{\mathcal{G}} f(Y)$, and $X <_{\mathcal{F}} Y$ iff $f(X) <_{\mathcal{G}} f(Y)$.

17.3.2 Archimedean Ordered Fields

The following [108, page 233] simplifies the remainder of this study.

Theorem 17.3 *Every ordered field contains (a subfield order-isomorphic to) the ordered field of all rational numbers.*

An ordered field is *Archimedean*[1] iff every field element is bounded above by some positive integer.

It is clear that any ordered subfield of the Reals must be Archimedean. So both the Rationals and the Reals are Archimedean. In fact [108, page 241], every Archimedean field is (order-isomorphic to) a subfield of the Reals. Thus, the subfields of the Reals are essentially the only Archimedean fields.

Archimedean fields have axioms that can be shown to be consistent using ACL2. So one way to deal with the real values a, b, and d in the generalized 91 recursion of (17.6) is to assume they are elements from an arbitrary Archimedean field. Then prove the claims about the generalized 91 recursion are true over any Archimedean field, instead of just over the Reals.

The Axioms for Archimedean Fields in ACL2

Here is one possible way to axiomatize, in ACL2, an arbitrary Archimedean ordered field

$$(\mathcal{A}, <_{\mathcal{A}}, +_{\mathcal{A}}, \cdot_{\mathcal{A}}, -_{\mathcal{A}}, /_{\mathcal{A}}, 0_{\mathcal{A}}, 1_{\mathcal{A}}).$$

By Theorem 17.3, the Rationals are contained in any Archimedean field, so it is safe to use the more familiar 0 and 1 for the field constants $0_{\mathcal{A}}$ and $1_{\mathcal{A}}$, respectively.

An **encapsulate** is used to introduce and constrain ACL2 versions of the following functions.

---

[1] This definition is an algebraic version of the "Archimedean axiom" from geometry: Starting from a point P, a given line segment PQ can always be laid off in the direction PR a whole number of times so that the last end point lies beyond any given point R.

♦ The predicate $\mathcal{AOFp}$. This is the test for membership in the Archimedean Ordered Field, *i.e.*, $X \in \mathcal{A}$ iff $\mathcal{AOFp}(X) \neq \text{nil}$. Recall that nil is used in ACL2 for false.

♦ The relation $<_\mathcal{A}$. This satisfies the type, transitive, and compatibility order axioms. Note, nothing is said about trichotomy at this point.

♦ The operations $+_\mathcal{A}$, $\cdot_\mathcal{A}$, $-_\mathcal{A}$, and $/_\mathcal{A}$. These satisfy the closure, commutative, associative, distributive, identity, and inverse field axioms. The nontrivial axiom is redundant because ACL2 already knows that $0 \neq 1$.

♦ The function Nat-Int-Bound. This is needed to state the Archimedean property.

Additional constraints enforce the containment of the Rationals, fill in for the missing trichotomy order axiom, and axiomatize the Archimedean property:

Rational Containment. For all Rationals X and Y,

♦ $\mathcal{AOFp}(X)$,

♦ $(X <_\mathcal{A} Y) = (X < Y)$,

♦ $X +_\mathcal{A} Y = X + Y$ and $X \cdot_\mathcal{A} Y = X \cdot Y$, and

♦ $-_\mathcal{A} X = -X$ and $/_\mathcal{A} X = /X$.

Trichotomy. The trichotomy axiom is equivalent to the following two constraints. Here $X \leq_\mathcal{A} Y$ is used to abbreviate $Y \not<_\mathcal{A} X$. For all $X, Y \in \mathcal{A}$,

Asymmetry. if $X <_\mathcal{A} Y$, then $X \leq_\mathcal{A} Y$;

Antisymmetry. if $X \leq_\mathcal{A} Y$ and $Y \leq_\mathcal{A} X$, then $X = Y$.

Archimedean Axioms. For all $X \in \mathcal{A}$,

♦ Nat-Int-Bound(X) is an Integer, and

♦ if $0 \leq_\mathcal{A} X$, then $X \leq_\mathcal{A}$ Nat-Int-Bound(X).

The Rationals are used as a witness to the consistency of these new constraints. Over the Rationals, ACL2's **numerator** function satisfies the constraints on Nat-Int-Bound.

Exercise 17.4 *The trichotomy axiom says that exactly one of the relations, $X <_\mathcal{A} Y$, $X = Y$, $Y <_\mathcal{A} X$ is true. It naively translates into the conjunction of the following:*

1. *At least one of the relations is true*
   $X <_\mathcal{A} Y$ or $X = Y$ or $Y <_\mathcal{A} X$;

2. *At most one of the relations is* true

    (a) if $X <_A Y$, then $X \neq Y$;

    (b) if $X <_A Y$, then $Y \not<_A X$;

    (c) if $X = Y$, then $X \not<_A Y$ and $Y \not<_A X$;

    (d) if $Y <_A X$, then $X \neq Y$ and $X \not<_A Y$.

A. *Use* **defstub** *to introduce a new function for $<_A$ and use* **defmacro** *to introduce notation for $\leq_A$. State and prove, in ACL2, the following equivalences.*

    (i) Formula (1) is equivalent to the antisymmetry constraint.

    (ii) Formula (2b) is equivalent to the asymmetry constraint.

B. *Clearly there is some redundancy in the formulas of (2). Use ACL2 to show that all the other formulas in (2) follow from (2b). Use* **encapsulate** *to introduce $<_A$ and state (2b).*

Exercise 17.5 *A ring with unity is a structure,*

$$(\mathcal{R}, +_\mathcal{R}, \cdot_\mathcal{R}, -_\mathcal{R}, 0_\mathcal{R}, 1_\mathcal{R}).$$

satisfying the following. Here $\mathcal{R}$ is a set, $+_\mathcal{R}$ and $\cdot_\mathcal{R}$ are binary operations, and $-_\mathcal{R}$ is a unary operation, while $0_\mathcal{R}$ and $1_\mathcal{R}$ are constants.

Ring with Unity Axioms. *For all $X, Y, Z \in \mathcal{R}$,*

    Closure. $X +_\mathcal{R} Y \in \mathcal{R}$, $X \cdot_\mathcal{R} Y \in \mathcal{R}$, $-_\mathcal{R}X \in \mathcal{R}$, $0_\mathcal{R} \in \mathcal{R}$, $1_\mathcal{R} \in \mathcal{R}$;

    Associative. $(X +_\mathcal{R} Y) +_\mathcal{R} Z = X +_\mathcal{R} (Y +_\mathcal{R} Z)$, $(X \cdot_\mathcal{R} Y) \cdot_\mathcal{R} Z = X \cdot_\mathcal{R} (Y \cdot_\mathcal{R} Z)$;

    Distributive. $X \cdot_\mathcal{R} (Y +_\mathcal{R} Z) = (X \cdot_\mathcal{R} Y) +_\mathcal{R} (X \cdot_\mathcal{R} Z)$, $(X +_\mathcal{R} Y) \cdot_\mathcal{R} Z = (X \cdot_\mathcal{R} Z) +_\mathcal{R} (Y \cdot_\mathcal{R} Z)$;

    Identity. $X +_\mathcal{R} 0_\mathcal{R} = X$, $X \cdot_\mathcal{R} 1_\mathcal{R} = X$, $1_\mathcal{R} \cdot_\mathcal{R} X = X$;

    Right Inverse. $X +_\mathcal{R} (-_\mathcal{R}X) = 0_\mathcal{R}$.

A. *Axiomatize, in ACL2, an arbitrary ring with unity. Specifically, use* **encapsulate** *to introduce and constrain ACL2 versions of the following functions.*

    ♦ *The predicate $\mathcal{R}p$. This is the test for membership in the ring, i.e., $X \in \mathcal{R}$ iff $\mathcal{R}p(X) \neq$ nil.*

    ♦ *The operations $+_\mathcal{R}$, $\cdot_\mathcal{R}$, $-_\mathcal{R}$, and the constants $0_\mathcal{R}$ and $1_\mathcal{R}$. These satisfy the closure, associative, distributive, identity, and right inverse axioms for a ring with unity.*

B. *Verify, in ACL2, that in any ring with unity, the additive identity
and additive inverses behave as expected on the left as well as on the
right. That is, prove for all $X \in \mathcal{R}$,*

♦ $(-_{\mathcal{R}} X) +_{\mathcal{R}} X = 0_{\mathcal{R}}$ *and*

♦ $0_{\mathcal{R}} +_{\mathcal{R}} X = X$.

*Hint: Show $0_{\mathcal{R}}$ is the only additive idempotent in the ring. That is,
prove if $X +_{\mathcal{R}} X = X$, then $X = 0_{\mathcal{R}}$.*

C. *Verify, in ACL2, that addition is always commutative in any ring
with unity. That is, prove for all $X, Y \in \mathcal{R}$, $X +_{\mathcal{R}} Y = Y +_{\mathcal{R}} X$.
Hint. Consider the two ways the distributive axioms can be used to
expand $(X +_{\mathcal{R}} Y) \cdot_{\mathcal{R}} (1_{\mathcal{R}} +_{\mathcal{R}} 1_{\mathcal{R}})$.*

17.3.3 Satisfiability of the Generalized 91 Recursion

The purpose here is to outline the argument that starting with an Archi-
medean field $\mathcal{A}$ and arbitrary choices of $a, b, c, d \in \mathcal{A}$, with $0 <_{\mathcal{A}} b, d$ and
with c a positive integer; there is at least one total function, acceptable to
ACL2's definitional principle, defined on $\mathcal{A}$, that satisfies the generalized
91 recursion in (17.6).

The key observation is found in Theorem 17.1, the very theorem this
study is formally verifying. There Knuth tells us that, often, any function
that satisfies the generalized 91 recursion in (17.6) also satisfies the simpler
recursion in (17.7). So the plan is to turn Knuth's observation around and
use the simpler recursion of (17.7) to define a function acceptable to the
definitional principle, and then prove that such a function must also satisfy
the generalized 91 recursion.

There is a small complication to this plan: At least when the parameters
a, b, c, d and the inputs are all restricted to be integers, the recursion, in the
simpler recursion (17.7), can be seen to terminate, by using an analogue of
the measure function in (17.5), *provided* that $d - (c-1) \cdot b > 0$. On the
other hand, it is easy to believe that the recursion in (17.7) does not halt
when $d - (c-1) \cdot b \leq 0$. So when $d - (c-1) \cdot b \leq 0$, the definitional principle
is not going to accept the definition suggested by the simpler recursion of
(17.7). This setback is overcome by observing: Even when $d - (c-1) \cdot b \leq 0$,
there are total functions that satisfy the recursive equation (17.7). Namely,
for any fixed constant n,

$$K(x) \stackrel{\text{def}}{=} \text{if } x > a \text{ then } x - b \qquad (17.8)$$
$$\text{else} \quad n.$$

Using concrete choices for the values of the parameters a, b, c, d to check
whether functions defined by (17.8) actually satisfy the generalized 91 recursion in (17.6), soon shows that n *must be no larger than* a. For example,

with $a = 100$, $b = 11 = d$, $c = 3$, and $n > a = 100$; assuming K, as defined by (17.8), also satisfies the generalized recursion in (17.6) leads to the contradiction: $n = K(100) = K(K(K(111))) = K(K(100)) = K(n) = n - 11$. Similar experiments suggest that *any constant* $n \leq a$ in Definition (17.8) produces a function that satisfies the generalized 91 recursion, provided $d - (c - 1) \cdot b \leq 0$.

So now the plan has evolved to use both the simpler recursion of (17.7) and Definition (17.8) (with $n \leq a$) to define functions, K_1 and K_2, acceptable to ACL2's definitional principle, and then prove these functions must also satisfy the generalized 91 recursion.

Additionally, by choosing a value for n in the definition of K_1 that differs from the value chosen for n in K_2, it is easy to arrange for $K_1 \neq K_2$, when $d - (c - 1) \cdot b \leq 0$.

Definitions for K_1 and K_2. First, some notation: For X, Y in an Archimedean ordered field $\mathcal{A}$,

- write $X >_{\mathcal{A}} Y$ for $Y <_{\mathcal{A}} X$,

- write $X -_{\mathcal{A}} Y$ for $X +_{\mathcal{A}} (-_{\mathcal{A}} Y)$, and

- write $X /_{\mathcal{A}} Y$ for $X \cdot_{\mathcal{A}} (/_{\mathcal{A}} Y)$.

Letting E be the constant $d -_{\mathcal{A}} (c - 1) \cdot_{\mathcal{A}} b$, define K_1 and K_2 so they are almost identical:

$$K_1(X) \stackrel{\text{def}}{=} \text{if } X >_{\mathcal{A}} a \text{ then } X -_{\mathcal{A}} b \qquad\qquad (17.9)$$
$$\text{else if } E >_{\mathcal{A}} 0 \text{ then } K_1(X +_{\mathcal{A}} E)$$
$$\text{else } a.$$

$$K_2(X) \stackrel{\text{def}}{=} \text{if } X >_{\mathcal{A}} a \text{ then } X -_{\mathcal{A}} b \qquad\qquad (17.10)$$
$$\text{else if } E >_{\mathcal{A}} 0 \text{ then } K_2(X +_{\mathcal{A}} E)$$
$$\text{else } a -_{\mathcal{A}} b.$$

Defining K_1 and K_2 in ACL2

Start with the ACL2 theory for an Archimedean ordered field $\mathcal{A}$. Use **encapsulate** to introduce and constrain ACL2 versions of the constants a, b, c, d so that

- $a, b, d \in \mathcal{A}$ with $0 <_{\mathcal{A}} b$ and $0 <_{\mathcal{A}} d$,

- c is an integer with $c > 0$.

Any positive integer is a witness to the consistency of these constraints.

A measure is needed to show the recursions in (17.9) and (17.10) terminate. Recall that the function, Nat-Int-Bound, is guaranteed, by the

Archimedean axioms, to return Integer values such that for all $X \in \mathcal{A}$, if $0 \leq_{\mathcal{A}} X$ then $X \leq_{\mathcal{A}}$ Nat-Int-Bound(X). Nat-Int-Bound is used to define another useful function, Least-Nat-Bound, that returns the least nonnegative integer strictly *larger*, in $\mathcal{A}$, than its input X. Least-Nat-Bound is used to define the desired measure: For $X \in \mathcal{A}$,

$$\text{measure}_1(X) \ \overset{\text{def}}{=} \ \text{if } X >_{\mathcal{A}} a \tag{17.11}$$
$$\text{then} \quad 0$$
$$\text{else if} \quad E >_{\mathcal{A}} 0$$
$$\text{then} \quad \text{Least-Nat-Bound}[(a -_{\mathcal{A}} X)/_{\mathcal{A}} E]$$
$$\text{else} \quad 0.$$

When $E >_{\mathcal{A}} 0$, for $X \in \mathcal{A}$, with $X \leq_{\mathcal{A}} a$, $\text{measure}_1(X)$ counts the increments of size E required to move, from X, beyond a.

Exercise 17.6

A. *Use* **encapsulate** *to introduce and constrain ACL2 versions of constants* a, b, e, n *so that* e *is a rational with* $e \leq 0$. *Use the ACL2 versions of* a, b, n *to formally state and admit Definition (17.8) in ACL2. Next state and formally prove, in ACL2, the recursive equation*

$$K(x) \ = \ \text{if } x > a \text{ then } x - b$$
$$\text{else} \quad K(x + e).$$

B. *Use* **encapsulate** *to introduce and constrain ACL2 versions of constants* a, b, e *so that* a *and* e *are integers with* $e > 0$. *Use these constants to formally state and admit the following definition, intended for integer inputs* x, *in ACL2.*

$$K(x) \ \overset{\text{def}}{=} \ \text{if } x > a \text{ then } x - b$$
$$\text{else} \quad K(x + e).$$

Use the following measure:

$$\text{measure}(x) \ \overset{\text{def}}{=} \ \text{if } x > a \text{ then } 0$$
$$\text{else} \quad a + 1 - x.$$

Since the inputs to both K *and the measure are intended to be integers, non-integer inputs may be coerced to be integers by the ACL2 function* **ifix**.

K_1 and K_2 Satisfy the Generalized 91 Recursion

Before the defining equation for the generalized 91 recursion can even be stated in ACL2's logic, iterations, such as $F^i(x)$, of a function $F(x)$ must be defined. *Iteration of applications of F*, Iter-*F*, is recursively defined for nonnegative integers i by

$$\text{Iter-}F(i,x) \overset{\text{def}}{=} \text{ if } i = 0 \text{ then } x \qquad (17.12)$$
$$\text{else } F(\text{Iter-}F(i-1,x)).$$

The *key fact* verified using ACL2, but not proved here, about iteration of the K_j is that for Integers $i > 0$ and $X \in \mathcal{A}$,

$$K_j^i(X) = \text{Iter-}K_j(i,X) = K_j(X -_{\mathcal{A}} (i-1) \cdot_{\mathcal{A}} b). \qquad (17.13)$$

Now it is easy to argue that the K_j satisfy the defining equation for the generalized 91 recursion: For $X \leq_{\mathcal{A}} a$,

- $K_j(X) = K_j(X +_{\mathcal{A}} E)$.

  Proof. By cases.

  $E >_{\mathcal{A}} 0$. According to the "else if" clauses in (17.9) and (17.10), $K_j(X) = K_j(X +_{\mathcal{A}} E)$.

  $E \leq_{\mathcal{A}} 0$. Since $X +_{\mathcal{A}} E \leq_{\mathcal{A}} X \leq_{\mathcal{A}} a$, by the "else" clauses in (17.9) and (17.10), both $K_j(X)$ and $K_j(X +_{\mathcal{A}} E)$ are equal to the same constant, either a or $a -_{\mathcal{A}} b$.

- $K_j(X) = \text{Iter-}K_j(c, X +_{\mathcal{A}} d) = K_j^c(X +_{\mathcal{A}} d)$.

  Proof. By the previous item, the fact that $E = d -_{\mathcal{A}} (c-1) \cdot_{\mathcal{A}} b$, and the key fact (17.13),

$$
\begin{aligned}
K_j(X) &= K_j(X +_{\mathcal{A}} E) \\
&= K_j[(X +_{\mathcal{A}} d) -_{\mathcal{A}} (c-1) \cdot_{\mathcal{A}} b] \\
&= \text{Iter-}K_j(c, X +_{\mathcal{A}} d) = K_j^c(X +_{\mathcal{A}} d).
\end{aligned}
$$

17.3.4 The Generalized Recursion Implies the Simpler Recursion

ACL2 can now verify that any total function, on an Archimedean field $\mathcal{A}$, that satisfies the generalized 91 recursion must also satisfy the simpler recursion of (17.7). Once again encapsulate is used. This time new ACL2 functions K and Iter-K are introduced and constrained to satisfy the defining equations, similar to (17.6) and (17.12), for the generalized 91 recursion and the iteration of K. The functions K_1 and Iter-K_1 witness the consistency of these constraints.

When the number of iterations, c, in the generalized recursion, equals 1, it is trivial that the generalized and simpler recursions coincide. When

$c > 1$, the *key result*, proved by induction on j, is for $X \in \mathcal{A}$ and Integers
$i > j > 0$,

$$K^i(X) \;=\; \text{Iter-}K(i, X) \qquad\qquad\qquad (17.14)$$
$$= \text{Iter-}K(i - j, X -_{\mathcal{A}} j \cdot_{\mathcal{A}} b) \;=\; K^{i-j}(X -_{\mathcal{A}} j \cdot_{\mathcal{A}} b).$$

When i, j, and X are replaced by $c, c - 1$, and $X +_{\mathcal{A}} d$, respectively, so
$i - j = 1$, in this key result; then for $X \leq_{\mathcal{A}} a$,

$$K^c(X +_{\mathcal{A}} d) \;=\; K^1[(X +_{\mathcal{A}} d) -_{\mathcal{A}} (c - 1) \cdot_{\mathcal{A}} b]$$
$$= K(X +_{\mathcal{A}} d -_{\mathcal{A}} (c - 1) \cdot_{\mathcal{A}} b).$$

Thus K satisfies the simpler recursion of (17.7).

17.3.5 How Many Functions Satisfy the Generalized Recursion?

The properties proved about the functions K_1 and K_2 demonstrate that
whenever the constraints, on page 294, in Section 17.3.3, on the parameters
a, b, c, d, are satisfied, then there is always at least one function, defined
on $\mathcal{A}$, that satisfies the defining equation of the generalized 91 recursion.
Additionally, $K_1 \neq K_2$ whenever the constant $E = d -_{\mathcal{A}} (c - 1) \cdot_{\mathcal{A}} b \leq_{\mathcal{A}} 0$,
so in that case there are multiple distinct functions satisfying the defining
equation.

When $E >_{\mathcal{A}} 0$, the function K, as constrained in Section 17.3.3, is
unique. This is verified in ACL2 in three steps:

♦ Use encapsulate to introduce and constrain a new function G_1 to
  satisfy the simpler recursion of (17.7). The function K_1 witnesses the
  consistency of this constraint.

♦ Prove, by induction on $\text{measure}_1(X)$, for all $X \in \mathcal{A}$, if
  $E = d -_{\mathcal{A}} (c - 1) \cdot_{\mathcal{A}} b >_{\mathcal{A}} 0$, then $G_1(X) = K_1(X)$.

♦ Since K also satisfies the simpler recursion, use functional instantiation to replace G_1 with K in the previous item.

17.3.6 When the Generalized Recursion Halts

When $E = d -_{\mathcal{A}} (c - 1) \cdot_{\mathcal{A}} b \leq_{\mathcal{A}} 0$, the possibility of terminating recursive
calls is ruled out, because there are too many functions that satisfy the
defining equation.

That is, *whenever the recursion always terminates, there can be only
one total function that satisfies the defining equation.* This is because each
distinct input value produces a finite sequence of recursive calls that computes some output value. This finite sequence of recursive calls can easily

be viewed as a finite sequence of equalities showing that the computed output value must be a logical consequence from the result of substituting the given input value into the defining equation.

Exercise 17.7 *This exercise shows that the existence of a unique total function, satisfying a given recursive equation, is not enough to guarantee termination of the recursion in Common Lisp and ACL2.*

A. *Use* **encapsulate** *to verify, in ACL2, that the Common Lisp function,* **identity**, *is the unique total function satisfying the equation*

$$f(x) \quad = \quad \text{if} \quad f(x) \quad \text{then} \quad x$$
$$\text{else} \quad x.$$

Make sure this equation is not added as a rewrite rule.

B. *Use* **encapsulate** *to verify, in ACL2, that the function with two inputs that always returns the constant 0 is the unique total function satisfying the equation*

$$g(x, y) \quad = \quad \text{if} \quad \text{zp}(x) \quad \text{then} \quad 0$$
$$\text{else} \quad g(x - 1, g(x, y)).$$

Recall that **zp** *is one of ACL2's idioms for testing whether its input is 0 (see* **zero-test-idioms**). *Make sure this equation is not added as a rewrite rule.*

Now suppose $E >_{\mathcal{A}} 0$ and the function K, defined on $\mathcal{A}$, is known to satisfy the defining equation of the generalized 91 recursion. Then the recursive calls occur for $X \leq_{\mathcal{A}} a$:

$$K(X) = K^c(X +_{\mathcal{A}} d) = K(\cdots K(X +_{\mathcal{A}} d) \cdots).$$

So K is recursively called, first on $X +_{\mathcal{A}} d$, then on $K(X +_{\mathcal{A}} d)$, then on $K^2(X +_{\mathcal{A}} d)$, $\cdots$, and finally on $K^{c-1}(X +_{\mathcal{A}} d)$. Thus, using measure$_1$, as defined by (17.11), to demonstrate termination, incurs the following proof obligations for each $X \in \mathcal{A}$ and each Integer i, such that $0 < i < c$:

◆ Measure$_1(X)$ is an ordinal less than ϵ_0. Inspection of Definition (17.11) easily dispatches this obligation.

◆ If $X \leq_{\mathcal{A}} a$, then measure$_1(X +_{\mathcal{A}} d) <_{\epsilon_0}$ measure$_1(X)$. Since $d >_{\mathcal{A}} E$, $X +_{\mathcal{A}} d$ requires at least one less increment (of size E) than X to move beyond a.

◆ If $X \leq_{\mathcal{A}} a$, then measure$_1(K^i(X +_{\mathcal{A}} d)) <_{\epsilon_0}$ measure(X).

Here is an argument that can be formalized in ACL2, for this last obligation.

First, some useful notation: For each Integer i, with $0 < i \leq c$, let E_i be the constant $d -_{\mathcal{A}} (i-1) \cdot_{\mathcal{A}} b$. Then $0 <_{\mathcal{A}} E = E_c \leq_{\mathcal{A}} E_i$, and for each $i < c$, $E_i -_{\mathcal{A}} b = E_{i+1}$.

For each $X \in \mathcal{A}$ and each Integer i, such that $0 < i < c$;

♦ $X +_{\mathcal{A}} E \leq_{\mathcal{A}} K(X +_{\mathcal{A}} E_i)$.

    Proof. By induction on $measure_1(X +_{\mathcal{A}} E_i)$.

      Base Case. For $X +_{\mathcal{A}} E_i >_{\mathcal{A}} a$,

$$X +_{\mathcal{A}} E \leq_{\mathcal{A}} X +_{\mathcal{A}} E_{i+1} \;\; = \;\; X +_{\mathcal{A}} E_i -_{\mathcal{A}} b$$
$$= \;\; K(X +_{\mathcal{A}} E_i).$$

      Induction Step. For $X +_{\mathcal{A}} E_i \leq_{\mathcal{A}} a$, since K also satisfies the simpler recursion, $K(X +_{\mathcal{A}} E_i) = K(X +_{\mathcal{A}} E_i +_{\mathcal{A}} E)$. Since $measure_1(X +_{\mathcal{A}} E +_{\mathcal{A}} E_i) < measure_1(X +_{\mathcal{A}} E_i)$, by the induction hypothesis,

$$X +_{\mathcal{A}} E <_{\mathcal{A}} X +_{\mathcal{A}} E +_{\mathcal{A}} E \;\; \leq_{\mathcal{A}} \;\; K(X +_{\mathcal{A}} E +_{\mathcal{A}} E_i)$$
$$= \;\; K(X +_{\mathcal{A}} E_i).$$

♦ If $X \leq_{\mathcal{A}} a$, then $measure_1(K^i(X +_{\mathcal{A}} d)) <_{\epsilon_0} measure_1(X)$.

    Proof. First, note that the key result (17.14) on page 297 also holds when $i = 1$ and $j = 0$. Then replacing j and X, in the key result, with $i - 1$ and $X +_{\mathcal{A}} d$, respectively, shows that

$$K^i(X +_{\mathcal{A}} d) \;\; = \;\; K^1[(X +_{\mathcal{A}} d) -_{\mathcal{A}} (i-1) \cdot_{\mathcal{A}} b]$$
$$= \;\; K(X +_{\mathcal{A}} E_i).$$

    By the previous item, $X +_{\mathcal{A}} E \leq_{\mathcal{A}} K(X +_{\mathcal{A}} E_i) = K^i(X +_{\mathcal{A}} d)$. Thus the desired result follows by Definition (17.11) of $measure_1$, because $K^i(X +_{\mathcal{A}} d)$ is at least one step (of size E) closer to a than X.

The description of the use of ACL2 to formally verify Knuth's theorem 17.1 is now complete. All the meta-corollaries on page 288 have been formally verified for an arbitrary Archimedean ordered field, $\mathcal{A}$, in place of the Reals.

Continuity and Differentiability

Ruben Gamboa
Logical Information Machines, Inc., Austin, Texas
Email: ruben@lim.com

Abstract

This case study shows how ACL2 can be used to reason about the real and complex numbers, using non-standard analysis. It describes ACL2(r), a modification of ACL2 that includes the irrational real and complex numbers. It then shows how ACL2(r) can prove classic theorems of analysis, such as the Intermediate Value and Mean Value Theorems.

Introduction

Readers familiar with ACL2 will know that ACL2 supports the rational and complex-rational numbers, but it does not include the irrationals. It is not too difficult to show that the exclusion of the irrationals is complete. For example, it is easy to prove that

```
(equal (* x x) 2)
```

is false for all values of x. Such readers may also fear that the classical way to introduce the irrationals will not work well with ACL2. In particular, axioms such as the least upper bound axiom are naturally expressed in set theory, but they do not appear to have a similar expression in the language of ACL2.

There is a way out, however. Non-standard analysis, first formalized by Robinson [91], gave a rigorous foundation to the informal reasoning about infinitesimal quantities used by Leibniz when he co-invented calculus and by engineers and scientists ever since. A convenient feature of many arguments using non-standard analysis is that mathematical induction and recursion replace the usual limit and compactness arguments. This suggests that non-standard analysis can be formalized in ACL2. Such a formalization is outlined in the next section; a more complete presentation can be found in [37, 36]. This section is followed with proofs of the Intermediate and Mean Value Theorems in ACL2.

Exercise 18.1 *Using ACL2 (not ACL2(r)) prove the following theorem.*

(not (equal (* x x) 2))

18.1 Non-Standard Analysis

From the viewpoint of non-standard analysis, the integers can be divided into two groups. The *standard* integers include 0, ±1, ±2, ... There is at least one non-*standard* integer, say N. The sum or product of two *standard* integers is also *standard*, so $N\pm1$, $N\pm2$, ... , $N\pm k$ are non-*standard*, for any *standard* values of k. This implies there is no least non-*standard* integer. A rational number is *standard* when its numerator and denominator are both standard.

If a number is smaller in magnitude than all positive *standard* numbers, it is called *i-small*. Similarly, a number is *i-large* if it is larger in magnitude than all *standard* numbers; otherwise, it is called *i-limited*. Two numbers are *i-close* to each other if their difference is *i-small*. These properties have simple interpretations over the integers: The *i-limited* integers are precisely the *standard* integers, the only *i-small* integer is zero, and no two integers are *i-close* to each other.

The reals have a richer structure. Besides zero, there are an infinite number of *i-small* numbers or infinitesimals. These include rationals like $1/N$, where N is the *i-large* integer seen above. It also includes irrationals, such as π/N. It is not the case that all *i-limited* reals are *standard*. For example, the only *standard* number that is also *i-small* is zero, and we have already seen two other examples of *i-small* numbers. But any *i-limited* real x is *i-close* to a *standard* number $^*x$; that is, x can be written as the sum of the unique *standard* number $^*x$ and an *i-small* number ϵ: $x = {}^*x + \epsilon$. The number $^*x$ is called the *standard-part* of x.

One of the benefits of non-standard analysis, particularly in the context of automated theorem proving, is that the new predicates possess simple algebraic properties. For example, $x + y$ is *i-small* (*i-limited*) if both x and y are *i-small* (*i-limited*). If x is *i-limited* and ϵ is *i-small*, $\epsilon \cdot x$ is *i-small* and for x not *i-small* and $\epsilon \neq 0$, x/ϵ is *i-large*. If x is *i-close* to y and y is *i-close* to z, then x is *i-close* to z. As all of these properties illustrate, the predicates really do capture the intuitive notion of "infinitely small," "finite," "infinitely large," and "infinitely close."

Standard-part also obeys simple algebraic rules. For example $^*(x+y) = {}^*x + {}^*y$ and $^*(x \cdot y) = {}^*x \cdot {}^*y$ for *i-limited* x and y. The restrictions to *i-limited* numbers is not necessary for the addition rule, but it is necessary for the product rule. The inverse operations follow similar rules: $^*(-x) = -{}^*x$

and $^*(1/x) = 1/^*x$, but the division rule is only true when x is *i-limited* and not *i-small*. Finally, when $x < y$, it follows that $^*x \leq \,^*y$. Notice the last inequality is not strict. Although this list is far from complete, it shows that the rules for the non-standard predicates can easily be captured in an automated theorem prover, such as ACL2(r).

However, one major problem remains. We have seen that the sum of two *i-small* numbers is also *i-small*. Using induction, it would appear that $n \cdot \epsilon$ is *i-small* for any positive integer n and *i-small* ϵ, but letting $n = N$ and $\epsilon = 1/N$ for N any *i-large* integer provides a simple counter-example.

What this illustrates is that induction must be restricted in the presence of non-standard notions. ACL2(r) contains a modified induction principle that deals with this problem, but for the purposes of this chapter, it is sufficient to simply disallow induction on formulas using any of the functions of non-standard analysis. Similarly, we disallow the use of recursion to define a function using any of the new notions.

From now on, we will refer to formulas not using any of the non-standard functions as *classical* formulas. In general, functions defined using any non-standard function are automatically non-classical, although we will later introduce a definitional principle that allows non-classical formulas to define classical functions, but only when strict conditions are met. Note that all classically-defined functions are necessarily standard, but that standard functions can have non-classical definitions. For example, the function defined as $^*x - \,^*x$ is standard, since it is identically zero, but this definition is non-classical, since it uses the non-standard function *standart-part*. Using this terminology, our restriction limits the use of induction and recursion to the classical formulas only.

But we began this chapter by saying that non-standard analysis makes heavy use of mathematical induction and recursion, where these often replace limit and compactness arguments. How can this be when induction and recursion are disallowed for non-classical formulas? The answer is simple. In the next section, we will see an inductive proof of the Intermediate Value Theorem. A key lemma there will be that for any partition $\{a, a + \epsilon, \ldots, a + n\epsilon = b\}$ of the interval $[a, b]$ if $f(a) < 0$ and $f(b) > 0$ there must be some i, $0 \leq i \leq n$, such that $f(a + i\epsilon) < 0$ and $f(a + (i + 1)\epsilon) \geq 0$. This lemma can be established with induction on n, the size of the partition. The Intermediate Value Theorem follows by applying this key lemma to an *i-large* value of n, or equivalently to an *i-small* ϵ.

Non-standard analysis has one more pleasant surprise. Given a classical formula $F(x)$, if $F(x)$ is true for all *standard* values of x, it is also true for *all* values of x. This is known as the *transfer principle*, and it can be explicitly invoked in ACL2(r) by using the event **defthm-std** in place of **defthm**.

Similarly, a *classical* function $f(x)$ can be defined by specifying its values only for the *standard* values of x. This is the only way a non-classical body can be used to define a classical function, and it is only permissible when the value of $f(x)$ is *standard* for every *standard* x. We say the function $f(x)$ is implicitly defined by its values on the *standard* elements. Functions can be defined implicitly in ACL2(r) by using the event `defun-std` instead of <u>`defun`</u>. Notice that the newly defined function $f(x)$ is *classical*, even though its explicit definition for *standard* values of x may not be. A common technique is to define $f(x)$ as the *standard-part* of some value. Theorems about $f(x)$ can be proved by using `defthm-std`, which requires only that the *standard* values of x be considered.

This section was a whirlwind tour through non-standard analysis in ACL2(r). These concepts will become clearer in the next section, where we will show how non-standard analysis can be used in ACL2(r) to prove some basic results from calculus. Readers interested in a more thorough introduction to non-standard analysis should consult [90, 24, 82].

18.2   Continuity

Intuitively, a function f is continuous if $f(x)$ is close to $f(y)$ whenever x is sufficiently close to y. This intuition is muddied using standard analysis, but it is represented faithfully in non-standard analysis, where the formal notion *i-close* replaces the informal notion of "sufficiently close."

In ACL2, we can introduce an arbitrary continuous function as follows.

```
(encapsulate
 ((rcfn (x) t))
 (local (defun rcfn (x) x))
 (defthm rcfn-standard
   (implies (standard-numberp x)
            (standard-numberp (rcfn x)))
   :rule-classes (:rewrite :type-prescription))
 (defthm rcfn-real
   (implies (realp x)
            (realp (rcfn x)))
   :rule-classes (:rewrite :type-prescription))
 (defthm rcfn-continuous
   (implies (and (standard-numberp x)
                 (realp x)
                 (realp y)
                 (i-close x y))
            (i-close (rcfn x) (rcfn y))))
 )
```

The function `rcfn` is axiomatized as a real, continuous function. These constraints are made in `rcfn-real` and `rcfn-continuous`. Notice the natural expression of continuity in non-standard analysis. Its only surprise is the hypothesis that x should be *standard*. Without this hypothesis the constraint on `rcfn` would be stronger: `rcfn` would become uniformly continuous.

In the current version of ACL2(r), **encapsulate** always introduces *standard* functions. All *standard* functions map *standard* arguments to *standard* values. However, the current version of ACL2(r) does not contain this axiom scheme, which is why we added `rcfn-standard` as a constraint. This may not be necessary in a future version of ACL2(r).

According to the Intermediate Value Theorem, if a, b, and z are reals such that $a < b$, $rcfn(a) < z$, and $rcfn(b) > z$, there is some c between a and b such that $rcfn(c) = z$. We can prove this theorem by finding a suitable value of c. Consider the points $x_0 = a$, $x_1 = a + \epsilon$, ... $x_n = a + n\epsilon = b$ for a fixed but arbitrary positive integer n. Using a simple induction, it is easy to show that for some index i, $0 \le i < n$, $rcfn(x_i) < z$ and $rcfn(x_{i+1}) \ge z$. So far neither continuity nor non-standard analysis has been used in the proof, but they will take center stage from this point. First, notice that since `rcfn` is continuous, $rcfn(^*x) = {}^*rcfn(x)$ for *i-limited* x. This follows because $^*x$ and x are *i-close* and $^*x$ is *standard*, so by continuity their `rcfn` values are *i-close*. Moreover, since $rcfn(^*x)$ is *standard* it must be equal to $^*rcfn(x)$, as no two distinct *standard* numbers are *i-close* to each other. Now, consider what happens when ϵ is *i-small* and a, b, and z are *standard*. Then x_i and x_{i+1} are *i-close*, so $^*x_i$ and $^*x_{i+1}$ are equal and also *i-close* to x_i and x_{i+1}. Moreover, $rcfn(^*x_i) = {}^*rcfn(x_i) \le {}^*z = z$ and similarly $rcfn(^*x_i) = rcfn(^*x_{i+1}) \ge {}^*z = z$, therefore $rcfn(^*x_i) = z$. To complete the proof, it is only necessary to show that $a \le {}^*x_i \le b$, but this trivially follows from the fact that $a \le x_i \le b$ and a and b are *standard*. This proves the Intermediate Value Theorem for *standard* values of a, b, and z. Using the transfer principle, it follows that the Intermediate Value Theorem is true for all real values of a, b, and z.

This argument can be formalized in ACL2(r). We begin with the lemma that $rcfn(^*x) = {}^*rcfn(x)$ for *i-limited* x.

```
(defthm rcfn-standard-part
  (implies (and (realp x)
                (i-limited x))
           (equal (rcfn (standard-part x))
                  (standard-part (rcfn x))))
  :hints ... )
```

This lemma is a simple consequence of the continuity of `rcfn` at $^*x$ and the fact that two numbers that are *i-close* have the same *standard-part* provided at least one of them is *i-limited*.

The second key lemma is the discovery of the number x_i with its specific properties. This number can be found using the following function.

```
(defun find-zero-n (a z i n eps)
  (declare (xargs :measure (nfix (1+ (- n i))))))
```

```
(if (and (realp a) (integerp i) (integerp n) (< i n)
         (realp eps) (< 0 eps)
         (< (rcfn (+ a eps)) z))
    (find-zero-n (+ a eps) z (1+ i) n eps)
  (realfix a)))
```

This function recurses "from i to n" looking for the first index i so that $rcfn(a + (i + 1) \cdot \epsilon) \geq z$, and it returns $a + i \cdot \epsilon$ (for simplicity, the value of a is incremented each time through the recursion).

It is trivial to show that find-zero-n returns a value of x_i so that $rcfn(x_i) < z$.

```
(defthm rcfn-find-zero-n-<-z
  (implies (and (realp a) (< (rcfn a) z))
           (< (rcfn (find-zero-n a z i n eps)) z)))
```

This follows directly from the fact that $rcfn(a) < z$. It is also easy to prove that the value of x_i satisfies $rcfn(x_i + \epsilon) \geq z$, from the fact that $rcfn(b) > z$.

```
(defthm rcfn-find-zero-n+eps->=-z
  (implies (and (realp a) (integerp i) (integerp n) (< i n)
                (realp eps) (< 0 eps)
                (< (rcfn a) z)
                (< z (rcfn (+ a (* (- n i) eps)))))
           (<= z (rcfn (+ (find-zero-n a z i n eps)
                          eps)))))
```

Notice the term (+ a (* (- n i) eps)) is always equal to b. Without too much difficulty, it is also possible to prove that $a \leq x_i \leq b$. Notice that all these theorems use induction to prove properties of find-zero-n, a recursive function.

Since $a \leq x_i \leq b$ for *standard* a and b, it follows that x_i is *i-limited*, hence $^*x_i$ is *standard*. We can therefore use defun-std to implicitly define a function that agrees with $^*x_i$ on all *standard* arguments. This function should return the right choice of c to satisfy the Intermediate Value Theorem.

```
(defun-std find-zero (a b z)
  (if (and (realp a) (realp b) (realp z) (< a b))
      (standard-part
       (find-zero-n a
                    z
                    0
                    (i-large-integer)
                    (/ (- b a) (i-large-integer))))
    0))
```

The built-in function i-large-integer introduces an *i-large* positive integer into ACL2(r).

To prove that find-zero satisfies the requirements of the Intermediate Value Theorem, we have to transfer the properties already proved about find-zero-n to find-zero. The properties about find-zero-n were proved using induction; now we will use defthm-std to transfer these properties to find-zero. The lemma rcfn-find-zero-n-<-z can be transferred as follows.

```
(defthm-std rcfn-find-zero-<=-z
  (implies (and (realp a) (realp b) (< a b)
                (realp z) (< (rcfn a) z))
           (<= (rcfn (find-zero a b z)) z))
  :hints  ... )
```

Because defthm-std is used to prove rcfn-find-zero-<=-z, ACL2(r) assumes the extra hypotheses that a, b, and z are all *standard*. Because of this, the definition of find-zero can be opened and replaced with $^*x_i$. The remainder of the proof follows simply from the fact that if $x < y$, $^*x \leq {}^*y$. Notice how the strict inequality has been replaced. The transfer principle can also be used on rcfn-find-zero-n+eps->=-z to conclude the following.

```
(defthm-std rcfn-find-zero->=-z
  (implies (and (realp a) (realp b) (< a b)
                (realp z) (< (rcfn a) z) (< z (rcfn b)))
           (<= z (rcfn (find-zero a b z)))))
  :hints  ... )
```

Similarly, we find that (find-zero a b z) is somewhere between a and b. All of these lemmas can be proved by applying the transfer principle applied to the corresponding lemmas about find-zero-n. Collecting all of these results gives the Intermediate Value Theorem.

```
(defthm intermediate-value-theorem
  (implies (and (realp a) (realp b) (< a b)
                (realp z) (< (rcfn a) z) (< z (rcfn b)))
           (and (realp (find-zero a b z))
                (< a (find-zero a b z))
                (< (find-zero a b z) b)
                (equal (rcfn (find-zero a b z))
                       z)))
  :hints  ... )
```

Exercise 18.2 *Prove a version of the Intermediate Value Theorem applicable when* (rcfn a) *is greater than z and* (rcfn b) *is less than z. Hint. Functionally instantiate the Intermediate Value Theorem.*

Exercise 18.3 *Using ACL2(r) show the existence of some x such that* (equal (* x x) 2). *Hint. Use the Intermediate Value Theorem.*

The proofs of other familiar facts about continuous functions follow the same pattern. For example, the proof of the maximal and minimal theorems—every continuous function achieves its maximum and minimum values over a closed interval—differs from the above only in the choice of the function find-zero-n. The remaining details are very similar. Using induction we establish that $rcfn(x_i) \geq rcfn(x_j)$, for all the x_j points in an ϵ-grid from a and b. Then $rcfn(^*x_i) = {}^*rcfn(x_i) \geq {}^*rcfn(x_j) = rcfn(^*x_j)$. Notice how continuity is used in this last step to justify moving the *standard-part* out of *rcfn*. For an arbitrary $x \in [a, b]$, we can find the x_j in the ϵ-grid that is closest to x. If x is *standard*, we have that $rcfn(x) = {}^*rcfn(x_j)$ since x and x_j are *i-close*. It follows that for an arbitrary *standard* $x \in [a, b]$, $rcfn(^*x_i) \geq rcfn(x)$. By the transfer principle, this is true for all $x \in [a, b]$, not just the *standard* ones, so *rcfn* achieves its maximum at $^*x_i$. We leave the reader to formalize this argument in ACL2(r).

Exercise 18.4 *Define a function* find-max-rcfn-x *and prove that* rcfn *achieves a maximum over* $[a, b]$ *at the point* (find-max-rcfn-x a b).

Exercise 18.5 *Define a function* find-min-rcfn-x *and prove that* rcfn *achieves a minimum over* $[a, b]$ *at* (find-min-rcfn-x a b). *Hint. Instantiate the theorem from the previous exercise.*

Exercise 18.6 *Prove that the sum and product of two continuous functions are continuous. Hint. Use two constrained functions,* rcfn-1 *and* rcfn-2.

18.3 Differentiability

Intuitively, we find the derivative of a function f at a point x by taking the slope of the chord between $f(x)$ and $f(x')$ for a point x' infinitely close to x such that $x \neq x'$. In standard analysis we say that as x' approaches x, the slopes of the chords approach the derivative of f at x. The derivative exists if the slopes of the chords have a limit. In the language of non-standard analysis, we say that the slope of the chord is *i-close* to the derivative at x if x is *i-close* to x' and $x \neq x'$. In order for the derivate to exist, the slope of the chord between $f(x)$ and $f(x')$ should be *i-close* to the slope of the chord between $f(x)$ and $f(x'')$ whenever x is *i-close* to both x' and x'' and distinct from both of them.

A differentiable function can be introduced into ACL2(r) as follows.

```
(encapsulate
 ((rdfn (x) t))
 (local (defun rdfn (x) x))
 (defthm rdfn-standard
   (implies (standard-numberp x)
            (standard-numberp (rdfn x)))
```

```
    :rule-classes (:rewrite :type-prescription))
(defthm rdfn-real
  (implies (realp x)
           (realp (rdfn x)))
    :rule-classes (:rewrite :type-prescription))
(defthm rdfn-differentiable
  (implies (and (standard-numberp x)
                (realp x)
                (realp y1)
                (realp y2)
                (i-close x y1) (not (= x y1))
                (i-close x y2) (not (= x y2)))
           (and (i-limited (/ (- (rdfn x) (rdfn y1))
                              (- x y1)))
                (i-close (/ (- (rdfn x) (rdfn y1))
                            (- x y1))
                         (/ (- (rdfn x) (rdfn y2))
                            (- x y2))))))
)
```

We will prove Rolle's Theorem for the function rdfn: Given reals a, b
with $a < b$ so that $rdfn(a) = rdfn(b)$, there is a point $c \in [a, b]$ so that the
derivative of rdfn at c is 0. The proof depends on the maximal and minimal
theorems of continuous functions. First, observe that rdfn is a continuous
function. Therefore, according to Exercises 18.4 and 18.5, rdfn achieves
its maximum and minimum. If the maximum is equal to the minimum,
rdfn is a constant function, and its derivative is zero everywhere on $[a, b]$.
Otherwise, either the maximum or minimum occurs inside (a, b). Assume
without loss of generality that the maximum occurs at the point $c \in (a, b)$,
and let c' and c'' be two points i-$close$ to c with $c' < c < c''$. Then the
slope of the chord from $rdfn(c)$ to $rdfn(c')$ is non-negative, but the slope
from $rdfn(c)$ to $rdfn(c'')$ is non-positive. Since these slopes must be i-$close$,
their $standard$-$part$—i.e., the derivative at c—must be 0.

So first, we must show that rdfn is continuous. Comparing the constraints on rcfn and rdfn, it is obvious that only rcfn-continuous needs
to be established for rdfn. This follows from the constraint rdfn-differ-
entiable by letting y1 and y2 be equal to y. Then the difference quo-
tient $\frac{rdfn(x)-rdfn(y)}{x-y}$ is i-$limited$ and since $x - y$ is i-$small$ that follows that
$rdfn(x) - rdfn(y)$ must be i-$small$, too; i.e., rdfn is continuous. This argument can be easily carried out in ACL2(r).

```
(defthm rdfn-continuous
  (implies (and (standard-numberp x)
                (realp x)
                (i-close x y)
                (realp y))
```

```
          (i-close (rdfn x) (rdfn y)))
    :hints  ... )
```

It is now a simple matter to define the functions find-max-rdfn-x and find-min-rdfn-x that find the points at which rdfn achieves its maximum and minimum respectively. The relevant theorems are functional instances of the theorems in Exercises 18.4 and 18.5, so they are trivial to establish. It is also simple to prove that if the maximum and minimum are equal, the function is a constant on $[a, b]$.

```
(defthm min=max->-constant-rcfn
  (implies (and (realp a) (realp b) (< a b)
                (realp x) (<= a x) (<= x b)
                (= (rcfn (find-min-rcfn-x a b))
                   (rcfn (find-max-rcfn-x a b))))
           (equal (equal (rcfn (find-min-rcfn-x a b))
                         (rcfn x))
                  t))
  :hints  ... )
```

Notice this theorem is being proved about rcfn, since it holds whether the function is differentiable or not. It is a simple matter to functionally instantiate this theorem to the differentiable function rdfn.

The remainder of the argument relies heavily on the slope of the chord from $rdfn(x)$ to $rdfn(y)$, also known as the difference quotient of x and y. We are particularly interested when y is i-close to x; that is, when y can be written as $x + \epsilon$ for some i-small ϵ.

```
(defun differential-rdfn (x eps)
  (/ (- (rdfn x) (rdfn (+ x eps)))
     (- eps)))
```

Similarly, the derivative can be defined as follows.

```
(defun derivative-rdfn (x)
  (standard-part
   (differential-rdfn x (/ (i-large-integer))))))
```

Notice that the choice of ϵ is arbitrary since rdfn is differentiable.

The first key lemma is that when rdfn is a constant function, any difference quotient of the midpoint of $[a, b]$ must be 0.

```
(defthm rolles-theorem-lemma-1
  (implies (and (realp a) (realp b) (< a b)
                (realp eps)
                (< (abs eps) (/ (- b a) 2))
                (= (rdfn (find-min-rdfn-x a b))
                   (rdfn (find-max-rdfn-x a b))))
           (equal (differential-rdfn (/ (+ a b) 2) eps) 0))
  :hints  ... )
```

ACL2(r) requires a hint to use the lemma `min=max->-constant-rcfn` to
deduce that `rdfn` is constant given that its minimum and maximum values
are identical. The condition on `eps` being less than half the width of $[a, b]$
ensures that both endpoints of the chord are inside $[a, b]$.

The remaining lemmas are all similar. For example, when `rdfn` achieves
its maximum somewhere in the range (a, b) and ϵ is positive, the difference
quotients to the right of the maximum point will be non-positive.

```
(defthm rolles-theorem-lemma-2a
  (implies (and (realp a) (realp b) (< a b)
                (realp eps) (< 0 eps)
                (< a (- (find-max-rdfn-x a b) eps))
                (< (+ (find-max-rdfn-x a b) eps) b))
           (<= (differential-rdfn (find-max-rdfn-x a b)
                                  eps)
               0)))
```

This is obvious from the geometry, since the value of $rdfn(x + \epsilon)$ is at most
equal to $rdfn(x)$ and yet $x + \epsilon$ is greater than x. Hence the chord can not
have a positive slope. Similar theorems apply to the other cases; *i.e.*, when
ϵ is negative or when the minimum is used instead of the maximum.

There is an important technical point remaining. When we look at a
point x in $[a, b]$ we can only look at its difference quotient with respect to ϵ
if we are guaranteed that $x + \epsilon$ is also in the range $[a, b]$. When a and b are
both *standard* and ϵ is *i-small*, it is clear that $a + \epsilon$ and $b - \epsilon$ are in $[a, b]$. In
fact, $x \pm \epsilon$ will be in $[a, b]$ for any *standard* $x \in (a, b)$. Otherwise, x would
be *i-close* to either a or b, but no two distinct *standard* numbers can be
i-close to each other. In particular, this holds for the midpoint $(a + b)/2$
and for the values of x at which `rdfn` achieves its maximum or minimum.
To verify this, we need only observe that the maximum and minimum are
achieved at *standard* values of x.

```
(defthm standard-find-min-max-rdfn
  (implies (and (standard-numberp a)
                (standard-numberp b))
           (and (standard-numberp (find-min-rdfn-x a b))
                (standard-numberp (find-max-rdfn-x a b))))
  :hints  ... )
```

We also need to prove the claim above that $x \pm \epsilon \in (a, b)$ whenever x, a,
and b are *standard* and ϵ is *i-small*. The following lemma proves half of this
claim.

```
(defthm small-squeeze-standard-1
  (implies (and (realp a) (standard-numberp a)
                (realp x) (standard-numberp x)
                (< a x)
```

```
                    (realp eps) (< 0 eps) (i-small eps))
            (< a (- x eps)))
  :hints  ... )
```

The other half is similar.

It is time to define the point that will satisfy Rolle's Theorem, the so-called critical point of rdfn.

```
(defun rolles-critical-point (a b)
  (if (equal (rdfn (find-min-rdfn-x a b))
             (rdfn (find-max-rdfn-x a b)))
      (/ (+ a b) 2)
    (if (equal (rdfn (find-min-rdfn-x a b)) (rdfn a))
        (find-max-rdfn-x a b)
      (find-min-rdfn-x a b))))
```

Intuitively, the point x at which rdfn achieves its minimum will work. However, it is important to consider the special case when the minimum occurs at either of the endpoints. Notice that rolles-critical-point always chooses an interior point in (a, b). To complete the proof, it is only necessary to consider each of the cases implied by the definition of rolles-critical-point. This yields the proof of Rolle's Theorem in ACL2(r).

```
(defthm rolles-theorem
  (implies (and (realp a) (standard-numberp a)
                (realp b) (standard-numberp b)
                (= (rdfn a) (rdfn b))
                (< a b))
           (equal (derivative-rdfn
                    (rolles-critical-point a b))
                  0))
  :hints  ... )
```

This theorem resembles Rolle's Theorem from classical analysis; however, there is an important difference. The theorem rolles-theorem explicitly requires that the endpoints a and b of the interval are *standard*, whereas no such restriction is made in Rolle's Theorem. Consider, for example, intermediate-value-theorem where no such restriction is made. What is the difference between these two? The reader will no doubt realize that at no point in the proof of rolles-theorem did we use the transfer principle. In the proof of the Intermediate Value Theorem, the transfer principle was used in the proof of the key lemmas rcfn-find-zero-<=-z and rcfn-find-zero->=-z. That is why the final statement of the theorem makes no assumption about its parameters being *standard*. A similar technique is required to complete the proof of Rolle's Theorem. A first attempt may be to replace defthm with defthm-std in the proof of rolles-theorem. However this will fail, since `derivative-rdfn` is a non-classical function. To correct this problem, it will be necessary to modify key parts of the proof.

Exercise 18.7 *Modify the proof of* `rolles-theorem` *to prove the classical Rolle's Theorem. Hint. Consider* `defun-std` *and* `defthm-std`. *A solution can be found in [67].*

Rolle's Theorem is typically used to prove the Mean Value Theorem. Given a differentiable function f on a closed interval $[a, b]$ such that $f(a) = f(b)$, Rolle's Theorem tells us that there is a point $c \in [a, b]$ with $f'(c) = 0$. The Mean Value Theorem is a generalization used when $f(a) \neq f(b)$. In these cases, we can find a point $c \in [a, b]$ so that $f'(c) = m$ where m is the slope of the line from $(a, f(a))$ to $(b, f(b))$. The Mean Value Theorem can be proved by applying Rolle's Theorem to the function $g(x) = f(x) - m \cdot (x - a) - f(a)$. Notice that when $g'(x) = 0$, $f'(x) = m$.

The first step is to define the function $g(x)$ in ACL2(r). We would like this function to be defined solely in terms of x, but notice that the definition given above depends on a and b as well. A simple way to accomplish this is to axiomatize the range $[a, b]$ by introducing the functions (a) and (b) of no arguments.

```
(encapsulate
 ((a () t)
  (b () t))
 (local (defun a () 0))
 (local (defun b () 1))
 (defthm realp-a
   (realp (a))
   :rule-classes (:rewrite :type-prescription))
 (defthm realp-b
   (realp (b))
   :rule-classes (:rewrite :type-prescription))
 (defthm standardp-a
   (standard-numberp (a)))
 (defthm standardp-b
   (standard-numberp (b)))
 (defthm a-<-b
   (< (a) (b)))
)
```

The definition of g is now straightforward.

```
(defun rdfn2 (x)
  (+ (rdfn x)
     (- (* (- (rdfn (b)) (rdfn (a)))
           (- x (a))
```

```
            (/ (- (b) (a)))))
      (- (rdfn (a)))))
```

Since we intend to apply Rolle's Theorem to `rdfn2`, we must show that it is differentiable. That is, we must show that it satisfies all the constraints of `rdfn`: `rdfn-standard`, `rdfn-real`, and `rdfn-differentiable`. The first two are trivial. The last one is more interesting. It can be proved directly from first principles, defining the functions `differential-rdfn2` and `derivative-rdfn2` in analogy to `differential-rdfn` and `derivative--rdfn`, respectively. It can also be proved indirectly as a consequence of lemmas about the differentiability of composition of functions. This is left as an exercise.

Exercise 18.8 *Prove that the sum and product of two differentiable functions are differentiable.*

It is now possible to invoke Rolle's Theorem on `rdfn2`:

```
(defthm rolles-theorem-2
  (implies (and (realp a) (standard-numberp a)
                (realp b) (standard-numberp b)
                (= (rdfn2 a) (rdfn2 b))
                (< a b))
           (equal (derivative-rdfn2
                     (rolles-critical-point-2 a b))
                  0))
  :hints (("Goal"
           :by (:functional-instance rolles-theorem ... )))
```

The theorem `rolles-theorem-2` applies for any *standard* range $[a, b]$. We are particularly interested in the range when a is (a) and b is (b). That is, we wish to find a specific instance of `rolles-theorem-2`. Notice that the points (a) and (b) are *standard* reals by their constraints, and that (a) is less than (b). Moreover, from the definition of `rdfn2` it follows that `(rdfn2 (a))` and `(rdfn2 (b))` are both zero. Therefore, when we specialize `rolles-theorem-2` we can remove all of the hypotheses.

```
(defthm rolles-theorem-2-specialized
  (equal (derivative-rdfn2
           (rolles-critical-point-2 (a) (b)))
         0)
  :hints (("Goal" :use ((:instance rolles-theorem-2
                                    (a (a)) (b (b))))
           ... )))
```

The only remaining lemma relates the derivative of `rdfn` to the derivative of `rdfn2`. The following lemma can be proved directly by algebraic manipulation or indirectly by using properties of the difference quotients of sums and products. We chose to follow the direct proof.

```
(defthm mvt-theorem-lemma
  (implies (and (acl2-numberp eps)
                (not (= eps 0)))
           (equal (differential-rdfn x eps)
                  (+ (* (+ (- (rdfn (a))) (rdfn (b)))
                        (/ (+ (- (a)) (b))))
                     (differential-rdfn2 x eps))))
  :hints ... )
```

The Mean Value Theorem follows from this lemma, the specialized version of Rolle's Theorem, and some simple reasoning about *standard-part*.

```
(defthm mvt-theorem
  (equal (derivative-rdfn
          (rolles-critical-point-2 (a) (b)))
         (/ (- (rdfn (b)) (rdfn (a)))
            (- (b) (a))))
  :hints ... )
```

18.4   Conclusions

ACL2(r) extends ACL2 with the capability of reasoning about the real and complex numbers. This chapter illustrates how ACL2(r) can prove some of the classic theorems from elementary analysis, and Kaufmann's article in this book presents more profound theorems from analysis. But the focus of ACL2(r) is not to become a platform for theorem proving about the real numbers. Rather, it is to continue in the tradition of Nqthm and ACL2, to prove theorems about algorithms and mathematical models of circuits. Many algorithms use properties about the real numbers, indirectly by using functions such as the exponential or trigonometric functions or directly, *e.g.*, finding the maximum of a function by finding the roots of its derivative. The point of ACL2(r) is to make these functions and their mathematical properties available to users of ACL2, making ACL2 applicable to even more domains.

Disclaimer

We have decided to view ACL2(r) as a separate program and logic, but with the expectation that it will be released with ACL2 2.5. Thus, even when it is fully incorporated, ACL2 will not have an official connection with ACL2(r) Version 2.5, other than that they share the same source files and are released together. Future releases may integrate ACL2 and ACL2(r) more fully.

Bibliography

1. R. Bellman. On a routing problem. *Quarterly of Applied Mathematics*, 16(1):87–90, 1958.

2. W. R. Bevier. KIT: A study in operating system verification. *IEEE Transactions on Software Engineering*, 15(11):1368–81, November 1989.

3. W. R. Bevier, W. A. Hunt, Jr., J S. Moore, and W. D. Young. An approach to systems verification. *Journal of Automated Reasoning*, 5(4):411–428, December 1989.

4. R. J. Boulton, A. D. Gordon, J. R. Harrison, J. M. J. Herbert, and J. Van Tassel. Experience with embedding hardware description languages in HOL. In V. Stavridou, T. F. Melham, and R. T. Boute, editors, *Theorem Provers in Circuit Design: Theory, Practice and Experience: Proceedings of the IFIP TC10/WG 10.2 International Conference*, IFIP Transactions A-10, pages 129–156. North-Holland, June 1992.

5. R. S. Boyer and J S. Moore. A mechanical proof of the unsolvability of the halting problem. *JACM*, 31(3):441–458, 1984.

6. R. S. Boyer and J S. Moore. Mechanized formal reasoning about programs and computing machines. In R. Veroff, editor, *Automated Reasoning and Its Applications: Essays in Honor of Larry Wos*, pages 147–176. MIT Press, 1996.

7. R. S. Boyer and J S. Moore. *A Computational Logic Handbook*. Academic Press, second edition, 1997.

8. R. S. Boyer and J S. Moore. Single-threaded objects in ACL2, 1999. See URL http://www.cs.utexas.edu/users/moore/publications/-acl2-papers.html#Foundations.

9. R. S. Boyer and Y. Yu. Automated proofs of object code for a widely used microprocessor. *Journal of the ACM*, 43(1):166–192, January 1996.

10. B. Brock. Defstructure for ACL2, 1997. See URL http://www.cs.-utexas.edu/users/moore/publications/acl2-papers.html#Utilities.

11. B. Brock and W. A. Hunt, Jr. Formally specifying and mechanically verifying programs for the Motorola complex arithmetic processor DSP. In *1997 IEEE International Conference on Computer Design*, pages 31–36. IEEE Computer Society, Oct. 1997.

12. B. Brock, M. Kaufmann, and J S. Moore. ACL2 theorems about commercial microprocessors. In M. Srivas and A. Camilleri, editors, *Formal Methods*

in Computer-Aided Design (FMCAD'96), pages 275–293. Springer-Verlag, 1996.

13. B. Brock and J S. Moore. A mechanically checked proof of a comparator sort algorithm, 1999. See URL http://www.cs.utexas.edu/users/moore/-publications/csort/main.ps.Z.

14. R. E. Bryant. Symbolic Boolean manipulation with ordered binary decision diagrams. *ACM Computing Surveys*, 1992.

15. J. R. Burch. Techniques for verifying superscalar microprocessors. In *Design Automation Conference (DAC '96)*, pages 552–557, Las Vegas, Nevada, June 1996. ACM Press.

16. J. R. Burch, E. M. Clarke, K. L. McMillan, D. L. Dill, and L. J. Hwang. Symbolic model checking: 10^{20} states and beyond. *Information and Computation*, 98(2):142–170, June 1992.

17. J. R. Burch and D. L. Dill. Automatic verification of pipelined microprocessor control. In *Computer-Aided Verification (CAV '94)*, volume 818 of *LNCS*, pages 68–80. Springer-Verlag, 1994.

18. A. Cimatti, F. Giunchiglia, P. Pecchiari, B. Pietra, J. Profeta, D. Romano, and P. Traverso. A Provably Correct Embedded Verifier for the Certification of Safety Critical Software. In *Proc. Computer-Aided Verification (CAV'97)*, Haifa, Israel, June 1997. Also IRST-Technical Report 9701-04, IRST, Trento, Italy.

19. A. Cimatti, F. Giunchiglia, P. Traverso, and A. Villafiorita. Run-time result formal verification of safety critical software: an industrial case study. In *FLoC'99 workshop "Run Time Result Verification"*, Trento, Italy, July 1999.

20. E. M. Clarke and E. A. Emerson. Design and synthesis of synchronization skeletons using branching time temporal logic. In *Workshop on Logics of Programs*, volume 131 of *LNCS*. Springer-Verlag, 1981.

21. Common Lisp Hyperspec (TM). See URL http://www.harlequin.com/-support/books/HyperSpec/.

22. T. H. Cormen, C. E. Leiserson, and R. R. Rivest. *Introduction to Algorithms*. MIT Press, 1989.

23. D. Déharbe. *Vérification Formelle de Proprietés Temporelles: Études et Application au Langage VHDL*. PhD thesis, Universite' Joseph Fourier, 15 Nov. 1996.

24. F. Diener and M. Diener, editors. *Nonstandard Analysis in Practice*. Springer-Verlag, 1995.

25. E. W. Dijkstra. A note on two problems in connection with graphs. *Numerische Mathematik*, 1:269–271, 1959.

26. K. Doets. *Basic Model Theory*. CSLI Publications, 1996.

27. E. A. Emerson. *Branching time temporal logics and the design of correct concurrent programs*. PhD thesis, Division of Applied Sciences, Harvard University, August 1981.

28. E. A. Emerson. Temporal and modal logic. In J. van Leeuwen, editor, *Handbook of Theoretical Computer Science: Volume B: Formal Models and Semantics*, pages 995–1072. Elsevier, Amsterdam, 1990.

29. E. A. Emerson. Model checking and the Mu-Calculus. In N. Immerman and P. Kolaitis, editors, *Proceedings of the DIMACS Symposium on Descriptive Complexity and Finite Models*, pages 185–214, 1997.

30. E. A. Emerson and E. M. Clarke. Characterizing correctness properties of parallel programs as fixpoints. In *Proceedings 7th International Colloquium on Automata, Languages, and Programming*, volume 85 of *LNCS*. Springer-Verlag, 1981.

31. E. A. Emerson, C. S. Jutla, and A. P. Sistla. On model checking for fragments of the Mu-Calculus. In *Proceedings 5th International Conference on Computer Aided Verification*, volume 697 of *LNCS*, pages 385–396. Springer-Verlag, 1993.

32. E. A. Emerson and C.-L. Lei. Efficient model checking in fragments of the propositional Mu-Calculus (extended abstract). In *Proceedings, Symposium on Logic in Computer Science*, pages 267–278, Cambridge, Massachusetts, 16–18 June 1986. IEEE Computer Society.

33. M. Fitting. *First-Order Logic and Automated Theorem Proving*. Springer-Verlag, second edition, 1996.

34. A. D. Flatau. *A verified implementation of an applicative language with dynamic storage allocation*. PhD thesis, University of Texas at Austin, 1992.

35. L. R. Ford, Jr. and D. R. Fulkerson. *Flows in Networks*. Princeton University Press, 1962.

36. R. Gamboa. *Mechanically Verifying Real-Valued Algorithms in ACL2*. PhD thesis, The University of Texas at Austin, 1999.

37. R. Gamboa and M. Kaufmann. Non-standard analysis in ACL2, in preparation.

38. S. Gilfeather, J. Gehman, and C. Harrison. Architecture of a complex arithmetic processor for communication signal processsing. In *SPIE Proceedings, International Symposium on Optics, Imaging, and Instrumentation*, volume 2296, pages 624–625. Advanced Signal Processing: Algorithms, Architectures, and Implementations V, July 1994.

39. W. Goerigk. On Trojan horses in compiler implementations. In F. Saglietti and W. Goerigk, editors, *Workshop on Safety and Reliability of Software-based Systems*, ISTec Report ISTec-A-367, ISBN 3-00-004872-3, Garching, Germany, Aug. 1999.

40. W. Goerigk, A. Dold, T. Gaul, G. Goos, A. Heberle, F. Henke, U. Hoffmann, H. Langmaack, H. Pfeifer, H. Ruess, and W. Zimmermann. Compiler correctness and implementation verification: The *Verifix* approach. In P. Fritzson, editor, *Proceedings of the Poster Session of CC '96 – International Conference on Compiler Construction*, pages 65–73, IDA Technical Report LiTH-IDA-R-96-12, Linköping, Sweden, 1996.

41. W. Goerigk, T. Gaul, and W. Zimmermann. Correct programs without proof? On checker-based program verification. In R. Berghammer and Y. Lakhnech, editors, *Proceedings ATOOLS'98 Workshop on "Tool Support for System Specification, Development, and Verification"*, Advances in Computing Science, pages 108–122, Wien, New York, 1998. Springer-Verlag.

42. W. Goerigk and U. Hoffmann. Rigorous compiler implementation correctness: How to prove the real thing correct. In D. Hutter, W. Stephan, P. Traverso, and M. Ullmann, editors, *Applied Formal Methods - FM-Trends 98*, volume 1641 of *LNCS*, pages 122–136, 1998.

43. J. Goldberg, W. Kautz, P. M. Melliar-Smith, M. Green, K. Levitt, R. Schwartz, and C. Weinstock. Development and analysis of the software implemented fault-tolerance (SIFT) computer. NASA contractor report 172146, National Aeronautics and Space Administration, Langley Research Center, Hampton, VA 23665, 1984.

44. M. Gordon. The semantic challenge of Verilog HDL. In *Tenth Annual IEEE Symposiom on Logic in Computer Science*. IEEE Computer Society Press, 1995.

45. D. A. Greve. Symbolic simulation of the JEM1 microprocessor. In *Formal Methods in Computer-Aided Design – FMCAD*, Lecture Notes in Computer Science. Springer-Verlag, 1998.

46. D. Hardin, M. Wilding, and D. Greve. Transforming the theorem prover into a digital design tool: From concept car to off-road vehicle. In A. J. Hu and M. Y. Vardi, editors, *Computer-Aided Verification – CAV '98*, volume 1427 of *Lecture Notes in Computer Science*. Springer-Verlag, 1998. See URL http://pobox.com/users/hokie/docs/concept.ps.

47. J. Harrison. *Theorem Proving with the Real Numbers*. PhD thesis, University of Cambridge, 1996.

48. S. Hazelhurst and C. H. Seger. A simple theorem prover based on symbolic trajectory evaluation and OBDDS. Technical report, University of British Columbia, Technical Report 93-41, 1993.

49. U. Hoffmann. *Compiler Implementation Verification through Rigorous Syntactical Code Inspection*. PhD thesis, Faculty of Engineering, Christian-Albrechts-Universität zu Kiel, Kiel, 1998.

50. J. E. Hopcroft and J. D. Ullman. *Introduction to Automata Theory, Languages, and Computation*. Addison Wesley, 1979.

51. R. Hosabettu, G. Gopalakrishnan, and M. Srivas. A proof of correctness of a processor implementing Tomasulo's algorithm without a reorder buffer. In L. Pierre and T. Kropf, editors, *Correct Hardware Design and Verification Methods, 10th IFIP WG10.5 Advanced Research Working Conference, (CHARME '99)*, volume 1703 of *LNCS*, pages 8–22. Springer-Verlag, 1999.

52. W. Hunt, Jr. and B. Brock. A formal HDL and its use in the FM9001 verification. *Proceedings of the Royal Society*, 1992.

53. W. Hunt, Jr. and B. Brock. The DUAL-EVAL hardware description language and its use in the formal specification and verification of the FM9001 microprocessor. *Formal Methods in Systems Design*, 11:71–105, 1997.

54. *IEEE Standard for Binary Floating Point Arithmetic*, 1985. IEEE Standard 754-1985.

55. IEEE-1076. *IEEE Standard VHDL Language Reference Manual*, 1993.

56. IEEE-WG1076.6. *IEEE P1076.6/D2.0 Draft Standard For VHDL Register Transfer Level Synthesis*, 1999. See URL http://vhdl.org/vi/-vhdlsynth/vhdlsynth.html.

57. M. Johnson. *Superscalar Microprocessor Design*. Prentice Hall, Englewood Cliffs, New Jersey, 1991.

58. M. Kaufmann, P. Manolios, and J S. Moore. *Computer-Aided Reasoning: An Approach*. Kluwer Academic Press, 2000.

59. M. Kaufmann and J S. Moore. Design goals of ACL2. Technical Report 101, Computational Logic, Inc., 1994. See URL http://www.cs.utexas.edu/users/moore/publications/acl2-papers.html#Overviews.

60. M. Kaufmann and P. Pecchiari. Interaction with the Boyer-Moore theorem prover: A tutorial study using the arithmetic-geometric mean theorem. *Journal of Automated Reasoning*, 16(1–2):181–222, 1996.

61. H. J. Keisler. *Foundations of Infinitesimal Calculus*. Prindle, Weber and Schmidt, Boston, 1976.

62. H. J. Keisler. *Elementary Calculus*. Prindle, Weber and Schmidt, Boston, 1976, 1986.

63. D. E. Knuth. Textbook examples of recursion. In V. Lifschitz, editor, *Artificial Intelligence and Mathematical Theory of Computation: Papers in Honor of John McCarthy*, pages 207–230. Academic Press, 1991.

64. D. Kozen. Results on the propositional Mu-Calculus. *Theoretical Computer Science*, pages 334–354, December 1983.

65. H. Langmaack. Contribution to Goodenough's and Gerhart's theory of software testing and verification: Relation between strong compiler test and compiler implementation verification. *Foundations of Computer Science: Potential-Theory-Cognition. LNCS*, 1337:321–335, 1997.

66. T. Lynch, A. Ahmed, and M. Schulte. Rounding error analysis for division. Technical report, Advanced Micro Devices, Inc., 5204 East Ben White Blvd., Austin, TX 78741, May 1995.

67. Supporting files for "Computer-Aided Reasoning: ACL2 Case Studies", 2000. See the link from URL http://www.cs.utexas.edu/users/moore/acl2.

68. K. Mainzer. Real numbers. In J. H. Ewing, editor, *Numbers*, Readings in Mathematics, chapter 2, pages 27–53. Springer-Verlag, 1991. Authors: H.-D. Ebbinghaus, H. Hermes, F. Hirzebruch, M. Koecher, K. Mainzer, J. Neukirch, A. Prestel, R. Remmert.

69. W. McCune. A Davis-Putnam program and its application to finite first-order model search: Quasigroup existence problems. Tech. Report ANL/MCS-TM-194, Argonne National Laboratory, Argonne, IL, May 1994.

70. W. McCune. MACE: Models and Counterexamples. See URL http://www.mcs.anl.gov/AR/mace/, 1994.

71. W. McCune. Otter 3.0 reference manual and guide. Tech. Report ANL-94/6, Argonne National Laboratory, Argonne, IL, 1994. See URL http://www.mcs.anl.gov/AR/otter/.

72. W. McCune. Automatic proofs and counterexamples for some ortholattice identities. *Information Processing Letters*, 65:285–291, 1998.

73. W. McCune and L. Wos. Otter: The CADE-13 Competition incarnations. *J. Automated Reasoning*, 18(2):211–220, 1997.

74. K. L. McMillan. *Symbolic Model Checking*. Kluwer, 1993.

75. K. L. McMillan. Verification of an implementation of Tomasulo's algorithm by compositional model checking. In A. J. Hu and M. Y. Vardi, editors, *Computer Aided Verification (CAV '98)*, volume 1427 of *LNCS*, pages 110–121. Springer-Verlag, 1998.

76. J S. Moore. Piton: A verified assembly level language. Technical Report 22, Comp. Logic Inc, Austin, Texas, 1988.

77. J S. Moore. *Piton : A Mechanically Verified Assembly-Level Language*. Kluwer Academic Press, Dordrecht, The Netherlands, 1996.

78. J S. Moore. Symbolic simulation: an ACL2 approach. In G. Gopalakrishnan and P. Windley, editors, *Formal Methods in Computer-Aided Design (FMCAD'98)*, pages 334–350. Springer-Verlag, 1998.

79. J S. Moore, T. Lynch, and M. Kaufmann. A mechanically checked proof of the AMD5$_K$86 floating-point division program. *IEEE Trans. Comp.*, 47(9):913–926, September 1998. See URL http://-www.cs.utexas.edu/users/moore/publications/acl2-papers.-html#Floating-Point-Arithmetic.

80. M. Müller-Olm. Three views on preservation of partial correctness. Technical Report Verifix/CAU/5.1, CAU Kiel, Oct. 1996.

81. E. Nelson. Internal set theory. *Bulletin of the American Mathematical Society*, 83:1165–1198, 1977.

82. E. Nelson. On-Line Books: Unfinished Book on Nonstandard Analysis. See URL http://www.math.princeton.edu/~nelson/books.html, in progress.

83. J. O'Leary, X. Zhao, R. Gerth, and C. H. Seger. Formally verifying IEEE compliance of floating-point hardware. *Intel Technical Journal, Q1'99*, 1999.

84. C. H. Papadimitriou. *Computational Complexity*. Addison-Wesley, 1994.

85. D. Park. Fixpoint induction and proofs of program properties. In B. Meltzer and D. Michie, editors, *Machine Intelligence*, volume 5, pages 59–78. Edinburgh University Press, 1969.

86. C. Pixley. A computational theory and implementation of sequential hardware equivalence. In *CAV'90 DIMACS series*, volume 3, June 1990. Also DIMACS Tech. Report 90-31.

87. A. Pnueli. The temporal logic of programs. In *18th Annual Symposium on Foundations of Computer Science*, pages 46–57, Providence, Rhode Island, 31 Oct.–2 Nov. 1977. IEEE.

88. J. Profeta, N. Andrianos, B. Yu, B. Jonson, T. DeLong, D. Guaspari, and D. Jamsek. Safety critical systems built with COTS. *Computer*, 29(11):54–60, November 1996.

89. J. Queille and J. Sifakis. Specification and verification of concurrent systems in CESAR. In *Proc. of the 5th International Symposium on Programming*, volume 137 of *LNCS*, 1982.

90. A. Robert. *Non-Standard Analysis*. John Wiley, 1988.

91. A. Robinson. Model theory and non-standard arithmetic, infinitistic methods. In *Symposium on Foundations of Mathematics*, 1959.

92. A. Robinson. *Non-Standard Analysis*. Princeton University Press, 1996.

93. D. Russinoff. Specification and verification of gate-level VHDL models of synchronous and asynchronous circuits. In E. Börger, editor, *Specification and Validation Methods*. Oxford University Press, 1995.

94. D. Russinoff. A mechanically checked proof of IEEE compliance of a register-transfer-level specification of the AMD-K7 floating-point multiplication, division, and square root instructions. *London Mathematical Society Journal of Computation and Mathematics*, 1:148–200, December 1998.

95. D. Russinoff. An ACL2 library of floating-point arithmetic, 1999. See URL http://www.cs.utexas.edu/users/moore/publications/others/-fp-README.html.

96. D. Russinoff. A mechanically checked proof of correctness of the AMD-K5 floating-point square root microcode. *Formal Methods in System Design*, 14:75–125, 1999.

97. W. J. Savitch. Relationship between nondeterministic and deterministic tape classes. *J. CSS*, 4:177–192, 1970.

98. J. Sawada. *Formal Verification of an Advanced Pipelined Machine*. PhD thesis, University of Texas at Austin, Dec. 1999. See URL http://www.cs.-utexas.edu/users/sawada/dissertation/.

99. J. Sawada and W. A. Hunt, Jr. Trace table based approach for pipelined microprocessor verification. In *Computer Aided Verification (CAV '97)*, volume 1254 of *LNCS*, pages 364–375. Springer-Verlag, 1997.

100. J. Sawada and W. A. Hunt, Jr. Processor verification with precise exceptions and speculative execution. In A. J. Hu and M. Y. Vardi, editors, *Computer Aided Verification (CAV '98)*, volume 1427 of *LNCS*, pages 135–146. Springer-Verlag, 1998.

101. C. H. Seger and J. J. Joyce. A mathematically precise two-level formal hardware verification methodology. Technical Report TR-92-34, University of British Columbia, 1992.

102. N. Shankar. *Metamathematics, Machines, and Godel's Proof*. Cambridge University Press, 1994.

103. M. Srivas and M. Bickford. Formal verification of a pipelined microprocessor. *IEEE Software*, pages 52–64, Sept. 1990.

104. G. L. Steele, Jr. *Common Lisp The Language, Second Edition*. Digital Press, Burlington, MA, 1990. See URL http://www.cs.cmu.edu/afs/-cs.cmu.edu/project/ai-repository/ai/html/cltl/clm/clm.html.

105. A. Tarski. A lattice theoretic fixpoint theorem and its applications. *Pacific Journal of Mathematics*, 55:285–309, 1955.

106. K. Thompson. Reflections on trusting trust. *Communications of the ACM*, 27(8):761–763, 1984. Also in *ACM Turing Award Lectures: The First Twenty Years 1965-1985*, ACM Press, 1987, and in *Computers Under Attack: Intruders, Worms, and Viruses*, ACM Press, 1990.

107. P. Traverso and P. Bertoli. Mechanized result verification: an industrial application. *To appear in International Journal on Software Tools for Technology Transfer*, 3(1), 2000.

108. B. L. van der Waerden. *Algebra*, volume 1. Frederick Ungar Publishing Co., 1970. Translated from the German *Algebra*, seventh edition.

109. M. N. Velev and R. E. Bryant. Superscalar processor verification using efficient reductions of the logic of equality with uninterpreted functions to propositional logic. In L. Pierre and T. Kropf, editors, *Correct Hardware Design and Verification Methods, 10th IFIP WG10.5 Advanced Research Working Conference, (CHARME '99)*, volume 1703 of *LNCS*, pages 37–53. Springer-Verlag, 1999.

110. L. Wang, M. Abadir, and N. Krishnamurthy. Automatic generation of assertions for formal verification of powerpc microprocessor arrays using symbolic trajectory evaluation. In *Design Automation Conference Proceedings 1998*, pages 534–537. ACM Press, 1998.

111. M. Wilding. A mechanically verified application for a mechanically verified environment. In C. Courcoubetis, editor, *Computer-Aided Verification – CAV '93*, volume 697 of *Lecture Notes in Computer Science*. Springer-Verlag, 1993. See URL `ftp://ftp.cs.utexas.edu/pub/boyer/nqthm/-wilding-cav93.ps`.

112. M. Wilding, D. Greve, and D. Hardin. Efficient simulation of formal processor models. *Formal Methods in System Design*, to appear. Draft TR available as `http://pobox.com/users/hokie/docs/efm.ps`.

113. M. M. Wilding. Robust computer system proofs in PVS. In C. M. Holloway and K. J. Hayhurst, editors, *LFM97: Fourth NASA Langley Formal Methods Workshop*. NASA Conference Publication no. 3356, 1997. See URL `http://atb-www.larc.nasa.gov/Lfm97/proceedings/lfm97-wilding.ps`.

114. N. Wirth. *Compilerbau, eine Einführung*. B.G. Teubner, Stuttgart, 1977.

115. L. Wos with G. Pieper. *A Fascinating Country in the World of Computing: Your Guide to Automated Reasoning*. World Scientific, Singapore, 1999.

Index

Underlined words are the names of links in the online documentation. From the ACL2 home page, http://www.cs.utexas.edu/users/moore/acl2, select the link to the User's Manual and then the link to the Index of all documented topics.